Voices without Votes

Revisiting New England: The New Regionalism

Series Editors

This series presents fresh discussions of the distinctiveness of New England culture. The editors seek manuscripts examining the history of New England regionalism; the way its culture came to represent American national culture; the interaction between that "official" New England culture and the people who lived in the region; and local, subregional, or even biographical subjects as microcosms that explicitly open up and consider larger issues. The series welcomes new theoretical and historical perspectives and is designed to cross disciplinary boundaries and appeal to a wide audience.

For a complete list of books available in this series, please visit www.upne.com

Ronald J. Zboray and Mary Saracino Zboray, *Voices without Votes: Women and Politics in Antebellum New England*

James W. Baker, *Thanksgiving: The Biography of an American Holiday*

Monica Chiu, editor, *Asian Americans in New England: Culture and Community*

Aífe Murray, *Maid as Muse: How Servants Changed Emily Dickinson's Life and Language*

Scott Molloy, *Irish Titan, Irish Toilers: Joseph Banigan and Nineteenth-Century New England Labor*

Joseph A. Conforti, editor, *Creating Portland: History and Place in Northern New England*

Deborah Pickman Clifford and Nicholas R. Clifford, *"The Troubled Roar of the Waters": Vermont in Flood and Recovery, 1927–1931*

JerriAnne Boggis, Eve Allegra Raimon, and Barbara A. White, editors, *Harriet Wilson's New England: Race, Writing, and Region*

Kimberly A. Jarvis, *Franconia Notch and the Women Who Saved It*

Christopher Johnson, *This Grand and Magnificent Place: The Wilderness Heritage of the White Mountains*

William Brown and Joanne Pope Melish, editors, *The Life of William J. Brown of Providence, R.I.*

Denis R. Caron, *A Century in Captivity: The Life and Trials of Prince Mortimer, a Connecticut Slave*

David L. Richards, *Poland Spring: A Tale of the Gilded Age, 1860–1900*

Paul M. Searls, *Two Vermonts: Geography and Identity, 1865–1910*

Judith Bookbinder, *Boston Modern: Figurative Expressionism as Alternative Modernism*

Donna M. Cassidy, *Marsden Hartley: Race, Region, and Nation*

VOICES without VOTES

Women and Politics in Antebellum New England

RONALD J. ZBORAY AND
MARY SARACINO ZBORAY

UNIVERSITY OF NEW HAMPSHIRE PRESS
Durham, New Hampshire

Published by University Press of New England
Hanover and London

University of New Hampshire Press
Published by University Press of New England
One Court Street, Lebanon NH 03766
www.upne.com

Manufactured in the United States of America
Designed by Katherine B. Kimball
Typeset in Monticello by Integrated Publishing Solutions

University Press of New England is a member of the Green Press Initiative. The paper used in this book meets their minimum requirement for recycled paper.

Library of Congress Cataloging-in-Publication Data
Zboray, Ronald J.
Voices without votes : women and politics in antebellum New England / Ronald J. Zboray and Mary Saracino Zboray.
p. cm—(Revisiting New England : the new regionalism)
Includes bibliographical references and index.
ISBN 978-1-58465-867-2 (cloth : alk. paper)
ISBN 978-1-58465-868-9 (pbk. : alk. paper)
1. Women—New England—History—19th century. 2. Women—Political activity—New England—History—19th century. 3. Women—Books and reading—New England—History—19th century. 4. New England—History—1775–1865
I. Zboray, Mary Saracino, 1953– II. Title.
HQ1438.N35Z36 2010
320.974082—dc22 2009047981

5 4 3 2 1

Contents

List of Illustrations vii
Acknowledgments ix

Introduction 1

Part I: The Rise of the Second Party System 19

1. *"I Shall* Weep *If* Jackson *Is Reelected":* Harriett Low and the "Reign" of "King Andrew" Jackson 21

2. *"Becoming Interested in Politics":* Women at the Birth of the Second Party System 36

3. *"The Most Intellectual Woman in Washington":* Eliza Davis as Political Wife 50

4. *"Siding with You in Politics":* Women's Political Polarization during the Van Buren Administration 64

5. *"Whig to the Back-bone":* Women and Mass Politics in the 1840 Campaign 79

6. *"But* I Will Think *the More":* Persis Sibley Andrews and the Politics of Covert Partisanship 98

7. *"Shame on the Woman Who Encourages the Lawless Proceeding":* Women Encounter Radical Democracy in the Dorr Rebellion 112

Part II: Party Dissolution and Formation 131

8. *"The Shouts and Responses of the Multitude":* Sarah P. E. Hale as Enthused and Disaffected Whig 135

9. *"A Most Unprecedented Act of Invasion":* Women, Mexico, and Taylor 151

10. *"Such a Lukewarm Spirit":* Women Divert Their Attentions during the 1852 Campaign 163

11. "I *Am Fremont, How Is It with You?":* Women and Sectionalism 179

12. *"I Read the Papers as Hard as I Can":* Women Face the Nightmare of Civil War 197

Epilogue 218

Abbreviations 227
Notes 235
Bibliography 265
Index 285

Illustrations

1.1. Harriett Low 22

3.1. Eliza Bancroft Davis 52

4.1. Mary Pierce Poor 75

5.1. Annie Bigelow Lawrence 93

6.1. Persis Sibley Andrews and her daughter Lotte 109

7.1. Catherine R. Williams 121

7.2. "Rhode Island Mass Meeting!!!" 126

8.1. Joshua Sheldon, *Whig Mass Meeting on Boston Common* 136

8.2. Sarah Preston (Everett) Hale 137

10.1. F. E. Worcester, "Scene at the Revere House" 172

10.2. *The Death of Daniel Webster* 177

11.1. Charlotte Forten Grimké 184

11.2. "John and Jessie" Frémont 1856 campaign ribbon 194

12.1. Elizabeth Dwight Cabot and Ellen Twisleton 198

Acknowledgments

In our long journey from archive to book manuscript we accumulated far too many debts to rehearse here. Some stand out more than others, of course. Among them are those to three institutions that provided early financial support: the Schlesinger Library (1993 study grant), the Massachusetts Historical Society (1994 Benjamin F. Stevens Fellowship), and the American Antiquarian Society (1992 NEH-AAS Fellowship). The book's endnotes brim with citations to about thirty other archival repositories we visited in the 1990s, each of which we thank, while apologizing for not having room to mention them. In 2003, the project received a Carrie Chapman Catt Prize for Research on Women and Politics (Honorable Mention), from the Carrie Chapman Catt Center for Women and Politics, at Iowa State University. For this honor, we are grateful.

On many occasions we delivered conference papers with research related to this book. Venues included the Organization of American Historians (1997), the Group for Early Modern Cultural Studies (1998), the Cultural Studies Association (2003), the Penn State Conference on Rhetoric (2003), the Society for Historians of the Early American Republic (2003, 2008, 2009), the Fourth Biennial Feminism(s) and Rhetoric(s) Conference (2003), the National Communication Association (2004, 2005, 2008, and 2009), the American Culture Association (2007), the American Literature Association (2007), the American Studies Association (2007), and the Eastern Communication Association (2008). Our deep appreciation especially goes out to Amy S. Greenberg, who arranged for us to give a major paper on our work at the George and Ann Richards Civil War Era Center, Pennsylvania State University, in November 2003. We are grateful to the many scholars who have discussed the project with us, including Catherine Allgor, Jacqueline Bacon, Anne Boylan, Stephen H. Browne, Joan Cashin, Daniel A. Cohen, Janet Coryell, Elaine Forman Crane, Edith Gelles, Kimberly Harrison, Anya Jabour, Julie Roy Jeffrey, Carol Lasser, Bruce Laurie, Carolyn Lawes, Carol Mattingly, Jonathan Prude, Amy Slagell, Tamara Plakins Thornton, Deborah Van Broekhoven, Elizabeth Varon, Martha Watson, Susan Zaeske, and Rosemarie Zagarri. Mary Kelley and Michael Pierson deserve our double thanks for the early interest they showed in our work and, more recently, for ever-so-thoughtfully reviewing the manuscript.

We addressed issues similar to those treated in this book in two journal articles. We are grateful to then-editor Barbara Cloud for shepherding our "Political News and Female Readership in Antebellum Boston and Its Region" into print in *Journalism History* 22.1 (Spring 1996) and to the Association for Education in Journalism and Mass Communication, History Division committee, chaired by Karen List, that awarded the article the 1997 Cathy E. Covert Prize. We also thank Michael Morrison and John Larson for editing our "Whig Women, Politics, and Culture in the Campaign of 1840: Three Perspectives from Massachusetts" for the *Journal of the Early Republic* 17.2 (Summer 1997), scattered passages of which appear in these pages, often in revised form.

Finally, we must acknowledge the helpfulness and enthusiasm of Revisiting New England series editor Siobhan Senier and past-and-present UPNE editors M. Ellen Wicklum and Richard Pult. Our copyeditor Will Hively and production editor Amanda Dupuis both deserve our special thanks for their care and vigilance in shepherding the manuscript into press.

Voices without Votes

Introduction

Let us eavesdrop on conversations in New England women's letters and diaries dating from Andrew Jackson's presidential administration to the Civil War. We start with the 1830s. "I did not dream of entering into politics when I began," a longtime Worcester politician's wife recalled in February 1833. "Did not find much in the papers except *politics* to interest," a young Salem woman wrote later that year. "Clay party triumphed in all towns," a twenty-year-old Connecticut schoolteacher "becoming interest[ed] in Politics" told her 1834 diary, in reference to Henry Clay's new anti-Jacksonian Whig Party. During the Panic of 1837, one Bostonian claimed that she, her mother, and her sisters preferred "the long columns of politics" in partisan newspapers. A Brookline minister's daughter reported to her parents that "I never heard so much about politics as I have this Summer" on an 1838 trip to Maine. She explained later, "I feel almost as much interest as the voters can."[1]

We continue with the 1840s, kicked off by the Log-Cabin presidential campaign. One woman, reading a Whig economic speech with a nephew, informed her husband, "we discuss politics with much *ability* & at least meet on equal grounds." Regarding a Democratic governor's speech, a retired Cambridge physician's spouse observed that "every lady says something about it," before giving her own thoughts. "All Worcester people call me a Loco," a woman suspected in her Whig circles of having Democratic sympathies notified her brother in July 1840. "I have not made up my mind, whether to be a Democrat, or Whig," a teachers'-training-school student penned in her diary that October as the campaign heated up. "If he *does* vote," a woman boasted to her fiancé of her efforts to get a brother-in-law to the polls, "I shall . . . attribute it in *some measure* to the wonderful eloquence I have been displaying for the few last evenings." A woman haunting the halls of Maine's State Capitol to hear debates confessed in 1841, "I take too much interest in Legislation for a lady." In 1846, an elderly Connecticut farmwoman shouted with her hard-of-hearing neighbor "on Politics . . . about an hour." One year later, a sometime Lowell millworker averred that "no one more reverences the democratic principle than myself," before criticizing the party's drift. In 1848, a Canton, Massachusetts, uncle teased his niece that she "did not take much interest in 'Political affairs'" to which the partisan teenager rejoined, "I told him! no!"[2]

We conclude with the years from the 1850s to the war's outbreak. A Democratic politician's wife in rural Maine simply proclaimed, "I love politics—political life excitement & all." An elderly Rhode Island spinster noticed in an 1851 letter to a niece, "I have not said a word of politics. . . . Do they continue to be an exciting subject with you?" Not all women were excited. "I am really very unhappy in my political mind," a Whig woman told her sister in 1854 amid her party's demise and a coalition between nativist Know-Nothings and Democrats. By the presidential contest of 1856, there was a new party, the Republican, with John C. Frémont as its standard-bearer. "*I* am Fremont, how is it with you?" a rural Vermonter asked her cousin, a Democratic politician. "I *think* you are the same, I am sure you are not Buchanan. . . . I do feel *very much* interested in the present election." War clouds gathering left the interest unabated. "Politics are rather exciting here this week for the South continues to bluster a good deal," a Bostonian wrote to her sister in England just after Abraham Lincoln's election. "We think of nothing but 'politics' & 'hard times' now," another woman wrote as secession fever took hold.[3]

Readers are unaccustomed to hearing such political sentiments as these, sustained over generations, from women in this time and place. Despite disfranchisement, women confess interest and excitement over elections and partisan contests. As nonvoters, they nevertheless identify themselves with mainstream political parties, and define themselves against the opposition. They write fluently and confidently about their political engagement, ranging from forming opinions through reading to influencing voting through arguing. They do not refrain from confronting issues like the economy or absorbing themselves in details of local elections. Yet there is little trace here of the domesticity, religion, benevolence, or reform that so much dominate accounts of women's history before the Civil War. Rather, these women demonstrate that they could and did speak in a decidedly unalloyed political register.

The seeming paradox of these political voices without votes is the subject of this book.[4] We argue that despite the separate-spheres ideology, discussed below, that relegated politics to the sphere of men, ordinary women pondered mainstream political issues and took part in political activities beyond moral reform and benevolent work. Such engagement gave women, who remained without the vote nationally until the next century, a role to play in politics by campaigning for elections, persuading voters, affecting lawmakers, and generally stimulating the "campaign talk" essential to the health of the democracy.[5] In such talk, which includes writing, women summoned a political rhetoric, usually uninflected by domesticity, benevolence, or reform, that was similar to men's. The topics women engaged, too, mirrored male concerns. Women tackled the economy and banking, analyzed party splintering, and pondered military affairs. They were far less likely to target obviously gender-specific political subjects including women's property rights bills or suffrage, or use them as justification for politicization. Thus, women in antebellum New England not only had a consciousness of politics; they had an active presence in it, with definite roles to play. As they wrote and conversed, acted and argued, they were civic participants trapped, solely by virtue of their sex, in a nonvoting status short of full citizenship.[6]

Below, we discuss how we came to this project and how we handled the material we uncovered. We then sketch women's place in the region's landscape of political culture, before we address the relevant scholarship. We end by pondering the political meaning of letter writing and diary keeping, before setting forth the book's organization and pondering the significance of our findings.

Project History and Methods

We first encountered these voices without votes accidentally in 1993. We were embarking on a large research project on what antebellum New Englanders read and what it meant to them. Our chosen method was to probe into manuscript family papers, mostly letters and diaries, by both men and women, and read through them systematically. That required a fine-tooth comb to identify every instance of participation in literary culture we could find. As we read through the material to transcribe relevant passages, we noticed a surprising frequency and depth of women's references to party politics. The references often were germane to our literary project, insofar as we aimed to record everything read, even political newspapers and speeches. But women also discussed politics in letters and diaries that did not directly refer to their reading.

Realizing how difficult it would be to recover these references later, we decided to record every passage in which a woman mentioned politics or parties, or any secondhand reports by men or women of women's involvement in the partisan mainstream. All this would occur alongside our hunt for reading. Thus began a six-year odyssey that led us to over thirty libraries, most of them in New England.[7] We transcribed just over two million words by 936 diarists and correspondents, 448 of them women who produced 2,202 documents, more than half of all those we collected.[8] Because we sought to generalize about literary practices for the entire regional population, we developed a socially representative base of testimony givers, from just about every New England county. This enabled us to measure, among the largely literate general population reflected in the transcribed material, the proportion of women referring to politics or newspaper reading.[9]

Through close textual reading, backed by exhaustive reference work in online newspaper and genealogical resources, we then analyzed this mountain of material for both projects. During the late 1990s, we produced interim reports in a dozen or so refereed journal articles and essays in books, two of which specifically dealt with our political project.[10] As the literary project eventually resulted in two books in 2005 and 2006, respectively, work continued on the women-and-politics one.[11]

With the help of a database, we coded the textual corpus for the presence of either politics or newspaper reading.[12] The results exceeded even our initial impression of the prevalence of politics in women's diaries and letters. Of the 448 women, 41 percent mentioned politics and an equal percentage showed unambiguous evidence of reading newspapers; 27 percent did both. Of the 2,202 documents, about one-third contain one or more references to politics and one-fourth to newspaper reading. Since many letters had specific purposes beyond politics, the percentage of diaries mentioning politics (53.96) more precisely indicates the surprising extent of the political presence in records of women's lives.

What is a striking number to us may not seem so to those unfamiliar with antebellum diaries, which can be disappointing in their spotty coverage, terse entries, and focus on business, agricultural, or domestic affairs. Even the wordiest ones written by men often elide important cultural, social, and political events. Glenn Altschuler and Stuart Blumin found among about fifty men's diaries only "a small number . . . that reveal . . . a lifelong engagement in political affairs." One-third were "kept by men who express in them little or no interest in politics, and who voted with little or no comment about the election or their participation in it." While they see that such diaries indicate voters' low-level engagement, other scholars dispute their findings, some of whom show that the rank and file beyond the few party leaders industriously organized rallies and avidly consumed political material culture.[13] We maintain that diaries, exposing but a fraction of all activity and thought, reveal only the tip of an iceberg of political engagement. Having at least as much and arguably more political coverage than men's journals, women's diaries only begin to suggest the true extent of female involvement.

Having established the prevalence of politics in women's life writings, we put much effort into analyzing the material for depth and quality of engagement. We did this mainly in two ways. First, we looked closely at women who wrote about politics extensively enough to develop a distinct and individualized partisan voice. In these women's writings, partisanship and identity fused; the writer rhetorically crafted her written expression in a manner that showed sure grasp of public affairs discourse, facility with modes of contemporary argumentation, and creative deployment of vernacular language and personal disclosure to highlight points being made.[14] Seen another way, from the fluidity and vibrancy of the partisan voices resounding through these diaries and letters, these women did not simply parrot other people's opinions garnered from print matter or conversations. They took proud ownership over what they wrote or said. "I have said my say," was the way one woman defiantly put it after she gave a "speech" on economic policy during a household argument. These women's agency was obvious, even in their occasionally discriminating decisions *not* to discuss a certain matter in a partisan way, or *not* to follow the party line.[15]

Second, we organized and read through the full body of material in chronological order to consider the collective evolution of the women's engagement with politics. To do this, we reshuffled the database to break up distinct diary entries. We chronologically interfiled them with letters to form a cross section of what several women had to say about each unfolding political moment. Common resonances within this collective voice particularly bespoke women's general civic awareness and participation, against which the individual voices sang along, at times, in counterpoint.

This dual strategy of analysis informs *Voices without Votes.* Its twelve chapters unfold in rough chronology from Jackson to the Civil War. Chapters focusing on the construction and expression of individual voice over time are interwoven with those broadly sketching the collective one, although in the latter, we sometimes provide extended treatment of individual cases. Women from diverse walks of life populate the collective chapters, while those featured in individuals' chapters tend to be politicians' kin with close "insider" intelligence who are vocal enough over lengthy time spans to provide us prodigious material. This is not to say that women who appear only briefly offer inferior insights. Rather, those insights provide essential building blocks of the whole picture. They, like their loquacious counterparts, are seeming anomalies of the separate-spheres ideology, which theoretically could silence even the most politically connected women. As we will see, it did not. We now turn to suggest some reasons for this by way of a synchronic overview of the culture out of which women's politicization emerged.

Women in Antebellum New England's Political Culture

Some degree of political socialization, regardless of gender, was virtually inescapable in antebellum New England, for it was an environment saturated with open and unambiguous expressions of partisanship. The near-universal extension of the male franchise regionwide (with the notable exception of Rhode Island, as we discuss in chapter 7) during the early nineteenth century ushered in a participant type of civic culture.[16] It differed from the earlier "deference democracy" of colonial-era town meetings, at which freeholders, loosely defined, voted and held offices but power clustered in an elite.[17] Still, even in the earlier time, deference did not preclude political mobilization of nonfreeholders or nonvoters for insurgencies and uprisings, not the least of which was the American Revolution.[18] So there was a rich local tradition of the politicization of the disfranchised upon which antebellum women could draw. In chapter 1 we hear echoes of this tradition in one woman's republican disdain for "King Andrew" Jackson.

The sense of civic belonging was also enhanced during the early Republic by nationalistic rituals, like Independence Day celebrations, in which everyone participated, young and old, men and women (see chapter 2).[19] Speeches and sermons commemorating the Revolution often intoned the rhetoric of republicanism to heterogeneous assemblages, thus reinforcing for everyone the political underpinnings of national self-definition. Little wonder that striking New England millwomen in the mid-1830s could easily invoke the memory of the American Revolution to bolster their claims.[20]

The final civic development was the rise of mass partisan politics, signaled locally by the election of Boston's Mayor Josiah Quincy in 1823 and nationally by Andrew Jackson in 1828.[21] The concomitant speechifying on the stump and editorials in partisan newspapers reached out to the widest public in order to get out the vote in often narrowly contested elections. As the parties coalesced during the 1830s into the Second Party System of Democrats and Whigs, they synergized with popular culture to inscribe it with the partisan divide. Partisan affiliation became a marker of identity, both for individuals and for groups.[22]

That such strident partisan advocacy fell on the ears and before the eyes of women was only natural, for in broadcasting their messages widely, politicians could not afford to discriminate narrowly by gender. Better to reach the most men, even if it meant reaching women, too. New England women were particularly well prepared to receive the message. Their literacy rates had been among the world's highest since the turn of the previous century. There was, too, a local culture of teaching and learning that included women, in both home and neighborhood settings, in the classroom, and, for a rare few, the female seminary.[23] Heterosocial spaces for conversing about a wide range of matters had been established, and women availed themselves of educational listening opportunities like the public lecture and the sermon.[24] Above all, there was much reading aloud, even of newspapers, in which women partook, as both auditors and readers. Often, discussion accompanied these oral readings, ultimately socializing news reception across genders.

Partisan news particularly flourished in this rich discursive environment. The same news gained force when it came from several directions—aurally, through word of mouth in casual conversations or newsboys hawking papers in the streets, or visually, in dense newspaper columns or in personal letters received. Conflicting news from varied sources could occasion critical assessment of the information's veracity. Our diarists and correspondents puzzled through the news to form a remarkably accurate account of political situations. Only a handful of women erred in fact, substance, or interpretation. Indeed, reading through the material chronologically offers a political history of the entire era, because writers did not focus on women's issues to the exclusion of other matters. So well apprised were many women, they could be called highly informed "opinion leaders" who were well situated to guide low-information voters.[25] One did not have to be such an active recipient to encounter news, however. Thanks to early nineteenth-century innovations in communication, particularly important news moved rapidly through the culture through "contagious diffusion."[26] Such waves did not discriminate by gender. Women could not but help soak in news.

To be sure, gender discrimination remained deeply embedded in the political culture. Not only were women barred from voting; they could not attend closed political caucuses, and even at many "open" meetings they were sequestered in a "ladies' gallery" or other sex-segregated areas. Female activists of all sorts had to endure scorn and name-calling. Controversy flared over women speaking before "promiscuous audiences," that is, made up of men and women.[27]

Changes were afoot, however, largely due to the interparty competition required to assure high voter turnout. The parties needed all the help they could get. Women could and did attend mass meetings and listened to speeches. They witnessed partisan parades and torchlight processions and demonstrated support with gestures like waving handkerchiefs. Their attendance not only upped the numbers reported in newspapers as evidence of a party's popularity but also countered public suspicion that mass demonstrations were akin to mobocracy.[28] They held ladies' fairs with thinly disguised partisan valences. They were present at party conventions, facilitating the proceedings by putting up boarders, feeding the masses, and listening to speeches. At election time, they lobbied fiancés and relatives to vote the right way. They sang partisan songs and presented homemade banners with political mottoes. They embraced a broad material culture of partisanship, from candidate pincushions to campaign badges. They even were able to organize a few partisan events, especially picnics and clambakes, as we shall see in chapters 5 and 7. There, too, we see that during the Log-Cabin Campaign and Dorr Rebellion, a few women took the podium before mixed-gender audiences.[29]

Among these participants were many politicians' women family members, who became essential to running their kin's or spouse's successful public careers. They might keep up on the news and digest it for busy or traveling male politicos, manage the welter of newspaper subscriptions and correspondence entering the home, undertake business account keeping to allow time for the man's politicking, sample local opinion and report on it to him, arrange for visits of supporters and colleagues, write letters to distant family members and acquaintances to coordinate political activities, and even draft or edit the politician's speeches and other public pronouncements. Little wonder that such women often acquired reputations as members of a team or, indeed, politicians in their own right.

Whether politicians' kin or not, partisan women did not employ a rhetoric of assisting someone else, a position that would have been consistent with traditional expectations of the feminine role as helpmate. While part of their political socialization was passively secondhand—women gained awareness from family members' and neighbors' partisan involvements or from moments they encountered politicians visiting town—this sort of indirect involvement happened to men, too. Instead of conceiving of themselves as auxiliaries, women most often described themselves as engaged in a common enterprise, usually indicated by their use of "we." "We have made him our representative," one woman wrote of a local politician in 1843, while another writing to a brother observed, "Our party seems now to be moving along." A rural Maine woman, on receiving President William Henry Harrison's 1841 inaugural address, proclaimed, "We Whigs think it first rate." But the first-person singular could be used, too. One supporter of Rhode Island's Dorr Rebellion dubbed herself a "'lifelong Democrat.'" The aforementioned "*I* am Fremont" may be the clearest identification with a candidate. Even young Emily Dickinson referred in 1845 to "my Whig feelings." Of the Harrison inauguration one woman admitted, "I am too much of a Whig not to enter into the general rejoicing." She trod carefully because she was one of many women who differed in their partisan affiliation from family members—another indication that such women thought for themselves and were not simply helping out loved ones. In short, as much as partisan political culture was inescapable in antebellum New England, women were ineradicably present in it as autonomous thinkers and actors.[30]

Histories of Antebellum Women and Politics

Voices without Votes emerges from American women's history as a field. The book hopes to contribute to it by widening the scope for conceptualizing antebellum women's experiences to include partisanship. As the field of women's history coalesced in the 1960s and 1970s, it struggled to recover information about women who left little trace in public records that figured centrally in the then-regnant top-down presidential synthesis adhered to by many historians. Women's history was part of the new social history that began writing history from the bottom up.[31] However, women, especially white middling ones who long enjoyed educational advantages, were not as inarticulate as other subjects of social history. Consequently, women's historians found, in archives, rich troves of testimony, especially in diaries and letters written by women themselves. Suddenly, these women's worlds, as seen through their own eyes, were open for us to view. This vast panorama of private writing made the shadows of women flitting through public records seem paltry by comparison. Who wants to chase shadows?[32]

Two broadly organizing concepts for understanding early American women quickly came to the fore. "Republican Motherhood," applied to women in the Revolutionary era by Linda Kerber, retained a civic role for women not as primary actors but secondary nurturers of males participating in politics.[33] Depending on the viewpoint, whether one measured the distance from full civic participation in modern societies or from women's limited education and civic roles in traditional ones, Republican motherhood was a glass either half empty or half full. In any case, it gave early American women a history connected with mainstream political history.

For the early nineteenth century, however, the dominant concept became "woman's sphere," a contemporary ideology that proscribed women from partisan politics as being outside their proper sphere. The concept as historical explanation traces its origins to Nancy Cott's *Bonds of Womanhood* (1977). Cott argued, based on her survey of private letters and diaries written by New England women during the early Republic, that "woman's sphere," as a "prescriptive 'canon' of domesticity" publicized through emergent mass print media, aligned with "middle class women's experience and concomitant outlook." Looking back after twenty years, she described her goal as "trying to capture the ways that ideology and experience were reciprocally influential or mutually constitutive." Some of the power of her explanation owed to that very claim of mutuality that allowed for, in subsequent historians' hands, public discourse to be read as a window into actual lived experience. Moreover, the claim led historians to contain the often inchoate experience reflected in diaries and letters by interpreting it through a commonly understood set of principles discernible in the discourse.[34]

"Woman's Sphere" soon dominated presuffrage women's history. Confined to the home, prohibited from most public activism, and barred from the ballot box, women were depicted as having little political involvement, except as it concerned appropriate religious or moral reform issues. These two areas almost immediately became foci for other women's historians unwilling to separate historical women entirely from the nation's civic development. By their accounts, despite woman's sphere, a relatively few forward-looking women devoted themselves to reform politics, such as women's rights, temperance, and antislavery, while fewer still dared to speak in public.[35] These historians saw that it was these pioneers who, through acquiring organizational skills in voluntary associations, paved the way toward woman suffrage in the twentieth century.[36] And it was these women who heroically challenged the ideological constraints of woman's sphere to create behavioral and attitudinal precedents for modern American women.

Republican motherhood, woman's sphere, and women's nonpartisan-yet-public activism together formed a solid and robust structure for the field of American women's history. Much excellent scholarship was produced using any one of the three or all in some combination. Thanks to these generations of women's historians, within a relatively short time, early American women emerged from the shadows.

As women's history came to light in ever greater detail and diversity, evidence of women's eruption out of woman's sphere into scenes of partisan politics clearly had to be addressed. Recent work on the Revolutionary era excavated women's direct involvement in politics that went far beyond Republican motherhood. One scholar has even seen the antebellum woman's sphere as a backlash against women's earlier politicization.[37] The crucial role of parlor politics at the hands of women in the nation's capital during its nascence was firmly established, while political couples and individual political women have been put on the map.[38]

Perhaps the greatest challenge became understanding women's relationship to the mass politics that emerged around 1840. Women's presence in this political pageantry had been acknowledged as far back as Robert Gray Gunderson's definitive 1957 book on the 1840 campaign. Claiming that "Whig women took a conspicuous, but passive, role in the mummery of their men," he merely situated women within a few scenes, mostly without inquiring what was on their minds or assaying their motives. The claim of inconsequence still echoed nearly a quarter of a century later in an article insisting that such women acted only within the constraints of their gendered role. "Men denied women the central experiences of the popular style," the writer observes, "not only the ballot but also the experience of mass mobilization." Another historian dismissed the significance of women at partisan events as "symbols" deployed within "strategies of electioneering." One historian argued that the very notion that "women's partisan participation was more prevalent than voluntary activism" casts them as "stupidly willing to waste their time or the dupes of men"—thoughtless bystanders simply emotionally swept up by the tide of politicking.[39]

In the 1990s a few historians, we among them, began to take women's involvement in mass politics more seriously or perhaps less cynically. In a 1992 article, Jayne Crumpler DeFiore, citing mostly newspaper sources, sketched out the depth of women's participation in the 1840 and 1844 campaigns. Using similar sources with a few diaries and letters, Elizabeth Varon in a 1995 article posited "Whig womanhood"—a fusion of Republican-womanhood-style patriotism with partisanship—as a way of explaining Virginia white women's presence and involvement in the 1840 and 1844 campaigns. She saw Whig womanhood as more an extension of benevolent organizing than originating in evangelicalism. As Varon's article appeared, our first report on our findings about New England women reading political news was already in press. We argued that the Boston-area women whose letters and diaries we examined demonstrate not only "a knowledge of political events" but also an "accompanying political consciousness" at odds with what "woman's sphere" might predict. A year later, in another article, we homed in on the experiences of three women in the 1840 campaign to show their rational engagement with issues, sustained party loyalty, and participation in a "cross-gendered, political culture of Whiggery." In both articles, as in this book, we attempt to shift the focus of discussion from whether women appeared in the political scene at all, to what they self-reportedly did in campaigns, how they in their letters and diaries conceived of their unfolding political experiences, and how they expressed their partisanship in writing about those activities and experiences.[40]

Inscribing the Political

What does it mean for a woman to write about politics in this time and place? When pen touched paper to write down words referring to politics, it already was an act of transgressing the normative expectation that women should not be political, and it created hard evidence of that transgression. It also prompted questions: Who is this woman writing about politics? Does she know what she is talking about? Her level of understanding was betrayed by the very words she used, the syntax she adopted, her style or tone, the knowledge she demonstrated, or her rhetorical savvy. Who stood in judgment of this? The woman herself, of course, but also those who would subsequently read the letter or the diary, neither of which writers could assume would be private. Letters were read aloud and shared in circles of kin and neighbors, excerpts sent into social networks, and they were at times opened in transit for the amusement of loungers in post offices or by mail carriers with time to kill. Diaries, few of which were protected by lock and key, were themselves read aloud, shared, and exchanged. In short, letters and diaries were stages for complex performances before some known audiences and potentially several unknowable ones. Letters and diaries provided opportunities for writing oneself, socially, into being, in this case into being political.[41] No wonder writers generally observed careful decorum in their productions.

What were these writings' purposes? Diaries recorded events for later retrieval, but they also served as a scratch pad for thinking through issues, which could result in phrases or entire paragraphs destined for letters. Incisive thoughts in diary entries could be shared in conversation, too. And diaries were mirrors to be held up, when rereading them, after passages of months or years. To pen the political was to inscribe it in the recorded life. Political references and discussions in letters had even wider purpose. They signaled that the writer was in the political game, helped her to coordinate activities or viewpoints with recipients, provided eyewitness or hearsay accounts, served as a platform for analysis, and functioned as their own vehicles of political socialization for recipients not as attuned to party politics. These letters and diaries are at once both records and products of political actions. Through them, on the page, we encounter evidence of the aforementioned campaign talk, while we recover traces of the moment the woman wielded the pen politically, at risk of violating woman's-sphere proscriptions.

Some of the most outspoken women who "talked" politics occasionally employed what we call a "rhetoric of diffidence" to ensure that their expressions—often perilously akin to men's campaign talk—would not be silenced. By employing a kind of "pragmatic rhetoric," women could act politically and even influence voters without social reprobation. After all, women unabashedly demonstrating an independent civic identity necessarily undermined the intellectual foundation for a gender-based franchise.[42] They did not want to hazard sacrificing influence by seeming to overreach for suffrage. Unsurprisingly, then, none of our women expressed a desire to have the vote.

Because a "diffident style" allowed private women to have a political voice, it functioned somewhat like the "feminine style" adopted by public speakers needing both to act in a feminine manner and to "demonstrat[e] expertise, authority, and rationality" before audiences accustomed to hearing male orators. While the diffident style held much in common with the public feminine style, including inductive argumentation and liberal referencing to personal experience, the form was utilized by women in their informal everyday communication. They made no ostensible claims to authority and were not obliged to legitimate it directly; yet they wrote authoritatively and evidently were conscious that the content of their writing legitimated their right to expound upon politics. After all, such rhetors were little expected to withstand comparison with public ones, so it allowed for them a differently configured discursive space.[43] They could be more subtle.

As we will see throughout the book, women campaign talkers sometimes used four pragmatic strategies to convey political intelligence: carefully deployed denials, self-reproaching statements, obfuscation by literary quotation, and feigned ignorance. Denial of political interest was typical of the diffident style, especially as summoned by young women with a dawning political consciousness. Awkward and abrupt, these defensive disavowals were usually conditional, often begging pardon for a subsequent barrage of political talk. Besides denials, self-reproach effectively deflected any suspicion of women's-rights radicalism. Unlike disclaimers, rebukes directly attacked self-acknowledged acts of politicization and often applied "humor arising from the comic frame," which implied acceptance of the social order. Women comic-rebukers assured they posed no serious threat in their overt politicization, while they deflected any charge of radicalism and avoided victimization.[44] Literary quotes could also obscure partisanship by diverting attention away from temporal and immediate issues toward timeless and universal dilemmas. These citations from Shakespeare or the Bible often referred to male political engagement: they might punctuate an election recapitulation, comprise a postscript to male epistolary campaign talk, or comment upon politicians' woes. In other words, they seemingly said little about the citation maker's opinion, but actually implied support or disapproval. Feigned ignorance, the least-used formulation of diffidence, was perhaps the most effective one for persuasive dialogue. Unlike the denial, rebuke, or quote that modulated political statements, feigned ignorance supplanted politicized utterances with strategic silence, in order to shepherd the talker to the right conclusion, gently.[45] While the rhetoric of diffidence could be used by men as much as women, the latter found it a particularly powerful tool for voicing politics in an age that otherwise would try to muzzle them. That this was a rhetoric, and not an unmediated expression of a naturalized feminine diffidence, suggests that women chose to call upon it to help them do something with words: in this case, to think and act as partisans.[46]

Organization

The book's chronological organization differs from that of histories influenced by woman's-sphere scholarship, which usually mix evidence drawn from several decades, even on a single page. When we look at these women's diaries and letters politically, there is too much flux to be encompassed by an approach that generalizes a big temporal picture. Rather than reciting the familiar litany of family news, household experiences, and religious expression, with an enduring sameness over decades, these women in their letters and diaries demonstrate deep engagement in rapidly unfolding political events. The apt timeliness of this engagement would be lost by a bird's-eye topical approach. Instead, the chronological presentation allows us to show these women variably negotiating a multitude of discourses circulating throughout the culture, among which woman's sphere is but one, and not the most common.

So partisan are these voices without votes that they closely align with the fates of two party systems, which we summon to divide the book into two parts: "The Rise of the Second Party System" and "Party Dissolution and Formation." In the first, we see women coming to political voice in the early 1830s and exercising political agency within the Whig-Democrat political culture at decade's end, while helping to nurture it to maturity in the mass politics of the 1840s. The book's second part begins at a high tide for women's activism in both parties, and it then traces the way women renegotiated their politicization in a time of Second Party System decline, realignment, and new party formation leading to the Third Party System, of Republicans and Democrats. Women's partisanship became vastly more complicated, in some ways weaker than before but in any case different and more varied, at least until Abraham Lincoln swept into the presidency in 1861 and into a war in which lines between partisanship and patriotism blurred. Finally, in an epilogue, we gauge what the foregoing political presence of New England women may have meant for women's civic future, and why that presence would be largely forgotten by the twentieth century.

Reimagining Women and Antebellum Party Politics

What does it mean that New England women were so engaged in antebellum party politics and that they were able to give voice to their politicization? First, it elucidates the mind-set of women who participated in political events. They were far from being stupid or "dupes of men" either in their political consciousness or in their actions surrounding mainstream politics.

Indeed, in our women's diaries and letters evidence of partisan awareness and activity is vastly more present than reports about involvement with or consciousness of voluntary associations, whether related to benevolence, reform, or evangelicalism. This underscores the ordinariness of these women, who were not leaders of such groups and, in most cases, not joiners. Even if specific issues that such associations grappled with come up, like temperance or antislavery, as they do frequently in the 1850s, they are generally discussed in a partisan spirit. Furthermore, before the 1850s, most of our politicized women were generally conservative regarding the immediate abolition of slavery and therefore unlikely to join antislavery groups.[47] In this they were no different from most mainstream Whig and Democratic men of the Second Party System.

Second, these women's diaries and letters probably represent but a minute fraction of how much women who did not leave such testimony thought and acted politically. There is little evidence that the women who did write were in any way singular or remarkable for their politicization. So, undoubtedly, there were many more like them who did not choose to articulate in writing either their partisan activities or their political thinking. For many women down the class scale, any kind of lengthy articulation through writing was a luxury afforded by leisure time, access to writing materials, and expendable energy that they may well not have frequently enjoyed. This is not to say there are no diaries and letters by working-class women or poorer farm women, for there are plenty, but they tend to record parsimoniously only bare essentials, whose meaning, political or otherwise, must often be teased out.[48] No matter the class position, the specific diaries and letters written by any woman may not be the ones in which she developed and exercised a political voice, for not all women sustained an engagement with politics evenly throughout their lives, and not all their manuscripts have survived.

Third, woman's-sphere rhetoric may have been in part a reaction to women's expressed and latent politicization continuing and gaining force since the Revolutionary era. As such the rhetoric did not as much constitute the reality (for Cott, "women's experiences") as try to constrain and condition its perceived tendencies not in alignment with the rhetoric. It is clear from our evidence at least that woman's-sphere ideology did not prevent many women from being aware of party politics, writing about it, and participating in related activities. The rhetoric of nonpartisan volunteer activism, however, needs to be set alongside pragmatic everyday political realities experienced widely by women. The price of women's increased visibility as nonpartisan activists and organizers may have been to disavow partisanship, lest they seem too threatening. For them, a hint of partisanship could become a taint to be used against them.[49]

Fourth, we should assume that women's role in antebellum party politics made a difference, however small, in some cases, in electoral outcomes, policy formation, and municipal, state, and local governance. It should be clear in the pages that follow that women acting and thinking politically were not simply whistling in the dark to keep themselves amused. Many had purpose and commitment. Their sense of efficacy should not be dismissed as mistaken, when they were so little mistaken in their analyses of political situations. After all, many elections were very close, especially at the local level due to vote scattering, so their advocacy to sway even a handful of votes could, in many instances, be decisive.

In short, when future historians imagine the lives and consciousness of women in this time and place, they should account for the distinct possibility of their partisan commitment alongside their domesticity and nonpartisan voluntarism. Conversely, when imagining antebellum politics, historians should not too readily eliminate the possibility of women's civic participation and awareness. Although they could not vote, women had voices that spoke incisively and articulately to their times. They can still be heard in ours.

I

The Rise of the Second Party System

I

The Second Party System, which came about in the later 1830s, well after the First Party System's collapse in 1817 as Democratic-Republicans triumphed over Federalists, afforded new opportunities for women to become politically involved, as this part of the book will demonstrate. Yet this generalization, while true enough, casts women as mere passive beneficiaries of men's actions and not as themselves political actors, that is, coparticipants in the construction of the Second Party System. As ensuing chapters show, however, women were very much involved in the discourse networks through which political controversy, particularly anti-Jacksonism, flowed before a Second Party System was even dreamed of. And they had a hand in on-the-ground political positioning that enabled the Whig Party's emergence on the local level; as counterpoise, women could be found on the inside of Democratic campaign machinery in the 1830s. Women just after helped politics go mass; as Whigs particularly, they became persuaders of the electorate, organizers of campaign events, leaders in the logistics of conventions, participants in publicity, and trusted advisers to high and mighty men. But as democracy was on the move, through mass mobilization without regard of gender, it hit brick walls of privilege such as Rhode Island's property-based franchise rules, which severely limited the universe of voters. A largely Democratic-led unsuccessful attempt to kick down those walls, even by force, in 1842 saw fiercely partisan women fighting with words, and occasionally threatening to use harsher means, for the extension of male suffrage. These advocates became a fixture of Democratic conventioneering leading up to election of 1844, with Whig and Democratic women facing off. By that year, then, women had become crucial to successful electoral outcomes in the closely contested races of the period.

In the following seven chapters, our women move from political awakening in the late 1820s, amid increasingly organized opposition to President Andrew Jackson, to partisan identification by the mid-1840s (chapters 1 through 4). We show how much women were present as the new party system emerged to spawn an age of mass politics in the campaign of 1840 (chapter 5) but also how such identifications could cause tensions in personal relationships with those affiliated with the opposition party (chapter 6). The part climaxes with a case study of the Dorr War—that democratic uprising and its Democratic women (chapter 7).

Did Whig and Democratic women equally embrace the political realm? While we located more written testimony from Whig women than from Democratic ones, it remains debatable whether or not "the women were all Whigs," as 1840 campaign slogans had it. It is plausible that most of the family records we used were preserved in older collections created by largely Whig institutions. It is also possible that Whig-leaning women were more prone to written expression, while Democratic-sympathizing women were more guarded. The two parties, however, claimed variant gender styles that could hamper or foster women's politicization. The "Jacksonian Mystique" permeated the Democratic Party; in 1840 Democrats exhibited "masculine, if not often macho, posturing," and by 1848 they had become defenders of the patriarchy. Whigs conversely exhibited feminine or cultivated qualities; Daniel Webster's affective oratory stands out. A "Whig ethos," as one scholar argues, "opened up political spaces for women." Furthermore, Whigs were more likely than Democrats to recruit women for electioneering. Before 1844, Boston's Democratic editors ridiculed these solicitations and the women who answered them.[1] So while it stands to reason that Whig women outnumbered Democratic ones, the tantalizing traces of politically active Democratic women that appear in this book suggest there are yet more to be recovered. Whigs may have led the way with politicized women, but Democrats were sure to follow.

1

"I Shall Weep *If* Jackson *Is Reelected"*

Harriett Low and the "Reign" of "King Andrew" Jackson

When twenty-year-old Macao sojourner Harriett Low took up her pen in April 1830 to write her parents in New York, a political vision seized her imagination: "Were I now to sit down between you, I think I should find much to say to you that at this moment thrusts itself forward to be put upon paper, to be sent across the great waters, to inhabit that happy country, now undergoing a 'reform.'" The "reform" was the newly elected president's agenda to root out corruption in government through retrenchment and "rotation" of appointed officials. "But this word *reform* brings our friend General Jackson to my thoughts," she continued, as if flattering "Old Hickory" from her chamber halfway around the world. Her sarcasm only became evident as the ink flowed more freely: "I cannot give him anything better than General, for if he had justice done him he would not have that. I fear he will ruin our government." After condemning Jackson's military credentials, his cabinet, and his other appointments, Harriett boldly declared, "It is a shame, a disgrace to our country, to have such a man president." Fearing her parents' censure for what seemed like an obsession with worldly affairs, she offered a disclaimer: "Do not think I am entering deeply into politics, but I'll assure you one feels these things when among Englishmen particularly, much more than when at home." She had been in Macao for only seven months, but already its complex political, cultural, and social climate had induced the once-diffident merchant's daughter to express her opinions forcefully. Three more years in Macao would allow Harriett Low to hone her newly discovered political voice (fig. 1.1).[1]

FIGURE 1.1 Harriett Low, painted by George Chinnery. Photograph courtesy of the Peabody Essex Museum, Salem, Mass. (negative M18709)

Unlike most of her female contemporaries' political voices, Harriett's emerged under highly unusual, indeed, drastic conditions. After all, she was thrust into an environment radically different from the New England maritime town, Salem, where she was born and had lived her entire life. She was suddenly surrounded by people accustomed to rigid class distinctions or monarchical forms of government, whether they be subjects of the Portuguese king, vassals of the Celestial Emperor, or British denizens sporting aristocratic airs if not actual titles. Against these, Harriett fashioned herself as the epitome of republicanism. Consequently, the juxtaposition of republicanism and monarchy laces through her political thinking, conversations, and diary, kept primarily for her sister Mary Ann. Harriett's reading, too, reflected a deep concern for the formation of republics, the rise of independence movements, and royal successions. History, literature, and political news columns occupied her days.

Away from dramatic "reform" at home, her republican ideals, descended from Revolutionary patriots and Founding Fathers (and Mothers), had crystallized in time. She looked backward—to a deference-based society with limited suffrage, governed by informed men of standing who answered to their own conscience rather than the popular will—instead of forward, toward increasing democratic participation. Her outlook was closer to that of the bygone Federalists than the current National Republicans. Thus, her essentially conservative but nonetheless fiery rhetoric was disdainful of Jackson, the first president to embody and speak putatively for the recently franchised "common man." Yet Harriett's unshakable faith in the Republic shines through her most scathing political raillery, which foreshadowed the future Whig Party's anti-Jackson rhetoric. Woman's-sphere ideology hardly constrained her desire for political engagement or for forming, effectively arguing, and defending her opinions.[2] Her own partisan voice, though not expressed via the polls, resounds today—a shrewd reminder that disfranchised women figuratively "voted" with their pens and ink, their persuasive tactics, and their rhetorical strategies. Below, we follow Harriett Low's two eventful journeys, one from Salem to Macao and back again, and the other through the troubled political waters of Jackson's two administrations, in hopes of reconstituting her distinctive political voice and the climate in which it was nurtured.

Reading Politics

Andrew Jackson, inaugurated in March 1829, had been president for only two months when Harriett boarded the *Sumatra*, Macao-bound from Salem, Massachusetts, to seek her fortune among the wealthy bachelor merchants trading with Canton, China. Her attitude toward Jackson remains uncertain because her early correspondence shied away from overtly political declarations. As the daughter of Seth Low, a Salem-based drug and medicine merchant pushed by limited local horizons to relocate to New York in 1828, she probably inherited a skepticism of Old Hickory and his party, the Democratic Republicans—directly descended from the party of Thomas Jefferson, Jackson's paragon of republican governance. After all, it was Jefferson's Embargo Act of 1807 that all but ended foreign trade in ports like Salem. Jackson's populist reforms harking back to his agriculturalist forebear would, according to Harriett's thinking, further damage commerce—including her hometown's already languishing maritime economy. Harriett's uncle William Henry Low also felt the pinch. Seeking to improve his fortunes in Canton, he beckoned Harriett to sail with him in order to nurse his ailing wife, Abigail, who would accompany him. He likely held similarly unfavorable views of the "General" since Jackson saw the powerful northeastern commercial class—of which Low was a member through his partnership in the China-trade commission house Russell and Company—as a force to be contained in the name of "liberty" for the common man. Four years at the firm's Canton countinghouse would secure William's fortune.[3] A creature of her class, region, and family background, Harriett Low was predisposed to spar with Jackson. Among her piles of luggage, books, and vivid memories of home, therefore, she carried a bleak view of the new administration with her on the high seas.

Harriett's political awareness upon embarking extended beyond contemporary American politics into history and international affairs, all informed by her reading, which, by age twenty, she avidly pursued. Like many other young women who obtained an education in the new nation, she probably imbibed the ideology of "Republican motherhood," which posited that schooling would provide valuable intellectual foundations for raising children to be good citizens. Mrs. Ward's Salem school for young women, which she attended, no doubt sharpened Harriett's literacy skills and critical thinking. By the time she left Salem's port, she had acquired a rudimentary knowledge of French and some skill in drawing.[4] On board the *Sumatra* and in exotic Macao, where several historical, political, and cultural traditions merged and often clashed—Chinese imperial rule, Portuguese and Spanish monarchy, and British colonialism via the East India Company—her attention increasingly turned away from novels toward European history, philosophy, and travel, the subjects relevant to her present situation.

It was not long, less than a month after setting sail, before Harriett began shunning the French and British novels in the ship's library to pick up Lucy Aikin's *Memoirs of the Court of Queen Elizabeth*. Perhaps reading about England's tumultuous history, the legacy of which would be ever present in Macao, made her homesick. For, while poring over Aikin, Harriett helped hatch a New England–style Independence Day scheme that included her uncle and a clerk for Russell and Company, Salemite Philip Ammidon, Jr. "We have agreed to day to choose a committee to wait upon Mr. Ammidon and request him to deliver an Oration on the 4th of July," she wrote on June 10. Her uncle was "to write an ode for the occasion" while Harriett herself would "read the 'Declaration of Independence'" before sitting down to "a *good dinner*." The basic scenario—oratory and food—was not unlike commemorations back home.[5]

In the meantime Harriett, would plod through Aikin, finishing the story of Elizabeth I on June 13. She concluded, "there are many things in her reign that I do not like exactly." Two days later, upon delving into Elizabeth Ogilvy Benger's *Life of Anne Boleyn*, she "got so enraged with Henry 8th, I wanted to chop his head off—a merciless wretch." The biography provoked nightmares: "I dreamed that I was to be crowned Queen of England of all things in this world! Never should I *deign* to think of it in my waking hours: hardly tolerate it in my sleeping moments." Undaunted, Harriett took up George Chalmers's *Life of Mary Queen of Scots* and after that another book that would invoke her wrath for its account of abuse of power—Walter Scott's *Napoleon*. This biography's appearance (1827) coincided with anti-Jackson rhetoric during the 1828 campaign. Presidential incumbent John Quincy Adams's partisans suggested an affinity between "tyrants" Jackson and Napoleon and a fate similar to France for the United States should "the General" win. As we will later see, "King Andrew's" high-handed, "imperial" manner reminded her and other Jackson critics of Napoleon.[6]

When the Fourth finally arrived, Harriett was disappointed by its pro-Jackson spirit. Ammidon located among the ship's pickings a printed speech praising Andrew Jackson delivered on July 4, 1828, in Boston's Faneuil Hall. "Mr A[mmidon] read to day H[ardy]. Prince's Jackson Oration," she grumbled and added with scorn, "*for want of a better*." She was not pleased. By underlining "for want of a better," she registered skepticism about his excuse.[7] To her mind, he simply had not tried hard enough to find something politically neutral.

This first hit at Old Hickory appeared in her diary shortly before an entry seething with disgust for Napoleon—"the most selfish mortal that ever lived—of the most unbounded ambition, with the attending evils." Upon finishing Scott's biography on July 20 she condemned the general who betrayed the French Revolutionary spirit to declare himself emperor and king of Italy. He was "a man of the most inordinate ambition and selfish in the extreme." She could not but think "That all he did was for his own glory, not out of any regard for France or her good." Was he all bad? "I now find in hunting for his virtues (I am pulling up vices) he had but few virtues." She feared power's corrupting influence over innately "good-hearted" national leaders who would trade noble aims, indeed, liberty itself, for self-serving ends. She ultimately satisfied herself that he was "brought to know that he was a *mortal* man" through his defeat, exile, and consequent death.[8]

After tussling with court intrigue and the rise and fall of Napoleon, Harriett tackled less emotionally taxing works that gave meaning to her travels and prepared her for life among an international group of government officials, merchants, missionaries, and settlers. As her ship plied the seas, she read about India, England, Holland, Scotland, Switzerland, and France. A month away from anchoring at Macao, she sharpened her French by reading François de Salinac de la Mothe-Fénelon's *Télémaque* and delved into William Paley's *Moral and Political Philosophy*.[9] She could now converse with the most cosmopolitan of merchants who vacationed in Macao after trading season closed in Canton.

A Republican among Monarchists

On September 29, 1829, Harriett Low finally reached Macao, then a Portuguese territory whose citizens fell under the jurisdiction of a royally appointed governor. The Chinese, however, were sovereign over Macao and exercised ultimate authority, when necessary, over sojourners and inhabitants of the peninsula. She and her aunt Abigail would remain in Macao while her uncle William and other merchants did business in Canton's "Factory" area, where foreign women were forbidden by imperial decree.[10] Soon Harriett would become cognizant of how antithetical to a republic Macao's governance was and how much the volatile clash of Portuguese and Chinese rule could affect her.

Until that time, Harriett only indirectly experienced Portuguese dominion and, for the most part, occupied herself with society parties, theatricals, Spanish lessons, sketching, sewing, conversation, and, especially, reading. Newspapers periodically arrived from home, and books came from the local company library or friendly lenders. As one of only a few Americans in Macao, she came to personify her country, and her reading reflected a growing recognition of her nation's unique qualities. Increasingly, she took sides against British travel writers in America. After reading Captain Basil Hall's *Travels in North America*, she lashed out. "I do not think he does the Americans justice, nor do I believe any Englishman ever will," she sniffed on March 6, 1830. "He is constantly drawing comparisons. I feel quite enraged with him at times. . . . He in some places makes the Americans appear quite ridiculous." Reading on, she discerned that "he is vexed that we are so *well* off *as we are*."[11] The country's prosperity in 1827 and 1828, the years of Hall's visit, was dear to her, and she hoped that under Jackson it would remain so.

Such wishes, built upon a growing consciousness of repressive royal governance and purportedly haughty British attitudes toward America found in books and in conversation with British society, prompted her April 1830 letter home (which opened this chapter), filled with fear that Jackson would "ruin our government." Because of the slow and circuitous shipping routes, Harriett received news via word of mouth or newspapers only months after the fact; evidently, she was only just hearing about the political fallout from Jackson's arguably weak appointments and replacements. Immersed in maritime culture, her thoughts naturally fixed upon a naval appointment. "Think of his appointing that Swazey, [*sic*] Esq., that cannot write his own name, to be naval officer, and many others no better," she moaned. In the same letter she spilled forth her building disdain for aristocracy as fashioned in European colonies and reported by British sojourners. "We had some gentlemen who had been residents in C.[alcutta] many years here the other evening," she explained; "It appears to me Macao is far preferable to Calcutta, for unless we had a title in Calcutta we should not be noticed." She then posed a rhetorical question and emphatically answered it by alluding to the new nation's democratic government: "Now is this pleasant? No! . . . It would not suit my republican ideas at all." Despite her claims to the contrary, she was already "deeply into politics."[12] Circumstances prevented her from being otherwise.

More than ever, Harriett eagerly anticipated newspapers from ships, awaited verbal reports from seamen and passengers on board, or welcomed callers who would discuss politics with her. A "good American *dish* of conversation" gratified her immensely. A pleasant morning during the merchants' vacation season went as follows. "Presently in drops King, then Uncle with lots of Boston papers up to the middle of April, so we all set to read them," she wrote in her diary on August 3, 1830. "In comes Talbot, he begins. Ha the bell again, a levee day. . . . Now fancy a busy set," she glowed, "every one bursting out now and then with a bit of news." At times she thought the chatter's content newsworthy enough for her journal. Her April 14, 1830, entry described how dinner party guests "brought us news that the *New Jersey* brought from Cadiz respecting the affairs of Russia and Turkey, [and] the Independence of Greece." Independence movements across Europe and especially the reinstatement of France's republic thrilled her. "Most wonderful of all," she gleamed, "Lafayette's being at the head of the National Guards again, after such a lapse of time. We hear that this revolution was a bloodless one." Reminded of monarchy's shadow in Macao, she rejoiced, "It is thought that Spain and Portugal will follow the example of France, and throw off the yoke, too." Although interested in European nations' freedom, however, she wrote nothing about emancipation for slaves in her own country.[13]

Before long, however, Harriett felt how much her own freedom was restricted—and, indeed, her life imperiled—by an imperial edict barring foreign women from entering Canton's Factory area. Although two British women were allowed to bend the rules, no American had yet done so; Harriett and her aunt felt duty bound to chip away at the barriers. Her daring, however, may well have sparked an international crisis. After the viceroy of Kwangtung and Kwangsi provinces actually enforced some bans in 1830, including the one on women, William, Abigail, and Harriett determined to uphold the British who had defiantly sent some marines and two cannon to the Factory, where servants accused of murdering a Dutch merchant were being held. On November 5, 1830, the three sailed up from Macao to Canton. "I daresay you will think we were wrong to attempt it, thereby breaking the laws of even the Chinese," Harriett apologized in a letter home. When officials found out, Harriett and Abigail were ordered to leave; if not, Russell and Company's trade would be terminated. The women left, with Low still fuming days later at the violation of the freedom she expected as an American citizen. "So we were obliged to give in. . . . but I could not bear to let the Chinese know they could do anything with the Americans." Word got to the emperor himself. "I hear the last report was that the Emperor's answer had been received, forbidding *any* lady to visit Canton henceforth," Harriett wrote with dismay, failing to tell the most frightening part—that, in the future, boats bringing foreign women into Canton would be fired upon if they resisted orders to go back to Macao. Upon the women's return to Macao, the new governor ordered the Low family to depart. "He says he shall not resort to force to drive us away, but, I assure you, it is not very pleasant to be threatened from one place to another," she admitted in a March 1831 letter. The fundamental rights to come and go at will seemed dearer than ever. Rumors of the imminent dissolution of the East India Company in May that year only darkened her horizon all the more. In her sleep, she even dreamed she was back in Salem, so great became her need for escape.[14]

Talking Politics

Harriett sought a modicum of relief in newspapers that allowed her to keep abreast of international events and the doings under Jackson's administration. Much to her chagrin, though, all was not well at home. By April 1831, four members of Jackson's cabinet had resigned, including the secretaries of state (Martin Van Buren), war (John Eaton), the navy (John Branch), and the Treasury (Samuel D. Ingham). Attorney General John McPherson Berrien soon followed suit. Harriett only learned of it in September after the supercargo of the *Atlantic* sent over some papers. Disgruntled with Jackson's appointments from the start, she would now infuse her remarks about the cabinet dissolution with a sly rhetoric of tyranny and "foreignness," perhaps adopted from anti-Jackson editors. "It seems our *King* is following the fashions of the rest of the world and dismissing his Cabinet." While some newspapers drew invidious comparisons to Louis XV's indiscriminate dismissal of ministers, others were more forgiving, pointing out that in Britain and France cabinet changes were the norm. However, the event was unprecedented in the United States; Jackson's dissolution of a cabinet whose members were approved by the Senate implied an authoritarian presidency.[15] Harriett's republican values, her understanding about the foibles of monarchs from reading history, and her own tenuous experiences with Chinese imperial rule all conspired to paint Jackson's purported high-handedness in a negative light.

From then on, Harriett began to "talk politics" with male callers. While she always had been privy to discussion about politics, she distinguished between polite conversation about international events and partisan argumentation. To her, "talking politics" meant taking a stance. "Mr. Baynes called; we talked *politics*," she cryptically wrote in October 1831. What she and the East India Company's "Select Committee" member discussed remains unknown, but the emphasized word, politics, suggests it was a fiery topic. A few days later she corralled another social caller into the political ring: "[Dr. James] Bradford spent an hour with me. We talked politics." This time, Harriett betrayed the content. He "Brought me his sister's letter, giving me the scandal of Washington, the real cause of the dissolution of the Cabinet. Seems there was a Lady at the *Bottom* of it." The "Lady" Harriett spoke about was the former secretary of war's wife, Peggy Eaton, who, though castigated by the cabinet wives because of her rumored sexual impropriety while still married to John Timberlake, was nonetheless ardently defended by Andrew Jackson. Although he stood by the Eatons, some cabinet members did not. He could not abide cabinet disharmony nor sustain the scandal's dire effect upon the administration. To Jackson's mind, the "petticoat affair" was a "conspiracy" conjured by Vice President John C. Calhoun's factions to ruin his chances for reelection. The cabinet resignations ensued, kicked off by Van Buren. Although unsavory stories about the Eatons had circulated for years in Washington, the *Telegraph* publicized the scandal in May 1831. Possibly, some damning tidbit of information linking Eaton to the resignations (the press had offered diverse reasons) appeared in the letter Harriett read. Her saucy pun on the word "Bottom" suggests a salacious letter indeed. Months later she was still amusing herself with Jackson's political impasse. When her language tutor came to call with "a variety of topics of conversation" on March 30, 1832, Low relished the time they spent "abusing our *beloved* president Jackson and his *whole cabinet*"—probably in Spanish. Again, a wicked play on words unveiled her partisan stance. The "whole" cabinet was, actually, in shambles, or full of "holes." She could afford to laugh, for she had yet to learn that, despite the scandal, Jackson would run for and win a second term as president in 1832.[16] But for now, with Anglo-Chinese relations turning bellicose and the East India Company's charter renewal looming (the lack of which could lead to the British monopoly's dissolution), she could only hope her uncle could accomplish his company's work so they could all head for home.

During the summer of 1832 the idea of home became more tangible, independence dearer than ever, and Jacksonianism less provoking as the "old soldier" approached his first term's end. "Liberty, how prized—our country, how happy. . . . growing in every sense of the word," Harriett radiantly greeted yet another Fourth of July. Jackson's America was indeed prospering—in wealth, manufacturing, industrialism, urban growth, and westward migration. Her own family's fortunes grew with the nation's improved transportation; her father's 1828 business relocation to New York City, linked to the Erie Canal, exceeded all expectations. "We ought not to complain of *General* Jackson," she averred, "for certainly his has been a good reign." After meting out an ounce of praise, she retracted—"although I do not think we owe it to him." The backhanded compliment, characterizing what she considered an increasingly imperial president favored only by circumstance, was followed by a sardonic analogy to her favorite military villain. "His turn came in a happy time, like Napoleon's, only a different sort of *glory*," she snickered, confident that, like the French general, "General Jackson" had met his political "Waterloo" in the Eaton scandal. Certain that his would be a one-term presidency, she sneered, "The domestic discords however do him no honor." These drowned out the chords of peace and prosperity that attracted even English laborers to migrate in unprecedented numbers to America and its burgeoning factories.[17]

Harriett's spirits soon took another turn downward during her last year in Macao amid distressing news from America and her own failed gambits at marrying. For one, she belatedly learned that Old Hickory had survived his cabinet breakup and was running for a second term as president. "Am afraid our poor country is in a *bad way* from all accounts," she penned in March 1833, with only dim recollections of toasting America's abundance during happier times. "I think I shall *weep* if *Jackson* is reelected." Hopes of returning home to a country steered by a new administration were dashed. Other dreams died that year too, notably, marriage. "The fact is," she wrote shortly before disparaging the "poor" country, "I am in a *bad way*." Two promising courtships—one with the company's chaplain and one with an editor—had ended in disaster. She finally poured out her heart to her diary. "I thought I had found one . . . on whom I could lean. I thought—but there it is vain, let it pass." Despondency she had earlier described as a "weight hanging upon my spirits" now suffocated her. "Fear this will be the *longest* year," she wrote on April 7, 1833, with only eight months left to endure.[18] The final weeks in Macao would seem like an eternity.

King Andrew versus Nullification

Little wonder then that on May 4, 1833, combined news of Jackson's victory at the polls in 1832 and South Carolina's threats of secession from the Union overwhelmed her. "Uncle brings us dreadful news from America," she scribbled in a panic. "That is the re-election of Jackson and the Declaration of Independence of the S.[outh] Carolinians." The news struck like lightning, not only because the American papers Harriett received were relatively few and far between, but also because events proceeded rapidly. The July 1832 Tariff Bill, deemed by some Southerners protectionism for Northern industry at the expense of their region, led South Carolina's legislature to call for a November "Nullification Convention" that passed the "Declaration," to which Harriett referred, that the 1828 and 1832 tariff laws were "null and void" in that state and would not be enforced. Federal efforts to enforce the law would be met with resistance and secession from the Union. "It is a disgrace to the country and I shall be prepared to hear any thing," Harriett despaired, her mind racing through a hellish future scenario. "The dissolution of the Union will follow I dare say. And the next thing Jackson will be declared King, Emperor or something of the kind, and about the time we are ready to come home there will be civil war and all sorts of evils may be anticipated." She was not exaggerating the possibility of hostilities. Jackson himself maintained that civil war would be a consequence of nullification. Although, like him, she was staunchly supportive of the Union, she blamed him for the troubles nonetheless. "Well I shall no longer fight for the happiness of our government, when such a man as Jackson can fill the highest station," she vowed. Ultimately, however, she held the voters accountable. Wondering just how viable was democratic governance by the masses, she punctuated her remarks with a peevish declaration: "by consent of the *people* too." After defending the manners of ordinary Americans so vociferously, she found little room in her heart to forgive them now. "Well it is 'truly awful' I think that the *people* should choose such a man." The republic that she dearly loved could ill afford this much democracy.[19]

Even those friends accustomed to Harriett's firebrand argumentation noticed this new level of exasperation. Her "political talk" had turned to invective. "I have been scolding furiously about it," she fulminated as she wrote, knowing she had risked social approbation by airing political grievances. The therapeutic effect of reconstructing one testy conversation registered on the page.

> Miss Low, "hope you have recovered?
>
> Thank you I have quite but was not aware I had been ill.
>
> Why you did not patronize the Concert last night."
>
> "Well," I said, "I did not send word I was sick—I said I was *lazy*," which certainly was my excuse.

Acknowledging the transgression of sociabilities, Harriett summoned a quote from the Bible (Isaiah 48:22) to quell the political fire consuming her: "'There's no peace for the wicked.'" It is difficult to tell to whom she refers as the "wicked" one—she herself for being a political hothead, or Jackson for provoking the South Carolinians with all his blustering.[20]

More dire, but outdated, news reports about secession threats filtered in throughout the spring and summer of 1833, causing Harriett no end of grief. After all, she had no way of knowing that a new "Compromise Tariff" signed into law in March 1833, bolstered by a "Force Bill" allowing Jackson to use military force to quell rebellion, had already resolved the conflict. A paper issued in December 1832 that she only received the following May offered little comfort. "The Carolinians seem to be taking a decided stand," she worried. "I fear for the peace and quiet of the Union—a division seems to be at hand." After what must have seemed an endless time, papers arrived on June 7 with news that gave her a faint glimmer of hope in Jackson's leadership, if not the crisis's denouement. In December 1832, in response to the Ordinance of Nullification, Jackson published a strongly worded proclamation denouncing it as subversive of the Constitution and the pending disunion as treasonous. Harriett applauded it. "Was exceedingly pleased with the President's Proclamation with regard to Carolina and think with him that they ought to be *whipped* if they do not behave." While reading the document, largely written by Secretary of State Edward Livingston, she rightly detected a tone and syntax unlike the general's. "I do not give the old gentleman the credit of writing this spirited and elegant production, but that he has had the good sense to subscribe to such sentiments has raised him some degrees in my estimation." This would be the one unqualified commendation she would grant Jackson. "I do not feel very anxious now about the division," she rightly assumed, "as I think the Carolinians will certainly yield." For her, however, American politics was part of an international drama in which republicanism and monarchy battled. "There seems to be terrible times in Europe too," she noted as she scanned the sheets finding "rebellion here and rebellion there, and all about this said *independence*, a spirit which is placed in every human breast." The fate of the world, of which she was now virtually a citizen, seemed to hang on a slender thread. No wonder she "Did not find much in the papers except *politics* to interest."[21] All issues beyond the crucial ones—war and peace, tyranny and independence—receded into the background. Newspapers, rather than books, became her lifeline to the future.

On the last Fourth of July she would spend in Macao, Harriett made a desperate toast to "The glorious birth day of our Independence!" Would the spirit of independence, she wondered, be extinguished by disunion? She prodded her diary for an answer. "How much I should like to know if *Union* and *peace* is still preserved." Around the same time she asked her parents for answers, knowing well that their reply would take months to arrive. Writing home, she again pondered the fate of the young and seemingly fragile Republic. "What a shame that the Union should begin to totter with the death of the Signers!" she regretted. By this time she had probably read about the increasingly violent rhetoric, the legislature's antiproclamation resolution, the marshaling of volunteer regiments, and other signs of unrest in the Palmetto State. Her initial reaction to Jackson's proclamation soured upon reflection. It "seems hostile and the reception of it by the Carolinians worse," she observed. She was vainly hoping for an update from home before leaving Macao. "I assure you we feel very anxious to know our country's fate." Harriett simply could not resign herself to four more years of Jackson and reuniting with a country wracked by war. Only the Bible offered consolation. "But as I have said before," she reassured her parents, "'Patience must have her perfect work'" (James 1:4).[22]

On July 17, reports of the Compromise Tariff finally dripped in, lifting Harriett's spirits. "Do not see any other news of importance except that peace is restored in America by the modification of the Tariff," she sighed in relief. "So I hope they have done with nullification and that our President will presume no more upon *veto's* [*sic*]." Jackson liberally used his veto power—more so than any president before him—even against bills that left little doubt about their constitutionality (the precedent set for vetoing). She perhaps understood that the mere threat to veto created in the Congress deference to the president, which to her signaled an imperial executive intrusion upon legislative prerogative. Although Harriett was heartened by the Compromise Tariff, she never forgave Jackson for, as she saw it, putting the Republic in peril. Having read about and experienced firsthand life under imperial rule, she loathed the very thought of a backlash against republicanism. She would later avow her family's commendation of the Whig Party, which, in adopting its name from those who opposed the monarchical party in England, instinctively appealed to the fiercest of anti-Jacksonians.[23]

Homeward Bound

One of the last political conversations Low had before leaving Macao on November 19, 1833, on the *Waterloo*—a name that must have greatly amused her—focused on "the merits of republics and monarchy's [*sic*]." In the heat of an August evening, she, her uncle, and her aunt spent time together without guests, perhaps vigorously assailing the Celestial Emperor, the British Crown, and the Portuguese king while weighing the merits of their own country, jeopardized as it was by disunion during the previous autumn and winter. Nonetheless, Harriett was anxious to return, and no doubt William was also. After all, relations between China and English merchants were fast becoming a powder keg that would finally explode in the Opium War (1839–42). In addition to the worsening conflict, the severe demands of Russell and Company were taking its toll. William had served the company well while accumulating his wealth, but he lost his health as a consequence. Nagging coughs that constantly alarmed Harriett were symptomatic of tuberculosis, which eventually took his life at Cape Town on the way home. While he did not live to see how much the nation had changed since he left Salem in 1829, his niece and wife did.[24]

The voyage home, ending in September 1834, took nearly a year—a long time for seasick passengers and world-weary politicos. Much was happening at the capital before and during the 1833–34 congressional session unbeknownst to Harriett, who could only feed upon morsels of news coming to her at irregular intervals. Jackson's war on the Bank of the United States had intensified, the Treasury secretary, reluctant to move deposits into state banks, was summarily dismissed, and the Senate had resolved to censure the president. Banknotes were being phased out for hard money. During this tumultuous time a new anti-Jackson party, called the Whig Party, was being born. For most of her time on the high seas, Low was kept in the dark. But on June 8, 1834, an outward-bound American ship loaded with papers and mail delivered its bounty to her vessel. Starved for news, she and her aunt Abigail hungrily studied the sheets all day long. "[P]olitics . . . are in such a state," she reported to her diary that evening. Another nullification crisis, probably the one involving Alabama and its claim to Creek Indian land, had struck around the time she was packing in the fall of 1833. Dreading a replay of the showdown with South Carolina, she prayed, "I hope we shall not find civil war when we get home." That day Low also arraigned Jackson for "sounding the people," probably during his grand national tour, with a stop among her own Salemites, during the summer of 1833. Or maybe she meant his populist appeals made through the *Globe* for currency reform or for his "pet banks." Whatever the case, she was certain "Our old general . . . seems to be wishing to play 'Napoleon' or dictator"; she would have doubtlessly rooted, along with the Senate, for his censure. The "Many failures . . . on account of his measures" began "worrying" Harriett about the economic health not only of the nation but also of her own family. Their fortunes and hers were wrapped up in administration reforms that were purportedly shaking the very foundations of the monetary system. "I have looked in vain for my dear father's name in the advertisements in the *Journal of Commerce* where he always appears, but alas it is not there. What is the reason?" Fearing his business failure, she could only "hope nothing has happened to him." Seth Low's business was yet intact, but he blamed a later financial panic (he suspended payments in 1837) on Jacksonian "removal of deposits" and "metallic currency."[25] Consequently, Low and his family became zealous Whigs throughout the 1840s.

On September 21, 1834, only a few days before she stepped back onto American soil, Harriett, who had been so anxious to see familiar locales, curiously imagined herself a visitor about to enter a new land. "I cannot explain how I feel. It is a sort of all *overness* and yet it appears to me that I am going to a strange place as I have been to so many before." True, Jacksonianism had transformed the political and economic landscape, but nonpolitical events would dramatically alter her life trajectory. Within two years she would, ironically, marry London banker John Hillard, move to England, and meet the famed author Harriet Martineau, who tried, unsuccessfully, to persuade her to publish her Macao journal. Instead of becoming an "*authoress*," as she once fancied, Low opted for a domestic existence, caring for her five daughters and her husband, who, upon becoming insolvent in 1848, took her back to New York. During the years in London, however, Harriett corresponded with her brothers, who filled her in on Whig victories, campaigns, and other timely events.[26] Could she have voted on American soil, she, like most other anti-Jackson women we located, probably would have cast her ballot for William Henry Harrison in 1840. It is not hard, however, to imagine Harriett "talking politics" with her male British friends, who, falling under the spell of her argumentation, passion, and conviction, voted precisely as she wished.

·· 2 ··

"Becoming Interested in Politics"

Women at the Birth of the Second Party System

Sarah Watson, a schoolteacher in Hartford, Connecticut, carefully followed the 1834 election returns for her state's representatives. For her, the results were good. On April 7 she wrote in her diary that the "Clay party triumphed in all towns [I] hear of excepting Glastonbury." As if those victories had ushered in an era of partisanship for her, she added, "becoming interested in Politics." A few days later she learned of the "triumph of the *right party* in N.Y." in municipal elections. The "right party," like the "Clay party," was actually the nascent Whig Party, a coalition of anti-Jacksonians spearheaded in Congress by Henry Clay. As leader of the opposition party, he first uttered the term "Whig" in a Senate speech that March. It had been adopted only the year before in parts of the South and was not yet widely used, nor was the party fully developed. So it comes as no surprise that Watson would not call 1834 candidates "Whigs," even though some local papers did. Whatever she labeled them, the partisans appealed to her and opened unexplored vistas of political consciousness. She was witnessing the birth of an entirely new party system—the Second Party System, which pitted Whigs against Democrats—and she wanted to be part of it.[1]

Like the men who voted Whig that spring, some women, too, clamored for change in government. But the buildup of support for the party was slow in coming. It began with an anti-Jacksonian stance, similar to the one Harriett Low expressed, that only gradually found voice under the banner of "Whig." If male politicos were slow to unite under that banner, so too were women. But they eventually did. The presidential election of 1840 drew sustenance from these women all over the country who, for the first time, in massive numbers, called themselves Whigs. They generally avowed Henry Clay's "American System": a strong Bank of the United States, extensive internal improvements, tough protective tariffs, and a robust manufacturing system. They celebrated when Whig president William Henry Harrison took office in 1841. A few of the women featured here, at the very nascence of the Second Party System, would later add their unequivocally partisan voices to the chorus.

In this chapter we trace the evolution of political consciousness and the first inklings of Whig partisanship among New England women during Jackson's two-term presidency. While they did not assume, at this time, any party name—National Republican, Anti-Mason, or Whig—they were fixedly anti-Jackson. Few had anything good or even neutral to say about him. From his triumph in 1828 to his last days in office, they made cutting remarks. Anti-Jackson women impugned his character, ridiculed his manners and looks (one alleged he was "chewing his cud"), disregarded his economic agenda, and disparaged his Indian removal policy.[2] Emphatically, there was more than personal animosity in this opposition; rather it was based on what he stood for. For example, anti-Jackson feelings might only have been intensified by what these women would have objected to anyway in the removal policy. While some early foes of Jackson evidently never turned Whig, others did. Short of calling themselves that by 1834, however, they would, in hindsight, have passed the "duck test," because of their espousal of certain politicians and causes. Far fewer might have been "Democrats." Still others discussed and read about political issues at home and abroad without taking any apparent side. Their lack of partisanship, however, made them no less politically curious. In this chapter we see them, and their more openly partisan counterparts, puzzling through the maze of political developments during this crucial moment in U.S. political history. We also witness the first female national petition campaign and early attempts by women to head fund-raising associations for civic and international causes.

Because of the overwhelming evidence of anti-Jacksonianism among these women, we will begin with their voices, followed by those who either admired Jackson or remained open-minded. Other statesmen also intrigued women who read about them in papers, visited their birthplaces, or studied their speeches. But none appealed more than Daniel Webster, to whose reception we devote the next section of this chapter. We will then move beyond engagement of larger-than-life politicians to explore women's incipient activism in two case studies: the war for Greek independence and the struggle to finish the Bunker Hill Monument in Charlestown, Massachusetts. Although women were not yet actively campaigning, they kept abreast of local, state, and national elections, and so their take on these contests forms the basis of the next section. We end with a nod toward those civic holidays—"Election Day" and Independence Day—that elicited women's patriotic and sometimes partisan sentiments.

Women and Jackson

Long before the Whig Party coalesced in 1834 in defiance of Jackson, women began to think of themselves as antagonists of the administration. Some remained faithful to the National Republicans under John Quincy Adams, the incumbent in 1828. So news of his defeat set off alarms, even across the ocean. The wife of the U.S. ambassador to Spain, Lucretia Everett, who was once confident that Adams's reelection was in the bag, was crushed. "I had thought . . . that a good Providence would have hardly permitted so bad a man as the General to be elevated to so high a dignity as presiding over a free people," she wrote from Madrid to her sister-in-law Sarah P. E. Hale in Boston. "I trust he will not be permitted to do much mischief," she surmised, while fearing the "general change" or reform that Harriett Low detested. She worried that her husband, Alexander Hill Everett, appointed by Adams in 1825, would lose his post and that Hale would "have the pleasure of seeing us at home"—which she did in 1829. Inauguration Day on March 4 of that year left Lucretia "anxious to hear . . . what they mean to do at Washington." On that same day, a fellow skeptic named Elizabeth Pierce simmered over noisy observances in Northampton, Massachusetts. "Much time & powder has been wasted here today by the friends of President Jackson," she disburdened to her diary.[3] As we will see, she became a fierce opponent of Jackson's Indian removal.

The Indian Removal Act of 1830, the first major piece of legislation Jackson signed into law, was sharply opposed by many women who felt it was cruel and unjust to Native Americans. The act authorized him to "exchange" eastern Indian-owned land for unorganized land in the West and effectively to relocate Indians there who insisted on abiding by their own law instead of that of U.S. states. The Removal Bill passed only after heated debate in the Senate and House of Representatives. To register their disapproval prior to its signing, Northern women inundated Congress with antiremoval petitions, inspired by educator Catharine Beecher's 1829 "Circular Addressed to Benevolent Ladies of the U. States." Thus the earliest female national petition campaign was launched. Others simply read, attended lectures, or joined charitable societies promoting missionary work among Indians.[4]

One such antiremoval woman was the above-mentioned Elizabeth Pierce, a Brookline, Massachusetts, Unitarian minister's daughter who was nursing her shopkeeper grandfather in Northampton when legislation was in motion. Her dedication to Native American rights began with her 1825 reading of the just-published *Memoir of Catharine Brown*, a Cherokee convert to Christianity. "It awakened in my heart," she wrote in her commonplace book, "an ardent &, I trust, invincible desire to dwell with & instruct that injured race." She did neither, but instead imbibed anything and everything about the Cherokee. Sometime in 1829, she read a poem on the death of Catherine Brown that had been published in the *Cherokee Phoenix* in March as an example of "Indian Poetry." Pierce diligently copied the lines in her book of literary extracts. In March, she recorded favorable gossip about the excellent singing, reading, and spelling bee performed in a local meetinghouse by "3 Indian children" who pulled upon the heart strings (and purse strings) of generous auditors. That summer, a *New York Observer* essay on Sequoyah, who devised a Cherokee alphabet, enlightened her: "The sagacity of our red brethren is very remarkable."[5] He and the well-read Elizabeth Pierce shared a regard for literacy.

Elizabeth took a political turn after reading the annual "Message of the President"—today known as the State of the Union Address—with her grandfather and cousin Anne in December 1829. In Jackson's first address she immediately saw the destructive writing on the wall of justice. "I am grieved & distressed at the proposed treatment of the Indians," she despaired over Jackson's well-laid plan for removal. "Will not the judge of Heaven be felt in this land, once termed a land of Freedom?"[6] She could only hope that divine intervention would derail him.

Soon enough, this modest minister's daughter was presuming that ordinary women like her should not submit to Jackson's will—at least not without a struggle. Shortly after the new year began, Elizabeth and her friend Harriet Clark, who was also "warmly enlisted for the Indians," imagined the possibilities of resistance together over tea. Moved by Harriet's eloquence, Elizabeth could almost see her on the podium: "Although I should be unwilling that a lady should plead in public, I should like much to have her gain the private ear of some influential characters." Harriet, armed with a copy of Beecher's "Circular," took matters a step further. Elizabeth's journal reported what she said. "'If the gentlemen do not interest themselves sufficiently the ladies ought to exert their influence,'" Harriet reasoned; after all, "'the English ladies petitioned Parliament & exerted a powerful influence.'" To soften the political thrust, she summoned the Old Testament figure alluded to in the circular, Esther, who saved Persian Jews from genocide with her suasion. "'Besides,'" Harriet averred, "'Mordecai said to Esther when exhorting her to plead for the poor condemned Jews Who knowest but thou art come to the kingdom for such a time as this.'" Putting herself in Esther's shoes, she rhetorically asked, "'Who knows but females in this country have been permitted to possess an influence, that it might be effectually exerted in the cause of them that are ready to perish at this time. We must share in the curse & disgrace that may be expected to rest upon our country in consequence of this unjust oppression.'" Harriet now had Elizabeth where she wanted her. "I told Harriet," Elizabeth responded, "that those who should be sufficiently ardent to carry out the plan, would do it without judgment" of God. "I think the present crisis, is one of deep interest, & if it be the duty of females to lift up the supplicating voice," Elizabeth conceded, "I hope they will not remain silent." She might have even signed a petition. But she was far from optimistic about changing the course of history. "I fear, it will be too late," she regretted, "perhaps it is already."[7] Indeed, the Indians' fate soon would be sealed.

But Elizabeth did not give up just yet. A mélange of evils, "Indian oppression, masonic delusion, Sabbath profanation, anatomical dissection," would collectively "awaken & agitate the public mind," she was certain. She searched for a ray of sunshine in reading materials. While a pro-removal article in the January 1830 *North American Review* that "hardly . . . viewed the subject in *all* its bearings" disappointed her, a speech on the "Ind[ian] question" by Senator Theodore Frelinghuysen, who strenuously opposed removal, surely comforted her. When Harriet Clark stopped by again in March, they chatted over these readings and "the ever interesting Indian subject."[8] If they could not speak in public, they at least could speak to each other.

After Jackson signed the Indian Removal Bill in May 1830, Elizabeth Pierce was still waging her own war against official policies. By the summer, she and her little sister Mary were meeting with an "Indian Society" to sew quilts and other articles to sell for the cause. After reading in December a "spirit stirring" speech by antiremoval senator Peleg Sprague delivered during the heat of debates, she once again invoked spiritual rectification: "Will not the cry of the oppressed ascend to God & call for vengeance upon our guilty land." Sprague's oration was but one in a volume of congressional *Speeches on the Passage of the Bill for the Removal of the Indians* (1830), which appeared within months of the bill's signing. Elizabeth was not alone among a reading public wanting to "hear" the fiery barrage of naysayers. In reading aloud at least two other speeches from the collection to her grandfather, she role-played the male public rhetor. "A fine effort," she asserted after sounding Representative Henry Randolph Storrs's speech; but she added, with chagrin, "Alas! How unavailing!" Even superior oratory could not save the Indian. Not long after reading it, her grandfather died, and she, too, fell silent on the matter. "May the Lord peacefully succeed the efforts of their friends!" was her last lament to her diary.[9]

After the Removal Act was passed, many women sided with defiant Indians. The Cherokee Nation even took its suit against the state of Georgia all the way to the U.S. Supreme Court in 1831, but to no ultimate avail. The next year, Chief Major Ridge and *Cherokee Phoenix* editor Elias Boudinot, also known as Buck Watie, toured New England to plead for aid. "The Cherokees are here getting sympathy and money, both I dare say in plenty," Eliza Davis, a Worcester, Massachusetts, homemaker wrote in March 1832 to her husband, a U.S. representative in Washington, D.C. One bigwig dished out fifty dollars. She commended her father, a Unitarian minister, who "did wonders in the way of an address" at one meeting and castigated a local who "spoke on the wrong side and was hissed, laughed at, and spit upon." In Boston, the Cherokees drew in even greater audiences. A young woman who went "sliding, slipping and slumping down" to a lecture on a wet April day in 1832 to hear them "never was in . . . a fuller church." Boudinot, who "talked like a man of sense and education" but was "sometimes dry and uninteresting," left her cold. But the next guest, possibly Major Ridge, who spoke "with all his heart and soul," struck a chord of commonality. "He was sometimes vehement," she exclaimed, "and Gen. Jackson had one or two side knocks, to my great satisfaction." Neither persuasion nor money, however, could turn back the tides. Under the next Democratic president, Martin Van Buren, the thousands of Cherokee still remaining in Georgia in 1838 were forced down the "Trail of Tears" to Oklahoma—or to their own deaths along the way.[10]

Indian removal was not the only issue at stake for anti-Jackson women. Some denounced the president's high-handed manner, purported misuse of executive power, and seeming violation of the Constitution—all rallying points for congressional Whigs-in-the-making, especially after Jackson's 1832 veto of the Bank's recharter. Among those was Harriet Prescott, a failed sea captain's wife living in New Castle, New Hampshire. In one 1830 speech by U.S. senator John Holmes, an associate of Henry Clay, she found fodder against the administration. "If every *honest* man in the United States would *read* it," she posited, "I think the 'high flying' Autocrats at Washington would soon find that *it is not* for *them* to make havoc of the Constitution which the Father's' [*sic*] purchased with their blood." Holmes's speech on the unconstitutionality of executive removal and replacement of officers during Senate recess resonated with Prescott, who had recently read about the 1829 politically motivated dismissal of Baltimore naval officer William B. Barney and his wife Mary's letter of protest to Jackson that was widely reprinted, publicized, and—in Democratic newspapers—vilified. They "think there is too much *nerve* in it to have been the production of a *lady's* pen," Prescott jeered. "If . . . to see a husband and children beggared will not give energy even to a female's pen—then there is nothing in human events that can have sufficient power to do so." Prescott condoned Barney's public appearance in print for justice' sake. Like Prescott, Eliza Davis inveighed against Jackson's supposedly mercurial and, ultimately, self-serving interpretation of the Constitution. "General Jackson sees every thing one day, nothing the next," she characterized him in 1833, and joked that "women had better take the reins." Playing upon a common sexist stereotype, she chortled, "We can do things in as summary a way as even Jackson might desire, and if we vacillate it is but in character." Sophia Peabody, future wife of author Nathaniel Hawthorne, also railed against Jackson's perceived abuse of presidential power—his "semblance of royalty"—in March 1834. "He is nothing but a great puppet," she sniped, "which Van Buren & the rest of the ministry have set on the throne to amuse people, while they play mad pranks in the cabinet." Regarding Jackson's war on the Bank of the United States, she was "angry" that he "should influence" people's purses and cursed, if wrongly, "King Andrew" for the economic downturn after his 1833 removal of deposits into state banks.[11] Anti-Jackson women undeniably spoke their minds.

But what did pro-Jackson women have to say? Little, to be sure, although one Massachusetts state representative's wife, Jane Woodbury Rantoul, whose extant letters are few, was powerful because of her relation to Levi Woodbury, secretary of the Treasury. While state Democratic leaders were throwing their weight around in 1836 over the new collector for the Port of Boston's appointment, Jane was quietly contemplating if and when to spring into action on behalf of Marcus Morton, a state Supreme Court associate justice. "I shall not give him my influence if he will not make my husband judge of the Court," she coolly calculated. Some Democratic women were spotted by others. "He is a warm Jackson-man and his daughter is a warm politician of the same kidney" was the way one man described Democratic New Hampshire congressman Henry Hubbard and his scion Sarah at an 1834 Worcester party. We found one woman writing shortly after Jackson's presidency ended, but she let others speak for her. During an 1839 Boston omnibus trip, she overhead a passenger "who seemed to have great compass of thought" praise the general: "'For my part I do not think so ill of Gen. Jackson as many do,'" he opined. "'I believe he wished to do right & when he had an object in view, he was very determined.'" That she transcribed the "interesting talk" in her diary and later belittled controversial Whig legislation hints at Jacksonian favoritism.[12]

Some apparently nonpartisan women simply noted Jackson's existence. Mary Hall, a Lowell mill operative, recorded in her diary in June 1833 that "General Andrew Jackson the President of the United States visited Concord." She penned, "I have been in town to day and seen him." On an 1831 steamboat trip, another woman relished hearing "Col. [Davy] Crockett," the House member from Tennessee, speak "cooly of the administration he 'knowed' a thing or two" about. Although he opposed Indian removal, "he said he was still a Jackson man but Jackson was now a Van Buren Man." In depicting for her diary a fellow traveler, the Jacksonian senator Felix Grundy, as having "a very florid complexion," she even likened herself to Washington newspaper editor Anne Royall. She shared Royall's mission to "describe members of Congress whenever I meet them as natural curiosities."[13] Nonpartisanship did not preclude fascination with politicos.

Women and Webster

Women were more likely, however, to write about politicians who would gradually align with Whigs. They devoured John Quincy Adams's speeches, rooted for presidential candidate Henry Clay in 1832, and followed the career of Josiah Quincy III from lawyer to mayor of Boston to president of Harvard College in 1829. Above all, they reserved a special place in their journals and letters—even if it was sometimes an equivocal one—for Daniel Webster. During Jackson's heyday, Webster, a formidable orator and lawyer, served as a U.S. senator from Massachusetts. The first news of his devastating replies to South Carolina senator Robert Hayne in the late-January 1830 debate over a resolution to limit sales of public lands was eagerly awaited by Sarah P. E. Hale and her editor-husband in Boston. "We look out very anxiously for Mr. Webster's speech, we have heard such great accounts of it," she wrote on February 2 to her brother. "Mr. Hayne[']s has just reached us, and I suppose before long we shall see the other." As a trial lawyer, too, Webster won women's affection. When he assisted the state's prosecution in the 1830 murder trial of John Francis Knapp of Salem, Harriet Prescott, who once walked a "long distance" just to see his house, hailed him. "Our favorite Mr Webster—seems to reap laurels even from the cypress of death," she wrote to her daughter. But Prescott detected partisan reaction. "I have heard that the Jacksonians made a charge against him of 'dastard measures.'—because he declined being counsel for the prisoners," she reported. She chalked it all up to politics as usual: "the friends of *Jacksonianism* can not love Mr Webster—too mighty is the mark of his right onward mind to meet with their approbation." As news spread in 1835 that Webster was seeking the presidency, Prescott was oddly let down. Preferring him in the Senate, she argued, "Almost *any* man can discharge *well enough* the functions of President,—but the place that Daniel Webster occupies can hardly find another such occupant." With such renown ringing throughout New England, it is no wonder that Mary Pierce, a Northampton, Massachusetts, Gothic Seminary student, was "highly *honoured*" when he showed up in July 1836 to examine her history class. "He . . . asked us some questions, which we answered, I can assure you, to the very best of our ability."[14] She would later become a devoted Whig.

Although Webster enjoyed widespread celebrity in New England, he was not above reproach. Sarah Hale's sister-in-law Charlotte Everett thought Webster was a "capricious, odd creature," who "*condescended*" to shake hands when she once visited the Senate to hear speeches. Sophia Peabody agreed that "Webster is not sound at the core," maybe because of his warming up to Jackson in 1833 over his adamant stance in the nullification crisis. For whatever reason, she judged that "Webster, in his failings, shamefully belies his godlike nature."[15] Even deities had flaws.

Activism

Not always content to just read about politics, some women acted upon their politicization. The 1830s saw waves of benevolent, reform, and abolitionist societies that women flocked to, to cure social ills or end slavery. As we have seen, the first women's national antiremoval petition campaign was also launched at this time, followed by large-scale antislavery petition drives. But women's groups devoted to national or international mainstream political causes also sprouted up in New England. The Greek war for independence from the Ottoman Empire (1821–29) won over hearts in Boston, Dedham, and Dorchester, Massachusetts. These coteries, roused by Whiggish physician and volunteer Samuel Gridley Howe, who lectured on his experiences, held "Greek meetings" in the spring of 1828 to impel fund-raising drives, organize purchasing committees, and sponsor sewing circles for war victims' benefit. Sarah P. E. Hale participated in one such Boston event. "You will see by the papers that our ladies have had a Greek meeting," she informed her U.S. representative brother Edward, who had earlier plugged the cause in the *North American Review*. Despite poor planning, the turnout was phenomenal. "Parthenon [Hall] was so crowded that we were obliged to adjourn to [John] Pierpont's meeting room, and that was crowded in a moment with ladies . . . who seemed to take the deepest interest in the matter." There the women could join committees, adopt resolutions, or simply hear rousing speeches. According to Hale, "now the whole female population of the town is in a stir." Yet women's public political advocacy came at a price. "There is a most scandalous coldness among many people," Hale testified; "indeed they tried their hand to turn this little attempt of the ladies into ridicule," probably through news reports. So plans for "getting up a gentlemans meeting" were abandoned.[16] Female-instigated mobilization of men was out of line for some folk.

Two years later women took up a patriotic cause nearer at hand—the completion of the Charlestown, Massachusetts, Bunker Hill Monument, commemorating the famous 1775 Revolutionary War battle. To shame lackadaisical locals who had let funding dry up, Sarah Josepha Hale (no relation to Sarah P. E.), the editor of Boston's *Ladies' Magazine and Literary Gazette*, turned to her readers. In her February 1830 editorial "The Worth of Money," she urged the "ladies in this city" to donate cash otherwise allocated for luxuries. Wanting this to be a solely feminine endeavor, she advised that "neither husbands, fathers, or brothers are to be importuned." Hale was sure to get men on board, however, and even wrote to anti-Jacksonian state legislator Henry A. S. Dearborn, son and namesake of the acclaimed Revolutionary War hero, hoping "the gentlemen will take sufficient interest . . . to encourage the ladies to proceed." Hale deferentially assured him "if I were convinced the measure would increase the vanity of my sex to be *distinguished* as *publick benefactors* rather than for their *domestic virtues* I would oppose it." Of course, Hale and the throngs of women who answered her call were making a public and arguably even partisan statement, for the men who founded the Bunker Hill Monument Association in 1823—Daniel Webster, Edward Everett, and *North American Review* editor William Tudor—and those keeping it afloat thereafter, were proto-Whigs. By March 11, 1830, a society of Boston women sprang up that included Committee of Correspondence members Sarah P. E. Hale and Lucretia Everett, whom we have met, along with novelist Lydia Maria Child and Katherine Bigelow Lawrence, wife of Boston industrialist Abbott Lawrence, among others. They composed a circular, printed in periodicals and distributed as a lithograph, enjoining others to "form societies in their respective towns." Subsequently, newspapers throughout New England beseeched women to unite. Contributions streamed in from the Charlestown convent, Roxbury, Watertown, Medford, and West Cambridge in Massachusetts, and Portsmouth, New Hampshire, among other places. Amounts varied; one Bostonian "pleased with the sum" a Gardiner, Maine, friend donated, was appalled by stinginess in more populous Portland. By the end of May, New England women amassed three thousand dollars—no small amount then. Thereafter, the fanfare about feminine bankrolling died down as news of renewed male financing spread. But some women carried on, even if informally. In 1835, Sarah P. E. Hale was peddling monument association subscriptions through word of mouth. By the end of the decade, money was only dribbling in as construction lagged. Women came to the monument's rescue again, however, when, nudged by editor Hale, they hosted a huge Bunker Hill Monument fair that just happened to coincide with the September 1840 Whig Bunker Hill convention.[17]

Elections

Long before the 1840 presidential election drew unprecedented numbers of female partisans into the campaign fray, many women preoccupied themselves with municipal, state, and, to a lesser degree, national voting, if not electioneering. We have already seen how much Lucretia Everett and Harriett Low were betting on Jackson's downfall in 1828 and 1832 and how thrilled Sarah Watson was to hear of Whig victories in 1834. Other New England women invested elections with varying degrees of emotional and intellectual involvement. Elizabeth Pierce seemed sure that the state representatives elected in May 1828 would promote stricter Sabbath legislation. After the protracted polling for Boston's mayor, Sophia Peabody trusted in 1829 that Harrison Gray Otis would "be as indefatigable a Mayor as Mr [Josiah] Quincy," the immediate predecessor. She wrongly predicted he would "certainly be Governor next year," unseating Levi Lincoln, Jr. Despite her allegiance to Quincy, she admired Otis's "very splendid & eloquent address in Faneuil Hall," delivered on inauguration day. Harriet Prescott bemoaned the rancorous partisan fighting leading up to the March 9, 1830, New Hampshire gubernatorial election. Referring to a February 1, 1830, Democratic editorial in the *New Hampshire Patriot* accusing Republican candidate Timothy Upham of "traffic in British goods" during the embargo preceding the War of 1812, Prescott deprecated the "shameless miscreants who stop at no falsehood however black that can stain the fair fame of an honourable man who has perhaps no other fault but different political views." In praise of the candidate she prematurely deemed "governor elect" (he lost), Prescott applauded Upham's subsequent decision to sue for libel.[18]

The presidential election results in 1832 shocked some women who never dreamed Jackson would win. Eliza Davis, for example, was optimistic after the 1831 Baltimore Convention met to enlist Henry Clay as National Republican contender. "Get in Clay," she told her U.S. representative husband, John, "and we will have a Thanksgiving feast of American manufacture." Of course, Clay and his running mate John Sergeant lost to Jackson and the "Little Magician," whom she wished would somehow magically disappear. When the second session of Congress convened, Eliza sarcastically asked John "to alter the Constitution to suit Gen Jackson and make Van Buren ineligible after his first term."[19] What better way to hang the Democrats on their own petard, she reasoned—than through stretching the Constitution?

Although Eliza Davis became more and more of a Whig partisan with time, Harriet Prescott would become more politically cynical as election after election passed. Her support of the anti-Jackson gubernatorial candidate in 1830 did not presage a slavish loyalty to Whigs in the March 1835 municipal elections in Calais, Maine, where she was then living. After being toppled (and spurning a Whig male relative of hers), they "acted, in every particular," according to her, "precisely as we have been accustomed to believe *only* the administration party would act." A year earlier, with the very idea of partisanship disgusting her, she prayed the "present spirit of patriotism and the still holier spirit of the Gospel shall not be crushed and annihilated in the sharp collision of opposing interests and dissimilar sentiments." Still, Prescott evidently wanted a U.S. Bank during the 1836 presidential election season, even though she did not seemingly favor any of the Whig candidates, including Daniel Webster.[20] Indeed, none of the politically aware women we located, except Eliza Davis, who snubbed Democratic nominee Van Buren, candidly revealed preferences in fall 1836. But that would change dramatically four years later.

Civic Holidays

One way that women could be civically active without necessarily showing their partisan cards was by participating in the rituals and hospitality surrounding spring "Election Day." No longer for actual voting, the day (sometimes a week) marked the annual "election sermon," the opening session of the state legislature accompanied by festivities honoring the newly elected. Election Day drew in hordes of travelers, statesmen, militia, and even showmen and hawkers. Those who could not attend asked others for particulars. So special was it that in 1831 Mary Hall, then working in Lowell, Massachusetts, noted the date it was held in her hometown, Concord, New Hampshire. Had she been there she could have seen the military escort of the legislature to the local meetinghouse where Nathan Lord, president of Dartmouth College, sermonized. She might have heard natter about who was elected Speaker of the House. Although she was home for Election Day in 1832, 1833, and 1836, by then the forty-seven-year-old state tradition of procession and sermon had been abolished—but not the usual "noise, hubbub, & confusion, drunkards, auctioneers, legislators, & tenpedlars, shows, caravans, alligators & nondescripts." The holiday could test domestic skills. New Hartford weaver and farmer Samantha Barrett and her sister Zeloda spent two days in May 1828 and 1829 "cooking for election." What they whipped up remains a mystery. The impressive cavalcade of the "Horse Guards" and three artillery, infantry, and rifle companies escorting the governor into Hartford, the marching band, and the sermon preached by Benjamin Munro Hill in 1829 attracted visitors, some of whom may have dined on the way with the Barretts. Perhaps they baked traditional "Hartford election cake," a yeasty, fruity, spicy confection provided since the colonial era.[21] In these small ways, women fortified the democratic process.

Another holiday saw even more pomp, patriotism, and sometimes partisanship than Election Day: the Fourth of July. Like Harriett Low, many New England women of the Jacksonian era revered the day—as they had done since 1777, the first anniversary of declared independence from Great Britain. Although the Fourth inspired revelry—parades, picnics, and entertainments—it also generated politicized activity and partisan commentary. Women marked it with solemnity. Mary Hall, the Lowell weaver, spent the holiday in moral instruction. In the early morning of what would be a "very warm" Fourth in 1834, she listened to "important and useful remarks" by William Austin, the Lawrence Company's mill agent, and at ten o'clock that morning she heard "a highly interesting Oration," probably a Whiggish one given the political leanings of the company's founders, in the Unitarian church. In the afternoon Hall "walked in prossession [*sic*]" to Chapel Hill Grove, a Lowell neighborhood, "where the audience were addressed by diferent [*sic*] Clergemen [*sic*] belonging in town."[22]

For some women, solemnity turned into sorrow for the state of the country. "I have been endeavouring [*sic*] to celebrate this day by the exercise of patriotic emotions, ardent desires for the prosperity of my beloved country &c," Elizabeth Pierce told her diary on July 4, 1829, adding "With sorrow do I see the extravagance etc. which prevail, the rapid declension from primitive simplicity of manners & habits." She pleaded for stricter Sabbatarian observances against, "particularly the increasing & alarming violations of *holy time* in thought word & deed, by myself & others," to curtail the erosion of Republican virtue. Independence Day grief took on an implied partisan edge for anti-Jacksonian Harriet Prescott. "And now for the day," she began in an 1829 letter to her daughter, written from New Castle, New Hampshire, on the first Fourth since Jackson's election. "The sun has even hidden his bright beams." Of festivities in her town, which had voted for the vanquished John Quincy Adams just months earlier, she noted, "Not a single peal of rejoicing has broken the almost portentous silence." Whatever noise came from the "usual *national salute* . . . almost sounded like the 'minute guns' upon some funer[al] occasion." Even the annual parade was suspended. An acrid Prescott spat, "there was 'nothing like "Independence" in it—after all.' . . . tho' now that *independence—is no more*!" Fearing that virulent Jacksonianism would infect the entire "body politic," she quoted Isaiah (1:5):

"And to the *body politic* may now be applied with truth the prophets lament—'the whole head is sick—the whole heart faint—. It is full of wounds and bruises and putrefying sores.'"[23] For the sick "head" of state, Jackson, there was no seeming cure.

Conclusion

Women living during the Jackson years saw political winds blowing in a different direction—toward the formation of a two-party system of Whigs and Democrats. While many could not foresee what was to be after 1834—an era of mass politics and intense partisan warfare—most could discern emerging sets of dichotomous values. The majority of our women took proto-Whig, anti-Jacksonian, positions claimed by politicians and laymen alike. They decried key Jacksonian initiatives, such as Indian removal, expansion of executive powers, and the war on the Bank. They lauded Whiggish politicos, especially Daniel Webster, without foreseeing the tremendously important role they would play within the florescence of the Second Party System. They even injected civic holidays with anti-Jackson venom. Those who favored the general scarcely signaled it in their personal writings. Those who either sat on the fence or eschewed taking sides could exercise their political acumen through reading about national and international events and honoring civic holidays. Whatever their predilections, however, none unambiguously signposted "I am a Whig" or "I am a Democrat." Even during the presidential election of 1836, which guaranteed a four-year extension of Jacksonianism under Martin Van Buren, the former vice president, they did not vocally rally around any candidate. However, as we will see in chapter 4 highlighting the Van Buren years, women began to understand the polarization on the national, state, and local levels not just as pro- or anti-Jacksonian but as Whig or Democrat, and began to see that they could have roles to play within that tug-of-war.

One woman, Eliza Davis, the subject of the next chapter, took advantage of these roles as she made a slow but steady retreat from Jackson-neutrality into the arms of the Whig Party. All the while she learned what it meant to be a political wife, with its attendant frustrations—and latent powers. She used those powers to influence her husband, a U.S. senator during the Van Buren years, and eventually to help orchestrate the enormous 1840 Massachusetts state Whig nominating convention for governor, lieutenant governor, and electors who seated the first Whig president. Incumbent Martin Van Buren met his match that year. But well before then, he could predict that Davis, whom he called the "most intellectual woman in Washington," would be a force to be reckoned with.[24]

3

"The Most Intellectual Woman in Washington"

Eliza Davis as Political Wife

Eliza Davis had just returned from the nation's capital where her husband, John Davis, was serving as U.S. senator, when a local acquaintance, Mrs. Willard, visited to verify some gossip. "She was full of her enquiries as to how I liked Washington, and Jackson, Van Buren, and every body else," Eliza wrote from Worcester, Massachusetts, on June 11, 1836, to John, stuck in Washington until July when the Senate would adjourn. Besides making queries, the nosy neighbor put words into Eliza's mouth: "'You must like Van Buren,'" she bluntly assumed; "'he was so polite to you.'" Davis, partisan foe of the current Democratic vice president and soon-to-be president, delivered a snide retort. "I told her on that principle there were others I should feel obliged to like better." Willard pressed on. "'Indeed, then you must feel flattered—he says you were the most intellectual woman in Washington.'" Scorning vanity, Davis shot back. "I assured her it was a remark that Mr Van Buren never made as he would lose more favor by it than he would gain." The tart response dismissing the vice president as a self-serving party hack left Willard "quite shocked," but she should have known better than to spar with one whose wit was so razor sharp and whose allegiances were so Whig. Yet Willard's words were conceivably credible. Indeed, Eliza's mother, Lucretia Chandler Bancroft, heard the same—back in February—and passed it on to her son George, who would soon become collector of customs of the Port of Boston under Van Buren's administration.[1] Whether or not the "American Talleyrand" ever said such a thing, there was a kernel of truth to it. Eliza was undeniably erudite and, above all, politically savvy.

Few could have thought otherwise during her stay in Washington between December 1835 and March 1836.

Eliza was not always such a passionate partisan, nor was she very politically minded when her husband first entered politics in 1825 as U.S. representative from Massachusetts. She would, however, be slowly and inevitably dragged into the fray through the slew of letters (sometimes one a day) with which John barraged her, and through the Worcester gossip mills that had a vested interest in her husband's affairs. Not that she would have remained ignorantly blissful of politics for long—she was far too curious for that. But the mental walls that she erected to hold back the tide of partisanship—including a faith in the elected powers that be—began to crumble as the Whig Party was emerging in the mid-1830s out of the ashes of National Republicanism and the smoldering embers of anti-Jacksonianism. Whig issues spoke to her. At a time when her own family's fortunes looked grim, Whigs devised an economic plan that seemed to her down-to-earth. Appealing to her disdain of demagogues, they appeared to act out of conscience, not out of desire for political gain.[2] Although she was hesitant to call herself a Whig, she thought and acted like one.

As she was becoming aware of the Whig agenda, she was also easing into her role as "political wife," understanding well the social and even political power accorded to spouses of government officials. As a political wife Eliza read prodigiously, tackling newspapers, speeches, history, and biography. She developed the arts of conversation and diplomacy. When constituents called, she gave them an "insider's" view of Congress, but more likely she coaxed information from the most tight-lipped movers and shakers to pass on to John. She confidently advised his move up the ladder, and even coached him in speechwriting. No wonder she earned the moniker "Aunt John" in old age (fig. 3.1).[3]

This chapter traces Eliza's transformation from apolitical domestic partner to partisan political wife over the course of fourteen years—from 1825 through early 1840, a time covering Jackson's and most of Van Buren's Democratic administrations. Much of this chapter's story unfolds during sessions of Congress, usually held from December to spring or early summer, when Eliza was sending letters to John in Washington. These letters are packed with spirited reactions to congressional speeches and debates. They also spin out intelligence gathered in the hushed parlors of Worcester. First, we outline Eliza's childhood background and newlywed days, when she was testing the waters of political wifedom. As it became clear around 1831 that John was in politics for the long run, Eliza took the plunge, becoming immersed in the tumultuous seas at Capitol Hill. After John is elected Whig U.S. sena-

FIGURE 3.1
Eliza Bancroft Davis.
Courtesy of the American Antiquarian Society, Worcester, Mass.

tor in 1835, we find her confidently swimming—sometimes against the tides—in deep partisan waters. By early 1840, she is ready to navigate John's bid for governor of Massachusetts and to help helm the June Whig state nominating convention.

Testing the Waters

By the time that Martin Van Buren's purported statement trickled throughout the Worcester grapevine, forty-five-year-old Eliza was a ten-year veteran of John's political career.[4] She could tell the difference between speech making and hot air, party loyalty and party-lining, open debate and backstabbing. She had watched the political climate change from heated National Republican Party infighting under President John Quincy Adams to fiery opposition-party-driven all-out warfare under President Andrew Jackson.

All the while she herself had politically matured. She first supported Henry Clay's American System, then disparaged Van Buren, and finally allied with the Whigs. But her partisan awakening was slow in coming.

Her background prepared her for the harsh political world. Raised in Worcester, Massachusetts, by the Unitarian minister Aaron Bancroft, a pivotal figure in the early nineteenth-century schism that divided Congregationalists into orthodox and liberal factions, Eliza must have heard about political infighting—of the religious sort. Shortly before her birth in 1791, Bancroft's followers formed their own second parish rather than submit to the conservative elements in Worcester's first Congregational Church. Despite the exodus, Bancroft suffered emotionally, physically, and monetarily. He even composed a memoir for his children, describing his torment. Perhaps the bitter aftertaste of religious controversy and the social reprobation the family endured thereafter temporarily blinded Eliza to secular battlefields. But soon after she married Yale-educated lawyer John Davis of nearby Northborough, in March 1822, she was forced to open her eyes, for in 1824 he would win a seat in the U.S. House of Representatives.[5]

At first Eliza steered clear of politics in her letters. That was fine with John, considering how much he longed to hear about the children (they then had two), the Northborough farm, neighbors, and kin. Hungry for Worcester news, he also solicited papers from home. John kept business separate from family, only briefly alluding—in a patronizing tone—to happenings in Congress. He assumed Eliza would be bored. James "Buchanan of Pennsylvania has delivered a very sens*ible Speech* which cannot be a matter of much interest to you," John wrote her in January 1826. The ink flowed over ladies' fashion, dinner parties, and bookstores, topics he thought would amuse Eliza. His pen also raced when owning up to his paralyzing fear of speaking before the House.[6]

Eliza's earliest forays into public political wifedom involved everyday socializing. Neighbors who were naturally inquisitive about John's adventures at the capital trotted down to Eliza's for updates. She also rubbed elbows with power brokers useful to John. Because consorting with the opposite sex while the spouse was away could raise eyebrows, Eliza first got John's OK. "As for Mr. Sheriff I have no hesitation in saying that you ought to call," John assured her in 1826, "for he is a person whom I must meet and with whom I must have frequent intercourse." With time, she would trust her instincts, make the right contacts without consultation, get the scuttlebutt, and brief John. So independent did she become that in 1833 her mother squawked that "Mr D gives her liberty to do what she pleases, and go where she pleases that is so much more than I should chuse [*sic*]."[7] Eliza remained undaunted.

At the end of 1829, as John began his third term as representative, Eliza began to feel more comfortable in her role. Politicized humor inflected her writing. For instance, after taking in boarders to ease their financial pinch, she bantered, "I am as ready to hear the call for retrenchment, as the strongest Jackson man among us." Eliza apparently was still backing the administration. To an extent, so was John. He did, after all, compliment Jackson's pet cause, Peggy Eaton, for her "self possession equal to that of some of my kinsmen" at an 1829 social function where she "recd but few civilities." And he dined on fine food and aged Madeira in 1830 with Secretary of State Martin Van Buren without a hint of displeasure.[8]

Soon enough, Eliza began reading congressional speeches, especially ones that hit home. She endorsed Jacksonian representative Richard Coulter's March 1830 speech against a resolution to reduce congressmen's overtime pay when sessions extended beyond the normal time, which they often did. Hearing about Eliza's approbation from John, Coulter rejoiced that "the ladies were on his side" and vowed to supply her with additional speeches. At this time John was also digesting Senate floor discussion for Eliza. His stirring January 1830 account of the Webster-Hayne debates must have delighted her. Still, by March of that year, he was convinced that oratory held "no interest" for her. "As you have no occasion to make speeches," he asserted, "I will not force you to enter into my reflections upon the subject."[9] Because women could not speak in public, John supposed they cared little about men who did.

Taking the Plunge

By the summer of 1831, however, things began to change just as anti-Jacksonianism was intensifying. As John gave Eliza the latest murmurings, he started to treat her as a sounding board. In February he announced "war has broke out in good earnest between the two great leaders," Jackson and his first vice president, John C. Calhoun, "and promises to rage with fury & bitterness." The "war" stemmed from Calhoun publishing correspondence (with Jackson) regarding his opposition, as secretary of war, to the general's 1818 insubordinate invasion of Spanish Florida. John sent Eliza a piece of the printed correspondence. He also dissected the politics of committee appointments for her at the start of the Twenty-second Congress in December, when he, reelected as National Republican representative, was placed by Jacksonian Speaker of the House Andrew Stevenson on the Committee on Commerce. John thought he would be ineffectual there. He was acknowledging not only Eliza's concern for politics but also her wisdom. Regarding former Federalist U.S. representative William Gaston, John was sure his wife had "heard of him as one of the most eminent men of the age."[10] His condescension had ceased.

As John encouraged her politicization, Eliza blossomed. By early 1832, her letters sported a clever anti-Jacksonian lexicon. Regarding John's severe headaches, she referred to Jackson's penchant for rejecting legislation: "This drawback put a *veto* on my hopes." She was also reading speeches as quickly as John could relay her opinions to their authors—even to the great Daniel Webster. John told him Eliza wanted his 1832 speech on the centennial of George Washington's birthday "bound with the farewell address" delivered by the first president in 1796 upon declining a third term. She also began to attack House members verbally. An 1832 speech by John Quincy Adams supporting a bill for the "adjustment and settlement of the claims of South Carolina against the United States" enraged her. The state sought repayment for woolen blankets purchased for servicemen during the War of 1812—a minor expenditure. Eliza was familiar with the topic since John, as the governor's agent, had been able to procure over four hundred thousand dollars for Massachusetts in 1831. "What a miserable manager Mr. Adams must be to tuck in Massachusetts & her claims under those Blankets of South Carolina." Deeming it self-serving and ultimately self-destructive to reason that Massachusetts could "come in, on the same principle, for perhaps about a million of dollars," when other representatives argued that *any* state, sometimes their own, was not entitled to trivial claims, she jibed, "I think I could do better than that," adding, "I should think he would need somebody, always ready to pick him up, if he stumbles and blunders in this way."[11] Eliza's hallmark stinging wit was already evident.

During this time, Eliza also assayed her husband's speeches, comparing them to his colleagues'. After reading Henry Clay's February 2, 1832, Senate speech advocating a strong protective tariff, Eliza told John, "Your speech two years ago was as good as his is as far as it went." This was not mere flattery, for her appraisal of John's May 1830 defense of the tariff claimed it did not fly as high as Clay's. Eliza was confounded that antitariff legislators "shut their eyes from truths." "The employment given to classes who without this 'American System' would be without means to get money, enables them to purchase more." To her it was as plain as day: tariffs on competitive imports fostered more home manufacture and thus more jobs and greater demand for goods. To be a good political wife meant being a good political analyst.[12]

As Eliza was becoming emboldened to speak freely about doings in Congress, she was also developing a partisan stance. Not only did she espouse the American System; she also, as we have seen in chapter 2, backed National Republican Henry Clay for the presidency in 1832. At the same time, she was becoming solidly antiadministration. In a May 11 letter to John she referred to the Democratic candidates—the incumbent Jackson and his running mate Van Buren—as pesky insects: "I shall certainly have a thanksgiving if the present swarm of patriots that fills the high places disappears" come November. Eliza had it in particularly for the vice presidential hopeful: "It will leave Van, as you call him, flat in the gutter. Oh! Lucifer!" she reveled, "son of the morning, how art those fallen." She worried, however, about the Anti-Masons, who enlisted their own candidate in September 1831 at the first national nominating convention. Because they shared some of the same anti-Jackson values as National Republicans, they could steal Clay's votes. "I hope we shall not realize Esop's [*sic*] fable . . . of the swarms of flies, though if Antimasonry had a chance I think we might." Here she alluded to Aesop's "The Fox and the Hedgehog": a fox that swims across a river only to be attacked by bloodsucking flies on the other side foolishly dismisses a hedgehog's help to shoo them away because a new, hungrier crop would supplant the now-sated bugs. In Eliza's version, the well-fed pests would be Jacksonians, while the bloodthirsty gnats would be Anti-Masons. Clay could not escape third-party vampirism.[13]

Worcester's approaching Fourth of July in 1832 summoned the worst of party tensions, and the best of Eliza's sleuthing—an important skill for political wives. She got wind of an "*anti party* meeting"—read: anti-Clay meeting—convened to counteract U.S. representative Edward Everett's invitation to give the annual address. There, a "few dough faces [i.e., malleable politicos] among the Clayites objected to having a party celebration and have united with the Jacksonites and Anti Masons to get up another oration." Impatient with the halfhearted partisans, Eliza angrily proffered, "I wish they would ask me to preach. I would take for my text he that is not with us is against us, and cast them all out as evil spirits." Her temperature rose as she wrote. "They are traitors to their Country," she roared; "it is no time for luke warm patriots." Alarmed by the intensity of her partisan fire, Eliza dampened it with a deferential bow to John. "But after all my zeal is only because of you, so I will say no more about it." It sounds somewhat disingenuous.[14]

By early 1833, the budding partisan offered insights on momentous national events. The 1832–33 South Carolina nullification crisis that frightened Harriett Low only strengthened Eliza's analytical muscle. She penned, "Woe to us if one state may say to the rest she only can expound the constitution, if the rest do not agree she will secede." She asked, "Where was the need of any bond of union if such could be the result[?]" The hemming and hawing that followed South Carolina's threat to secede and effected the adoption of Henry Clay's "compromise tariff," which lowered duties, left Eliza "sick" of the "everlasting debate about the Tariff." She wished that Congress and the "old General" himself could be shipped "off into the Oregon territory, or the Texas," where they could "work out their own salvation." Eliza could hardly pretend anymore that she was a political naïf. "I did not dream of entering into politics when I began," she confessed to John, "but as it [is] your vocation just now I shan't apologize." She evidently never did again.[15]

Just as Eliza was staring her own politicization in the face, she was also giving John feedback on his popularity. "I heard a person say that a Gentleman said you were the most useful man in Congress," she fawned, "that your opinions were the most respected, and you had the most influence, and the *true* interests of the country were more advanced by your exertions than by those of any other individual." Everyone it seemed wanted to read his speeches. Yet all was not rosy; she held nothing back. One guest at a ritzy January 1833 Salisbury family party "went on to intimate that the trouble with the South [i.e., the nullification crisis] was the result of the tariff and that Gentlemen who had been zealous supporters of it were now at a loss how to act" to resolve the crisis. John, of course, was one of those "Gentlemen" who now had to decide whether to chance civil war or back Clay's budding idea to compromise by preserving high tariffs in the short run to please northeastern protectionists in exchange for reducing or eliminating them after several years to please the South. Predicting that John would hold to his "old principles" of protectionism, Eliza bit back at her interlocutor: "I told him that there was something more than the tariff to be put aside at the South." She then spelled out the impossible bind in which this detractor was putting John. "If you vote one way, why you don't prize the union," she riposted; "if the other, you are sacrificing your Constituents: so you may expect abuse any how."[16] What did she relish more: defending John (who would in February vote against Clay's compromise bill), or savaging an opponent?

Eliza's aspirations were by now one with John's, and so she felt compelled to help manage his career. After all, she had the scoop on Massachusetts politicos and voters who determined his fate. Yet John's health was waning. The stress of being away from family made him vulnerable. And Eliza dreaded separation every December when he left for the capital. A mutually beneficial solution was to have John at home as state attorney general. "There will probably be many aspirants after the office . . . ," she gathered from her informants in March 1832, "but I should think you might stand some chance of getting it, that is if you wish." Weighing the odds, she bet that Perez Morton, "the present incumbent cannot look to it for himself" (he would retire), "and the Solicitor is not far behind him." The governor, however, appointed James T. Austin. Eliza nonetheless had set wheels in motion for John's homecoming. He would run as a National Republican for Massachusetts governor in 1833, surprisingly, against her wishes.[17]

When John asked her if she was "ready to set up for Governor's Lady" in December 1832, she replied, "I do not just now feel like relishing it at all." Although she balked at the greater expenses incurred with the exalted office, she mainly feared John "might be turned adrift in a year or two," or out of a job. To trade his reputation as congressman for the untried seemed risky. She also smelled something fishy. Although trusted sources swore that John was a shoo-in to replace retiring governor Levi Lincoln, Jr., skeptics warned that the arrangement was a trap: Lincoln was stepping down because he coveted the vacancy that would open for John to fill upon U.S. senator Nathaniel Silsbee's retirement. "If you are to be *any thing* but what you are," she pleaded in January 1833, "let it be Senator & that is *just* where the Gov., does not want you should be, he had rather be Senator himself." Soon after, Eliza learned from William Lincoln that his brother would first set his eyes on John's House seat—a professional stepping-stone to the Senate. "What do you say to this?" Eliza asked John, as if to say, "I told you so." The nomination of gubernatorial candidates was postponed that March until the fall, so Eliza still had some time to buy. But John, "being pressed and urged" by his friends, was dead set on running. Accordingly, Eliza sighed, "if you quit Congress my interest in its affairs are ended too."[18] It sounded almost like an ultimatum.

Eliza's crystal ball proved reliable. John was nominated by the National Republicans in October 1833 and ran, even though he had been reelected to Congress. After the November election returns showed no majority, meaning John's "friends" had abandoned him, the decision was thrown to the state legislature. Eliza made one last-ditch effort. "If you must serve the public I should rather you serve where you are," she scolded in December. "I cannot see any good that will grow out of it." Anti-Mason contender John Quincy Adams, Davis's most formidable rival, withdrew from the race, handing John the governorship on January 1, 1834. John resigned from Congress on January 14 and took the governor's oath on January 21. On February 17, Levi Lincoln, nominated by National Republicans for U.S. representative, won and occupied John's vacant House seat. John, now a Whig, was reelected governor in November 1834 by a vast majority. How Eliza managed as "Governor's Lady" is unclear—she had no need to write to John about it. By some accounts she shunned all ostentation and lived frugally, perhaps even unsociably so. Parties were expensive.[19] For two years she certainly remained isolated from the vortex of national politics.

Swimming in Deep Waters

That ended in December 1835. After six turbulent rounds of votes in the state House of Representatives, John was elected U.S. senator (then, there was no popular vote for that office). He had easily smashed his nemesis, Levi

Lincoln, Jr., but slowly inched ahead of former House colleague John Quincy Adams. This time, when John departed for Washington, he took Eliza with him, perhaps to nurse his fragile health. She could not have been happier. Her letters home teemed with excitement. "Members of Congress, and Governors were as thick as grasshoppers," she wrote her mother of fellow travelers heading south. Almost everything at the capital fascinated her: the White House, where she gawked at the "immense chandeliers"; Daniel Webster's, where she dined; and the Capitol building, where she heard rousing oratory—her "principle [*sic*] amusement." "I enter just enough into politics to enjoy a debate," she disclosed to a friend, "without feeling so much interest as to care who speaks, provided it is well done."[20] What she could once only read after the fact, she could now hear in the making.

Some things, however, disappointed her. Just the sight of administration men brought out her venom. After glimpsing the president, his department heads, and Postmaster General Amos Kendall at a senator's funeral, she jested, "You may shake our native citizens of Worcester in a bag and draw half a doz. my life on it they will look more like Statesmen than they." She diminished Jackson. "He is hardly thought of except as a peg on which to hang Van Buren." She even kept anti-Jackson columnist Matthew Livingston Davis (no relation), known as the "Spy in Washington," in stitches, with caustic vocalizations about Van Buren and his sycophants in the Senate. The "Spy" was still chuckling after Eliza left for home: "When I hear certain individuals of that grave and dignified body thundering or muttering (as the case may be) into the Ears of the Vice president, I smile, involuntarily, at some of the remarks (may I not say sarcasms) which have fallen from your lips, in my presence."[21] Eliza could make a callous journalist giggle. When Van Buren pronounced Eliza "the most intellectual woman in Washington," did he really mean the most acerbic woman in Washington? Was he was glad to be rid of her in March?

Once she arrived home, visitors, such as the nosy Mrs. Willard who opened this chapter, bombarded her with queries, gossip, and predictions that she passed on to John. Even on the ride north she collected intelligence that the "Van Buren party has been pretty well harpooned lately" by newspapers in Connecticut around state election time. In Worcester, "not a voice in favor of Van Burenism" could be heard as presidential election season was gearing up. "If I have seen a Jackson man, he has not dared to speak out," she informed John. Some people knew to be mum with Eliza. She also heard disturbing rumors that last winter that "our friend and relative"—possibly her brother George Bancroft, once a National Republican but now a Democratic Party organizer and spokesman—was bad-mouthing John in letters to John Quincy Adams, who "speaks *meanly* of" her husband. Eliza refused to believe it. "It seemed to be guess work or inference, and I had no time to pump him," she said of the storyteller; "when he comes again . . . I intend to cross question him." For the first time Eliza felt betrayed by vicious liars—or, dare she think it—ambitious kin. After all, George was becoming a hardened Democrat, and his once warm epistolary relationship with John had devolved into a partisan hollering match.[22]

Eliza grew suspicious of George as his friendship with her husband further deteriorated during the Senate recess. At George's behest, his sister Lucretia Bancroft tried to find out if John would actively damage her brother's chances of seeking office. "I have not been unmindful of my promise My dear brother," Lucretia wrote him, "& have touched on politics with Mr Davis whenever opportunity offered." Taken aback during one of Lucretia's confrontations, "Eliza alluded ironically" to George's "exertions to get [John] elected Senator." In other words, Eliza insinuated George had scarcely lifted a finger. John, in turn, accused George of "heaping invective on the Whigs." Lucretia dutifully reported to George that John "has conversed on politics enough with you. He would rather avoid the subject when with you." She felt sure John "would not do any thing inconsistent with perfect integrity" but also would not help his brother-in-law.[23] Political sisters, like wives, were caught in the partisan cross fire. And they could shoot at one another, too.

That fall, Martin Van Buren narrowly won the presidency, notwithstanding competition from three Whig candidates, William Henry Harrison, Daniel Webster, and Hugh Lawson White, while George Bancroft lost his bid for U.S. representative without any apparent interference from John. Congress, however, was still controlled by Democrats. Jackson would remain in power until the March 4, 1837, inauguration. Such was the political atmosphere facing John when he returned to Washington in December 1836.

This time John, much improved in health, left Eliza at home, where she buried herself in reading. Most of it was political and historical material, some supplied by politicos and pundits in Washington with whom she maintained a friendship independent of John. U.S. representative from Massachusetts Caleb Cushing sent Eliza his *Address Delivered Before the American Institute* in December 1836 and his 1834 *Eulogy on Lafayette* "& two other addresses" in January 1837. After reading the *Address*, she remarked, "the only thing on earth I ever envied are knowledge and intellect," little recognizing her own prodigious mind. She also feasted on the first volume of Matthew Livingston Davis's *Memoirs of Aaron Burr*, the former vice president (under Thomas Jefferson) who had just died. Evidently the "Spy" himself gave it to her and promised to dispatch the second volume upon completion. William Lincoln's *History of Worcester*, hot off the press, did not impress her though: he "made one mistake" that left her mother "indignant." The Lincolns could never redeem themselves.[24]

That winter Eliza put down her books long enough to enjoy a good rant about partisan politics. She was outraged that at the start of the second session of the Twenty-fourth Congress three Whig senators, Daniel Webster, Henry Clay, and her husband, lost chairmanship of committees to Democrats Silas Wright, William R. King, and James Buchanan, who would become John's archenemy. She groaned, "but what a change!" "This is only the begin[ning] of degradation," she predicted. "They are a fit troop for Dick Johnson," the new vice president, "to preside over." As if partisan chair selection was not enough, the January 16, 1837, Senate vote to "expunge" Henry Clay's resolution censuring Jackson for his conduct in the removal of deposits from the Bank of the United States made her blood boil. Jackson, according to Clay and other senators, had acted illegally and deserved formal rebuke. But nearly three years later, the secretary of the Senate could literally "write across" the 1834 resolve in the Senate journal. "The deed is actually done!" she shook her head in disbelief. "Little did I ever think it would amount to more than a . . . humbug tolerated for the purpose of shouting praises to sooth the wounded vanity of the old man." A seasoned speech reader, she tore into the arguments of Democratic yea-sayers Thomas Hart Benton (sponsor of the resolution), William Cabell Rives, and James Buchanan. She had a field day with the latter's convoluted reasoning that "expunging" the record did not mean "obliterating" it. "And what have they gained?" she wondered. "If Gen Jackson did right he needed nothing from them to insure justice to his memory. . . . If his course was unconstitutional and if he did assume unlawful power, this certainly don't mend the matter." But to Democratic senators, "a black mark rectifies all errors," she protested. It was all too absurd. She half-seriously surmised that next Benton would argue the constitutionality of a "perpetual President."[25]

John came home early that year, just after the inauguration, but his break was cut short. The new president called Congress back in September for a special session. The fiscal tumult known as the Panic of 1837, resulting from an international influx of gold and silver into the country, stringent English credit policies, and payment suspension by domestic banks in May, alarmed Van Buren. He wanted Congress to assess the situation. His own solution was to create an independent Treasury for the federal government, reliant on state banks since 1833 when Jackson deposited funds in them.[26] John and fellow Whigs, insistent on a new national bank, fought the idea for three years.

At home, Eliza felt the rumblings of the panic and dissatisfaction with the current leadership. Her friends the Swans picked up stakes for New York in order to manage their property there themselves. Others bashed the administration. With the Warrens she "dished up van Buren, [and] turned up our noses at some of his great associates." Eliza could not tolerate anyone promoting an independent Treasury. Senator John C. Calhoun was one of them —though he had his own ideas of how it should operate. She even nixed subscription to a paper advancing his views, probably Richard Crallé's Washington *Reformer*. "Do pray drop this Calhoun paper," she ordered John; "it is not worth a pin. It has but one idea from week to week and I would not contribute to the *glorification* of Mr Calhoun."[27] Nullification was bad enough; now, it was an offensive economic program.

In December 1837 Eliza once again headed for the capital with John, for the second session of the Twenty-fifth congress. She felt winds of change in the Capitol building where she once savored debates. Slavery, a subject Eliza rarely broached, had seeped in. Van Buren, the first to utter the word in a presidential inaugural speech, saw it coming. Policy debates over Texas, which had just declared independence from Mexico, would necessarily bring up the issue of annexing land in which slavery was legal. Southern congressmen injected slavery even into independent Treasury argumentation. Abolitionists were flooding Congress with antislavery petitions. Beginning in 1836, a series of resolutions called "gag laws" that "tabled" these petitions, or forbade their reading or discussion, were passed in the House. Representative John Quincy Adams clamored to have them rescinded. The Patton Resolution, one of the "gag laws," was adopted the December Eliza was in town, but she never mentioned it. "Ever since I came here, one house or the other, sometimes both have been discussing slavery," she bellyached. "I am sick of the sound, and have rarely gone into the Capitol, where I could hear little else."[28] True, slavery filtered into debates, but certainly without dominating other topics. Yet for Eliza it was more than she could bear. If only she knew just how crucial and divisive an issue it would become.

Back in Worcester by April, Eliza was, as usual, debriefed by visitors. This time, John's February 28, 1838, speech countering the independent Treasury was the talk of the town. Someone said it was better than Daniel Webster's. Everyone expressed admiration except Samuel Burnside, a lawyer and stockholder in the Worcester Central Bank, who came around in a huff "to *talk politics*." Eliza told John, "He has left Van Buren, and why? Ostensibly because he thinks the policy of the administration ruinous to the country, but in truth, because it has left State street," the banking center of Boston, "empty." "By touching his purse you enlighten his understanding." Things were looking up for the Davises, however, who, with five children, set their eyes on a larger home. "I want a kitchen," Eliza pleaded with John in May, "and suitable accommodations for all the trumpery and newspapers that are accumulating in every corner of the house."[29] The very items that were lifelines to John were swamping her.

But Eliza was used to being in over her head and surviving. Indeed, the whole business of being a political wife was becoming so commonplace that the affairs of Congress were predictable—even boring. "There seems to be very little of interest going on," she grieved in January 1839, "or else I have lost my desire to engage in these matters." To her, local conversation was also running out of steam as the number of antislavery societies in Worcester County mushroomed. "There is nothing but abolition & Temperance talked of; and people seem to take less interest in Washington matters than usual," she observed. Adding to her misery was the recent death of her sister Sarah. Although she managed to commend John on his remarks in support of tacking funding for war veterans' pensions onto an appropriations measure for government operations, she flipped past a speech in the paper by U.S. representative John Bell. Perhaps she was getting too rhetorically sophisticated to be a passive consumer and hankered to author her own speeches. The next-best thing was tutoring John. After reading *City of the Czar* by Thomas Raikes, governor of the Bank of England during the currency crisis of 1797, she counseled John, "If you have any speech to make on Banks or Tariffs, or the benefits of domestic manufactures, I advise to the reading of the eleventh chapter. A sentence or two come quite to the point." Short of writing John's speeches, she masterminded his arguments.[30]

Despite her involvement in John's work, Eliza denied that she loved vicariously experiencing his fame. "Not that I am very ambitious," she assured John after praising his "reputation in the Senate."[31] Yet much belied her disclaimer. Over the fifteen years since John first sat in Congress as a diffident freshman, Eliza had been transformed from a complacent housewife wary of uttering a politicized word into a virtual collaborator with her husband. She could rightfully claim the word "ambitious" for her character. But the world was not yet ready for women's bold self-fashioning. Society was prepared, however, to let "Aunt John" have a central place within the local mill that kept "Honest John" in office.

The malaise that set in during winter of 1839 was hard to shake. Even the conflict known as the Aroostook War, arising over a boundary dispute between Maine and British Canada, simply annoyed her, though it terrified many other women, as we will see in the next chapter. The gubernatorial race mildly rattled her. It seemed all the more meaningless after her father died in August. While Eliza might scribble "an attack on locofocoism" in a letter or two to brother George, it would take the frenzy of the presidential campaign season, which in Worcester began early in 1840, to get Eliza going.[32] By that time John had set his sights again on the governorship. His fate, it seemed, was tied to the future president's, and Eliza, being a good political wife and Whig to boot, worked hard for both John's and William Henry Harrison's success. The price of that endeavor, however, would be peace of mind and familial goodwill, for Eliza locked horns with siblings George and Lucretia. She would long for the good old humdrum days.

4

"Siding with You in Politics"

Women's Political Polarization during the Van Buren Administration

Shortly after Martin Van Buren won the 1836 presidential election, Lucretia Bancroft wrote a mixed-message letter to George Bancroft, a newly minted Democrat. Though an adoring sibling, Lucretia was skeptical of her brother's party. "If I were a little more of a radical, I would congratulate you on Martin's success," she chided him, and added, "I can not yet bring myself to rejoice in the triumph of cunning & bribery." In her opinion Democrats resorted to trickery. But the opposition candidate from Massachusetts did not thrill her, either: "I am not Whig enough to mourn over Webster's defeat."[1] Though obliged to takes sides within the new arena of Second Party System politics, she found it impossible.

Her social status and principles were at odds. On the one hand, she abhorred the "riff-raff" with whom George associated. "There is but one thing which prevents me from siding with you in politics, and that is the companions you are compelled to be linked with." Anti-Mason editor Benjamin F. Hallett, who supported George's unsuccessful 1834 bid for the Massachusetts General Court, was at the top of her list. "Where will you find a man more despised by the respectable part of the community?" she asked. She preferred the company of elite Whigs and "plead[ed] guilty" to the "charge of aristocracy . . . so far as my own associates are concerned." On the other hand, she upheld Democratic Party principles. "On the floor of the Representatives' Hall I should be as staunch a republican as you."[2] In time, as we will see, her Democratic leanings would win out.

By 1836, women like Lucretia Bancroft were beginning to think of themselves not only as admirers or detractors of an administration but as affiliates of a party. They realized that a line was being drawn in the sand and that they could increasingly stand on either side with Whigs or Democrats. This chapter explores they ways women began to align during the Van Buren years (1837–41).

"Takings sides" usually meant being eased into partisanship by mothers, brothers, and other kin, beaus, and neighbors. They persuaded initiates with partisan reading matter and chitchat, or took them to political lectures. Politicians exploited their sisters' or wives' skills in electioneering. Still, budding female partisans had minds of their own, sometimes stubbornly resisting induction. But even recruits who were more compliant became, with time, independent of family members' influence. Throughout this chapter, we see these partisans-in-the-making negotiating the social relations of politics.

To explore side-taking among New England women at this time, we highlight state and municipal elections. These as opposed to presidential contests held the most interest for women before 1840. After all, they addressed local concerns; their outcomes affected everyday life more visibly than presidential race results. Also, they featured names and faces immediately familiar to constituents. Candidates could be seen in the neighborhood or pressing the flesh at cattle fairs, militia exercises, and public dinners. Gossip about them was often firsthand. Presidential hopefuls still shunned the limelight of open national campaigning.[3]

Of course, not all politically savvy women were partisan, nor were all political developments. The abolition movement, for example, touched the lives of some New England women in the 1830s. So did a "war" that was bipartisan: the 1839 Aroostook conflict over the border between Maine and Canada. Therefore, after discussing state and local elections, we turn to women's involvement in antislavery and then their engagement with the boundary war.

Elections of 1837, 1838, and 1839

In the state and congressional elections of 1837, 1838, and 1839 Whigs attracted long-term partisan followers and picked up a momentum that would usher in the first Whig president in 1840. Voter turnout for these elections was generally higher than before.[4] For the women whose "side-taking" was solidifying in these years, state and local elections would provide the platform for springing into action in 1840.

The 1837 Democratic losses and dramatic Whig gains in state legislatures were duly noted by those opposing Van Buren or favoring Whigs. The flagging economy that voters attributed to Democratic monetary policy was a decisive factor in the victories. Although women generally did not equate success at the polls with the recession, they were certainly aware of its effect on their own and others' fortunes. So heightened was female consciousness of the economy that the publishing industry responded with an outpouring of "panic fiction," or novels and stories situating middle-class women in trying circumstances.[5]

Women's awareness of the panic no doubt set the stage for their encounters with the 1837 elections. The day it began, May 10, 1837, Lucretia Chandler Bancroft, a staunch anti-Jacksonian, frantically wrote to her son George. New York banks had just "suspended payment," meaning they would not exchange gold or silver for deposits, checks, or their paper notes. Nearly eight hundred banks immediately followed suit. "We are quite well, notwithstanding all the trouble our country now abounds in" she told him. "There are so many banks, is it possible they can keep their credit?" she asked, referring, probably, to their inability to redeem their own notes from other institutions. She feared that George, heavily invested in a Cleveland, Ohio, bank that would falter a year later, was "among the loosers [*sic*]." As credit contracted more and more during May, shock waves passed throughout Boston Whig capitalist circles. In reaction to Van Buren's executive order that only hard money—not banknotes—would be accepted by post offices, some Bostonians held a meeting on May 17 at Faneuil Hall that resulted in a call for civil disobedience and, if necessary, forcible resistance to the law. These were frightening times for Hannah Lowell Jackson, whose father was neck deep in Boston real estate. Van Buren's order, she gasped, "produced such excitement . . . that a few words only would have been sufficient to cause the pulling down of the Postoffice." To ease her mind, she buried herself in newspapers, knowing her father was "not in the habit of talking about public affairs, in his family." A day after the meeting she rejoiced in the *Transcript*'s "good news, that the President has agreed to call the Congress together." She was referring to the special session convened in September to address the economy. Despite these efforts and a recovery between 1838 and early 1839, the recession would persist at least until 1843.[6]

Given the sagging economy, it was, perhaps, no surprise to some women in the Boston region that Whigs made great strides in 1837. The "New York tornado" that swept out Democrats in the state's legislature left behind a four-fifths Whig majority in the lower house. This boded ill for the president, a New York native, and Lucretia Chandler Bancroft was sure to let her son know it. "It is thought friend Van burin, [*sic*] must take cair [*sic*], now all his own state has forsaken him," she warned on November 12, 1837. That George was up for election as Democratic state senator the next day made her fret. "I don't know how it will affect your worldly concerns." She then not-so-subtly hinted he should stick to history writing. In Boston, Sarah P. E. Hale, whom we met in chapter 2, soaked in news of the December 1837 mayoral race. With no word of a winner on election night, she feared "there was no choice," due to the "numerous tickets." As many as fifteen ran against Whig victor Samuel A. Eliot, including George Washington Dixon, an entertainer from blackface minstrelsy who impertinently vowed not to serve if elected.[7]

For Katherine Lawrence, the wife of former U.S. representative and Boston-based industrialist Abbott Lawrence, the November 13 state election was an opportunity to convert her eighteen-year-old daughter Annie to Whiggery. Hoping her own excitement would rub off, Katherine wrote Annie, away at school in New Brighton, New York, that her father would preside "at a great political meeting at Faneuil [Hall] this E.[vening] for the first time," to rev up voters. Afterward, Katherine bragged of the "Whig victory going on" and the November 22 "Whig Jubilee" in New York to which a Boston delegation was sent. She also mailed Annie a steady stream of *Atlases* and *Transcripts*, Whig papers. Annie, however, could not care less. She even refused to answer Katherine's repeated pleas: "I wish you would acknowledge . . . if you receive the 'Transcripts' regularly."[8] She was stubborn, but her mother was more so.

She flooded Annie with more papers, for which her daughter was rarely, if ever, grateful and sent other politically charged reading matter including a pamphlet on the Cherokee, Henry Hallam's *Europe During the Middle Ages* (1818), and Emma Willard's *Universal History* (1836). She mailed letters about the December 1837 forced resignation of Whig U.S. congressman Richard Fletcher from the Ways and Means Committee, the February 1838 fatal duel between U.S. representatives William Jordan Graves, a Whig, and Jonathan Cilley, a Democrat, and a July "Webster Festival" at which the disgraced Fletcher spoke. Annie had heard an earful, but was still not budging. She wrote home about the latest fashions, visiting, and social events.[9]

Come November 1838, Katherine was still trying to mold Annie into a good political daughter. No issue was too complex to write about. She gave Annie the scoop about the Whig ticket for state representatives that split "owing to the friends & enemies of the 15 gall.[on] . . . license law." By forbidding sales of distilled liquor in amounts under fifteen gallons—thus making purchases expensive—the law was meant to curb intemperance. "Amory Hall" Whigs, who favored it, issued their own ballot in opposition to "regular" Whigs, who vowed to repeal it. "People are cross & excited," Katherine explained, because the three-way race resulted in decisive outcomes for only twenty of fifty-six seats for representatives from Boston. She was piqued that the "Party would be divided & that many . . . in the excitement of the moment would overlook all the evil consequences." Katherine enclosed a list of the Amory Hall upstarts, but whether Annie looked at it remains a mystery.[10] Time, however, was on Katherine's side. Annie would finish school, return to Boston in December 1838, and fall under her mother's direct supervision.

Unlike Annie Lawrence, Charlotte Rantoul of Beverly, Massachusetts, took the 1838 election by the horns. The twenty-two-year-old, who temporarily moved to Gloucester to nurse her sister-in-law Jane, wound up assisting her older brother Robert, Jr., a Democrat, in his bid for U.S. congressman. But aiding Robert meant lending a hand to Jane, who had been his secretary since 1835 when he became state representative. Jane, as we have seen in chapter 2, wielded considerable influence. Two weeks prior to the October 3 Gloucester caucus to choose delegates, Charlotte helped canvass and copy documents. "Instead of living in the dim reflected light of political excitement," she kidded, "I have enjoyed its full & immediate radiance." Robert's stiff competition, however, got Jane's goat. "Opposition has had its usual effect," Charlotte teased, adding that "in spite of her ill health" Jane "engaged all her faculties."[11] Democratic women could be as zealous as Whigs.

Charlotte cherished being involved, and her good humor spilled out in letters home. In them she lovingly barked orders to her father: "Much depends upon a full caucus tonight, do your best in Beverly to swell the number." In case she nettled him, she asked "Is Pa tired of my politics[?]" After playfully parroting a string of partisan banter—"See that your Beverly delegation are true men. . . . 'The majority must rule'; I manage Beverly. . . . 'After eight years I shall be willing to rotate out'"—she joshed, "I know something of the game they play at." Indeed, she did.[12]

Because the Democrats divided during their October 5 district nominating convention, with one faction wanting Joseph S. Cabot and the other Rantoul, they would eventually run against one another as well as Whig nominee Leverett Saltonstall. Once again, the 15 Gallon Law, which Rantoul advocated, was partly to blame. When Robert's friends, including Levi Woodbury, started a letter-writing campaign to counteract moves toward Cabot's "irregular" candidacy, Charlotte copied one missive for her father. As self-proclaimed "private secretary of the democratic party," she mock-boasted, "Let it fill a page & a half of a sheet of letter paper with the above & you have the letter verbatim." She was proud of her copying skills, as were many New England amateur scribes.[13]

Jocular-but-down-to-earth Charlotte had few illusions her brother would win. "Unless circumstances wear a new face, a couple of weeks more will bring me home. If Cabot goes to Congress assuredly & if Saltonstall probably, otherwise I cannot tell how long I may stay." Nevertheless, Charlotte gave it her all by "answering the letters from the Anti Slavery party." These were evidently from constituents energized by a recent Essex County convention's resolution to find out about candidates' positions and withhold votes for or vote against (writing in candidates to "scatter" votes) anyone "not favorable to" the immediate emancipation of slaves in the District of Columbia. "My skill in penmanship makes me a very convenient piece of furniture," she diffidently joked. While Charlotte claimed she only "acted the part of the private secretary," she, at the same time, could "not disclaim all share in the composition in as much as the views expressed are mine." In other words, Robert (who was antislavery) trusted her knowledge about abolitionist politics enough to give her free reign. But neither her eloquence nor the backing of George Bancroft, now the powerful collector for the Port of Boston, could help Robert.[14] He lost to Saltonstall.

For Mary Pierce, the daughter of a Brookline, Massachusetts, Unitarian minister, 1838 was an exciting year—one of both political and sexual awakening. Before then, partisanship and romance mattered little. But her life would change forever during a stay at her sister's Bangor, Maine, home during election season. There, the seventeen-year-old met Henry Varnum Poor, a Whig lawyer who gallanted her about town, steeped her in politics, and eventually married her.[15] Although Pierce's first duty was to her pregnant sister, she had time to socialize with local politicos, Henry and his brother Alfred, and with literary society members—all of whom turned her pro-Whig. "I never heard so much about politics as I have this Summer," she told her parents in early September. "The Messrs Poor are violent [i.e., fervent] whigs, and Alfred seems to think of nothing but the approaching election. He works night and day to secure governor Kent's election." After meeting the incumbent, Edward Kent, who called at her sister's, Pierce felt "quite interested in his success."[16]

Election Day, September 10, was electrifying. "I feel almost as much interest as the voters can." That morning she felt "little doubt that governor Kent will be elected in spite of the locos," who she sensed were up to no good. Referencing an incendiary article in the Bangor *Courier*, Pierce alleged that "*twenty two thousand dollars* had been sent by the United States government to aid the loco foco interest in this state . . . at the instigation of Reuel Williams of Maine." According to the paper, U.S. senator Williams withdrew federal funds placed in a Massachusetts pet bank for Democratic electioneering. She had faith the supposed cash infusion would not affect the outcome. But while having an evening snack at a neighbor's she found out Kent had lost to Democrat John Fairfield. Rumors spread that Democrats were "purchasing votes" and tricking Whigs into casting illegal ballots. "Some good firm whigs have been deceived by them, and put them into the box thinking that all was right," she grumbled, "when in fact they do not count for anything."[17] Pierce never questioned Whigs' integrity.

The calls of foul play only fixed her loyalty. The day after election she wrote home about "corruption and bribery," but she could nonetheless say "I never felt so much interested in politics before." This attraction flowed from partisanship: "It seems so evident which is the right side." Although she was not calling herself a Whig, she was clearly on their "side." Side-taking was also evident at a September 12 meeting of the "Bouquet," a literary society, when "the conversation took quite a political turn." One Whig editor member reassured the group of victories next year. During a subsequent visit to her sister Lucy's, he was "full of the tricks of the locos," who had supposedly discarded Whig votes. "Is not this a sad comment upon the *glorious right of suffrage* of which the newspapers boast so much and of which every citizen of the United States feels so proud?" Pierce wondered.[18] Yet it would not shake her faith in the system. As we will see, she campaigned for Whig William Henry Harrison in 1840.

The 1839 election, which was part of a "continuous campaign" for the 1840 presidential contest, registered among our women mainly through the Massachusetts gubernatorial race. On November 11, Democrat Marcus Morton narrowly defeated Whig incumbent Edward Everett largely because of the 15 Gallon legislation he upheld while governor. Because the ballot count was so close, it was debated in the papers until the state Senate made its official report on January 13, 1840. Eliza Davis was getting impatient by New Year's: "I really begin to feel as if I wanted to hear." The drawn-out election was a prop for Lucretia Bancroft's November 21 slam on her brother's politics. Not yet knowing "whether to congratulate or condole" George "on the result," she took the opportunity to question the legality of some Democratic votes and to half-blame the party for a neighbor's illness. "Sam Ward added to his fever by going out to give his vote," she taunted. "If he die in consequence, I hope his zeal will be properly appreciated, and a subscription [i.e., donation] taken up in your party for the family."[19] Such acrimony came with side-taking.

In his January 1840 inaugural address, Morton pushed for judicial reform, Democratic monetary policy, and repeal of the 15 Gallon Law. The speech was the feminine talk of the town according to Louisa Waterhouse, a Jacksonian sympathizer. "Every lady says something about it whether they know anything or not." While Waterhouse dismissed her Cambridge, Massachusetts, neighbors, perhaps because they were likely to lean Whig, she also chided herself. "I am not acquainted enough with statistics, with currency, banking, or judicial matters, to talk about them," she admitted. "I wish I was, this is one of the deficiencies of female education, they should understand business." Regarding the liquor legislation, however, she could, "give an intelligent opinion." "It is decidedly *aristocratic* & will not do with us *Republicans*," she opined. "It was wrong to make such a law. . . . Gov. Morton thinks so too if I understand him aright." The law was indeed repealed.[20]

Unlike Waterhouse, Annie Lawrence was only beginning to wrestle with politics in 1839. She began making a gradual transition from impish schoolgirl to sophisticated partisan daughter after coming home in December 1838. Then her attitude was still playful. She relished politicians making fools of themselves, flirting with her at parties: "Mr W.[ebster] was rather devoted which annoyed Father excessively much to my amusement." By the spring 1839 she more maturely handled social interactions. When Whig politicos Henry A. S. Dearborn and Winfield Scott showed up unexpectedly at her door, she was able to wing it, but awkwardly. "I was of course much embarrassed," she confided to her diary, "but acquitted myself as well as circumstances would admit & showed them the library &c." She reserved wisecracks for Martin Van Buren. While sojourning in Saratoga Springs, New York, that summer to revive her health, she met the president on his reelection campaign trail. "Two cheers & a half greeted his arrival & some few hisses, sufficient to testify the prevailing feeling towards him," she sniggered. A farmer's wife from Charlemont, Massachusetts, honeymooning in New York, had a similar, sour reaction to Van Buren: "I have the extreme honor (if it may be called an honor) of seeing him."[21] She and Annie were not impressed.

It was only after the election that Annie adopted a more serious comportment. Something clicked when her father Abbott, having been elected U.S. representative, left home for Washington in late November. She wept uncontrollably. Yet she hoped, despite her own "very great" sacrifice, that his service to the country would "all prove for the best." That evening she dried her tears and went out to hear famed phrenologist George Combe speak at the lyceum about "evils arising from our present government." In his politically inflected address he accused "those permitted to vote & even placed in offices of trust" of being "ignorant & ill fitted for their duties." By now, Annie had become a regular at the lecture hall. She listened to Whig Edward Everett's Lowell Institute speech on cultivating the intellect for "the good of our country." Then she heard Whig Charles Francis Adams, grandson of the second president, talk about his grandmother Abigail Adams's Revolutionary War letters, which he had just published. The former first lady became Annie's role model. "She was a woman of superior education & great firmness of character," she wrote in her diary. "Amidst the roar of cannon & the din of artillery Mrs Adams writes evidently agitated but trusting in God for protection. What an effect must such resignation and strength of principles exercise over the minds of others."[22] If Adams could suffer the hardships of a political wife in turbulent times, Annie could withstand the minor irritations of a political daughter in stable years. A seriousness about politics, previously absent, was now washing over her. That gravity would shape her experiences throughout 1840.

Antislavery

Most women did not politick with abolitionists, as Charlotte Rantoul did in 1838, or sign antislavery petitions and voice interest in abolitionist societies, as Glastonbury, Connecticut, farmwoman Hannah Hicock Smith did in 1835 and 1839. Indeed, only about 1 percent of the population nationally called themselves abolitionists in 1860, when divisiveness over slavery was its strongest. So it is not surprising that few of the women we located candidly espoused the immediate end of slavery, which was considered a radical stance. The subject, however, was in the air. It was difficult, especially in New England, to escape it. As Mary Pierce noted in 1837, while she was attending school in western Massachusetts, "The good inhabitants of Northampton are all alive upon the subject of Abolition." She even described it as "hackneyed." Still, she could count "but *one*" abolitionist within her circles.[23]

Women could help end slavery, however, without seeming radical. One way was by spending money at antislavery fairs. These fund-raisers organized by women and held in homes or meeting halls sold sundry items, many of them handmade domestic articles, to the public. Tickets, such as the ones Salem matron Sarah Browne bought for twelve and a half cents in December 1839, also raised revenue. Large fairs sponsored by the Massachusetts Anti-Slavery Society in Boston solicited upward of fourteen hundred dollars, smaller ones much less (the fair Abigail Lummis, a Lynn apothecary's wife, mentioned in her diary netted only five dollars and fifty cents). Fairgoers were treated to ornamented sales booths, foods for purchase, and faux "post offices" at which they could "mail" letters to attendees.[24]

Like fairs, antislavery lecturers attracted women. For some, these talks were entertainingly informative, like any other given in town halls, rural churches, and urban spaces. For others, they gave voice to a politicized position. Just as venues varied, so did speakers. Inelegant spouters could, as Mary Pierce observed, do "more harm to the cause, than good." So could seemingly condescending zealots determined to "enlighten the degraded minds of the ignorant inhabitants of Massachusetts." To reach an often resistant public, the American Anti-Slavery Society spent an unprecedented 50 percent of its 1835–36 annual income on lecturers.[25] Women were the beneficiaries.

But they could as easily learn about slavery from household members reading newspapers aloud. The *Liberator*, *Emancipator*, *New York Evangelist*, and many partisan periodicals as well disseminated relevant news. One female *Emancipator* reader in New Haven scanned an 1839 story on "the traffic of slaves in some of our southern states" after contemplating her Bible. That year her sister followed the trial of the Mendian slaves who seized the schooner *Amistad*, which had been carrying them to a Cuban plantation. Elizabeth Cheever of Hallowell, Maine, reacted passionately to another widespread story—the November 1837 murder of editor Elijah Lovejoy by an antiabolitionist mob in Alton, Illinois. To fence-sitting newsmen, she retorted, "what evidence we have in the different views of this tragic murder expressed by some of the various editors, of the corresponding influence of slavery in even destroying those true feelings of patriotism, and liberty, which do naturally burn in every breast."[26] Those against abolitionism were against republicanism.

While there were some antislavery enthusiasts at this time among our women, most, like Eliza Davis, generally ignored the subject in their diaries and letters. Those who did mention it by and large showed no commitment to the movement. Such an attitude underscores their partisanship, for they followed their parties in distancing themselves from antislavery advocates. Yet women were often curious about, even sympathetic to, the movement's aims. For them and for many male voters, holding the movement at arm's length was strategic. Applying an antislavery litmus test to candidates could wreak havoc on local elections, while an even tentative embrace of antislavery would repulse Southerners, leading to certain failure in presidential elections and internecine warfare in Congress. In the next two decades, however, as antislavery became an explosively political issue, New England women would take definite sides, despite the issue's potential divisiveness.

The Aroostook War

Just as antislavery could bring women into a politicized (but not always partisan) arena, so could war. Toward the end of Van Buren's administration, women faced the undeclared "Aroostook War," a bloodless conflict over the boundary between Maine and New Brunswick determined by the Treaty of Paris (1783) ending the American Revolution. The border was disputed for decades, meaning that a section of land, the Aroostook Valley, was claimed by both the United States and Great Britain. Britain valued it for defense—it allowed wintertime overland passage, via the St. John valley, between the Bay of Fundy and the St. Lawrence River. Maine prized its rich timberlands.

In January 1839, the state's new governor, John Fairfield, asked his legislature to finance a land agent and "suitably equipped" men to survey the area and deter what he saw as Canadian "pillage." On January 24, legislators empowered the agent and appropriated ten thousand dollars. In early February, Rufus McIntire and his "posse" trekked toward the disputed area. Matters thereafter escalated until early March, at which time more than ten thousand Maine militia stood ready to fight and Congress appropriated ten million dollars and authorized raising fifty thousand troops should war eventuate. Although prior censuses, surveys, and mappings of the area were undertaken, none had brought Maine to the brink of war.[27]

Most of the women who followed the conflict in their diaries and letters were irate. Although some historians have laughed in retrospect at the "Pork and Beans War," those with loved ones in the state militia were terrified. These included Mary Pierce, who was still with her sister in Bangor, Caroline Haynes, a resident of that town, and Harriet Prescott, of Calais. They did not make it a partisan issue, and in many ways it was not. Even though the Democrats needed Maine's support come election time, Van Buren would not hand Fairfield what he wanted on a platter. And, although this Democratic governor fanned the flames of war, Whig politicos shared the opposition party's "Anglophobia" enough to turn hawkish once the die was cast.[28] For women, diplomatic failure, rigidity on both sides, and an expansionist mentality caused the war.

Mary Pierce (fig. 4.1) first heard about the growing tensions while having tea at a minister's house on February 6, 1839, just after McIntire and his two hundred men left for the Aroostook. "A company of young men have been sent to the Northern part of the state to drive off some trespassers," she informed her parents, noting they earned "a dollar per day." She worried about her sickly neighbor, Frederick K. Bartlett, who she mistakenly thought had joined the posse, for the deep snow, sub-zero-degree weather, and lean diet of "raw pork and sea biscuit" he would have to endure. Days later, she was told his father had forbidden him to undertake "such a fool's errand."[29]

All of Bangor was on pins and needles. On Sunday, February 17, Mary watched onlookers gather like "swarms of bees" around sleighs carrying five Canadian prisoners taken by the posse. "Even the Sabbath day has given no rest to the agitated feeling which prevails on all sides," she protested. The next day, by order of Fairfield to raise one thousand troops, the names of men from each ward aged eighteen to thirty-five were entered into a draft lottery. According to the 1792 Militia Act, all nonexempted "able-bodied" men (white citizens) between the ages of eighteen and forty-four were to be carried on each state's rolls for military service; they had to arm and equip themselves. Having heard rumors her husband's name had been drawn,

FIGURE 4.1 Mary Pierce Poor. Courtesy of The Schlesinger Library, Radcliffe Institute, Harvard University, Cambridge, Mass.

Mary's neighbor Mrs. Appleton "cried and said she should certainly die if he went." Mary comforted her, telling her he could hire and outfit a replacement. She even instructed Henry Poor—now her fiancé—to find out more information. "I pitied her very much," she explained; "she appeared to be so much overcome." Poor returned with good news: it was a John Appleton who was drafted, not Mary's friend's spouse. Frederick Bartlett, however, began active duty on February 20, as a corporal in Captain Nathan Ellis's company of light infantry.[30]

Since Bangor was designated as the assembly point for departure, mobilization would take place right before Mary's eyes. "It will be a new and terrible sight for me to see a thousand men prepared for fighting." On February 19 the city hall floor "was carpeted with soldiers, lying with their heads upon their knapsacks" waiting to be dispatched. Soon companies were forming in the streets under mounted commanders. "I believe we shall have a war after all," she sighed in resignation. "It will be a sad thing for our country." Both sides, she decided, were bullheaded: "The disputed territory is of as much importance to both nations that neither will feel willing to give it up." Born in 1820, she had never experienced war, but now the grim realities were setting in.[31]

Further escalation deepened women's anxieties. Within the week after orders to draft an additional 10,343 on February 19 were given, militiamen were heading toward the Aroostook. The time was burdensome for Harriet Prescott because her son, Colonel Joseph Prescott, a commissioned officer, was certain to be called up. She was already in bed on the night of February 24 when a sharp knock at the door woke her. She panicked. "Immediately associating in my mind this *rap* with the news of the border conditions my heart withered and I could hardly command steadiness of voice to demand who it was that at such an unreasonable hour disturbed the quiet of a private family." It was General Ezekiel Foster's aide informing Joseph that he was on active duty. As she pondered the situation, Harriet grew more frustrated with the powers that be: "I feel that the whole tract in dispute—and the *honor of the State* to boot are not worthy [of] one widow's moan—one orphan & tear . . . the sacrifice of even one human life." Making matters worse were neighbors—including some women—who reveled as militia from the west poured into Calais, the early March rendezvous for several companies. These merrymakers were confident that brinkmanship would bring Sir John Harvey, New Brunswick's governor, to his knees. It was no laughing matter for Harriet, yet she too hoped the "commotion" would alert Harvey to "a sense of the injustice (if such it be)—of his measures and of the disastrous consequences of embroiling the two nations and involving them in a war." In response to rumors that forces would sweep all of Canada, Harriet fumed: "when a craving for conquest takes possession of a nation or rather its rulers—*right* is forgotten—*justice* disregarded—and humanity outraged." Unnecessary acquisition of land was immoral.[32]

While Prescott was seething in Calais, other women were scouring the papers and swapping news. In New Haven, Connecticut, Elizabeth Jocelyn, the daughter of an artist, read printed correspondence between Fairfield and Harvey, and puzzled it out with a visitor who "explained a little difficulty in it." One afternoon she divided her attention between "a long piece in the paper, concerning the 'Boundary War,'" and her baby sister. Her older sibling Sarah kept pace: "Read in this evening's paper that the danger of war had assumed a very serious aspect, although many are of the opinion that it will be amicably adjusted." In Bangor, Mary Pierce was sick of the only topic of conversation. "We hear nothing of importance here," she sent word home, "but wars & rumors of wars."[33] Like it or not, she was an important link in the chain of political communication.

Despite the many voices around her that were "decidedly for war," Caroline Haynes, the widow of a Bangor lawyer, put her stock in diplomacy. "Van Buren seems disposed to have the matter peaceably adjusted, and to discourage a war," she wrote on March 9 in the family diary. She was right. Even though Congress authorized him to raise fifty thousand volunteers, Van Buren did not want to use them. While in a special message to Congress he guaranteed he would defend Maine if attacked, he also warned Fairfield that aid would be withheld if his armed occupation lasted too long, thereby creating further incidents. Van Buren then sent Whig partisan Major General Winfield Scott to Augusta, Maine, where he corresponded with Governor Harvey and on March 21 arranged for a truce. Both Harvey and Fairfield complied, agreeing to withdraw forces. On March 25 the conflict ended with little more than a drunken brawl and an accidental death from a ricocheting bullet fired during peace celebrations to count among its casualties.[34] The boundary issue remained unsettled until the 1842 Webster-Ashburton Treaty.

Mary Pierce's sister Lucy could not have been happier about the peace. "We hope now that the war is over, and feel quite relieved at the present aspect of affairs," she wrote to her parents on March 30. "What a waste of money!" she exclaimed, adding that "a treaty is formed with the English to which they would gladly have acceded in the very beginning, without one grain of trouble or expense to us!" She may have been referring to the British foreign secretary Lord Palmerston's eagerness in 1837 to accommodate Maine and resolve the long-standing problem, after a surveyor was arrested in the disputed zone.[35] That was water under the bridge now.

By mid-April, militiamen were returning to Bangor. They camped at the barracks on Thomas Hill, the highest point in town, waiting to be mustered out. Frederick Bartlett was probably among them. Mary Pierce's brother-in-law, Henry Hedge, went with a neighbor, Caroline Farrar, to the hill to welcome them home. On April 14 Mary noted they marched, accompanied by music, to church, where they heard preaching from Joseph C. Lovejoy, who had served as army chaplain for the troops at the border. His brother, Mary was sure to mention in a letter to her parents, was editor Elijah Lovejoy, the abolitionist martyr.[36]

It would be several years before Mary Pierce would see another war—that with Mexico (1846–48) over the acquisition of western land. This time, antiwar sentiment would be partisan among the Whig women who blamed Democratic president James K. Polk for igniting war. In the meantime, however, there would be much to distract them from the haunting memories of 1839's first few months. After all, the 1840 presidential campaign was just getting under way, rallying all Whig women beneath the banner of "Tippecanoe and Tyler, too!" In the next chapter, they will guide us through the sensation known as the Log-Cabin Campaign.

5

"Whig to the Back-bone"

Women and Mass Politics in the 1840 Campaign

By late summer 1840 the "Log-Cabin" Campaign was in full swing, and Mary Pierce wanted to be part of it. On September 3 she rode out from her home, Brookline, Massachusetts, in a train of horse-drawn wagons to a Whig picnic about eleven miles to the southeast in Quincy. The cart in front of her sported a banner reading "whig to the back-bone," leaving no mistake as to the occupants' allegiance to presidential hopeful William Henry Harrison. Her own cart, packed with men and women, was similarly decorated. "Harrison Flags abounded on horses['] heads and indeed wherever they could be stuck on," she wrote to her fiancé Henry Poor. "There was a vacant seat in our omnibus and how I *did* wish you could have filled it." Never before had she done such a novel thing as public campaigning—and in mixed company, too—so she needed to reassure Henry that he remained foremost in her mind. But Mary was not alone in stretching the limits of feminine decorum. About fifteen hundred women—nearly half of the three-thousand-plus attendees—turned out for the rally sponsored, organized, and conducted by women.[1]

The 1840 campaign reached new heights of strategic electioneering. Whigs and, to a lesser degree, Democrats employed spectacle, disseminated politically themed material objects, and created image-making songs and slogans for both men and women to embrace. Women could be seen riding in processions, populating rallies, watching parades, and even hosting political meetings as they did in Quincy. Many purchased Harrison portraits and handkerchiefs, made pincushions emblazoned with party symbols, or stamped the candidate's likeness on hand-sewn books to announce their partisanship publicly.[2]

But the frenzied mass campaign was more than mindless to-do for women. The contest marked a turning point that set them on a course of increasing civic participation and party identification. They were now calling themselves or being called "Whigs" as they embodied a partisanship that seeped deep into their "back-bones." Democratic women were more diffident about announcing preferences, perhaps because that party was not nearly as encouraging of their exertions. Indeed, Whigs' visible mustering of women's activism was ridiculed in Boston's opposition newspapers including the *Bay State Democrat*, which George Bancroft helped to establish.[3]

This chapter looks at women who entered the era of mass party politics in 1840. They did not simply experience their public behavior within traditional gender roles, involving family, benevolent work, and Evangelicalism. If so, we would have seen abundant testaments to the rhetoric of moral suasion, expressions of sympathy for the disadvantaged and oppressed, responses to Sabbatarian appeals, or hopes for the spiritual regeneration of the country upon electoral victories. Instead, their writings are filled with details of political infighting, complexities of economic issues, concerns about patronage and corruption, discussions of the nature of democracy and the republican legacy, discourse about modes of political communication, and fascination with electoral returns—a variety of interests that, in short, differed little from those of voting men. A blend of kin and neighborhood affiliation, party loyalty, and rational judgment of economic problems and politics motivated them, as it did men.[4]

Still, as we will see, gender restrictions generated unease as campaign experimentation and institutional chaos countenanced women's forays into the public sphere. For in their activism women explored relationships outside courtship and family—at political lectures, reading groups, and other social and cultural events—with male strangers or casual acquaintances who shared a common partisan purpose. Indeed, these affiliates could seem closer than kin holding contrary views.

This chapter follows campaign milestones, from the nomination of Harrison in December 1839 to his triumph in November 1840, through the eyes of three Massachusetts Whig women whom we have already met—Eliza Davis, Mary Pierce, and Annie Lawrence. Not merely spectators or passive consumers of partisan knickknacks, they reveal a level of involvement—ranging from sacrifice in the name of the party to introspection on the interrelationship of politics and gender—that intensified as the campaign unfolded.[5]

We will begin with Davis. We find her sizing up the political horizon early in the year for her Whig husband John, who has once again tossed his hat into the ring for the governorship. The section culminates with Davis's shining moments during the June 17 state nominating convention. We then turn to Pierce, home from Bangor and writing to Henry Poor in March about Whig activities in Brookline. Her disavowal of the use of feminine influence in favor of rationality to persuade voters marks a high point in her partisanship. After that, we look in on Lawrence, whose story picks up from chapter 4 in Washington, D.C., where she has joined her U.S. representative father, Abbott. Just as she is easing into her role as political daughter there, she must relinquish it and draft Abbott's resignation letter. We wrap up with a section on celebrations following Harrison's success. Throughout, voices from across the region will be heard.

Eliza Davis and the Massachusetts State Convention

In January 1840, a month after William Henry Harrison and John Tyler were nominated for president and vice president at the Whig national convention in Harrisburg, Pennsylvania, the campaign was already blazing in Worcester. Eliza Davis felt the heat, especially because her husband John wanted to be on the Whig ticket for governor come November 9. His bid would simmer along with Harrison's as slogans like "Old Tip and Honest John" paired the two. But hearing in January about the near defeat of Whig Robert C. Winthrop as Speaker of the House, and the tight race between the 1839 Massachusetts gubernatorial candidates—Democrat Marcus Morton would win—made Eliza uneasy about trends.[6]

That her brother George Bancroft was in town for the Democrats' February 12 county convention made matters worse. He was, as Eliza described him, "full of matter." "He hopes you dont mean to accept a nomination—certain failure if you do," Eliza wrote to John mocking George's scattered verbiage. "Morton inevitably be reelected. Whig house—Whig Senate may be. You be rechosen—better situation for you. All the country go for Van Buren."[7] To her, George was manipulative; he wanted John in the Senate to clear the way for Morton's reelection. Refusing to be a pawn, she weighed his undercutting words with enough security in her assessment to discount them.

With the Independent Treasury Bill having recently passed in the Senate, George held forth confidently on banking. Since Eliza was pro-Bank, she sarcastically recapped his one-man war on the state-chartered (once national) Bank of the United States in Philadelphia. "Don't know what to say to the Gov. of Pennsylvania," George steamed about David R. Porter's requesting credit from the flagging institution. "United States Bank better pay its own debts instead of loaning money," Eliza continued in his voice. "Wrong for the state to borrow of an insolvent institution. Charter ought to be taken away . . . Whigs *individualy* [*sic*] condemn—uphold as a *party*." She rejected his blustering, rigid stance: "I cannot but be provoked with his politics—for he has sense enough to do better."[8] The partisan slavishness that George attributed to Whigs, Eliza detected in him to a fault.

It played out in his oratory. "The paper you sent with Georges speech came yesterday," she informed John on February 15; "It is indeed 'exactly' like him." She chided her brother for stooping to vagaries for popularity's sake and wondered why "a legal mind, accustomed to the exactness of law phraseology should ever adopt such mean anything sort of language." She gave George a piece of her mind. "I broke out into quite an invective against it, which completely astonished him—he had not an idea that any body could be displeased." Rather than simply dismiss his rhetoric, she analyzed its causes: "George sees but one set of people and is so filled with his own notions that he . . . has not an idea on political matters beyond the tactics of his own party." Likening herself to him as a strategist, she cogitated, "He makes me think of my own skill as a chess player—I can lay a grand scheme—see my own moves far a head, but forget that my antagonist may not play exactly as I expect; so my scheme gives place to expedients to ward off threatened dangers."[9] Like brother, like sister: Eliza, too, was partisan "to the back-bone."

As gossip flowed about the Democratic meeting Eliza kept her eyes open, always on the lookout for the opposition's vulnerability. Whig retorts to Loco speakers tickled her. Editor Benjamin "Hallet[t] made a long flourish about banks; abusing them root & branch," she snarled. "Some one said it was not very kind in him, considering he was invited up, and in part *paid by two Bank Presidents*." When he rhetorically yelled out, "'Can any one tell me who Gen. Harrison is?'" Eliza learned that a Whig shot back, "'*An honest man*.'" She felt vindicated. "It must have thrown cold water on the fire of his eloquence." If she herself could not shout down blowhards, at least others did.[10]

Although Democrats showed signs of weakness in Worcester, they had been fighting hard on Capitol Hill for the subtreasury bill that John opposed in a speech on January 23. Eliza applauded it, little knowing what controversy it would stir up. "I think it one of the most conclusive arguments I ever read . . . and only wish it may be read by every body in the State," she glowed, urging him to make political capital of it. "You mean I hope to circulate it," she advised on February 15. "The Boston papers have not as I see republished it yet but I think they cannot fail to do it." It was reprinted and had the effect Eliza foresaw.[11]

John's speech was popular around town, even among women. Rebekah Salisbury, wife of a wealthy businessman, listened to her nephew read it aloud. "We discuss politics with much *ability* & at least meet on equal grounds," she wrote to her husband. Embarrassed by her grappling with hard-core economics, she entreated him not to tell her sister "that I am study[ing] the sub treasury scheme for she will laugh at me." Her mother-in-law had already. "Never mind," she told Stephen, "I have said my say." On her side against Van Buren, her domestic chimed in, "we might as well have a king, & house of Lords & commons at once, as to have a government which considered the people so little." Fervor that spread even to the "help" enthralled Rebekah. "I do want to have a little insight into matters which agitate the community at large," she explained, joking, "Besides you know I have to enlighten the household."[12]

While the speech was making its rounds, trouble was brewing between Eliza and her sister Lucretia Bancroft, who, as we have seen in chapter 4, labeled herself a Democrat in spirit. The trial began when Eliza's longtime friend "Mr Warren" visited in early March "full of anticipation for the whigs." Because George Bancroft and Warren were not on friendly terms, Lucretia sparred with him. "He and Lucretia will never agree; for she has all George's inveteracy towards him," Eliza protested. Lucretia called Warren "'worthless and unprincipled,'" and Eliza knew him to be anything but. To make matters worse, rumors spread that Eliza and Warren were publicly insulting George. "To nobody but you," she swore to John, "have I ever spoken of George in any way that he might not hear." Apparently Warren was telling people just how much his and Eliza's partisanship countered George's. "Warren by mixing up his own thoughts with what he says of me, has given an impression that I agree with him." The election was tearing Eliza in two. "I must either resign an old friend, or appear to George to have taken a part in the slanders which have been circulated." She upheld Warren, but asked him never again to speak of her and George in the same breath.[13]

Not letting the matter rest, Lucretia refused to dine with Warren. Eliza bristled at her insolence. "If I am to measure my intercourse with the world by any body's rule but my own or yours," she vented to John, "I shall give all up at once." Lucretia would not run her life. "If I shut out all who disapprove of George's political career," she seethed, "we shall lop off many we are glad to welcome." Put between a rock and a hard place, Eliza chose partisan friendships over Lucretia's demands. It was not only for John's sake that she put her foot down. She had developed a political mind of her own that carried her to the massive Worcester state convention about which Warren had just briefed her.[14] It would take place on the battle of Bunker Hill's anniversary on June 17 and would attract thousands statewide to designate the gubernatorial ticket and approve the presidential slate. She had no idea of the central role she would play.

In the meantime John's speech had prompted a belated rejoinder from

Democrat James Buchanan. On March 3 in the Senate, he charged that it grossly misrepresented his pro–independent Treasury position. Three days later John defended himself. The press ballyhooed the exchange, alarming Eliza. "Why under the sun have you not written since the Buchanan business," she chastised John on March 15. "I have been anxiously looking every day for a letter." Everybody was talking about it except Lucretia, who was still moping, "sure that George is right in all things." For news-hungry locals Eliza had no inside scoop. Left to her own devices, she assessed the local impact, which if overwhelmingly negative may have imperiled John's nomination. "The two sides give two versions," she reported. "Mrs Salisbury says her husband and all others agree that you have done nobly, she says she learned every body sustained you." Another assured her "every body sees through Buchanan's plan." Eliza gave the gist of the Whig response: "Mr B[uchanan] finding himself in the downhill course, resorted to this attack as his only mode of regaining his standing." With gallows humor, she offered the Loco viewpoint, referring to a cosponsor of the Independent Treasury Bill who seemed poised for a rejoinder: "The Post . . . affirms that you are dead and Mr [Robert J.] Walker is soon to pronounce your funeral oration." Referring to mourning dress, Eliza snidely asked, "Shall I get my suit of Sable ready?" But John was far from buried. In Vermont alone the speech was being reprinted by the "thousands" and was making "proselytes by hundreds." John was besieged with requests for it. "You cannot imagine what a demand there is," he wrote Eliza on March 18. "Letters come . . . from all parts of the country begging for a copy." He smirked, "it vexes the Locos beyond endurance" and was certain his detractors would be silenced for good.[15]

Eliza, however, knew better. Democratic papers were still slinging mud while incriminations about George's dirty hands surfaced. Eliza heard—she refrained from writing down her informant's name—that George was behind a slam of John's speech in the March 20 Boston *Post*. "I cannot divest my mind of the conviction that he was privy to it," was all she could say; "When I see you I will tell you why." Eliza would have pumped Lucretia to find out "if George admits the Editor of the Post to his house," but they had agreed to a truce. "I have weathered the storm, and such a storm I never was out in before." Not wanting a replay, she forgave her sister's outburst. "I think Lucretia meant right," Eliza conceded; "she thought me deficient in respect & affection for George. . . . I determined to forgive all unkindness towards myself, knowing that her means of judging George were less favorable for truth than my own." She breathed a sigh of relief. "Thank Heaven I am not caled [*sic*] to sit in judgement on George . . . I should be but too apt to condemn." Still, Eliza wanted to patch things up with him. She had long promised to visit but never got around to it. But because of the "storm" and the upcoming election, her absence could be misread. "I mean to go before the excitement becomes more intense, which it daily is," she wrote John on March 21. "Now I can see that during the next year political excitement is destined to usurp the place of kindly affections; but while I mean to maintain the right to select my own company, and to enjoy my own opinion I do not wish if I can help it to cut asunder the few ties I have to my kindred."[16] She wanted to have her cake and eat it too, but at a high price.

As Eliza was waiting for John's rebuttal to Buchanan to appear in the papers, the latest scuttlebutt sent Lucretia reeling "into a grave fit which lasted several hours." Alonzo Hill, Eliza's dinner guest on March 28, intimated that George had masterminded the Buchanan scheme. "George will do any thing for his party I dare say," she wrote to John, "but I am unwilling to think he would aid or abet in such a foul course of conduct." She suspected he "might know other people" who did, though. Whether George was involved or not, the plan backfired. John's speech became "the *whig tract* of the winter," part of a public forum in which, as one Democratic woman observed, "The baker & Milk Man are thinking & attending to *Banking* & the *Currency*." Even Hartford's postmaster admitted to George on April 7, after Democratic spring election defeats, that "Davis['s] speech had an effect which we could not counteract."[17]

When Eliza finally visited George in early May, she was "convinced he has not been guilty of any thing." He confessed Benjamin Hallett had authored the *Post* harangue but said nothing about coaching Buchanan. Eliza dared not ask. George warned her he would "buckle on his armor in defense of Judge Morton" but swore he would "never be personal in his mode of warfare." Eliza extracted this promise while reading his face for hints of self-doubt. "He is unwilling to think his days are numbered," she guessed, "but there appears an anxiety about him that contradicts the confidence of his assertions."[18] This was the news John needed to hear as the convention was approaching.

Released from family stress, Eliza focused her energies in June on becoming John's deputy during the state convention. Although she foresaw the "utter annihilation of Van Burenism," she fretted to John that "there will be a strong effort to suppress your nomination." After all an 1840 census taker was brazenly distributing Buchanan pamphlets and a torrid review of John's speech as he canvassed houses. But she was confident that ultimately the "democratic revolution" of 1840 would sweep John along with Harrison into office. "The *people* have taken political matters into their own hands, and mean to see that all goes to their own mind. . . . They dont ask where you can do the most good; but where they can hurrah loudest for you." In the age of mass politics, numbers spoke volumes.[19]

On June 10, with the convention only a week away Eliza expressed a willingness "to do all in my power to change the rulers of the Country." That included housing and feeding delegates. Convention committee members suggested she serve them simple "log Cabin fare." Eliza proposed a tavern-style menu of cold "Beef ala mode, tongue, ham, boiled beef & . . . leg of veal" and, of course, hard cider. Because strange men would be rooming with her while John was away, she argued its propriety: "Even Mary Stiles," who lived in an all-female household, "was called on as a whig & takes four." Some were sheltering fifty or more. "The Taverns are setting tables for a thousand a piece," Eliza shrieked. The numbers mobilizing were daunting. Trains would run hourly between Boston and Worcester to transport them.[20]

The night before the convention, Eliza thought she was prepared for anything, but chaos set in. She received word at the last minute that the entire Barre delegation would drop by the next day for dinner. Eliza scavenged some extra cider, cheese, and crackers. She had told the committee she could house eighteen, but twenty-five dripped in, one of whom "said he would sleep on the sofa." Since she represented her husband, she had to show them hospitality as if they were friends. She amicably called them "good & true whigs . . . [with] zeal enough to save the country any day." One guest grateful for her amiability exhorted the others, "'you shan't sleep in that bed to night if you dont promise . . . to make Mrs Davis a Governor's Lady.'"[21] Of course, they would.

Her convention efforts, though exhaustive extensions of domestic routines, edged her toward an increasingly public role. After sending off her delegates in the morning to the "Log Cabin," where speeches and nominations would be made, she and her domestics began "the tug of war for us at home." They cleared the breakfast tables, set them for dinner, sliced meats, and cut up cakes. In the meantime, as many as thirty thousand conventioneers were pouring into Worcester—nearly one-third of the entire county's population of 95,313. One woman counted "*4 acres* of men." About ten thousand, including thirty musical bands, were assembling for the 10:00 A.M. procession. There would have been more had a Boston-to-Worcester train wreck not held up some delegates. Though the news ruffled some women, no one was killed.[22]

When Eliza locked up her house and entered the streets' bustle, her public role began. She headed down to the Salisburys' for the procession, passing by buildings overflowing with women, stationed to wave to the marchers. Those who could not come implored observers for particulars. The parade, which took one and a half hours to run its course, had not yet passed when she arrived. But when it finally came, Eliza was flabbergasted. "What a shew!" she wrote to John: "Never, never shall I forget the deep and solemn feelings that agitated me as I beheld this magnificent spectacle!" She was overwhelmed by the sea of banners, the thundering "hurrahs," and deafening music. "One felt there was power for good or for evil in such a living mass," she shuddered and prayed, "God grant it may be for good." While Eliza was drinking it in, one of her companions stepped outside to indicate Eliza was at the Salisburys' window. The parade suddenly stopped and shouted, "Three cheers for the Lady of John Davis." Eliza jumped away, but the instigator led her back. "You must show yourself," he said. So she took out her handkerchief and waved to the roaring Suffolk delegation. After that, delegation upon delegation paused at the Salisburys' to salute Eliza. When one of her houseguests passed, she blew him a kiss. His platoon cried out, "'Again,'" but she curtsied this time and then over and over, amid cascades of "'once more.'" "Judge if you can what I felt," she told John, "but strange as it may seem, after the first five minutes I forgot myself entirely; and received it only as a part of the enthusiasm of the day in which, such is the power of sympathy, I fully participated."[23] Eliza took to the limelight.

As soon as the parade was over, she rushed home to greet the Barre delegation. Instead of the small group she expected, two hundred or so invaded her house with "banners, drums and trumpets." She panicked. "My heart sank within me—how on Earth should I feed them?" They were ravenous. "Dish after dish of ham tongue & crackers disappeared bread butter & cheese seemed to have wings, cold veal & ala mode beef were exterminated, while the rivers of beer, cider, wine & water, might have turned a cotton mill," she gasped. "And as for cake the way it went was a caution." As they wolfed down the food the delegates tested her mettle. When Eliza admitted she would never remember all their names—that "the name of whig was enough"—the delegation leader snapped back: "The only thing I like Van Buren for . . . is his memory of names—he never forgets any one." She thought on her feet and replied, "I hope . . . I am as unlike Van Buren in every thing else as that." Then she heard clapping; the day was saved. When they finished feasting, all two hundred lined up outside the house, asked Eliza to stand at the door—in another public display—and serenaded her with "Hail Columbia." After the leader made a speech praising her and John, she "had half a mind to speak in reply," and probably would have had not her overnight boarders showed up for leftovers before heading to the train station. The last trickled out around 6:00 P.M. The cars leaving Worcester were so packed that they inched their way along, engines coughing out. One Bostonian Whig woman stayed up until eleven o'clock waiting for her father to come home with news. She was awoken when the train chugged in at midnight with its musicians' horns blaring.[24]

The next day Eliza wrote about the convention in a long letter to John, who after reading it replied, "I could not suppress tears it so much affected me." He showed it to Daniel Webster, who deemed it "the very best letter I ever read in my life." It became campaign propaganda in the Whig press and a joke in opposition papers, including her brother's *Bay State Democrat*, in which one smart aleck quipped that John wept because the conventioneers had demolished his wine and cake and that Webster sniveled because Eliza was the better rhetor. Eliza's private words had become partisan fodder.[25]

John would win the governorship in November, thanks in large part to her sacrifices. But she won something too. "I shall be a lover of the people—shall ever believe and trust them," she effused when the convention was over.[26] This devoted Whig woman had become not only a public personage but a thorough democrat.

Mary Pierce Gets Out the Vote

After Mary Pierce left Bangor, where she became engaged to Henry Poor in February 1839, she exchanged letters from home with him, sometimes twice weekly. As we have seen in chapter 4, Henry introduced her to Whig partisanship during the 1838 Maine state election, so it was natural that they continue their political discussions in writing. In March 1840, when the campaign started flaring up in Brookline, Massachusetts, Mary began to apprise him of local happenings. "Of late politics are much attended to in our once peaceful village," she jested. "Last Saturday evening there was a whig meeting and a whig association was formed." Having read in a newspaper Henry sent her that he was secretary of the Penobscot County Whigs, she asked him to "write a letter of encouragement to our young society." It needed no nudging. By April they were meeting in farmer Jones's barn, and by late June she could report that "The Whig association . . . have been making a great fuss and everybody is so full of Harrison and log cabins that there is really a strong temptation to turn a Loco foco for effect." Women played a role in this hubbub. They collected funds for an Independence Day banner and presented it, along with a speech, to the association president.[27]

The association gave Mary occasion to test the waters with Henry about mixed-gender political sociabilities. Young men were eager to escort her to partisan affairs, including the July 4 banner presentation, but Mary feared Henry would nix the invitations. So she declined them. "John Howe invited me to go with him on the morning of the fourth . . . but the morning proved rainy and I concluded not to go," she divulged, adding, "Remained quietly at home all day." As if to humor Henry in case he was steaming, she told a joke: "'Why are the Locos like fishes thrown up by the waves?' Ans[wer] 'Because they are always *ly*ing ^(lie)^ about the banks.'" Laughing to herself, she wrote, "Is it not a good one?" Eliza Davis would have appreciated it. After Mary said no to another outing, Henry stepped in. "I trust I am not so narrow minded or exclusive as to suppose your love for me is incompatible with your enjoying the society of other young gentlemen," he heartened her. "Your own good sense will always lead you just right, and will always satisfy me."[28] His broad-mindedness was in touch with the times.

While Mary was sequestered at home on the Fourth, other women were being struck by its partisan overtones. Aurilla Moffitt, wife of a Providence, Rhode Island, stable keeper, wrote that the day had "been celebrated as usual" but with "a Harrison Convention at which a clam bake and chowder were served up." In Lexington, Massachusetts, student Mary Fiske studied despite "the excitement of the day," which included a Democratic fete and a Whig procession "with a Log Cabin drawn by thirteen white horses, and the big political ball, painted in gores, with mottos written in the spaces." Lucretia Bancroft, away in Vermont, longed to hear her brother George speak in Barre, Massachusetts, where Daniel Webster was also scheduled to address Whigs. It was a recipe for trouble, but she wanted to stir some up among townsfolk traveling to Barre along roads lined with rooting Whig women. "As all Worcester people call me a loco, I should have enjoyed following the Whigs of our town to the rallying point of both parties, & then deserting them for metal more attractive"—meaning the Democrats. Eliza Davis felt smug the Whigs outnumbered them.[29]

Two months later, with Henry's blessings, Mary ventured out with John Howe and a wagonload of Whigs to the Quincy picnic. Back in July, seventy-five townswomen had met at Quincy town hall to plan the outing, appoint an arrangements committee, and brainstorm on possible speakers. Soon the committee, mainly wives of lower-middle-class artisans and tradesmen, were mailing circulars all over Norfolk County and placing notices in the *Quincy Patriot*, inviting "*all the Ladies*" to come. That same paper warned women of the consequences: "Can any woman be so blind as not to see that she is by thus publicaly [*sic*] entering the political field, adding oil to the political fire. . . . Is she ignorant of the tendency it will have of turning her tea parties into political clubs—her fireside hearth into a political hall . . . ?"[30] The "ladies" said hogwash.

The turnout gave tiny Quincy "the appearance of Boston." Over two thousand purchased tickets, but hundreds more showed up at Hancock's Lot. There they joined a procession, led by the "Randolph Band" and the arrangements committee, to pick up speakers from Major Thomas Adams's. All snaked back to the amphitheater, where front rows were reserved for women only. The stage was flanked by mottoes, including "Martha Washington and Abigail Adams; / 'Tis glory enough to follow in their footsteps." John Davis's portrait hung among them. There, the picnic's president, Mary Boott Goodrich, wife of popular author Samuel G. Goodrich, a.k.a. "Peter Parley," asked Adams to introduce U.S. representative Caleb Cushing, whose speech encouraging women's political engagement ran well over an hour. Mary Pierce described it as "a short forever in length." The picnickers then marched to "an immense tent" adorned with flowers and overflowing with cakes and fruits that were beyond Mary's grasp. "There was *such* a pushing and scrabbling as I never witnessed before." So she recruited a gent whose "long arms reached every-where." John Howe—"not a very *gay*" gallant according to her—was evidently useless. His fiancée had just broken off their engagement. Nonetheless, Mary confirmed her fidelity to Henry. "As to being interested in each other we were on pretty equal terms as all ladies must be alike to him at present and I am sure all the gentlemen who were there were so to me." Refreshed, all headed back to hear Samuel G. Goodrich curse the independent Treasury and James Buchanan while he pointed to Davis's picture. After Josiah Quincy, Jr., had his say, a ball at the Hancock House capped the evening for lingerers.[31]

After this foray, Mary rode to the September 10 Bunker Hill Whig procession that flowed, fifty thousand in number, from Boston into Charlestown. Because she would fill in Henry when he next visited during one of "those long talks" they usually had, we know as little as he did from her September 19 letter. But she whetted his appetite with tales of shifting partisan allegiances: "I noticed in the great procession a young man whose father is one of our most violent locos & several who had once been of that party themselves."[32] She took almost personal satisfaction in the desertions.

The more Mary publicly announced her partisanship, the more she transgressed crumbling boundaries of feminine comportment. Shortly after the procession she "went into" a male sanctuary of newspaper reading and politicking not normally open to women. "Our Whig reading-room . . . is quite a new thing for Brookline and shows that we are looking up in the world," she glowed. As her partisan reputation spread, admirers tested her fidelity. One September evening, while she was congratulating Henry on Maine's state election, a mysterious young man camped outside her bedroom window to play "Harrison melodies" for her. "Whoever the youth is," she wrote Henry, "he certainly has a very good ear and plays quite well." She assured him that although she opened the window to savor the music, the blinds remained drawn.[33]

Oddly enough, as Massachusetts polling day, November 9, drew near, Henry urged Mary to use feminine wiles in persuading voters. "I know that you are a good Whig," he began his plea, adding that balloting in Maine "owed a great deal to the whig young ladies." He then recounted a story—similar to "Whig Lysistratas" tales plastered all over newspapers—about a woman who refused to marry a Democrat unless he cast a Whig ballot. "So you see . . . what good principles the Maine Ladies have and what *obedient* lovers they possess too." Mary was not amused. After congratulating Henry on Maine's returns and expressing hopes for a favorable outcome in Massachusetts, she slammed his strategy. "I do not *altogether* approve of the means the young lady you mentioned took to change her lover's political opinions," she scolded. "It was not right for him . . . to vote the whig ticket to please all the ladies in the world." Mary prided herself in using logic and rhetoric to convert wavering Democrats, such as her brother-in-law, Calvin Durfee. "If he *does* vote," she told Henry, "I shall flatter myself so much as to attribute it in *some measure* to the wonderful eloquence I have been displaying for the few last evenings . . . adhering as closely as possible to the Socratic mode of reasoning." By rejecting emotionalism for intellectual persuasion—she probably asked probing questions like Socrates—Mary demonstrated her preference that Durfee act according to principles of inner direction and rational assessments of the candidates.[34]

Whether or not he ever voted remains a mystery. He pledged to only if it was not raining.[35] Regardless, the state went for Harrison, Tyler, and Davis—and Mary, along with Whig women like her, had a hand in it.

Annie Lawrence and the Bunker Hill Meeting

When Annie Lawrence's Whig father Abbott won a seat in the U.S. House of Representatives in November 1839, she became more serious about politics, a topic she had resisted as a student despite her mother Katherine's cajoling. To fill the void left by him when he moved to Washington, she went to Whiggish lectures, including one on former first lady Abigail Adams, Annie's role model for becoming a conscientious political daughter. Her politics deepened in late January 1840 at age nineteen, after she joined Abbott at the nation's capital. There, among national decision makers, Annie sought information on timely issues, including economic ones. After watching Henry Clay argue before the Supreme Court on February 8, she deemed "his voice & manner . . . always delightful." A few days later she heard Representative Ogden Hoffman expound for an hour on a bill to continue construction of the Cumberland Road. She supped at the president's and had calls from "several Congressional gentlemen." These excursions were soon interrupted by a bout of "Typhus fever" that halted her diary keeping and nearly took her life.[36]

Annie recovered in time to follow the May 4 "Young Men's" convention in Baltimore, Maryland, that ratified the Whig nominees for president and vice president. It coincided with the Democrats' May 5 nominating convention in which the first national party platform was devised. So enthusiastic was the response from Washington that Congress voted for a recess. Annie noted the "large number of persons" absent, including Clay and Webster. Stephen Salisbury joined them, leaving wife Rebekah home to fret about news that "a Whig was killed in the procession." Annie, who remained in Washington, debriefed returning conventioneers. "The results surpassed the most sanguine expectations," according to them. "The procession," she heard, "was more than a mile in length composed of Delegates of Young Men from . . . every state in the Union." She may have also savored stories about the prodigious female showing.[37]

As election frenzy mounted, Annie's father was growing too ill to serve at the capital. "We shall soon be preparing to leave this," she sighed at the end of May, "not without regret however on my part." At home she continued to record Whig highlights, including the Worcester state convention and her chats with local big wheels. After hobnobbing with sometime Harvard Law School lecturer Charles Sumner, Annie complained: "persons of such intelligence never take notice of me. I am destined for some *ignoramous*."[38] Notwithstanding her greenhorn parlor-room banter, her schoolgirl days of ignorant bliss were well behind her (fig. 5.1).

Annie witnessed the extravagant Bunker Hill Whig meeting held on September 10, only days after the Quincy picnic. "All citizens . . . desirous of a change in the administration" were invited to watch the 10:00 A.M. parade wind from Boston Common to Bunker Hill in Charlestown. Annie was relieved that, the night before, Boston was "so busy a scene . . . , that the morrow promises an auspicious one." The next morning she stationed herself with her father on their porch to watch. As "Invited Guests" and Revolutionary War veterans passed by, some recognized Abbott. Annie was thrilled they "set up a shout, which was kept up by most of the Delegations which followed," the last of which came two hours later. Annie estimated fifty thousand had swept through. Displaying the Whig penchant for public order, she noted, "the decorum & order which was every where manifested was better than all." Reflecting upon the whole, she swelled with pride: "It will not soon be forgotten by those witness to this glorious spectacle." Sheer numbers made it memorable. At Bunker Hill, the terminus, one Rhode Island woman imagined "more people were assembled together than ever were before in this country." Annie guessed there were between eighty thousand and one hundred thousand participants.[39]

FIGURE 5.1
Annie Bigelow Lawrence, sculpted by Shobal Vail Clevenger (1812–43), 1839, stone, 55.88 x 45.72 x 30.48 cm (22 x 18 x 12 in.), gift of Miss Aimée and Miss Rosamond Lamb, 69.12. Photograph © 2010, Museum of Fine Arts, Boston

The day was not over for Annie with the last strains of the marching bands. She went to the "Horticultural Rooms" and was charmed with "a fine display of fruit." The exhibit, staged with the procession at the height of harvest season, showed off agricultural bounty and the advantages of Whiggish "book farming." In the evening, visitors from Virginia and Connecticut dropped in along with "part of the Ohio & New York Delegations," who gave three cheers, toasted her father, speechified, and vanished as suddenly as they had materialized. The following day she was unexpectedly greeted by "the Maryland Delegation" looking for Abbott, who was out. "I was obliged to see about 20 gentlemen," she revealed in her diary. "I endeavored in vain to appear self-possessed, until Father returned, which somewhat relieved me & I was enabled to converse with tolerable ease."[40] Like Eliza Davis at the Worcester convention and Mary Pierce on the Quincy excursion, Annie improvised her way through this new environment of mass politics.

The Bunker Hill procession was the focal point of varied events in which Annie participated that Massachusetts Whigs juxtaposed to their advantage to create a well-coordinated package. Besides the horticultural exhibit there was the "Ladies' Fair," which raised funds to complete the Bunker Hill Monument, and the performances of Viennese ballerina Fanny Elssler, who became unwittingly embroiled in partisan scuffles. Significantly, they all centered around the monument as a symbol of party identity, for it embodied the Revolutionary republicanism that the Whigs were appropriating as their own. Of course, Democrats, too, saw themselves as heirs of this tradition, but it became a wellspring of Whig women's political activities during the 1840 election.[41]

Deft timing and thematic interplay helped create these associations of political and cultural offerings. The ladies' fair, which opened two days before the procession, was long in the planning phase. Masterminded by Sarah Josepha Hale, once dubbed the "mistress over the house of Whiggery," it showcased American women's productivity (in a fashion reminiscent of the domestic products campaign of the Revolutionary era) as seen in their household manufactures, arranged by town and county on tables scattered throughout Quincy Hall. Hale's daily paper, *The Monument*, full of republican rhetoric, was printed there. Annie, who attended on September 11, found it so jam-packed that "one could hardly get a glimpse of the tables." Eliza Davis, who chaired the Worcester committee, oversaw its booth, which raised about eleven hundred dollars. She peddled unsold merchandise at the horticultural fair. Her report was printed in the papers.[42]

Five days later an astonished Annie, who had seen Fanny Elssler dance, called her "the most graceful creature I ever saw." During her Boston tour the danseuse witnessed the Bunker Hill procession, bought items at the fair, and, swayed by the campaign's outpouring of emotion, donated the proceeds from one of her performances toward the monument's completion. Legend has it her ballet slippers lie in the cornerstone. The Democratic press jumped on her donation: "the aid of *foreigners* in rearing the monument is repugnant to the patriotic pride of Americans." Sarah P. E. Hale shot back that since "every body, black white and gray," had contributed—why not Elssler? She was also the butt of jokes in the *Post* that romantically linked her to Whig congressman Caleb Cushing simply because he escorted her to the ladies' gallery in the U.S. House of Representatives. He denied the liaison: "all I did . . . was the performance of an act of every day civility, to a person of highest excellence in her profession."[43] Editors would stop at nothing as the election approached.

And no wonder. New England Whig women were everywhere busy campaigning throughout the late summer and fall. Some dispersed candidates' portraits. Katherine Lawrence gave Annie three Harrison cards to pass out. Of her own Harrison engraving, a Providence Quaker fancied that "if he would do as well as that looks he would make a very good president." Others populated rallies. Women "crowded" Worcester's Log Cabin in July to hear former governor Levi Lincoln rail about the Federal "Preëmption bill" granting squatters' rights to public lands. In Rutland, Vermont, Elizabeth Clement sallied off to an August 29 outdoor convention with baby Ann in tow, "the youngest whig on the ground," to hear a three-hour speech by a local lawyer. In early October, Sarah Jocelyn cheered on a New Haven Whig procession. The Pierce family cook, Abigail, sang Harrison songs at a Brookline Whig meeting, to Mary's mother's dismay. "I do rejoice that we shall soon have an end to Political meetings," she grimaced, noticing Abigail was still cavorting after 10:00 P.M.[44]

The effect of these rallies on women's partisanship was tremendous. A good case in point is Clarissa Harrington, a student in the nation's first state-supported teacher-training school in Lexington, Massachusetts. She heard former state representative Robert Rantoul, Jr., speak at a Democratic meeting there on October 9; a week later she attended a "Whig Lecture." Despite the Whig juggernaut under way, Rantoul evidently had made a good enough case for his party to stand up to the opposition, for on October 15 she scratched in her diary, "I have not made up my mind, whether to be a Democrat, or Whig." In subsequent diary entries, however, she leaned Whig. Within two weeks she, "with several of [her] sisters, attended a Whig meeting at the Baptist Church" featuring Salem mayor Stephen C. Phillips. When her classmates debated on October 17 the question "Is it best for females to attend Political Lectures," partisanship imbued the schoolroom.[45]

By mid-September, Annie's politicization had developed to such a degree that she scarcely resembled the social butterfly she was at school. But that month her ailing father decided to retire from Congress. When Sarah P. E. Hale found out, her thoughts flew to Annie's mother Katherine, who "regrets . . . giving up public life." Katherine's brother-in-law Amos Lawrence was sure that her "taste for public life is *so decided* . . . that it will be difficult to keep her in her proper *home* sphere." But Annie's heart was breaking too. "I am sorry on some accounts, for I should have an opportunity of seeing those to whom I am attached," she wrote resignedly; "but all is ordered rightly, & I will not say a word." These "attachments"—including Fanny Calderon de la Barca, wife of Spain's minister to Mexico—grew from political sociabilities. Annie underscored the sacrifice she made in forgoing political prominence by quoting a verse: "And oft the fav'ite wish denied, / Has proved the greatest good." Her knowledge of Whig economic stances was utilized, however, during her father's convalescence. "I have been occupied of late preparing Father's *resignation letter*," Annie recorded on September 19. In it she outlined the Whig plan for economic recovery, "the Currency—The Tariff, Internal Improvements—and The Public Lands—all of which demand the early and serious attention of Congress," and explained "that the majority of the people are convinced that the present Executive and his immediate predecessor have not administered the Government in accordance with the principles upon which it was founded." It was printed in the Boston *Daily Advertiser* on September 22. Like Eliza Davis's political letters that were sometimes read by others, Annie's written words became public property.[46]

The disappointment caused by her father's retirement from Congress made Whig gains in state contests no less electrifying for Annie. "The victory in Maine seems to have inspired all good Whigs," she glorified in September; "the city is rejoicing & sanguine of a glorious result in March next." She also exulted in Georgia's triumph, noting that, consequently, "the whole country is in a state of excitement which it has never before known." She added with undoubted melancholy, "what a winter to pass in Washington."[47] If times were thrilling in Boston, what would they have been like on Capitol Hill?

As the presidential race came down to the finish line, Whig women kept their fingers crossed. Since polls opened in late October or early November depending on the state, anticipation was sustained. While Whigs were already celebrating in New Haven on November 4, Sarah Jocelyn was hesitant to call the vote "because Harrison's election is depending now entirely upon the returns from Pennsylvania and New York." Understanding the winner-take-all rule, she realized "a small majority" in these key states "will be as good as a larger one for our country's Salvation." November 9 election-day tensions in Massachusetts got the best of Clarissa Harrington, who "wish[ed] there might be such a thing as having *two* Presidents that both parties might be satisfied." But by then the die was being cast. In what was a record presidential election turnout, Harrison would take nineteen of twenty-six states to receive a landslide 234-to-60 electoral vote. "What was equivalent to a revolution of this whole great country," Sarah P. E. Hale wrote her brother, "was accomplished without a drop of blood." She chalked it up to "a very deep feeling of dissatisfaction of the men and measures of the present government." In many ways she was right, for the Democrats' response to the financial panic and ensuing economic downturn seemed to have been their undoing.[48]

After Harrison's victory, Annie's father was courted for the U.S. Senate but demurred. She was crushed. "I cannot reconcile myself to this refusal of one of the highest positions in this country." Her own aspirations were frustrated. "Oh! this desire of earthly distinction will at times have its sway."[49] All was not entirely over, however. Abbott recovered and in 1842 acted as commissioner in the Maine-Canada boundary settlement. In 1849 he was appointed minister to Great Britain. By then Annie was married with children and out of the immediate orbit of his fame. Although she would remain a Whig, the glow of political life for her would never again burn so luminously.

In the Election's Aftermath

With Harrison's victory the expanded political sociabilities that Whigs offered continued. In Sarah P. E. Hale's Boston there was "singing and parading, till it seemed almost like childs play." New Haven, according to Sarah Jocelyn, planned a "grand illumination" to bring out residents to stroll among the rows of buildings ablaze with candlelight. At the Lawrences', Annie regaled guests—including John Davis—"with Whig Songs" until she "was hoarse." In Brookline, Mary Pierce popped into a barnyard hop, to which "all who call themselves whigs were invited." Mary was sure to tell Henry that she danced with several men, including a "vile loco" farmer's son. "Society here is much broken up into clans," Mary claimed, but "so many persons who were previously unknown to each other were there." This breakdown of family- or neighborhood-oriented socializing appears to have coincided, at least in Brookline, with the appeal of Whiggery as a cohesive force within the community. Yet Whigs advertised their avowed disdain for party platforms and other forms of political identification in order to create a putative image of nonpartisanship. So it is no surprise Mary savored the irony of another event to which "'All the *whigs* of Brookline are invited to attend without any distinction of party.'"[50] For Mary nonpartisanship was but a sham. She would stubbornly remain "Whig to the back-bone" until the party's 1850s demise.

While others were partying throughout the election's aftermath, Sarah Hale remained sober. She realized the real battle was only just beginning. "It now only remains to be seen how the Whigs will demean themselves when they get the upper hand," she wrote with some caution.[51] In chapter 6 we will find out, as we trace the next four years and beyond through the turbulent diary of a Whig married to a Democratic politician.

6

"But I Will Think *the More"*

Persis Sibley Andrews and the Politics of Covert Partisanship

William Henry Harrison, the first Whig president, was inaugurated in Washington, D.C., on March 4, 1841. That day, in Freedom, Maine, twenty-seven-year-old Persis Sibley was jubilant. "I am too much of a Whig not to enter into the general rejoicing," the farmer's daughter wrote in her diary. "Wish I was at Augusta," the state capital, "to dance," she wistfully sighed, but it was thirty miles away. She heard it would be a nonpartisan ball that "Locos seem to have anticipated . . . with as much pleasure as the Whigs."[1] It gratified Persis, who would search throughout the 1840s for any glimmerings, however dim, of harmony between the parties.

In 1841 Persis was as pro-Harrison as any of the women in chapter 5 who campaigned for him. But her life course ambled through Loco territory when she met and married the Democratic politician Charles Andrews.[2] Like John Davis, Charles understood how spouses could further political careers. He depended upon Persis to help him win elections, think through perplexing issues, and climb out of political quagmires. Because Persis loved both her husband and party politics, she tucked her Whiggery away inside her heart, which she opened only to her diary. At times the duplicity—a Whig supporter masking as a Democratic wife—overwhelmed her. At other times it allowed her to craft the bipartisan ethic she publicly avowed. In both cases, Persis was an unwitting vessel of the era's partisan struggle.

To some extent, a similar duplicity—or so said Whig congressmen—was in evidence on Capitol Hill. In March 1841 it seemed certain that the Whigs, having a president and majority in both houses, would undo Jacksonian economic measures, but a strange twist of fate changed the course of history. A month after Harrison took office he died, leaving Vice President John Tyler to take command. At first he acted more Whig-like than Democrat. He honored Harrison's cabinet appointments, dispensed political offices to Henry Clay's friends, and vowed, in his first message to Congress, to cooperate with the legislature in dismantling the subtreasury and distributing land revenues to the states. But he soon fought strenuously against reestablishing a Bank of the United States and increasing tariff duties. As the Democrat in Tyler assumed greater and greater presence, and as Whig losses in state and congressional elections multiplied, it became impossible for Whigs to implement their plans. Generally guided by republican values, Tyler's stances as he switched from Jeffersonian "Old Republican" to Democrat to Whig during his terms as U.S. senator (1827–36) were not easily pigeonholed into partisan categories. So it should have come as no surprise that he failed the Whig duck test as president. Yet Whigs expected him to adhere to their agenda as Harrison would have. When he did not, they "excommunicated" him from the party.[3]

Persis Sibley's partisan ethos was as complex and elusive as Tyler's. In this chapter we scrutinize her diary to get under the skin of a "covert Whig" who was writing about politics during the "Accidental President's" term.[4] Like Tyler, she at varying times deferred to, compromised with, or stomped upon the party with which she was nominally affiliated—in her case, Charles's Democratic Party. Living in this house of mirrors wearied her, as we will see. But Persis could not resist the lures of politics, even if it meant having a divided consciousness. As such she represents a variation of the political wife—one who could privately dispute her husband's party while publicly advocating it. Her story begins on January 1, 1841, with her first extant diary entry, and winds down in November 1844 when Democrat James K. Polk is elected president. Finally, we give a brief glimpse into Persis's future.

Living in a "World of Feeling"

"My history for the past year wo'd be one of the heart, for I have lived in a world of feeling." These first words of Persis's 1841 diary allude to her courtship by a slew of bachelors in and around Freedom, Maine. One was Charles Andrews, a Democratic state representative from Paris, with whom she became acquainted during an October 1840 visit to Augusta, the state capital. She had "long & firmly resolved never to have married," but Charles, whom she referred to in her diary as "Andrews" or simply "A," was giving her second thoughts. Although she tried to hide her affections from her parents—

they made courtship none of their business—she blushed at his mere mention. "There is one name that occurs frequently in Legislative proceedings that is rather difficult for me to speak without stammering." Since she scanned the papers with her family, it posed a problem. "It will embarrass me to read this kind of news aloud before them."[5] Her secret would soon be disclosed, however.

In late January Charles paid her a visit that set one jealous beau reeling. During it he evidently invited her to Augusta to witness the new legislature in action. Persis had followed its activities since it convened on January 6. Since both branches had Whig majorities, she felt "pleas'd with all they have done" so far, namely selecting a Whig Senate president, Speaker of the House, and governor, for whom there was no majority at the polls. Although she approved of Speaker Josiah S. Little, she would have preferred Democrat J. R. Chadbourne. This Whig was far from doctrinaire. Still, she was amused that town Locos who traveled to the capital craving appointments would be denied them "because none but Whigs will get any this year."[6] Persis, who despised office seekers, would soon watch them scurrying for crumbs.

On February 7, she rode off with Representative William Buxton and his wife for Augusta. There, she stayed at the Mansion House, a hotel pulsating with excitement as boarding senators, representatives, and other politicos and their wives darted about with news from the State House.[7] But the real action was taking place on the House floor. She arrived just in time for the fireworks.

Persis sat in the ladies' gallery, among some "old friends," to watch the face-off on February 9. Whigs were intent on passing resolutions denouncing the government's current financial policy and upholding Whig measures. One specifically "instructed" Maine's U.S. senator Reuel Williams to vote according to the other resolutions' spirit, which was anti-subtreasury, pro–national bank and tariff, and favorable to distributing public land sales funds to the states. Hoping to delay the resolutions' passage, Democrats filibustered. Persis understood exactly what was going on, nervously watching them "talking against time, w'h they commenced in good earnest." One windbag in particular annoyed her. "My friend Andrews takes an active part in these unworthy measures," she admitted, "but I was glad to hear him speak upon any subject." She had no illusions about Charles. He was as vain as he was ambitious. "I am sorry he thinks himself so good a speaker," she simpered; "it will prevent him from making improvements for w'h I think there is room."[8] Whether she realized it or not, she was anticipating political wifedom's advisory role.

When Persis left the House chamber for dinner, the Locos were still jabbering. At 11:00 P.M., Persis jotted down that they were "still killing time by their gift of gab." She was convinced that "Never was there such a scene in the House of Reps. in this State before." The hotel, too, "was confusion all night." Some representatives who dragged themselves in to nap were rounded up at 2:00 A.M. to vote. To break the quorum, Democrats walked out, but were ordered back by the sergeant at arms. The resolutions were finally passed, and the House adjourned at 3:30 A.M.[9] Persis barely slept a wink.

Despite her restless night, she went back for more. On February 11 she listened to a speech that was "racy—witty—full of comparison & apt quotation" in the Senate. Nowhere did she feel more at home than among battling politicians. "I take too much interest in Legislation for a lady," she whispered to her diary that evening; "I sho'd like to spend all my time at the Capitol if it were consistent." Instead of chatter about her "unfeminine" fascination with lawmaking, tittle-tattle spread that she and Charles were engaged.[10] It was untrue—for the time being.

Persis returned home on February 13 to a less-than-exciting routine of washing and ironing, picking up, cleaning bedrooms, and instructing Nancy, "a sort of adopted daughter," in letter writing. The arrival of newspapers on March 11 bringing Harrison's inaugural address brightened one routine day. He promised to serve only one term, use the veto temperately, and interfere as little as possible with Congress. "We Whigs think it first rate," Persis beamed, adding, "the Locos sneer at it—of course." She probably allied with some household members and sparred with others over the speech at the fireside that evening. Lively debate was common in the family, composed of her mother Charlotte, father William, brother William, Jr., Nancy, two male boarders, and a farmhand. "We have read the newspapers aloud," she penned on March 13, "discussing the grave questions of politics & the nation together—each drawing arguments from his favorite paper—Whig or Loco, for we have both."[11] This kind of good-natured partisan bickering probably kept her mind and heart open to Charles.

After the Augusta trip, Charles aggressively courted Persis. In mid-March he sent her a "story paper"—a large sheet studded with fiction—with an "unexpected penciling." (New Englanders mailed newspapers inscribed with simple messages instead of letters because the postage was cheaper.) What he scribbled remains a mystery, but it must have been pleasing, for Persis swooned, "How sweet is a pleasure that comes unexpectedly." His letters were "devour'd . . . over & over again." Yet marriage was out of the question, especially with him. For one thing, he was too poor; gossipers swore money passed through his hands like water. For another, he was too ambitious for political fame. Finally, he was too much a Democrat. "His politics too wo'd be in the way of us both," she realized. So the answer he received when he proposed to her in April crushed him. "A's wobegone countenance has haunted me as Banquo's ghost did Macbeth," she moaned. "I went & lay down, & covered my head with the bedclothes, but its ghostliness follow'd me." Afterward, Persis mailed him "a cold studied discouraging letter" that outlined her "reasons w'h wo'd have silenced any but a lawyer or a person in love."[12] Charles was both.

Her despondency deepened with shocking news of Harrison's death on April 4. The sixty-nine-year-old, hounded by office seekers, stressed by the domineering Henry Clay, and incautious about his health, had let a bad cold develop into pneumonia. He had had time to do little but form his cabinet, appoint some government officials, and respond to Clay's pressing for a special session of Congress. Persis deduced that the "arduous duties of his most responsible office & the consequent excitement have proved too much for his great age." She predicted the "loss will be bewail'd by the majority of this great nation."[13]

She was right. Women's outpouring of sorrow was tremendous. Some were thunderstruck at Harrison's precipitous passing. "He survived his inaugration [*sic*] just one month" an East Greenwich, Rhode Island, seamstress sighed in disbelief. Others imagined the divine hand of intervention at work. One pro-Harrison New Bedford teacher believed God was teaching zealous campaigners a lesson. "How mighty the effort which has been put forth to raise Wm. Henry Harrison to the Presidency. . . . but how soon has the Governor of all things shown how easily he can wither all the hopes of man." Many participated in obsequies. In New Haven, Sarah Jocelyn saw several women at a Harrison memorial procession wearing the traditionally male badge of grief, a black crepe armband. In Boston, Sarah P. E. Hale noted a similar parade that passed through the hushed streets to Faneuil Hall, where U.S. senator Rufus Choate eulogized. "It is so short a time since our convention procession last fall, when every thing was so gay and joyous, the streets dressed with banners and flowers and ringing with cheers and shouts," she wrote to her sister-in-law, "and for the same man the streets are again filled, but all was dark and solemn and quiet."[14] Log-Cabin fever was over in an instant.

Persis laid aside her grief to weigh the pros and cons of taking a teaching position at the "Young Ladies' High School" in Belfast. Although the pay was low, she loved teaching and supposed it would take her mind off "one unpleasant subject," namely Charles. She accepted the offer and left on May 14, the national fast day for mourning Harrison's death, a fact registered in her diary. In Belfast, a full schedule including teaching, attending a chemistry lecture series, and meeting with a Unitarian sewing society banished the gloom. But Charles would not let her forget him. "'The *handsome* Lawyer' of Augusta" sent her another paper with scribble begging her to reconsider marriage: "Will 'no never,' under any circumstances whatever always remain an obstacle insurmountable forever?" She thought to herself, "Who can ansr. such a question with certainty?" His charm was working its magic. More papers and letters followed. He even dispatched an envoy, a Belfast editor at the July Augusta Democratic convention, to give Persis "a welcome message." During her August break in Freedom, Charles, although sick as a dog, showed up.[15]

By this time, however, Persis was smitten with "Captain Cutter." During the last term he had lent a hand with paperwork, and she in exchange read to him. "I like his Sailorisms," she explained; "his jovial . . . cheerfulness has kept me in high spirits." She also relished their political discussions. Shortly after the August 14 Democratic county convention assembled in town, she, Cutter, and Universalist minister Rev. Andrew Pingree "had a rich dish of politics . . . —the first I have tasted this Summer." The Bank's fate was on the menu. "All parties are in anxiety to find whether President Tyler will veto the bank Bill passed at the present Extra Session of Congress," she declared on August 18, not yet knowing he already had. Tyler was willing, with reservation, to reestablish a national bank as long as states' rights were preserved. He therefore vetoed Henry Clay's Bank bill on August 16, because it did not allow state legislatures total authority to approve or reject branches. By the time Tyler had vetoed a revised bill on September 9, a mysterious coldness had set in between Persis and Cutter, who was embarking for sea.[16]

Persis engaged other politically minded companions. Pingree was always eager to chat. "Tho' I do not like his politics or religion . . . , I like to talk with him upon both subjects." Academy teacher George Field was also game. On September 13, state Election Day, she and Field together heard "uproarious bursts of clamorous rejoicing" at the nearby Democratic Party headquarters every time returns came in. "It is believed that the Loco-foco triumph is complete," she conceded. They took both houses and the governorship. That fall, Whigs lost six out of eight gubernatorial races and, by year's end, control of nine out of fifteen formerly Whig-dominated state legislatures. Voters had already lost faith in their ability to enact economic-recovery legislation.[17]

Charles, who rode this wave of voter disenchantment, confirmed in late September what Persis already knew—that he was reelected as state representative. "I am afraid his public career will ruin him." She thought him a slave to politics, and not a very good one at that. Yet she was drawn to him, against all logic. "How strange is my position with regard to him. I like what he appears to be—no mistake;—but I am always doubting him." After all, the buzz about him was not good: tongues wagged he was a deadbeat.[18] If she could not trust him, how could she marry him?

Persis left Belfast for home on November 18 with seventy dollars pay and some regrets. She would miss Pingree, the teachers, and, curiously, the students who troubled her the most. She traveled with a drunkard whom she granted "co'd talk temperance as fast as I co'd." While it was hard to readjust—she enjoyed teaching's daily grind—she eventually settled into a comfortable regimen that included family reading. "We have read President Tyler's Message this eveg.," she reported on December 13, six days after its delivery. "The Bank—the Bank, the Bank" was its drone to her, but in fact that subject occupied less than one-quarter of the message because Tyler left the detailing of his economic plan to the secretary of the treasury. Tyler's "Exchequer plan" called for a nonpartisan "Board of Control . . . for the safekeeping and disbursement of the public moneys" that some called a compromise between the independent treasury and the national bank. Persis stood firm on the Bank and presupposed most citizens were with her. "The President vetoes what the people wo'd have," she reasoned, and "the people won't have what he proposes." She suspected his new scheme would fizzle. "The Whigs & Locos both complain of him," she observed. Indeed, the exchequer bill was so unpalatable that both parties united to defeat it.[19]

The year 1841 ended with a visit from Charles, whom Persis greeted "with a heart palpitating with deep interest." They spent New Year's Eve reading together and feasting on apples. On January 2, he departed for Augusta, where "loaves & fishes are to be distributed" to "all the hungry office-seekers," as Persis snidely remarked. She could not reconcile herself to his profession. "It is strange that I feel so pathetic about the success of friend A," she admonished herself. "Individually I feel *perfectly* indifferent except for . . . the pleasure it affords me to see his wishes gratified, but as to final benefit to him I believe it wo'd be greatest to be disappointed." Politics brought out the worst in him, she imagined. Perhaps she wanted him to turn Whig. Whatever the case, Persis welcomed rumors he was routed as Speaker of the House. "A. . . . must be bitterly disappointed . . . tho' I believe it a salutary check upon his ambition." The next day, word came straight from the horse's mouth that he had won "'by a triumphant majority.'" Embarrassed, she wished "my last evg's reflections were cut out."[20] But they were permanently etched in her diary.

Falling deeper and deeper for Charles despite his nagging flaws, Persis contemplated marriage. As his wife, she would live in poverty. "I don't mean starvation or deprivation of the necessities of life, but I mean pinching along without the thousand & one luxuries that I habituated to." These she would "exchange . . . for care labor & love." To express her ambivalence she quoted Byron's "Don Juan": "'Marriage from love, like vinegar from wine— / A sad, sour, sober beverage—by time.'"[21] The unhappily wed Byron advised that marriage spoiled love. Persis turned a deaf ear to the poet.

By April 1842 she had said yes to Charles, evidently upon his word to quit politics for a while, start a legal practice, and "get religion." She may have promised to stifle her Whiggery, for notwithstanding the occasional grumble about Loco politicos she surely did—at least until 1844.[22] They were married on June 22 and settled in Dixfield, Maine.

Living with "Difficulty & Trial"

Married life was far from easy, as Persis's 1843 New Year's entry, in which she gives thanks for "strength in every time of difficulty & trial," shows. She was ill during her first trimester of pregnancy—her "'going to seed,'" as she called it. "There are some days when my stomach will not retain a particle of food." Charles's law practice languished, which meant hiring servants was infeasible. "It is only to save expense . . . that I do my own work in the present state of my health." Although a boarder did odd jobs while studying law under Charles, domestic labor, instead of politicized rumination, filled her hours. One bright spot for Persis was the literary company of "Dr [Albert Fisk] Stanley," who shared the same roof but once resolved "to have nothing to do" with Charles.[23]

By March, however, things were looking up. Persis could say Charles's "business is good, of late—very good." He even landed "an important case" that stirred the public. She could now hire Arvilla Leavett, a good cook and fireside reader. Around the same time Charles was undergoing religious conversion. He had often listened to Persis read sermons on Sunday mornings, a practice prevalent in rural New England, but on March 12 he prayed aloud. "It was a new & untried thing to kneel down before God," Persis imagined; "no wonder he felt it to be a great thing."[24] He was on the right path.

But the fires of political drive still smoldered. Representatives coming back from Augusta in late March after adopting a new "'Apportionment'" Bill gerrymandering the Fourth Congressional District to favor Democrats persuaded Charles to run for U.S. representative in September. "We expected it two years hence," Persis sighed in resignation. Their deal regarding his political respite was off. "Ambition is almost a ruling passion with him," she groaned. "There is great danger that the coming political campaign will distract his mind & draw it from the religious course he has recently entered." Charles, however, grew "stronger in prayer."[25] He would need divine inspiration to survive the coming election.

In early June, while delegates to the district convention in Lewiston were being chosen, supporters of Charles's opponent, Virgil Delphini Parris, waged a smear campaign. Persis was outraged at their "false, malicious stories, such as used to be bro't to me when I was hesitating to become his" wife. This time they centered on Charles's profligacy while Speaker of the House. Accused of not paying his board or tailor's bills, he buckled, frantically combing the house for receipts. "'It, will lose me the town, if I cannot find *those*,'" he yelped. He finally located them, showing every penny was paid, in his office. Despite the slander, his delegates were "elected three to one," but according to Persis, "he suffered more than the glory of office ever repaid." In August he won the Democratic nomination. Although Persis "co'd not consider it a matter for rejoicing," she would have to bear with it.[26]

After all, Charles wanted her involved in campaigning. He even regarded his candidacy as "theirs." "We are nominated," he would refrain. But acting the Democratic wife would not be easy for one so attuned to Whiggery. To ease the strain, she adopted, perhaps unintentionally, the Whig tactic of appearing to transcend party politicking. "Why did they invite only partisans (we only excepted)," she grieved after attending a private gathering. The sociabilities only made "party divisions greater, instead of doing something that wo'd have a tendency to unite." She thought it "Strange any can be so selfish as to think one party possesses all the good, the other all the bad." But taking the high ground scarcely eased the physical demands of campaigning. Persis was weak from the uterine infection she contracted after delivering "Lotte" in July. "My sufferings . . . were a thousand times worse than the birth," she recalled. Nevertheless, she would room and board Charles's political friends passing through town and at the same time dye yarn, knit socks, skim milk, churn butter, and make soap to save money as campaign expenses, like paying postage, printing ballots, and renting horses to canvass, accrued. "We have enough of everything for our table, but . . . scarsely [*sic*] enough to pay our rent & girl." Charles, too, troubled her with his drinking "ardent" liquor. As if that were not enough, the day before the September 11 polling, a local minister "preached a violent bolting sermon," instructing congregants not to vote for Charles.[27]

Election Day provided no relief from the mounting tension. "My poor husband is on the 'anxious-seat'"—the place where "sinners" sat awaiting conversion during religious revivals. She well knew that despite the gerrymandering, the election would be a close call. "The District is nearly balanced between Democrats & Whigs," she calculated; "then there is quite an army of Abolitionists & a few bolters." She speculated his election "wo'd be pretty certain were it not for the two last." The Liberty Party, which formed in April 1840 to run abolitionist candidates, would make quite a dent, especially in the gubernatorial race; abolitionist vote-scattering also cut into the mainstream parties' majorities. The sideshow only hardened Persis's stance against Charles's running. "I sympathize with him in his anxiety, because it is *his*—not because I have any that he sho'd be elected."[28]

Returns came in slowly, only to suggest no clear victory in most districts. "If elected it is by a small majority," she wrote on September 23. "The returns . . . differ so much that it is impossible for him to know with certainty until the votes are officially counted w'h will not be until 10th Oct." It seemed like an eternity. "O if he be elected What am I to do?" After calming herself, she determined, "I will not borrow trouble, it will come fast enough."[29] To the contrary, the contest dragged on.

Because the official count verified majorities in only three of seven districts, another election was scheduled for November 13. The delay gave rumormongers time to hatch new assaults on Charles's character. Meanwhile money was getting tighter as campaign costs soared. Persis took in three boarders to compensate. To break the camel's back, Arvilla quit to teach school, leaving Persis without assistance except that which boarders volunteered. And it was "off to baby every five minutes."[30]

Voting day came and went, again, without presumed victors. Persis finally let it rip on November 19. "This protracted political campaign is a continual drain upon the little change in husband's purse," she fumed. With a large does of sarcasm, she groused, Charles does not "dun any one because—forsooth—he is candidate for Congress, but he must pay everybody because he is candidate for Congress." She then vented about political wifedom. "Every low lived political miser who comes this way must stop the night with us, & get supper & breakfast, because 'we are Nominated,'" she hissed, summoning Charles's pet phrase. "We must be all agreeable" and say "glad to see you . . . *call when you come back* from us—, & all because we *are nominated*," she scrawled with growing rage. "If I were to recount the numerous ways that are tried to sponge something out of my dear spouse," she howled, "this book wo'd not contain the record." But in the end, she whimpered, "we must bear it all tongue-tied because forsooth the Col. is Candidate for Congress." She suffered silently until the official count was taken on December 12.[31]

On December 16 Persis read in the papers that Whig candidate Freeman H. Morse had won. "Then my spouse can say 'Farewell hopes of Laurel boughs,'" was her relieved response, which quoted poet Robert Burns.[32] She would not have to play Democratic "nominee" again for seven years.

Living to "Think Unbound"

On New Year's Day 1845, a year after the election trial, Persis Andrews awoke to a house empty except for the sleeping baby. Her help was away, and Charles was at Augusta arguing before the legislature for a new county with

Dixfield as its seat. The solitude inspired her to "*think* unbound . . . of other New Year['s]—days far back in the past—days of frolic & glee." Persis was giving herself rein to daydream. It is no wonder that during the past year she took license to ruminate over her own partisanship.[33] While she hardly reclaimed the strong Whig voice of her unmarried years, she hinted at a lingering fondness for that party during the 1844 presidential race.

By that time Charles's business was prospering, but only enough to sustain necessities, one domestic, a farmhand or two, and "Carlo" the puppy. Persis, however, would commission, for five dollars in January, a miniature portrait of herself and Lotte (fig. 6.1) and hope to purchase the new edition of the *Madison Papers*. In February, Charles had been given fifteen hundred dollars by Persis's father—the talk of the town—to buy the mortgage on their rented home and farm.[34] Life was getting easier.

By the summer, however, Persis was becoming restless, both physically and mentally. She wanted to "mingle with the world again." She argued, "I have been shut up at home so long, that I began to grow moody-depressed." So she made neighborhood calls and even visited friends in nearby Peru. That made her "feel, as one of the family of mankind again." In another display of independence, she broke her silence about Whiggery for the first time since her marriage, and voiced her preference for Henry Clay as president. "The Baltimore Conventions are over," she began her entry for June 2. "The Whigs have nominated Henry Clay as expected." The third-party candidate was also predictable: "The Tylerites" jumping off the Democratic bandwagon favoring Martin Van Buren chose "John Tyler, of course." "But the *Demo*-crats," she snarked, "have had to take a man never talked of, or they co'd not have effected a nomination at all." Indeed, when Van Buren failed to get a majority after seven rounds, James K. Polk, a young "dark horse," was placed on the ballot. With all three candidates now in place, she sounded the bugle: "Now for the battle. I shall not *say* much—family considerations—but *I will think* the more," she scrawled defiantly. In her mind, she could be as partisan as she wished. She probably favored Clay because he was against Texas annexation; it could lead to war, which she was resolutely against. Although he was a solid candidate, the mudslinging machine was stronger. "It will be strange if the horrid abuse heaped upon Clay does not elect him," she worried after counting twenty-nine "different slanderous articles" in one issue of Belfast's Democratic *Republican Journal*. Persis prized campaign-season fair play. No wonder a July picnic she attended, at which "partizens & bitter enemies mingled in the sociality of the scene," delighted her.[35]

But Persis's subtly partisan journalizing continued. In early August, Charles and other townsmen who attended a ratification meeting in Lewiston "came home full of enthusiasm & sure of success." Persis added with a

FIGURE 6.1 Persis Sibley Andrews and her daughter Lotte, c. 1844. Collections of the Maine Historical Society, Portland (collection no. 271)

touch of derision, "They feel so stout that they co'd elect Polk & Dallas without any help if they co'd have the privilege." What seemed like a shoo-in to the arrogant Charles was a tight race to Persis. In this combative frame of mind she tackled the August 29 Dixfield rally for Democratic gubernatorial and congressional hopefuls. Despite an unreliable domestic and a sick baby, she housed the "first class" main speakers, fed the rest ("a lot of lesser stuff"), and held a reception for ex-governor John Fairfield, with nary a grunt. But the "'hard handed Democracy'" who "preferred being about the grog-shops—Giving political harangues of their own" got her goat. "Never was so much noise drunkenness & disorder in this place before," she griped. "These Mass meetings, I am now convinced are a great curse to the country." A week later, however, when Charles's old foe Freeman Morse "bro't out quite a multitude," she had no objections.[36]

After state Election Day, Persis, Lotte, and Charles took off to visit family in Freedom; on the way they were bombarded with a "thousand inquiries" about election returns. "Husband wo'd pull out his list & read, then great joy if he were democrat, a long face if Whig." At Augusta, Charles was "sent for *twice*" during dinner by an editor, to Persis's dismay.[37] Politics stalked her relentlessly.

It greeted her warmly, however, when she returned in October to Augusta, where she would meet her father to discuss business. The Mansion House reawakened fond memories of staying there exactly four years ago, when she first encountered Charles. There she was free to think unbounded. "I spent the morn'g in agreeable reminiscences of that happy season," she wrote, though once-familiar faces had long left town. "I do not often see the most of those who then formed the circle here, but I occasionally hear from them, & always with great warmth of affection." Her world had changed, just as the political scene there had shifted. Then, State House Democrats in an adjourned session had been scrambling to revise election laws and choose a senator before the new 1841 Whig-controlled legislature would take charge.[38] Then, there had been hope for a Whig president in the White House. But those hopes were dashed.

Persis said little about Henry Clay's defeat. "There was great rejoicing among the Democrats at the election news bro't by last eve'gs mail," she noted on November 10. "It is now very certain that Polk will be elected."[39] After that, until Charles's untimely death from tuberculosis in 1852, she advocated only the Whig candidates her husband endorsed, too.

Their remaining years together were happy ones. In September 1845, Charles was elected clerk of courts for Oxford County. He then recruited Persis—"trying me little by little"—to answer his voluminous correspondence. "I love business, politics & such things as men have to do, & am most happy in this confidence he reposes in me," she wrote in November, before moving to the county seat, Paris, around New Year's Eve. On their fourth wedding anniversary, she assessed her lot in life and found it bountiful. "The right man for me is seldom to be met, but I did meet him," she glowed on June 22, 1846. "Call him scheming if you please:—he has honorable principles & will be governed by them." Looking back to a time of distrust, she protested: "I am not a 'woman deceived' . . . I am permitted to enter his deliberations to know him just as he is."[40] Time had healed all wounds.

In September 1850, Charles ran again for U.S. representative and Persis, again, resisted, though she admitted, "I love politics." Charles won and moved in November 1851 to Washington, D.C., where he "'neither *drank*—smoked—nor *chewed*'" tobacco, as Persis insisted. She remained at home, "keeping husband informed" of local opinion. "With every vote he casts *some* of his thousands of constituents are dissatisfied, offended or disappointed." Some even charged Charles with going "to Wiggerism." Perhaps she turned him around after all. One of the last things she wrote before Charles died showed how much she respected the party system—even as she was being wrought by it. "I am *in* with *both* sides—& they are *all* friends of Hus.—but not to each other," she ribbed. "I may be a *go-between* them & Hus. but not between each other."[41] This once-covert Whig, who cowered before partisan matches, had in the end become a respected and prized bipartisan referee.

7

"Shame on the Woman Who Encourages the Lawless Proceeding"

Women Encounter Radical Democracy in the Dorr Rebellion

On May 16, 1842, Thomas Wilson Dorr, a radical suffragist who was recently chosen governor in an unauthorized election, rode, with two hundred men, some carrying weapons, into Providence, Rhode Island, to the sounds of cheering masses. He was returning from Washington, D.C., where he had asked President John Tyler to legitimize his "people's government." Tyler, although a states' rights man sympathetic to constitutional reform in Rhode Island, urged conciliation with the official "Charter government," to which he had promised federal military aid in the event of armed rebellion. In defiance of Tyler's neutrality, the returning Dorr now brandished a sword he said was "dyed in blood," according to eyewitness Orson Moffitt, a Whig stable keeper. Women strained to glimpse Dorr in the procession that transported him to his headquarters. Some twelve hundred people joined in but not Aurilla Moffitt, Orson's twenty-six-year-old wife. "I did not trouble myself to go and see the parade," she wrote in her diary that day. "Shame on the woman who encourages the lawless proceeding by her presence!" Merely showing up sent a message: "insurrection and sedition."[1] She wanted nothing to do with that.

Many women, however, publicly fought to extend Rhode Island's white adult male franchise, severely limited by the state charter. Like Whig women before them, female Dorrites watched and sometimes joined parades, attended suffrage meetings, gave speeches, and sponsored picnics. The 1840 race had opened up new spaces for women's politicization that these female

Dorrites exploited. They arguably went a step further than their Whig predecessors, regularly publishing partisan periodical essays.[2] Like their 1840 counterparts who were demoralized by Harrison's untimely death and Tyler's betrayal of Whig principles, the female suffragists were dismayed by Dorr's exile, conviction for treason, and imprisonment.

This chapter recovers the diverse range of women's experiences during the tumultuous years of constitutional reform and its aftermath (1842–44) in Rhode Island. Some Whig-affiliated women, like Aurilla Moffitt, deplored the Dorrites and upheld the Whig-dominated state government. Others, like Louisa Park Hall, a Providence Unitarian minister's wife and daughter of a retired academy teacher who was a die-hard Whig, understood the Dorrites' frustrations but not their ways of registering them. Mary Avery White, a Boylston, Massachusetts, shopkeeper-farmer's wife, whose son Aaron moved within Dorr's inner circles, considered the state government repressive but fell short of endorsing Dorr. Some Dorrite women were mainstream partisans. Activist Catherine R. Williams, granddaughter of Rhode Island's former attorney general, pronounced herself a "'lifelong Democrat.'" Dorr himself, a onetime Whig, turned Democrat by 1839 and attracted sizable party support. While other Dorrite women were not necessarily calling themselves Democrats, they published in Democratic papers, and planned and participated in several joint Dorrite-Democratic rallies held after Dorrites and northeastern (particularly Rhode Island and Massachusetts) Democrats combined ranks for the 1843 and 1844 election seasons.[3] This period, then, represents the first widespread expression that we have uncovered of female Democratic partisanship on par with Whig women's.

As this chapter unfolds chronologically it weaves, throughout, the stories of the abovementioned women. We begin with Suffrage Association activism in April 1841 leading to the forging of a "people's government" in May 1842. We then turn to the rebellion itself—the May 18 attack on the Providence arsenal and the June showdown at Chepachet. The third section concerns Dorrite-Democratic women's exertions in 1842, 1843, and 1844 to agitate for further reform, liberate Dorr from prison, and elect Democratic officials. An assessment of the larger meanings of Dorr women's activism closes the chapter. Throughout, we see these women as dedicated activists, keen observers, and partisan rhetors.

The People's Government

On April 17, 1841, at the height of Harrison obsequies, Aurilla Moffitt remarked, "The free suffrage folks are having a great time to day." She noted they formed "a very long procession" that wended its way "to Jefferson's

Plains to partake of a collation." About three thousand people, many waving banners, joined the parade lead by butchers in aprons. "'Peaceably if we can, forcibly if we must'" was their motto. At the plains they roasted an ox, calf, and pig, and served a seven-hundred-pound, ten-foot-long loaf of brown bread.[4] The imposing barbecue boldly (and threateningly) advertised the Rhode Island Suffrage Association's cause—universal white male suffrage. With butcher aprons, boisterous mottoes, and behemoth-yet-humble brown bread, working-class symbolism naturally inflected the proceedings and put wealthier folks on notice that they could, only at their peril, impede the onward march of the age of mass politics.

The timing of the two events—Harrison's funeral observances and the Rhode Island Suffrage Association outing—was not entirely coincidental. The Log-Cabin Campaign, with its in-your-face style of voter mobilization, conceivably nudged the disenfranchised—well over 50 percent of white men—into action. Furthermore, the election had drawn 80.2 percent of the franchised population, more than any previous presidential contest. It is not surprising then that as the campaign was gaining momentum in March 1840, the Suffrage Association was born. By the time of Harrison's death, it was just getting off its feet. The April cookout was the group's first grand affair.[5]

Prior attempts to organize were fairly ineffective. Since the Revolution, individuals had occasionally championed revising the still-operational Charter of 1663 defining voters as "freemen" or landholders. Around 1832 artisans and tradesmen, notably carpenter Seth Luther, and some professionals agitated through publishing and speech making. In February 1834, "friends of a Constitution and Extension of suffrage" met at the State House to plan a convention. Around the same time the Rhode Island Constitutional Party, composed of moderates—mainly Whig businessmen and professionals—was instituted. Member Thomas Dorr won a seat in the state legislature that convened on May 7; he immediately pressed for a state-sanctioned constitutional convention. On July 4, a bill to hold one was passed. Dorr, reelected representative, was also chosen as a delegate to the September Providence convocation. Because only freeholders elected the delegates, they, like the legislature, reflected conservative elements keeping the Charter alive. Consequently, the convention, which at times could not even reach a quorum, failed to expand suffrage. After unsuccessfully running two candidates—one was Dorr—for Congress in 1837, the Constitutional Party dissolved and, with it, concerted efforts for change until the Suffrage Association's establishment.[6]

The association would take up the cudgel of reform. It issued the *New Age and Constitutional Advocate* and in December 1840 sent a petition to the legislature, which promptly tabled it. Soon after, the association flexed its muscle with the intimidating butchers' barbecue and a fearsome, partially armed procession at Newport in May. On Independence Day, suffragists staged a "very long" parade in Providence, according to Aurilla Moffitt. She was not yet candidly antisuffragist.[7]

Less than a year later she was. The Suffrage Association had been becoming increasingly militant, while the Charter government had been becoming more accommodating. The suffragists planned, without legal sanction, a "People's Convention" for drafting a constitution, and they held an election open to nonfreeholders in August for choosing delegates to their October gathering. There, delegates, including Dorr, produced a document that extended suffrage and reapportioned legislative seats to represent northern, industrial, and commercial residents better. At the government-sponsored counterpart "Landholders' Convention," delegates devised by February 1842 a similar constitution that enlarged the electorate but barely addressed reapportionment in the north.[8]

In December 1841 a high turnout of voters ratified the people's constitution. State supreme court judges shot back that it was not legally binding and that carrying it out would be treasonous. No wonder Moffitt recoiled. But not the nine Rhode Island lawyers who in March 1842 authored the Suffrage Party manifesto titled "Right of the People to Form a Constitution." One of these was Aaron White, Jr., the forty-four-year-old son of staunch abolitionist Mary Avery White.[9]

Besides the specter of treason, nativism turned Moffitt around. She feared that if propertyless Irish immigrants could vote—over 7 percent of Providence's population was Catholic in 1840—the "Roman" Church would dominate the United States. As far back as the 1820s, Rhode Island conservatives had been irrationally arguing the same; now Charterists were banging the same drum about the people's constitution. So after learning on March 24, 1842, that the Landholders' Constitution was "rejected by a small majority," Moffitt exploded. "These free suffrage advocates," she snapped, "*had they the power*, we should be delivered up to the tender mercies of *Roman catholic foreigners*, who . . . are at the beck and call of their priests as a *body*, the most corrupt and remorseless beings upon the face of even *this polluted* world." She paraphrased words then attributed Revolutionary War hero Marquis de Lafayette to fortify her position. "'If ever this republic is destroyed it will be by *Roman priests*!'" To her, suffragists were traitors.[10]

Members of the new "Law and Order Party" in the Charter government thought so, too. In response to the upcoming suffragist election for a "people's government," the legislature passed an act—called the "Algerine Law" by detractors, referring to the despotic dey of Algiers—under which unofficial officeholders, candidates, or organizers of illegitimate balloting would be imprisoned and fined. As a result, major candidates on the Suffrage ticket resigned, and moderates fled the party. Dorr, undaunted, stood for election as governor.[11]

As the April 18 election approached, Rhode Islanders trembled. After all, on April 4 the Charter governor, Samuel Ward King, had ordered company commanders to "'be in readiness at thirty minutes warning.'" He had also positioned guards at the arsenal. Even President Tyler reluctantly got involved. He agreed in an April 11 letter to send military aid, but only if a revolt broke out. Newspapers rattled the population with tales of Irishmen stockpiling arms.[12]

Fearful women left the state. But Louisa Park Hall stood firm. On April 11, her father John Park begged her "to take refuge with us" in Worcester, Massachusetts, "till the struggle between the political parties be over." Hall tried to quell his anxiety in her correspondence. Still he feared the worst as refugees streamed into Massachusetts. But on Election Day, Hall testified "The Free Suffrage Election went off peceably [*sic*]."[13] Dorr had won without bloodshed.

Dorr's inauguration day, May 3, was full of both excitement and dread. Thousands, including women and some men bearing weapons, filled the streets of Providence. A procession escorted Dorr and the "People's Assembly" to a foundry under construction—they were barred from the State House—where he would organize his new government. During the two-day session, they chartered a militia company, repealed the Algerine Law, authorized an expedition to inform President Tyler of their doings, and passed a resolution that all public property be turned over to the people's government. John Park fretted all the while, reacting to news that vigilantes pouring into Providence would storm the State House. Louisa assured him there was no rioting; in fact she made social calls with her husband Edward. Aurilla Moffitt, however, was intimidated. With two governments—one legal, the other, treasonous—both claiming legitimacy, she wailed, "I am fearful of the end of all this."[14] Indeed, the worst was yet to come.

The Dorr Rebellion

After Dorr's inauguration, warrants for arrest were served to people's government officials without delay. Others resigned from office in droves. By May 9 Dorr was in Philadelphia heading for the nation's capital. After Tyler essentially told him to work things out with the Charter government himself, Dorr sojourned in New York City, where "Tammany Hall" Democrats pledged their allegiance and backing. By this time Louisa was getting nervous. With Dorr due back, shops were shutting down. Armed Charterist sentinels surrounded the arsenal and other state properties. The streets were humming with residents' trepidation. Finally, on May 13 Louisa wrote her father that she, her daughter, and her nanny were on the way.[15] The day Dorr returned to Providence, May 16, Hall was safe in Worcester.

Aurilla Moffitt, instead, sequestered herself at home, cursing women who ventured out to see the huge procession that swept Dorr to "the house of Burrington Anthony on Federal Hill" near the arsenal. There, she said, "Dorr's men assembled . . . in some force" to guard him. The next day, Dorr called in people's militia from Woonsocket, Gloucester, and Pawtucket. He also sent his men to steal arms. Moffitt gulped, "they took the artillery's cannon." Companies of the Charter-government militia in Providence were put on alert, and some state militia units outside the city were ordered in. That evening, Moffitt's husband Orson sped to Warren to escort its troops into the capital.[16]

During the wee hours of the next morning, Dorr with more than two hundred men and two cannon headed for the arsenal amid the clanging of alarm bells. There, the commandant, his men, and the Charter governor's party stood ready and waiting. Orson, who was nearly hit by insurgent musket fire on his way there, infiltrated Dorr's lines. He heard Dorr order his men to fire, but evidently neither guns nor cannon ignited. One contemporary swore a woman tried to light one of the cannon but was "held back by someone." No blood was shed, and many rebels deserted before sunrise. By all accounts, Dorr bungled the uprising.[17]

Later that morning Orson and about eight hundred men stormed Dorr's headquarters "to take him dead or alive," according to Aurilla. "They entered the house and lo' the bird had flown," she sneered, adding "his governorship . . . left his followers to their fate." It was to her the "wisest thing he has done." Until June, Dorr would roam from Maine to New York. But many, including Moffitt herself, were upset by his imminent reappearance. "Our city is on the look out for the return of Dorr with a band of foreign ruffians. God in mercy grant that our apprehensions may be groundless." They were, for the time being, but Governor King would take no chances and demanded federal aid from Tyler. Unfazed, the "Ladies" in nearby Woonsocket were "coming round" to Dorr's side.[18]

In Boylston, sixty-four-year-old Mary Avery White worried that in this climate of fear, Dorr insiders, like her son Aaron, would be persecuted. "May the Lord dispose those in power to do justly by all," she prayed on May 21. But, in a veritable witch hunt, many allegedly Dorrite mechanics and workers were fired, and like-minded shopkeepers were boycotted. Arrests abounded. White's law practice in Woonsocket, Rhode Island, was spared, but only for a while.[19]

Writing in exile, Dorr adjured White to keep the movement alive. White suggested Dorr reconvene the people's legislature in Chepachet, Rhode Island, a tiny northern village just over the Connecticut state border where some Dorrite militia were by early June training for another round of aggression. Louisa Hall felt confident enough to return to her home in Providence at that time. But by midmonth Chepachet had become a magnet for lower- and working-class suffragists from nearby towns and Providence County awaiting Dorr's comeback. Aurilla Moffitt felt tensions rising in Providence, where, as she observed on June 18, "Preparations are being made all about the city for the reception of Dorr and his insurgent followers." She resigned herself to the worst. "We are in the hands of God. Oh, may he mercifully shield us as before!"[20]

Like Moffitt, Louisa Hall watched Providence unravel over the prospect of a rebel clash. On June 23 her home became a clearinghouse for news and a haven for emotional therapeutics. In the morning a frazzled neighbor dropped by, disclosing that last night four Rhode Islanders riding near Chepachet—two of them to gather intelligence—were abducted. Sixteen musket-bearing Dorrites, one shouting "'damned landholders, let's arrest them,'" seized the coach and made the travelers trudge, bound, twelve miles to a barn. No sooner had the overwrought visitor finished when teenager Eliza Peckham zoomed in. Her twenty-seven-year-old brother Samuel was one of the prisoners. As Louisa was calming Eliza, Harriet Bowen abruptly entered to announce that the men had been released. Sometime that day Edward asked Louisa to pack for Worcester.[21]

The next day the city, as Louisa described it, was "in great commotion—families leaving—merchants sending off goods for fear of conflagration." She read that five hundred Dorrites had "already collected at Chepachet, ready for anything." State militia companies were filing out of Providence not knowing "their destination, or how long they [would] be gone." Women were frantic. Louisa tried her best to console the "Mothers and wives and sisters . . . left behind in the most trying suspense." That afternoon Hepsy Wayland, wife of Brown University president and Baptist minister Francis Wayland, called "half sick with anxiety." Louisa knew well that her husband, a staunch law-and-order man who preached that God was on his side, was "particularly obnoxious to the rebels." He would be singled out. Louisa dared not remind Hepsy that Francis, a regiment chaplain, would be ordered to accompany his men should they be sent to Chepachet.[22]

All the while Louisa trusted reason would prevail. She was heartened by the General Assembly's conduct. They had "done all that can be reasonably expected . . . taking away all excuse for violence, & bringing all the respectable and truly conscientious suffrage men to the support of the laws." After all, they passed one act to call a constitutional convention (the carrot to satisfy radicals) and another authorizing Governor King to declare martial law (the stick to deter violence). She also was grateful that "the coloured population have shown an excellent spirit"—they formed a Battalion of City Guards—". . . and will probably now help us as well as the abolitionists." Members of both groups were incensed that the people's constitution did not enfranchise African Americans. Furthermore, the rebels acted rationally. "The hardness of the times has driven many, who were once working men, into idleness and desperation." Conflict "between those who have nothing to lose, and those who are blessed with character and property" was bound to happen. Dorr to her mind was "maddened by disappointed ambition and the ridicule that has been heaped upon him," especially after the armory incident. Compromise was key.[23]

Calm in the face of events, she hazarded out with Edward for tea at her friend Mrs. Brown's house. While they were walking, Edward "could not help bursting out occasionally—the thoughts of the misery inflicted so needlessly on innocent females did so stir his sympathies." His mood was infectious, so the sight of the Newport Artillery, ordered in that day by Governor King, saddened her. "As I looked at the Soldiers," Louisa disclosed, "my heart swelled for their wives and mothers left at home." Still, she took comfort in how "uncommonly well skilled" they were, "having had the advantage of seeing United States troops march." Once inside, tea with neighbors was a respite from troubles. But just as things were winding down cannon fire shattered the air. Louisa thought the Newporters were showing off. But Edward investigated and found out it was Dorrite fire on Federal Hill. He and Louisa sped home.[24]

There Louisa once again became ballast for unsteady neighbors. Harriet Bowen dashed in again, begging Edward to check in on her mother. "It will be a fearful night again for many," Louisa predicted. Despite the darkening clouds, she opened up the chapel as she usually did on nights the sewing society met. While waiting with one other courageous seamstress for the rest, she heard a "burst of martial music from the next street," a signal, she supposed, to fire. "When I heard the brass band strike up so unexpectedly, with a slow, noble movement, my heart misgave me." She locked up and scurried home. An hour later Eliza Peckham flew in to say the music had signaled a company's departure with two of her brothers. "No one knew why," she sobbed. "Poor girl!" was all Louisa could say. "I shall make arrangements tomorrow, if we get safely through tonight, lest there should be fires." In Worcester, her father was thinking the same thing. In fact, his letter urging her departure probably crossed hers in the mail. In the meantime, thousands of militia troops at Governor King's orders were preparing for duty.[25]

Early on Saturday Dorr arrived in Chepachet, only sixteen miles from Providence. Women were everywhere fleeing, but a female stay-put at the Burrington Anthony house—formerly Dorrite headquarters—hid her governor's sword so the Algerines "could not get at it." Aurilla Moffitt also decided to stick it out, unbeknownst to her mother who came by: "she was afraid that I should go out of town and she would not see me for a long time." By Sunday morning martial law was in effect. To the sound of "fife and drum denoting the entrance of companies into the city," Moffitt surveyed near-empty churches and streets "paraded by armed men." Over three thousand troops flooded Providence, many of whom were quartered at Brown University or in citizens' homes.[26]

On June 27 Orson and Aurilla's brother were sent to Chepachet, where as many as one thousand albeit ill-equipped insurgents had assembled. "May God in his mercy spare us!" Aurilla broke down. "Surely Dorr will not be mad enough to attempt an engagement with a force so much superior to his." He was not. That day, he had sent a letter to a friend, intercepted by the Charter government, stating he had dismissed his forces. So when the advance guard reached Chepachet at 8:00 A.M. on June 28, Dorr had already escaped. They took prisoners, many of whom were noncombatants in the wrong place at the wrong time. The next day over one hundred captives were herded into Providence with the returning companies, who, according to Moffitt, traversed streets "litterally strewn with flowers" thrown by jubilant handkerchief wavers. Some female Dorrites dared toss prisoners bouquets, but most "closed up all their shutters." On July 2 the scene was reenacted when the cadets came back. Aurilla with her brother "rode all around" the city near the parade. "Their march was quite a triumph," she gushed.[27]

It was not a triumph for Mary White, who learned that day Aaron "had his house broken into." She offered him sanctuary in Boylston and prayed "Lord . . . direct him in the paths which lead to peace & freedom." Only after he fled to Thompson, Connecticut, did Mary finally reveal her proclivities: "may . . . his foes soon be made to see the errors of their ways." In Thompson, Aaron would practice law and meet his future wife, Cordelia P. Barnes, a tavern keeper's daughter who, some say, secreted food to his woodland bastion where he remained for some time. The legend symbolizes women's increasing activism during the summer and fall of 1842.[28]

Dorrite-Democratic Women Take Up the Torch

One of the first things suffragist women did was to organize. The Providence Ladies' Benevolent Suffrage Association formed "*to discuss the affairs of the*

FIGURE 7.1 Portrait of Catherine R. Williams, c. 1835, oil on wood, painted by Susannah Paine. Courtesy of the Rhode Island Historical Society, Providence (negative no. RHi X3 4475)

State" sometime before mid-August, when they raised one hundred dollars for Dorr. According to its corresponding secretary, Catherine Williams (fig. 7.1), "It was ostensibly a benevolent association, though in truth a Political one." Its constitution's "'*Treasonable Language*' would have sent any man to prison," she boasted. Statewide, "Women of the Democratic Party . . . carried on their plots" and, "protected by their political disability" (meaning they were disfranchised), escaped charges of treason. Some invited fugitives to speak. Others raised funds for suffragists and visited prisoners. The Young Women's Suffrage Fair held in October 1842 sold confectionary for the cause.

Some groups, such as the Ladies Free Suffrage Association of Pawtucket, which published its constitution in the *Bay State Democrat*, gave print a whirl. These societies welcomed women from laboring, artisan, professional, and elite classes.[29] This would thus be a vast, multiclass exercise of mass politics: the "people" against the anachronistic rule of property.

Some women acting independently "talked politics" in letters to Dorr in New Hampshire and pledged their continuing allegiance. A liveryman's wife trusted the legislative process. "If you have the votes for the peoples constitution, let them be counted in Congress, and the President once more made acquainted with facts as they are." She even asked Tyler to visit and planned to form a "committee of suffrage ladies" with a male spokesman to "present the case of R.I. as it is." A total stranger wrote him a poem about Algerine "tyrants" and aligned her partisanship with "feelings that . . . have been handed down to us from the noble Washington and others who struggled for liberty." Recording secretary of the Providence Ladies' Benevolent Suffrage Association and physician's wife Ann Parlin reiterated the allusion to rebellion: "Our husbands have been prisoners of *War*, & now we *are* ready to be *so*." Most correspondents beheld a bright future. Catherine Williams rejoiced, "we have the countenance & approbation" of Connecticut's Chauncey Fitch Cleveland and Massachusetts's Marcus Morton, current and former Democratic governors of their respective states. A partisan unknown to the outcast reassured Dorr "the days of the tyrants are alreddy [*sic*] numbered. . . . the democracy of other States is comeing [*sic*] to the rescue."[30] These missives empowered their authors emotionally to sustain Chepachet's disappointment.

Women "took the lead," one male Dorrite conceded, in holding clambakes that demonstrated strength in numbers, attracted prominent spokesmen, and raised money for the cause. The line between these and Democratic assemblies often blurred as the party in Massachusetts united against Whig "Algerines" before the November elections. At the August 4 Seekonk, Massachusetts, clambake conducted and chaired by women, which attracted about four thousand, *Bay State Democrat* editor Lewis Josselyn spoke. There, in an adjourned meeting, a committee of eight women drafted resolutions, one asserting "the people have an unalterable and inalienable right to change, abolish, and institute government." The Whig *Atlas* sarcastically anointed one "Immortal Lady of the Clam-Bake" and called their proceedings a "petticoat Revolution."[31]

Unshaken by bad press, women poured out for subsequent preelection suffragist clambakes. Another Seekonk affair, held on August 30, the day delegates to the Charter government's constitutional convention were elected, attracted as many as fifteen thousand attendees. Although Democratic senator James Buchanan and Democratic surveyor of the Port of Boston John McNeil declined invitations, their letters of regret were published. Democratic gubernatorial hopeful Marcus Morton also said no, but his pro-suffragist "clam bake letter," later used by Whigs as campaign-season mud, was read at the event. Alongside president of the Massachusetts Democratic state convention Seth Whitmarsh, who made a speech, Ann Parlin exhorted "'Suffrage ladies present, to . . . liberate William Dean,'" arrested that day for participating in the arsenal attack. "'I am willing to be the first shot down,'" she reportedly roared. To Dorr she bragged, "I said a few words that have really made them afraid. The Algerines conclude we are rather treasonable characters; . . . we bear our suffrage badges at all times in open daylight." She evidently emboldened Catherine Williams, who at a September 10 Millville, Massachusetts, clambake "threw off her cloak" and marched "forward to the front of the Stand" to report on her New Hampshire trip to see Dorr. "[Y]ou might have heard a leaf move . . . so profound was the attention given," she divulged. At the same event, before possibly three thousand listeners, a "young lady" damned Massachusetts Whig governor John Davis for granting Governor King's requisition to apprehend exiles, one of whom was her brother. In an equally fearless move, the "ladies of Gloucester," Rhode Island, planned the September 28 suffragist clambake held at Chepachet. "I cannot describe my sensations while gazeing [*sic*] from the top [of] the hill," attendee Abby Lord, a carriage maker's wife, exclaimed; "to think of all the suffrage party had suffered in trying to gain their rights." Eight thousand heard speeches by Lewis Josselyn and Welcome B. Sayles, Speaker of the people's House of Representatives. Around this time women were also peopling Democratic Party clambakes. At the October 5 Southbridge, Massachusetts, partisan feast, three hundred women were among the two thousand who cheered on chair David Henshaw, Bay State party boss, and Speaker Sayles.[32] As the boundaries between suffragist and Democrat were dissolving, women walked the line.

This bold activism ruffled some male feathers. One Dorrite suggested Ann Parlin's militance was turning away women. Her hands-on initiatives also upbraided him. "Mrs. P. is determined to do the controlling part or distroy [*sic*] all—she takes up collections & says its [*sic*] no boddy's [*sic*] business how much or what she does with them." After she spoke on the abuse of suffragist prisoners—her husband was one—to a mixed-gender audience in New York City on November 4, she was derided in Rhode Island papers and in the Whig Boston *Atlas* as a "roving" wife deserving of her spouse's reprobation. She conversely claimed the audience was "stimulated" by "seeing a female taking so much interest in state affairs." Less daring activism could upset the applecart. One man planning to march in a November

Nashua, New Hampshire, clambake procession threatened to bolt if women walked beside him. "There's gallantry," Catherine Williams grunted; "a Widower too, pray heaven he never gets another wife."[33]

As Rhode Island's November 21–23 referendum on the new constitution drew near and Massachusetts' undecided November 14 gubernatorial election dragged out after several candidates, including John Davis and Marcus Morton, received no majority—Dorrite women joined the partisan brouhaha. Ann Parlin was "cheered with the prospect of . . . Massachusetts" voting Democrat. Confident that Morton would urge "all people to . . . fight [it] out" over suffrage, she vowed herself "to lead the army to death or victory." Catherine Williams congratulated Dorr in December "upon the result . . . in Massachusetts," probably referring to legislative victories ensuring Morton's election in January 1843 or his slight November lead over Davis. She was far from optimistic, however, about the referendum. "About this constitution, I rather think they will not attempt to vote it down." She faulted the disorganized mobilization effort.[34]

After Rhode Islanders ratified a constitution unacceptable to Dorrites, women remained active at suffrage meetings, Democratic rallies, in the press, and in the home. Women also attended Dorrite trials, including Francis Cooley's for treason, at which they took copious notes. In December, male suffragists united with like-minded Democrats in a Providence convention to revive the party and take the April 1843 elections. Women did their part. In the Democratic *Republican Herald*, one "Daughter of Rhode Island" spurred men to vote in the spring elections, while another in the *Bay State Democrat* praised the Democratic gubernatorial candidate, Thomas F. Carpenter. Catherine Williams urged Dorr to forge deeper bonds with Marcus Morton: "I take him to be a sound man. & fully believe that if you were to go to Mass. he would meet you cordially & prove himself a friend." In April 1843, Pawtucket-area women "*en masse*" welcomed Dorr, who wanted to be near the border with Rhode Island in case of expected Whig electoral defeats. Instead, they swept the state. "I am ashamed to own I belong here . . . since the last Election," Williams protested. Whigs controlled the first General Assembly organized under the new constitution.[35]

Dorrite women experienced the fallout. In June the legislature revamped the militia law requiring "every master or mistress of a family or dwelling-house" to provide tax assessors names of residents eligible for military service. When asked on August 24, Abby Lord gave tax man Jeremiah Briggs an earful. "I told him I had no one to train in his company; that we were all Dorrites." She explained her "oldest son was not 14" and thus was too young to serve and her husband Henry had "fought for the liberties of the American people" in the War of 1812 but was imprisoned for "daring to defend their rights" at Chepachet. Indeed, she harbored no eligible men—only three boys and a sixty-year-old husband. Yet on September 28 she and a number of other women were arrested upon "bench warrants" and hustled off to address grand jury charges. Local women, knowing the feisty characters involved, rushed to the courthouse for the sideshow. One of the apprehended smirked that if imprisoned "'I should not then have to hire a Tenement'" (pay rent). Another with infant boy in arms said she would "'Not at all'" mind jail, that she "'brought him on purpose'" to join her. When the attorney general suggested they were nescient, Lord piped up: "'They were not so ignorant as not to know that ignorance of the Law, was no excuse for breaking it.'" Lord pleaded not guilty to refusing contemptuously to provide her household members' names. After the arresting sheriff offered surety (legal liability), she was released. Lord spit out, "I should give no surety," as she stormed out of the courtroom. Female spectators must have relished the fiasco.[36]

In the meantime, Dorr, disillusioned with flagging support and bruised by Whigs' success in the April and August elections, slipped into Rhode Island in October, effectively guaranteeing his arrest. Throughout Dorr's incarceration many suffrage women remained loyal to him. Politicized letters flowed into prison. "I do not know your views in regards to the annexation of Texas," one importuned; "for myself I am most earnestly opposed to it. . . . How can good come of taking a country . . . with such a population, & heavy debts." Another woman admonished Dorr to serve God instead of politics. "Our political parties are corrupt," she pronounced. Other writers-for-print kept partisan flames burning. In November 1843 newspaper pieces, Catherine Williams denounced Whiggery and asked suffragists to vote Democrat in the 1844 presidential contest. Ann Parlin chastised New York *Courier* editor and turncoat James Watson Webb (he was pro-Bank) in a fiery February 1844 published letter. "I had not entirely forgotten the use of a *pistol*, that would enable me to teach you a lesson how to speak of a lady," she warned him after he lambasted her in an editorial. That year Frances Whipple Green published her history *Might and Right*. The introduction, probably by Catherine Williams, paints a Loco-centric retrospective vilifying Rhode Island's Federalists and Algerine Whigs while sanctifying the Democrats.[37]

Dorrite women were up in arms over Dorr's 1844 trial, imprisonment, and sentencing. They populated the courthouse during the hearing. Catherine Williams restrained one rabble-rouser "feeling it her duty to rise & give her testimony against the proceedings." Dorr was found guilty of treason on May 7 by an Algerine jury. Women's horror at the verdict and severe sentence on June 20 spread far and wide and was absorbed into Democratic Party machinery gearing up for the presidential campaign. Twenty-six women,

FIGURE 7.2
"Rhode Island Mass Meeting!!!" *Weekly Herald* (New York), Sept. 7, 1844, detail. Courtesy of the American Antiquarian Society, Worcester, Mass.

representing the states, marched in a July 4 Sullivan County, New Hampshire, Democratic Party procession leading a crowd of both sexes to an amphitheater where speakers railed against Whigs, rallied for Polk and Dallas; at dinner Governor Hubbard asked all to remember Thomas Dorr, "sentenced by judicial tyranny . . . '*to hard labor during his natural life!*'" The convict was placed in solitary confinement, barred from correspondence, and denied most reading material. In the wake of the harsh penalty, women joined the Dorr Liberation Society, of which firebrand Abby Lord was elected president. In August 1844, the Providence Ladies' Benevolent Suffrage Association implored clergymen to petition for Dorr's release.[38]

Later that month Providence geared up for the massive September 4 meeting of Dorrites and Democrats held about two months before the presidential election (fig. 7.2). John Park, in town visiting Louisa, noted Governor Fenner was "taking measures to preserve order" days before. On convention morning, at least seven hundred New York delegates on a steamboat bedecked with Democratic banners and Dorr's portrait were ushered from the wharf to speakers' podiums by a procession of between four thousand and six thousand people who poured in from New England and New Jersey. "Ladies"—about 270 according to Park but 1,000-plus by some papers' estimates—walked near the parade's head. One waved a banner with words attributed to Patrick Henry: "If this be treason, make the most of it." Park only caught the "well-tanned" women in milk carts riding with a "vulgar body of rabble." In all, five thousand women dotted the thirty-thousand-strong panorama of supporters who heard Marcus Morton, Thomas F. Carpenter, and New Hampshire governor Henry Hubbard, to whom one gave a bouquet, prompting the reply: "I say to you ladies, your Dorr will be set at liberty." Women were duly recognized by a New York delegation leader bearing a "Young Hickory" stick, who addressed his "Fellow Democratic Ladies and Gentlemen." After listening to letters from Martin Van Buren, Andrew Jackson, and James Buchanan, kerchief wavers saw the New York delegates off. The day was matched only by the September 6 Democratic Swampscott, Massachusetts, clambake with its "200 gallons of chowder," "1000 lobsters," five thousand women, and twenty thousand men. After the procession, where some women walked alongside banners hailing their incarcerated governor, some women marchers and many more female spectators joined in the culminating cheers for "Polk & Dallas, Bancroft and Childs, and Gov. Dorr."[39] The gulf between Democratic and Whig women's mobilization during presidential campaigns—at least in Rhode Island and Massachusetts—had all but disappeared.

Conclusion

In a tight race like the one in 1844, every vote counted. Of the 2,700,000 ballots cast, James K. Polk won by a very small number: 38,000. Rhode Island went Whig, unsurprisingly, for despite a new constitution widening the franchise, serious impediments to voting continued, especially for workers and immigrants, the latter for whom the old property-holding restrictions remained in place. Yet, by actively campaigning, Dorrite women at least gave Clay's supporters a run for their money. But Dorrites may have inspired Democrats in other New England states, too, especially New Hampshire and Maine, where Polk triumphed; during the campaign some editors had urged women on and had tallied their numbers at rallies. "Heretofore the ladies have not been permitted to join in our political gatherings," a reader wrote to New Hampshire's *Dover Gazette*; "I am heartily glad that this barbarous custom is to be done away with."[40] Democratic women could best their Whig counterparts.

To be sure, Democratic-Dorrite women helped elect a president. But not all of them immediately knew about it. Only in December, while docked at Gibraltar on the bark *Weybosset*, did the wife of Captain Westcott Harris of Providence, Rhode Island, finally hear that Polk won. "She is very much pleased," second mate John Congdon told his diary. At dinner she crowed, predicting "some of the tyrants of Algerines now in R I would get paid up," and with some other passengers branded Congdon a "Whig or an Algerine." The politically naive Congdon said little, thinking "it is from a woman she knows no better." But she would not let up. When a newspaper finally arrived in February 1845 confirming the hearsay, she "talked a considerable" amount and reiterated "some of the R I people would get paid up now." Even into November, the Dorrite could be heard—so whispered the supercargo—quarreling with her husband, who was the "other way." "Arent you ashamed of yourself to speak so and so to a man," Captain Harris would shout back; "well if you are not you ought to be."[41] Some Democratic women could not be silenced.

Whether or not Polk directly made law-and-order men "pay up" beyond his patronage of Rhode Island Dorrite-Democrats remains doubtful. But women took advantage of the new political milieu to further the state's party. The Providence Ladies' Benevolent Suffrage Association urged legislator Olney Ballou to push for Welcome B. Sayles as postmaster—someone members trusted to search for "*missing*" correspondence of private citizens, purloined by officials during their persecutions of suspected Dorrites. Author Frances Whipple Green suggested Dorr's father draft petitions to Congress and Polk, "setting forth the abuses of the Constitution of the Country and the violations of common Law" in Dorr's trial. As the inhumanely treated prisoner aroused more and more sympathy—thanks in part to women of the Dorr Liberation Society—Dorrite-Democrats and opportunistic Whigs formed a coalition, backed a "liberation" ticket in April, 1845, and defeated the law-and-order gubernatorial candidate. After the General Assembly pardoned Dorr on June 27, he was set free.[42]

With Dorr's liberation, a large element of suffragist women's mission was over. The Providence Ladies' Benevolent Suffrage Association immediately disbanded. But they and the countless other women who called themselves Dorrites left in their wake a long string of accomplishments. They "encourage[d] the lawless proceeding[s]" by participating in the mass uprising and acting during pivotal moments in the suffrage movement.[43] They spoke valiantly in public. They raised money for suffragist families and prisoners and organized highly visible, well-attended clambakes that drew in prominent Democratic speakers. In so doing they created alliances with party leaders that upheld Dorr's innocence and claim to the governorship. Most of all, they added their partisan voices—perhaps more boldly, zealously, and audaciously than their Whig counterparts in this chapter—to the growing chorus of women who, though deprived of the vote, nonetheless helped steer the nation along its ever-changing political course.

II

Party Dissolution and Formation

II

The Second Party System had reached its apogee during the mid-1840s on the wings of men's *and* women's partisanship. It did not stay so aloft for long, however. The system would begin its descent after 1844 as the Whig Party slowly began falling into inconsequence. By the mid-1850s it had vanished as a national force. The Democratic Party meanwhile remained airborne, although challenged by third parties such as the Free-Soilers or Know-Nothings and riven by sectional division before the Civil War.

That the Second Party System was becoming unstable raises the question of whether the involvement of New England women it had elicited and to some extent depended upon could be adapted to new circumstances. Put another way, did women's politicization rely upon stable parties to structure their understanding of public affairs and provide safe and predictable partisan environments in which to act? The simple answers are yes, many adapted, and no, they all did not need stable parties. The chapters below feature ample voices of women sustaining their partisanship through the internal division of the Whig Party in the late 1840s, its dissolution in the early 1850s, the confused period that followed, and into the formation of the Third Party System, in which coalescing Republicans and factioning Democrats squared off. That partisan women kept on going through these changes suggests that the wellsprings of their civic commitment resided in themselves and not solely in formal party organizations calling upon their allegiance.

Despite the fact of many women's continuing partisanship, the overall picture was now more diversified and complicated than before. For one, a generational succession was taking place. Some of the most partisan women whose voices we heard in part I become less present, even absent in part II. Replacing them are younger or newly active women more than willing to engage "divisive" issues like antislavery that gave many of the earlier women pause, but which were becoming common coin in electoral campaigns. With issue-oriented politics streaming through a welter of upstart parties and coalitions, women of the 1850s could choose their partisan fights and allegiances. In 1852, for example, former millworker Lucy Larcom maintained, "I am so unfortunate as to be neither a Whig nor a Democrat," explaining that she was "a little nearer Free Soilism than anything else."[1] In this part, too, more extensive commentary comes from women with working-class origins, like Larcom, while a few African Americans can be also heard for the first time in these pages. By contrast the women who withdrew, most of them Whigs, should not be viewed as apolitical. After all, they had already established themselves as partisan beings, so their departure must be seen as a political choice. Yet at the same time a few other women assumed a public visibility well beyond what was seen during the heyday of the Second Party System. As previous scholars note, individual women beginning in the late 1840s became more prominent as leaders, and women's presence at public events became accepted as normal enough to be routinely reported in newspapers, but partisan commentary by some of our diarists and letter writers, none of whom were leaders in associations, seems more restrained and less extensive than before.[2] Many of the women from the early 1840s, by their own accounts, were more partisanly active in public than their counterparts from the 1850s, so over the course of the two decades one can see little uniform movement among our diarists and correspondents from private reflection to public activism. In some cases, change went in the opposite direction. Amid the Mexican War, particularly, some chose to become less vocal about their politics, while others, perhaps no less antiwar, would paradoxically support a war hero as a Whig presidential candidate (chapters 8 and 9). Women closely followed disputes over new territory gained by the war that only buoyed political expression of the antislavery impulse in the North and prompted severe reaction to it in the South. In the 1850s the slavery issue, alongside mounting controversies over recent immigrants' citizenship rights and sales of hard liquor, worked to splinter parties into factions and often strange-bedfellow coalitions (chapters 10 and 11) and set the stage for a new entity, the Republican Party, that would sweep into victory in 1860.

Although our women assumed varying positions over time on these many vexing political issues in a way that demonstrated their fluency with the quickly evolving political vernacular, the general thrust, albeit with a few dissenters, was toward antislavery and the use of federal power, if necessary, to limit the spread of slavery and preserve the Union—even to the point of war (chapter 12). Nativism and temperance were largely set on the back burner, while the antiwar attitude that most of our women shared regarding Mexico in the 1840s gave way to a widespread pro-war stance by 1861. The difference was between what they saw as unjustified and justified violence. By the time hostilities broke out, partisanship for many women conflated with patriotism, even for some who were against the war.

8

"The Shouts and Responses of the Multitude"

Sarah P. E. Hale as Enthused and Disaffected Whig

During the 1844 campaign season, Whig women were determined not be shown up by their Democratic counterparts who, as we have seen in chapter 7, had entered the partisan ring—with a vengeance. In Massachusetts, where Whig delegates pledged the state for Henry Clay in September 1842, rallying began early. Women flocked to Faneuil Hall's March 4, 1844, Clay ball, where glowing painted transparencies depicting a Goddess of Liberty freeing a slave and a log cabin shimmered beneath the darkened galleries. Schoolteacher Mary Fiske, perhaps wishing she was there, recorded it in her diary. Around the same time Mary Poor in Bangor, Maine, was teaching eighteen-month-old Agnes to propagandize, so that by the time Clay was nominated at the national Whig convention in May the child was ready to stump. "When asked, . . . [']Who's going to be President?'" the baby replied "'Henry Clay.'"[1] Partisanship permeated the confines of home.

As the campaign intensified, women visited Whig reading rooms, presented patriotic banners, attended "Clay club" meetings, read partisan newspapers, and turned out in large numbers for party gatherings. They populated countywide and local rallies in towns like Thetford (Vermont), Falmouth, Roxbury, and Taunton (Massachusetts), Middletown (Connecticut), and Richmond (Maine), where the tariff, Texas annexation, and "Dorr Insurrection" were topics of the day. Some cadres among the "3000 Whig Ladies" at a September Litchfield, Connecticut, event "made a most imposing appearance" with their matching outfits. Urban convocations also drew in women like magnets. So many out-of-towners trekked to the October 11 Hartford convention that locals volunteered room and board for twenty-two "delega-

FIGURE 8.1 Joshua Sheldon, *Whig Mass Meeting on Boston Common, Sept. 19th, 1844* (Boston: Thayer and Co., 1844). Courtesy of the American Antiquarian Society, Worcester, Mass.

tions of LADIES." Women lined the streets for Boston's October 31 torchlight procession in which African Americans fearlessly marched, flanked on all sides by whites shielding them from bigoted troublemakers. "The *blacks* of Ward 6 are all coming forward at the election to vote as nobly for Clay as they did for Harrison," one Whig woman rejoiced. The regard given them, she was certain, secured at least "200 good black votes for Clay." Women created show-stopping dramas at the enormous September 19 Boston meeting that drew one hundred thousand Whigs, by passing out treats or throwing bouquets to marching delegations, who then paused to speechify or give "three cheers for the ladies" (fig. 8.1). After the hour-and-a-half-long procession ran its course, they scrambled to the Common for speeches.[2]

Among them was Sarah Preston Everett Hale, the forty-eight-year-old wife of editor Nathan Hale (fig. 8.2). Sarah had been a faithful, if reserved, Whig for years. She had long advocated her party's candidates in state and local elections, and hung on every word during the Log-Cabin Campaign, but apparently never frolicked at a Whig picnic. She met high and mighty politicians, who curried Nathan's favor and spots in his *Daily Advertiser*, and she even helped prepare copy for the partisan sheet, but never heard a stump

FIGURE 8.2 Sarah Preston (Everett) Hale, undated c. 1850s (Hale Family Papers). Sophia Smith Collection, Smith College, Northampton, Mass. (4689)

speech. She wrote letters filled with inside partisan gossip to her brother Edward Everett but seldom, if ever, watched a procession outside the confines of her home.[3]

In short, Sarah eschewed on-the-ground campaigning before the election of 1844. The party's unusual optimism that fall inspired her to take to the streets for Boston's October 31 torchlight parade. And the day of the September 19 convention, she "felt some curiosity to get a specimen of Stump oratory." Perhaps the morning procession she was "craning" her "neck to see" from her window beckoned her outdoors. In any case, after dinner she and her husband "strolled to the common" to catch the speechifying. The crowd around the stage was thinning when they arrived; conventioneers with rumbling stomachs were scavenging supper. So Sarah squeezed into the front ranks, close enough to see eye-to-eye Daniel Webster, who was winding down his speech and about to introduce Georgia senator John M. Berrien. Immediately Sarah was hooked. The way spectators barked back to orators, who threw out rhetorical questions like bones to hungry dogs, thrilled her. She lingered longer than she expected—enough to hear three or four stumpers. "This sort of speaking with the shouts and responses of the multitude was quite exciting." She was surprised at her own spirited solidarity; "I stayed about an hour." Woman's sphere be damned, she loved rough-and-tumble politics.[4]

These were exciting times for Sarah, whose partisanship had been maturing with the Whig Party for a decade. By the time Clay was nominated, the party was more cohesive than ever before in uniting behind the founding father of Whiggery, and Sarah was never happier to read, think, and write about partisanship. Like her, most Whigs were high in spirits about certain success in November. But Clay's defeat by a hair in the popular vote shocked the nation. And when Clay lost, Sarah lost something too.

Even though she pretended to be "more disappointed at Mr. Clays defeat" for her husband, who "seemed to feel all but certain of his success," the letdown evidently triggered in her a long downward spiral that bottomed out during the final phases of the U.S.-Mexico War in 1847. After that she seldom "talked politics" with the same enthusiasm again in letters. It seemed as if the party's postelection blame game and internal bickering over what went wrong depressed her. Mid-1840s divisions and party splintering into cotton and conscience factions incensed her. As the Whigs were inching toward their demise in the next decade, Sarah, too, was slowly but surely silencing her political voice.[5] Rather than watch the party creep along to its death, Sarah averted her glance.

This chapter presents the response of one woman to the Whig Party after it lost its big chance in 1844. While it might seem that a paucity of political discussion in women's personal writings signals a lack of political thinking, it could, instead, as in Sarah's case, indicate a choice to disengage—precisely because of fixed partisan positions. Sarah wanted to hear only about classic Whig issues: banks, the economy, the tariff, and internal improvements. With Polk's election and Texas annexation, however, the specter of slavery's extension would haunt most partisan debate. Sarah had kept her head in the sand about slavery, but after the election it was staring her in the face. She became increasingly vexed with abolitionist vote scattering, which disrupted elections, and Conscience Whigs, who would abandon her "side" to found the Free-Soil Party. The U.S.-Mexico War, which began in 1846, meant even greater focus on slavery because it would either be legalized or prohibited in any land wrenched from Mexico. But the militarization of the news, masculine bravado, and rising death toll ultimately laid her pen to rest. Whig antiwar unity would not keep her in the game, and war hero Zachary Taylor's 1848 presidential victory would not bring her back in.

The first half of this chapter traces Sarah's self-fashioning as a Whig during her early adulthood. Much of her partisanship was honed by assisting her husband and in letters to family, especially her politician brothers Alexander, who became a Democrat, and Edward, a resolute Whig. Writing to them would naturally test the nature of her own partisanship. For keeping in touch was more than simple nurturing for Sarah. Her letters were primary links for travelers, like her brothers, back to Boston's political circuits. She was privy to political intelligence few other women had. From her husband Nathan she heard breaking stories often before they were printed. During the nineteenth century, when the "press was the political system's central institution," big-city editors like Nathan formulated and disseminated party rhetoric and ideology, connected voters with candidates (sometimes literally), whipped up attendance at rallies, and kept partisan fires burning between elections. Nathan thus wielded considerable power—power that Sarah channeled.[6] A coterie of politicos, authors, and luminaries were at Sarah's fingertips. As we will see, she came to distrust one of these—her old friend Daniel Webster.

The chapter's second half traces Sarah's slow withdrawal from political reportage after November 1844 as she is forced to confront the abolitionist challenge to Whig Party unity and bear witness to war. Although her brother Alexander begged for battlefield news, she was loath to report it, especially to a Democratic war-supporter. We see the draining of lifeblood from her political correspondence as she herself sinks into a malaise. Sticking to family matters in letters was the only way to recovery. Like Persis Sibley in chapter 6, Sarah would have to "think the more" as she dug in her heels over the war. The Whig partisanship that had beamed so brightly as she was swept up in the speeches on Boston Common during the Clay mass meeting that September evening in 1844 would become dimmed through the fog of war.

The Making of a Whig Sister

Given her early life, it is not surprising that Sarah Hale, born in 1796, was so political. Her father, Oliver Everett, a liberal Boston Congregationalist minister, became in 1799 Dorchester judge of the Court of Common Pleas and in 1802 Federalist candidate for Congress. After he died that year, her two older brothers Alexander and Edward, one at and one destined for Harvard, instructed her. "[L]ittle had schools to do with [her] education," one son later claimed. This was not remarkable. Early nineteenth-century children were often homeschooled, and few young women enrolled in academies. Sarah literally married into politics on September 5, 1816, when, at age twenty, she wed Nathan Hale, publisher of the quondam Federalist *Boston Daily Advertiser*. Under his tutelage until 1863, when he died, it survived the "Era of Good Feelings," Jacksonianism, and the birth and death of the Whig Party. Because of Nathan's profession there was never a dull or nonpartisan moment in Sarah's life. During the 1820 Massachusetts constitutional convention, for example, Webster and U.S. Supreme Court justice

Joseph Story "were on terms of the closest intimacy at our house," according to her son, "and would come in almost every evening" to have Sarah emend and correct proofs of their speeches for the papers. She was trained by political giants.[7]

At thirty-two and a mother of four by 1828, Sarah still found time to correspond with her brothers during the Jacksonian years, when she developed an anti–"Old Hickory" stance. "What do you think the world is coming to with General Jackson for President?" she asked, expecting a sympathetic reply from Edward, a National Republican U.S. representative in 1829. Her other brother Alexander, already out of tune with her politically, reassured her that Jackson would never become a Napoleon. Sarah feared otherwise, so it is not surprising she emphasized the literary over the political in her letters to him. But she also saw Alexander's destiny in belles lettres and academe, and thus discouraged his political career, especially after he gravitated toward the opposition. She was more comfortable "talking politics" with Edward, for whom she foresaw even higher public office. She thus encouraged him by letting him know how eagerly she awaited papers with his speeches. And she made sure he had the best information at hand, even if it meant clarifying her husband's words. "The story Mr. Hale told us the day before you left home . . . about Mr. Calhoun, he meant for Mr. Crawford," she explained, correcting Nathan's mix-up of two 1824 presidential candidates, John C. Calhoun (he ultimately ran for vice president) and William H. Crawford. "I did not want a wrong story to go from *us*."[8] Her credibility mattered to her and to Edward.

By the late 1830s, Sarah's youngest children were over five, leaving her more time to write—letters, children's books, and translations of German and French literature for various periodicals—and to think about politics. But even prior to that, she dropped hints she was interested in the new Whig Party's progress. "You will probably learn from the papers as soon or before you get this," she wrote newly minted Whig Edward on February 21, 1835, "that Mr. [John] Davis was elected today by the Senate receiving on the 4th ballot 20 votes." With Alexander, who had run for state Senate as a Democrat that year, she was more circumspect, disclaiming interest in political news and side-taking. "I have read Mr. Adams speech on the fortification bill," which defended Jackson's stance on it, "and rather more of the Congressional debates in general, than I usually do," she practically apologized in February 1836. In November 1838, when Democratic Alexander was running for U.S. representative while Whig incumbent Edward was seeking the governorship, Sarah tagged herself a Whig to her son by referring to "our side" being "split up" into pro– and anti–15 Gallon Law factions. But she still had only goodwill toward Alexander. "I heard some one say that this difficulty about the License law would bring in Uncle Alexander." So determined to get the latest news was she that she teased her son, "you have been thought of notwithstanding the Election."[9] Politics could crowd out family matters.

This was not so with Alexander, who stood at the partisan spectrum's opposite end. On him, she lavished family news and literary affairs. She was "glad to see him entirely withdrawn from politics" and reunited with academe after losing his congressional bids in 1838 and 1840. He was inaugurated president of Louisiana's Jefferson College in June 1841. Despite his hiatus from government, she still walked on eggs when it came to politics. "The Election is over," she stiffly wrote in November 1841, "though it is not to be expected that such a matter should terminate to the satisfaction of all parties." She was brief and diplomatic about the race that reelected Whig governor John Davis.[10]

By contrast, Sarah lingered over election scoops with Edward, who left for Florence, Italy, after very narrowly losing the governorship in 1839. There, he would miss out on Log-Cabin madness, changes in Congress, and William Henry Harrison's victory, but Sarah carefully briefed him about stump speaking, rallies, and processions. After the election, she could exult, "The country was never I think before in such a state of excitement, at least not since the establishment of our government." Sarah conjectured about Harrison's cabinet with the sober qualification "it is rather premature to fix these things on paper" and dismissed some editors' advice "that neither Mr. Webster nor Mr. Clay ought to be in the Cabinet because they were before the public as candidates for the presidency" in light of Harrison's promise to serve but one term. With the administration distributing offices to loyal Whigs, Sarah subtly dangled opportunity before Edward. A trusted informant told her that if he were in the States, he would "have some of the appointments." Edward plainly told her he "certainly would not go to America for such an object." Wanting to stay abroad, however, Edward hinted to Representative Robert Winthrop, he would take a diplomatic post.[11]

With Edward's appointment as minister to England on September 13, 1841, Sarah began a four-year stint as Tyler administration pundit for him and others. She was a critic of the nominally Whig president, who was cast out of the party just after the Twenty-seventh Congress's first session. "You will be astonished to hear . . . what a snarl matters seem to have got into in the high places," she told Edward. She referred to Tyler's vetoing of Henry Clay's Bank bill on August 16 and, "when another had been prepared as it was supposed exactly to suit him," she huffed, "doing the same thing again" on September 9. She was stunned that his cabinet, excepting Daniel Webster, had abruptly resigned in response. "It is said by some," she intimated, "that he stays at the particular request of the President." Tyler's turning into a loose cannon unnerved her, happening so closely upon Harrison's death. "Our poor country has been so providentially carried through so many storms . . . , but when one thinks of the present state of things, and that it must flounder on with such a captain for four whole years, it looks a little dark." In her diffident manner, Sarah asked pardon for editorializing. "I suppose your political friends write you more fully and understandingly on these matters than I can—but every body is so busy and you must feel such interest in public affairs, that I have written, thinking that if you may not have heard, you would be glad of a meager disquisition."[12] True, he would get scuttlebutt from bigwigs, but none were as eager, caring, and, perhaps, as careful as sister "Sally."

Beginning in December 1841, when Edward was established in London, Sarah flooded him with letters thanks to regular English mail-packet service. In them she avowed the president's message to Congress gave "tolerable satisfaction" and assessed the mayorship that nearly escaped Whig incumbent Jonathan Chapman because of his anti–liquor law stance. "This was doing pretty well since there was another candidate [Charles Leighton] put up by the sellers of liquor . . . and Mr. [Nathaniel] Greene who is popular was the Loco foco candidate." She followed pro-Whig legislation including the "bankrupt bill," enacted in August 1841 and set to go in effect on February 1, 1842. "The news today," she wrote on January 31, "is the bankrupt bill is not repealed," by one vote. By now her political acumen and Whig credentials were widely recognized. "Yes, this is Mrs. Hale, sister to our minister in England Mr. Everett, and who would make a very good minister herself," is the way Katherine Lawrence, whom we have met in earlier chapters, introduced Sarah to Charles Dickens's wife at a party when the couple was touring Boston in January 1842. The ever-self-effacing Sarah was flustered: "I did as well as I could, and talked for a few moments with Mrs. D. but I think she must have thought Mrs. Lawrence a funny person."[13] Lawrence, though violating proscribed feminine roles, was merely stating what many knew to be true.

The Creation of a Webster Foe

Because of Edward's ties to Webster and her own investment in the Whig Party, Sarah kept tabs on the beleaguered secretary of state. He had been a close intimate of the family for years. After his first wife died in 1828, Sarah had even taken in his son. Yet now Webster was keeping away from her and others while home at nearby Marshfield for a rest between congressional sessions in October 1841. Sarah figured he was avoiding constituents disapproving of his remaining in the cabinet. After all, there was growing pressure for him to resign. Short of seeing him, she followed his path through newspapers and the grapevine. She could guess he was miffed he did not receive the Whig presidential nomination at the September 1842 Massachusetts Whig convention, which instead chose Henry Clay and passed a resolution to "separate" completely from Tyler's administration. Still, Webster tenaciously held on. His speech later that month at a Faneuil Hall meeting celebrating the Webster-Ashburton Treaty, which settled the U.S.-Canadian boundary dispute, Sarah learned, turned into a harangue against the convention. "People seem to have been somewhat startled, at his coming out as he did and blaming the Whigs for their nomination of Mr Clay," she informed Edward. Sarah thought it inexcusable: "He does not love Mr. Clay, I suppose, but he need not have mentioned it quite so plainly." Granting that Webster "could not have satisfied every body," she still could not condone divisiveness.[14] The party deserved better.

By the end of 1842, President Tyler, who was now determined to procure Texas, a slaveholding republic that had declared its independence from Mexico in 1836, had all but ousted his antiannexation secretary of state Webster, who sought escape from Washington. Sarah watched helplessly as he angled for her brother's plum position in London, about which she had labored so tirelessly to keep him informed during the time leading up to his appointment in 1841. But Webster first needed to finagle a new slot for Edward. Why not send him as far away as possible? In a December message to Congress composed by Webster, Tyler called for an emissary to China. In January, Webster wrote Edward he would recommend him for the post. No sooner had that happened when Sarah read in the papers that he had been confirmed as minister to China on March 3, 1843. "I dare say you opened your eyes as wide as the rest of us at the announcement," she presumed of her son. "I think it a little too bad in Webster after having sugared such a nice piece of bread and butter and put it already into the hands of his friend. . . . To snatch it back that he may swallow it himself." This was the last straw. "I do not know as I shall ever forgive Webster for acting so meanly." She apparently never trusted him again. Edward flatly refused the post, crushing the scheme. In the meantime Webster was nowhere to be seen or heard in Sarah's circles. But she spied a *Boston Times* extra asserting he would step down in early May. Frozen out of the president's confidence, Webster left Washington midmonth with no firm plans for the future. On his trek back, he stopped at Baltimore to speechify on foreign trade. Sarah remarked with a sprinkling of venom, "this is a funny way of retiring to come speaking it all the way home[;] he says Treaty now pretty much as he used to say Constitution."[15] Were his days as a great statesman numbered? Would he show his face to Sarah again?

Webster resurfaced in December 1843. He and his wife paid a surprise, "rather long . . . ceremonious visit," while Nathan was in Pennsylvania. Still recoiling from his fall from grace, Webster was less than vivacious. "Mrs. was smiling and polite, as usual," Sarah wrote her husband; "Mr. I thought somewhat pouty." He seemed annoyed Nathan was not at his disposal, snorting, "'Mr. Hale had had occasion to go to Philadelphia frequently this winter.'" His wife jumped in to mollify, explaining "public business kept" Nathan "constantly moving." Indeed, as a representative of Boston's State Street financiers, he was lobbying for measures to reduce Pennsylvania's debt largely incurred through public works, including railroads, which would allow new investment in rail construction. Having to deal on her own with Webster, Sarah found it "rather hard to get along," and fresh memories of the minister-to-China affair did not help. Conversation was strained. "I do not know whether Webster is perfectly wooden and felt nothing at all," she wondered, "or whether he felt a good deal at meeting us again." The old ties binding them together had finally unraveled. It was tragic, but it hardly dampened her enthusiasm for the party.[16]

The Emergence of a Campaign Pundit

Sarah initially channeled much of that enthusiasm into the upcoming presidential election by carefully watching over Nathan junior, who had been holding down the *Advertiser* office while his father was in Pennsylvania. She wanted him to boost the Whigs but without sacrificing accuracy. For example, upon hearing that longtime Democratic editor Nathaniel Greene joined a Henry Clay club in February 1844, her son vetted the information to Sarah's gratification. "He afterward . . . saw Mr. Harding who said he had seen the treasurer of the Clay Club, who stated that he had received Greene's entrance money," Sarah reassured his father of the story's veracity. After Sarah joined her husband in Pennsylvania she continued advising the fledgling editor. In March she recommended on her husband's go-ahead that he "come out as strong as he will against the annexation of Texas." Likely presidential nominee Henry Clay, afraid of alienating voters, had been sidestepping the issue during his winter southeastern stump to focus on his American System and other economic issues. No wonder Nathan junior had pause. Sarah knew on Webster's authority "that Mr. Clay and the Kentucky Senators are very strong on that point." Indeed, by late March, Clay had mentioned to Kentucky senator John J. Crittenden that he was considering making a statement—it would be the April 17, 1844, "Raleigh letter" laying open his antiannexation position. Sarah evidently had inklings of it. "Webster says Clay has written a letter which has been shown to Mr. Adams and with which he is perfectly satisfied." But she distrusted Clay's rival. "I am afraid of any thing Webster says."[17] After all, she had been hurt by his attempts to snatch Edward's position.

Having returned home as the election grew near, Sarah relayed the local excitement to Edward. She sent him word before most U.S. papers announced pro-annexation James K. Polk had been nominated by the Democrats on May 29. "I do not know how this will go," she told him on the thirty-first; "there seems to be division in their camp." She referred to Van Buren supporters who thought his nomination a done deed. "Our party," she beamed, emphasizing she and Edward were both Whig to the backbone, "seems now to be moving along rather more harmoniously than usual." Edward also heard, via Sarah's letter to his wife Charlotte, about the September Whig convention. "You can hardly imagine how your good old native town looks decked out in banners and strung in every direction with garlands and mottoes," she marveled, mentioning "the fairer portion of creation from windows and sidewalks" cheered on the procession. So partisan was she that when Alexander mailed her a pro-annexation *Democratic Review* essay of his, he hedged, "mine will not, I trust, be thought very heretical by the Whigs."[18] But she always respected her brother's differences, and he, his sister's intellect.

With the election only a month away, Sarah's hopes soared. In early October she was heartened by sanguine newspaper predictions for Maryland's gubernatorial and state legislature and Georgia's congressional contests. "The election news from the South seems to be quite exhilarating," she told her son, hoping these were signs of success in November. The *Advertiser* was indeed "so full of elections now," she wrote him, "that there does not seem much room for" anything else including her own translations. The rallies also filled her with optimism. She even boasted to Alexander about the "brilliant appearance" her younger sons made at one she attended. Attuned to changes in campaign strategy, she observed, "This torch light seems a new feature in electioneerings" especially suited for boys, who "like the fun of walking round with them and shouting." The ever-so-diffident Sarah Hale was letting a little fun into her life. But it would soon escape her.[19]

The Shaping of an Antiwar Correspondent

Clay was defeated in November, partly because of the Liberty Party's popularity and partly because of growing numbers of new Democratic votes over the past four years. Clay women, and especially abolitionists who decried the

Democratic platform advocating the annexation of Texas, were appalled. On Connecticut's polling day, farmer Hannah Hicock Smith, a widowed seventy-seven-year-old Glastonbury abolitionist, jabbed at a local-yokel parade of "ten yoke of oxen . . . with a cart full & a flag with Polk & Dallas on it." She spat sarcastically, "I cannot blame the oxen, they do not know any better." At the contest's end, Abigail Pierce saw the writing on the wall. "Alas, . . . we are to have James K. Polk for our President," she commiserated with her sister Mary Poor. "I do really hope that Texas will never be annexed to the United States. We have too many slaves among us already." Some women faulted party leadership. A Bostonian, "Mrs. Gorham," was "rampant about the loss . . . and furious with Webster for coming out so strong in the Native American way, and exasperating the Irish, which she said his speech," delivered at Faneuil Hall on November 8, "did in high degree," as word trickled in of Clay's losses in state elections held on previous days. In it, Webster pandered to growing anti-Catholic and antiforeigner sentiments in the Northeast by clamoring for stricter naturalization laws.[20]

Sarah tried to take the loss in stride. In vain she emphasized the positive: at least George Bancroft lost the governorship. "Whatever else happened," Massachusetts "will not set down under 'little Bran,'" she smirked. But still, the Whig debacle obsessed her. Although she believed Webster's speech had "aroused" Bay State voters "to do their very best"—Massachusetts did deliver a majority for Clay—she could not tolerate his rubbing elbows with nativists. "I think it is wicked in the extreme to make a party question of the matter," she groused. "Here we are with a body of foreigners domesticated with us, and instead of doing our duty and letting them learn by degrees," we "choose sides and endeavor to fight it out." In December, she would protest the "foolish division of our party into Native American and Abolitionism" that derailed Boston's mayoral election by depriving any candidate of a majority.[21]

Nativism was just one item on the postelection plate poking at Sarah. Controversy over "slavery is now so great," Sarah wailed, that Nathan senior and junior "generally both stay" at the office "till ten o'clock." It swamped her vista too. She was outraged that Samuel Hoar, delegated to challenge statutes permitting the seizure of Massachusetts's free black seamen at South Carolina's ports, was expelled from the state by its legislature and threatened with violence. Because his daughter was with him, Hoar was "guarded by an aristocratic mob, from being torn to pieces by one of the lower class," Sarah quivered. The insult and near injury made her rethink antislavery activism: "Verily such doings . . . will make Abolitionists of us all." To her, this was just the beginning of the rough ride to come. "The poor old ship of state will beat its way along some how or other for another four years," she moaned, wondering if First Lady Sarah Childress Polk could save the day. "Perhaps

Mr. and Mrs Polk together will make a very good President." She based her prediction on her neighbors, Katherine and Abbott Lawrence, who "together made a very excellent representative."[22] Women were not unmindful of First Ladies'—and congressional wives'—power. But any moderating effect Mrs. Polk may have had was lost on the president.

To Sarah's chagrin, Polk wasted little time to instigate conflict over Texas and other Mexican land. Even before his inauguration, he had urged Congress to set annexation in motion. Her state tried to nix it. Elated, she noted in January that Congressman Robert C. "Winthrop had got the floor for his Texas speech" to oppose Texas annexation and that plans were afoot for a Faneuil Hall, statewide, nonpartisan anti-Texas meeting. But only days before Polk's swearing in, Tyler signed a joint resolution allowing Texas to join the Union. The Texas Senate on June 16, 1845, accepted it. On Polk's orders General Zachary Taylor's troops stationed in nearby Louisiana marched into Texas territory and were encamped at Corpus Christi by July. That November, he commissioned John Slidell to pressure Mexico into selling New Mexico and California. With so much banging of the drum, no wonder Sarah awaited Polk's annual message to Congress. It urged Congress to admit Texas into the Union, which it did by act that December. Sarah said little about it.[23] As many Americans were raising their voices in support of Polk's war, Sarah began lowering her partisan register.

Sarah was dead set against war from the start. In February 1846, just as Taylor was getting ready to position his troops near the Rio Grande, the disputed border between Texas and Mexico, she divulged to her son that "news of peace seemed to be taking form and I cannot but hope that this Mexican wickedness is drawing to a close." She was grasping at straws. Because it could take three weeks or more for news reports from Mexico to reach Louisiana and spread outward, she remained unaware of the meltdown of talks between Slidell and the new Mexican president, who was adamant against selling land.[24] After major clashes along the Rio Grande, the United States declared war on Mexico on May 13.

The next month Alexander, who had been appointed minister to China, was headed for Macao. Sarah promised to keep him in the loop but kept her opinions to herself—including glee over Democratic senator William Henry Haywood's July resignation over the Democrats' tariff bill. "It is amusing to think [how] enragé all the Locos must be," she told her son. To Alexander she sparsely reported on the settlement of the Oregon boundary and the Walker Tariff's passage while assuring him that "I am more at home in my family narrative." With him she strained to be upbeat regarding the war. She wagered on a quick peace settlement. After all, she read Polk was asking Congress for two million dollars for negotiations with Mexico. In September, she allowed that exiled general Santa Anna's return to Mexico might change the war's course. "What will come of it, no one knows," she granted. In power, he kept on fighting the invaders.[25]

Although Sarah was against the war, she distanced herself from that wing of the Whig Party most vociferously opposed to it—the abolitionist Conscience Whigs. She would not countenance her Bostonian friends—lawyer Charles Sumner, secretary of the Commonwealth John G. Palfrey, and Boston *Whig* editor Charles F. Adams—who tried to pull the party in an antislavery direction before the 1846 fall election. She derogatorily referred to their followers as "semi bobalition" (a racial pejorative for abolitionist), because they remained within the party fold instead of going "bobalition entire." Her husband in his paper warned that their doings at the September Massachusetts Whig convention would antagonize Southerners. But "Sumner and his clique," as she called the Conscience Whigs, failed to enact their pro-abolition, antiwar resolutions there. Sarah felt "quite sorry" they had "degraded themselves so" and predicted they would wind up "settling down with the regular Abolitionists, whose mission seems to be to make as much useless fuss as possible" by upsetting elections. Her heart went out, however, to her former minister, Palfrey, who was nominated for U.S. representative that October by Whigs. His new pamphlet *The Slave Power*, she thought, would "dish his election" because it was "very violent and sweepingly written." Offensive to conservative Whigs, he failed to get a majority. She blamed abolitionists, who "had . . . candidates of their own, which was the more cruel, as the Dr. had shocked his old friends a deal by the very abolitionist ground he took.'" When Sarah wrote Alexander in January 1847 of Palfrey's victory in the December "extra election," he had been three months in China.[26]

As the war dragged on it was becoming more and more difficult for Sarah to write about it for Alexander. "I cannot give a very good account of the state of war," was her caveat in February 1847, "because, as you know, it grieves me so to think of it, that I do not read the accounts enough to know the state of the case." She implied he should get details from the papers himself. She had lost faith in peace, questioning Congress's sincerity to make it. "An amendment had been adopted" to the Civil and Diplomatic Bill in the Senate, "appropriating $50,000 for sending a commissioner to Mexico, in the event of peace being declared," she shrugged. "I suppose this is only another form of getting money to go on with the war." Despite her distaste for war news, she gave Alexander a wooden, sometimes sardonic roster of events: former minister to China Caleb Cushing—"he always had a taste for military glory"—was elected colonel of the Massachusetts Volunteers; former Kentucky state representative Captain Cassius M. Clay and his men were taken prisoner; troops engaged in a skirmish near El Paso; Santa Anna was indeed alive despite "rumors" that had "killed him some days since." Knowing literature was the key to Alexander's heart, she turned to Robert Southey's "After Blenheim," a 1798 antiwar poem invoking the War of the Spanish Succession battle that tolled over thirty thousand casualties. "'But what good is to come of it at last?'" she paraphrased a line to express her feelings of futility.[27] Artfully referring to literature in correspondence had the advantage of indirectly voicing otherwise controversial political stances with recipients likely to disagree with them.

Perhaps because Alexander's wife lamented they were getting no American papers, Sarah continued to chronicle what she could barely stomach. But she kept coverage concise, and commentary sharp. But even that amount of reporting was becoming painful. Sarcasm crept in. "Every thing about the war is successful on our side," she mordantly scoffed, "except that there have been many valuable officers and men lost," including, at Buena Vista, George Lincoln, son of former governor Levi Lincoln, and, at Vera Cruz, John Rogers Vinton of Providence. Almost pleading to retire from her role as news correspondent, she supplicated Alexander, "you know I hate this war and cannot bear to write or talk about it." The once liberating activity of reportage now imprisoned her. Only with her son Edward could she pour out her heart. Although many Whigs, especially men, were as eager as Democrats to embrace military glory as justifying the loss of life, Sarah was not. "I have thought a great deal of the poor Lincolns and other parents and friends of whom I know nothing but that their sons have fallen in this most needless and unrighteous war." "My only hope," she continued, "is that" God "will interfere to save us from the fruits of our sins and follies as a nation."[28] Major fighting would drag on five more months.

When Sarah wrote Alexander on June 23 she probably had no idea of how ill he was. Five days later he died. Although his wife sent word promptly, it would take months to arrive. Unaware, Sarah sent Alexander at least three more letters, all with terse snippets about the war. Her last to him went out about two weeks after Mexico City fell to General Winfield Scott, thereby effectively ending the conflict. Sarah only knew he was within seven miles of the capital.[29]

After the war, Sarah maintained a lively, but less politically nuanced, correspondence with her family. Even with Edward, who took Webster's place as secretary of state after he died in 1852 and a seat in the Senate in 1853, Sarah focused on literary topics. Perhaps after the war she could no longer distance herself enough from events to record them objectively for loved ones. Perhaps she thought politics was Alexander's undoing. More likely she lost interest in the Whig Party that cynically put up Zachary Taylor, who never voted and who was not Whig-identified. It was a long way from that evening in 1844 when she was so emotionally transported by stump speaking that one could easily imagine her grabbing the podium herself. The war had cooled her partisan fervor and hardened her stance against women in public life. After the 1859 fall election she admitted to Edward, "I am glad women do not have to enter these ranks" of politicians, adding "I never sympathized with the womans rights wing of the sex."[30] The winds of change were blowing in its direction, however. But Sarah, as politically accomplished as she was, chose to walk against them. She had little idea that partisans like her helped pave the way to the future.

The next chapter brings with it more women who, like Sarah Hale, detested the war with Mexico but who, unlike Sarah, refused to be silenced by it. Indeed, it even jarred some protesters, as we will see, into partisan ways of thinking.

9

"A Most Unprecedented Act of Invasion"

Women, Mexico, and Taylor

In her retrospective of the year 1848, just after Mexico ratified the Treaty of Guadalupe Hidalgo ending war with the United States, Hannah Hicock Smith, an eighty-one-year-old widowed Glastonbury, Connecticut, farmer, was still bashing the Democratic administration that ignited the conflict. "Its spirit of aggrandizement, not to say robbery, that plunged us into a war unjust & unnecessary . . . was most outrageous," she criticized in her diary. "It was a most unprecedented act of invasion on an independent Republic." Smith pummeled President James K. Polk for the "unprovoked aggression" that marked a "stain on our country." For this abolitionist, the election of pro-expansionist Polk was a turning point. She began to "talk politics" with friends, compiled lists of pro-war congressmen, read antiwar editorials and congressional speeches, and rooted for Free-Soilers in the 1849 spring elections.[1] The war sparked a greater concern with electoral politics.

The women we located who wrote about the war generally denounced it for reasons similar to Smith's—that it was unjustifiable, avoidable, a boon to pro-slavery forces, sinful, and a waste of precious lives. Their opinions were honed by prodigious reading of partisan news. Between 1844 and 1849 Smith, for one, subscribed to a pro-Whig weekly and scanned, among other periodicals, the *New York Tribune* and antislavery *New York Evangelist* issues her neighbor Emily Moseley supplied.[2] But books, printed speeches, and conversation also provided food for antiwar women's thoughts. Moreover, the loss of state or local residents and prominent figures in battle only hardened women's viewpoints.

Because these women were white and mostly middle class, they held a racially, socially, and indeed globally privileged position. Not surprisingly, their condemnation of the war little related to sympathy for Mexicans, particularly the Spanish-Mexican women who were economically disempowered by conquest.[3] Nor was their opposition always linked with antislavery. As has been shown in chapter 8, Sarah P. E. Hale was both antiwar and antiabolition. These women's stances, instead, reflected the antiexpansionist, antimilitaristic, and generally Whig partisan strain of reactions to Manifest Destiny—the supposed divinely ordained mission to conquer U.S. borderlands, coast to coast.[4] Their gravity contrasts sharply with the buoyant, chivalrous, martial imaginary in periodicals, music, art, and popular literature valorizing the fighting, to which even many Whig men subscribed.[5]

In this chapter we follow these women from the outbreak of hostilities in 1846, to various battles waged, and then to the 1848 peace treaty. Themes emerge throughout, such as fixation on casualties and futile hopes for peace at the war's inception. We then look at the 1848 presidential campaign and victory of war hero General Zachary Taylor. We spotlight Calista Billings, a rambunctious Whig teenager from Canton, Massachusetts, who gets so caught up in the three-way race that she provokes Charles Sumner during a stump speech for Free-Soil presidential candidate Martin Van Buren. As she found out, party leaders had no mercy on young, naive, partisan bystanders. A mixed bag of reactions to Taylor's triumph tops off the chapter.

Women Fight Mr. Polk's War

Women's fear of inevitable fighting with Mexico began not with any specific event such as Texas's independence from Mexico in 1836 or President John Tyler's pressuring Congress to annex the new republic. It sprang from a longtime ambivalence about expansion. Acquisition could lead to international strife and armed force to achieve ends. Women sometimes alluded to borderlands and border-disputed areas as arenas for male squabbling. Eliza Davis, for example, during the height of the 1833 nullification crisis recommended that all of Congress and President Andrew Jackson be shipped "off into the Oregon territory, or the Texas," where they could "work out their own salvation." A few years later, as chapter 4 shows, the 1839 "Aroostook War" rankled women who insisted that the boundary between Maine and New Brunswick could be settled through diplomacy instead of at gunpoint.[6]

Women's earnest attentiveness to potential embroilment with Mexico began during the 1844 presidential campaign season when Democrats and Whigs divided over Texas. We have seen in previous chapters how Sarah Hale urged her editor son to vilify annexation, how Hannah Hicock Smith ridiculed a local-yokel Polk-and-Dallas bandwagon, and how Mary Poor trained her toddler to announce Henry Clay would be president. Out in Dixfield, Maine, Persis Andrews secretly advocated Clay despite her Democratic husband. But prior to the first skirmishes between the United States and Mexico, Andrews was against bloodshed. "I am pleased with martial music & with military uniform," she avowed after watching militia muster in 1843, "but I am decidedly an 'anti-War.'"[7]

It is no surprise that she anxiously awaited Polk's December 2, 1845, first annual address to Congress. Thin ice on the Androscoggin River had stopped mail delivery. But on December 14, she recorded, "Yesterday they crossed . . . & at last we rec'd the Presidents Message." Its forceful call to admit Texas into the Union and belligerent tone regarding U.S. military presence near Mexico could not have pleased her.[8]

Shortly after the United States declared war in May, Andrews cried: "War! War! Is the only topic now." "Two battles have been fought," she grimaced, referring to Palo Alto and Resaca de la Palma, waged earlier that month under General Zachary Taylor's command. Like other women, she transcribed in astonishment the sometimes erroneous figures found in newspapers, including the improbable "700 Mexicans kill'd" during the early May siege of Fort Texas on the Rio Grande. Similar reports fabricated the annihilation of Matamoros, the Mexican city just across the river. She, like Sarah Hale in chapter 8, trusted editors predicting a speedy termination. "It is the opinion of most that it will be a short, small War, tho' every State in the Union is call'd upon to have troops in readiness." Regarding her own, she proclaimed "Maine for 1500 men." Volunteers nationwide were streaming out west.[9]

Given this climate, Andrews watched the spring 1846 U.S. Senate election pitting conservative candidates, acceptable to the "pro-slavery" faction of the Democratic Party, against the antislavery Democrat, Hannibal Hamlin. On May 24 she had faith that someone would "soon . . . be elected" by the state legislature "to fill the place of [George] Evans whose time expires." After all, she reasoned, her "old friend" Ebenezer Knowlton, the new House Speaker, would "set an example worthy to be imitated." But after two days of voting in which the Senate blocked Hamlin, who had the House majority, she sighed, "Senator question not decided." After six weeks of stalemate, Hamlin withdrew and was replaced by the more conservative James Ware Bradbury who finally won over the Senate.[10] Slavery was becoming more of a hot-button issue.

As the war stretched out women became resigned to its perpetuation, but not its legitimation. Hannah Smith registered her discontent in conversations and record keeping. One can only imagine what she literally shouted to her eighty-one-year-old neighbor Jonathan Wells during a spirited tête-à-tête. "We have been on Politics well agreed about an hour," she scratched in her diary on September 2, 1846. "But he is so deaf, it is hard talking to him, & I was somewhat out of breath," exhausted from yelling. She was so up on war news that one late October report of the bloody battle of Monterrey, detailed news of which had reached New England only around midmonth, seemed like "an old story." That December, she tallied up hawkish congressmen in her notebook, concluding "there is a furious long number of the rascals, upholding war & slavery." No sooner had she finished her roster, when she purchased the new 1847 *Liberty Almanac*, which "had them all in it." With so many warmongers in power, how could combat easily cease? Smith scoured the newspapers that winter for war news and speeches against slavery. But she studied only part of the president's 1846 annual address to Congress—a rationalization for aggression—and was presumably put off by its single-minded, repetitious character. "I do not care about reading all the message." Persis Sibley Andrews also balked. "It is very lengthy, much of it explanatory of the unhappy Mexican War." She opined, "I do not know but that he makes out justification, but I have always been inclined to think it an unnecessary war."[11] She was not alone.

For some women the cost of war hit home with the March 1847 battle of Vera Cruz. After days of bombardment, Mexico's foremost port, protected by the formidable San Juan de Ulúa fortresses, fell into U.S. hands on the twenty-ninth. In New Haven, an artist's twenty-two-year-old daughter, Elizabeth Jocelyn, heard on April 10 "the ringing of bells, and firing of cannon announc[ing] a great victory had taken place." She learned General Winfield Scott "has possession of . . . the castle of San Juan Ulloa and 4000 prisoners of war." Like others, she fastened on enormous figures recounted in the papers. She seemed baffled that "The foreign counsels had permission to leave the city, before the bombardment commenced which they did not at first accept, and afterwards, when they would have done so, were not allowed to leave." Scott indeed warned foreigners before the siege but refused to let them or even Mexican women and children flee once firing began.[12]

Even though only thirteen U.S. combatants were killed, one of them particularly tugged on women's heartstrings: John Rogers Vinton, Third Artillery captain from Providence who was appointed major just days before his death. The demise on March 22 of the region's West Point–trained, rising military star seemed as senseless as it was tragic. Some women, like Emily Morris of the Boston area, found solace in reading the Whig *American Review*'s tribute. Others took his fall as a dire omen. After telling her diary about Vinton's passing, Bostonian Annie Lawrence, now married to Benjamin Rotch, trembled: "Our nation must be cursed for so unrighteous &

needless a war." Assuming a prophet's voice she decreed, "'There really is a God who judgeth & will avenge.'"[13] It seemed just a matter of time.

Rotch felt vindicated that Polk's Boston visit in June to drum up war support flopped, notwithstanding (or because of) the military pomp and circumstance greeting him. "The rain," she icily commented, put "a decided damper on the little enthusiasm that might possibly have escaped" the spectators. Bostonians were notorious for their war antipathy. Nathan Hale's *Advertiser* even dared inhabitants to stay home. More welcoming of Polk's northeastern tour was Olive Worcester, a Swedenborgian minister's widow, who on July 3 heard Senator George Evans regale the president on the wharf at Gardiner, Maine. The guests of honor, she, and other onlookers then boarded the steamboat *Huntress* "amidst firing cannons & cheers" and cruised down the Kennebec River. Taylor-supporter Worcester probably went because it was a big deal in her tiny town, not because she admired Polk. Antiwar Persis Andrews could hardly care less when he appeared that day at the state's capitol to address the legislature. Her Democratic husband Charles returned home from Augusta glowing. "He says yesterday was a proud day . . . for Maine," she dryly etched in her diary, "but as the particulars will be a part of our State History I need not record it here."[14] For "covert Whig" Andrews, the less said, the better.

After taking Vera Cruz, Scott headed inland toward Mexico City. Elizabeth Jocelyn cited key clashes en route to the capital. "Heard on Saturday that another terrible battle had been fought by the Mexicans and our troops," she recorded in May of Cerro Gordo, a short but intense confrontation. She noted the other side "met with a heavy loss, thousands being taken prisoners." For Jocelyn, gains were punctuated by calculable human suffering, especially when in September tragedy struck on a local scale. "The paper this evening contains an account of the late battle between our troops and the Mexicans, in which the former were victorious," she wrote, alluding to the August conquest of Churubusco; "Major [Frederick D.] Mills, native of this city headed the list of those killed"—around 130. The Yale graduate died on August 20, pursuing Santa Anna's forces to the Garita de San Antonio, a gate to Mexico City.[15]

On September 14, Mexico City fell to Scott, but peace negotiations would flounder for months. In his annual message, Polk made it clear he would settle for nothing less than the Texas boundary at the Rio Grande, along with Upper California and New Mexico as indemnity (payment for war costs), in exchange for peace. He asked for more troops to back up his threats. Hannah Smith reacted negatively. "I have not read a word of the Presidents speech," she turned up her nose. "The editor thinks it is a great lie." She conversed, instead, with her daughter about a book she had borrowed, *Six*

Lectures on the Uses of the Lungs by Samuel Sheldon Fitch. She jeered, "he certainly tells some truth if the President does not." A few days later she "read in the paper, the answer to the Message from the Intelligencer," a Whig periodical. "It is capital," she smiled, no doubt. This abolitionist later found in pro-slavery senator John C. Calhoun a strange bedfellow. In his January 4, 1848, Senate speech he challenged Polk's argument that the war could "conquer a peace"; after all, with so many conquests, there was still no peace. "I have read Calhoun's speech & tho' heterogeneous matter, it has more verve & soundness than all congress beside," Hannah averred, allowing it would "not be altogether popular & there are many defects in it." She agreed further aggression would accomplish little and reckoned, "it is impossible to predict the end." On February 2, 1848, however, the Treaty of Guadalupe-Hidalgo was signed and, on March 10, ratified in the Senate. Polk finally devoured the land he craved.[16] But what would become of it regarding slavery? This question would hover over events for years to come.

For now, there were the dead to bury. Joining them was antiwar representative John Quincy Adams, mortally stricken on the House floor with a cerebral hemorrhage on February 21, shortly after he had voted against considering resolutions honoring military officers who served in Mexico. It was a signal demise that immediately sent women into public mourning and galvanized female presence in Boston at his March 10 obsequies. "The galleries of Faneuil Hall were filled with ladies," one reporter observed. At the April 15 eulogy delivered there by Edward Everett, one minister's daughter noted "there was a fearful crowd of ladies who attempted to get in after the galleries were filled & the doors closed." Women were scheduled to file into their segregated seats at 9:00 A.M., but they arrived hours earlier, packing them by eight o'clock. Latecomers buffaloed their way in; "it is a wonder that some were not seriously injured." She knew "several ladies who were in the crowd but only two who got into the Hall," both of them ticket holders up before dawn. It was a show of force in support of an icon who embodied "Conscience Whiggery," against the war and the territorial extension of slavery it heralded.[17]

All the while some war dead, mainly officers, were being shipped to the United States. Before the Civil War, there was no systematic procedure within the armed forces for burying the fallen; they were laid to rest near battlegrounds or camps. But some survivors journeyed to Mexico at their own expense to retrieve loved ones. State legislatures sometimes appropriated money for repatriation. Rhode Island, for example, financed Major Vinton's return. Aurilla Moffitt, whom we met in chapter 7, attended his May 12, 1848, funeral parade. "To me it was a very solemn scene." One Providence matron seemed disappointed that it was postponed a day. On July 11, 1848,

Elizabeth Jocelyn and two friends rode to New York City for the funeral of five of the state's military commanders. "It was a very imposing spectacle," she grimly wrote in her diary. She saw "the name of each officer in silver letters" upon the biers and the "black draperies" on the horses, trotting while the "band played a dead march." The cruel irony that they were "brought from Mexico on the 4th" was not lost on Elizabeth.[18]

Women Elect Zachary Taylor

Even before the last shots were fired, talk of recruiting General Zachary Taylor for presidential nominee filtered through the political grapevine. His exploits at Buena Vista and his "no party" position made him attractive to all—including nativists. "Both want him now," Persis Andrews wrote from Paris Hill, Maine, in August 1847, "but when the leaders have settled it, one party will be loud in praise of his virtues—the other as clamorous to noise abroad his faults." Echoing Polonius's conviction that Hamlet was mad, she quoted Shakespeare: "'Pity 'tis true.'"[19] To her, hypocritical politicos were slightly loopy.

As contenders jockeyed for the prized nomination, partisan fires flared among women. Lowell mill operative and author Harriot Curtis hissed venomously at the party that had instigated war. "No person can hold the *present genius* of the Loco Foco party in more utter contempt than myself," she seethed, although she herself was a longtime Democrat. "They have abjured democratic principles—abandoned its glorious aim—and remain banded together upon the principles of the banditti—for 'the spoils.'" At the moment, Democrats to her were unconscionable thieves. One Middletown, Connecticut, matron sparred with her Democratic spouse through caustic correspondence to her son early in 1848. "Mr Collins has been here and made a speech which your Father says has dun up the Whigs," she penned demurely before tossing in a punch: "so much for a *Locos* oppinion [*sic*]." "The Whigs would say it was all *Slang I* suppose," she added, dismissing the duo's "democratic eloquence." Whig loyalty was more genially expressed by New Haven native Charlotte Bostwick, who saw presidential hopeful Henry Clay at a March 1848 New Jersey rally. New Englanders' typical fascination with celebrities' physiognomy took hold: "his eyes are matchless in depth and richness of expression." Convinced he should win the prize, she asked, "Why is it that he cannot reign at the [head] of the people, when he does so entirely in their hearts?" Clay—whose son was slain at Buena Vista—was, by now, Taylor's chief rival.[20] Taylor triumphed, however, at the June Philadelphia convention.

The die was also cast by then for the Democrats, who at Baltimore in May had selected Lewis Cass, an advocate of "popular sovereignty" (the policy by which a territory's residents would determine its slave status). Persis Andrews became a local celebrity because her husband Charles was a delegate. "Men flocked about me as I came out of Church to inquire 'what news from the Col.,'" she mused on May 28 after getting word from a "Tellegraph" [*sic*] report—an innovation that had appeared four years earlier, revolutionizing newspaper reportage. Charles "had had a hand in the good work, & in their ardor co'd not be restrained . . . from almost doing *me* homage—as part of him."[21] Stardust rubbed off on political wives.

There was one more candidate nominated, making it a three-way race. New York's antislavery "Barnburner" Democrats, favoring Martin Van Buren, bolted the Baltimore convention because they could not accept a key condition that would allow them to be seated: to abide by the convention's decisions. Their rivals, the conservative "Hunkers," who did not want to discuss slavery, did promise to accept the outcome, and thus were seated as New York's delegation. Barnburners subscribed to the Wilmot Proviso, first introduced with a bill in Congress in 1846 that would have, if passed, prohibited slavery in any territory acquired from Mexico after the war. They joined ranks with Conscience Whigs and former Liberty Party men in August at Buffalo, New York, to nominate Van Buren as the Free-Soil candidate. The new party opposed the extension of slavery into free territory and advocated homesteading. "I should think . . . that the Van Buren fever has reached its heights," Eliza Davis gossiped to her husband John in early September. "Whether there will be a reaction in favor of Taylorism remains to be seen." Most Massachusetts Whig leaders, including Senator Davis, shunned the Free-Soilers and rallied behind Taylor. Webster reluctantly acquiesced. On September 1 he delivered a speech that disparaged Taylor's opponents but scarcely endorsed the Whig nominee. "Mr Webster was to speak in favor of Taylor in Marshfield," Eliza Davis wrote, bewildered, when he did not. "Why he speaks at all I know not." Unlikely rumors circulated he was paid a hefty sum. Eliza heard "he wants a hundred thousand dollars expected to get it is mad because he don't. Is he not to be pitied?" She snarled, "mine I am afraid is not a Christian pity." Godlike Webster should have transcended self-interestedness.[22]

Webster's speech marked the beginning of down-to-the-wire campaigning in Massachusetts. Seventeen-year-old Calista Billings relished the intensifying hoopla. She lived just south of Boston in Canton with her aunt Louisa and uncle Lyman Kinsley, an iron manufacturer and Whig state representative hopeful, three cousins, and three Irish servants. Calista's father, a severely alcoholic, faltering shopkeeper, could never provide for her like Lyman. Because of her uncle's wealth and political ties, Calista's days were leisurely and full of politicking. Across from her home the Massapoag Hotel, an eighteenth-century dwelling Kinsley had refurbished, hosted Whig events.[23]

Before one of these, Calista professed her love of politics. Her uncle James Dunbar, preparing for a September 4 Whig meeting while she was visiting, teased her about it. "He told me he supposed I did not take much interest in 'Political affairs.'" She volleyed back in good humor, "I told him! no!" When the meeting reconvened a week later Calista attended and heard two speeches. She returned on the twenty-second for more, but the orator stood up everyone. The next Wednesday she and her aunt Louisa lucked out with two "very good" crowd-pleasers.[24]

As the election drew near Calista was carried in a whirlwind of activity. First there was the October 25 "Water Celebration" marking the opening of pipelines from Lake Cochituate to Boston—an event party organizers appropriated. Calista, invited to a Boston friend's home, rode in the night before to catch a Whig procession, but it was rained out. After rising to bells, guns, and cannon, she headed down the gaily decorated streets to Charles Call's apothecary, where she met "a number of other Ladies" waiting for the noontime procession and sampling from a "table of refreshments." The parade—largely composed of statewide militia and fire companies, waterworks laborers, manufacturers, fraternal and charitable societies, and even "three or four ladies" in the mostly male cavalcade—was to Calista "a magnificent affair." With nightfall, public and private buildings lit up while Free-Soilers fired their torches for a massive procession. Not to be outdone, "a man got up on city-Hall piazza & made a Taylor speech" just as it started, according to Calista; fiery abolitionist Abby Folsom followed.[25]

Instead of romping through Boston during the October 30 Whig torchlight fete, Calista did homework. She missed what Kitty Lawrence called a "really splendid" affair; marchers, "sometimes six, abreast," wielded Bengola lights, "which sent forth brilliant stars" that Sarah Hale's daughter claimed made the Free-Soilers' blaze look like a "a miserable small '*sizzle*.'" Calista set her sights, however, on the November 3 Canton Taylor Club meeting. Members were already practicing songs. "Every one is betting & talking about" the election, she told her diary, adding, "I dont believe Taylor will be elected." Why she doubted remains unclear, but still she campaigned. After Samuel Noyes, a club officer, asked her to make a banner, she shopped for cloth, tassels, and fringe, whipped it up by 4:00 P.M. on the big day, and mounted it at the Massapoag, where a procession formed at 6:00 P.M. in front of her home. After Lyman fired a rocket and the parade took off, he drove his niece around to see the lights. "Fathers shop they said looked as well as any in town but it was partly out," she blushed with embarrassment. They tried to squeeze into the packed Town Hall for speeches but gave up and sang Whig songs with some neighbors. Back at the hotel they greeted "a party of young gents . . . from Roxbury" serenading in "*Sombraroes*" and the returning marchers. Calista gawked as they ate "like wolves" and then feasted herself, listened to champagne-laced toasts, and joined in song before dancing in the parlor. After leaving and locking up at home, she saw in the darkness "2 cigars come from the Hotel up our yard"—Noyes and a male relative of his armed with champagne. Once inside he toasted Calista's health. Her cousin Adelaide teased he "liked me pretty well." It was 3:00 A.M. before the two, excited by the day, went to sleep.[26]

Similar festivities were sprouting up over the region. In Lowell, Massachusetts, factory worker Mary Paul "went out to see the illuminations" during a November 3 Whig torchlight ceremony. "One entire block," she noted, glimmered "with the exception of one tenement which doubtless was occupied by a *Free Soiler* who would not illuminate on any account whatever." She could read the political aura: partisanship registered by lighting—and snuffing—candles. In Gardiner, Maine, the ladies, according to Olive Worcester, came out for former senator George Evans's speech "in favor of Gen Taylor's election" the day before polling.[27] It seems unfathomable that some Whig women upheld "Old Rough and Ready" despite their antiwar position, but four more Democratic years was unthinkable.

After a brief wee-hours nap, Calista was eager for more. She saw her Boston friends off at the station and popped in at the Massapoag with Adelaide. The hotel keeper's wife, whose son was still snoozing, asked them to awaken him. "So we took some sticks and pounded on the door & screeched Hurrah for Taylor then he gave 3 cheers for the Ladies." Partisanship and frolicking blended seamlessly. The indefatigable campaigners hounded Lyman to go to the Sharon Whig meeting that evening. Their horse-drawn cart "pushing along" with torchbearers from Waltham stopped at a church vestry for the convocation. Inside, Noyes sat with Calista, "& very affectionately put his arm on the back of" her seat. At least "the others thought so." She supposed he was cramped for space.[28]

After a peaceful Sunday came a raucous Monday for Calista and her friends, thirteen-year-old Hannah Stetson, the hotel keeper's daughter, twenty-three-year-old Sarah Davis, wife of a shovel maker, and twenty-three-year-old Caroline Lincoln, whose father Frederick was a copper manufacturer. They all went to hear the chairman of Massachusetts's Free-Soil central committee and guest of Canton's Free-Soil Club, Charles Sumner, who had attracted women auditors the previous month in Dorchester. He was aghast some locals questioned the Free-Soil candidate's legitimacy. After thundering "'such persons are either grossly ignorant or daringly audacious,'" he demanded names. Town painter William Fuller retorted, "'Lyman

Kinsley for one F[rederick] W[alter] Lincoln for another.'" Sumner roared, "'an intelligent man cannot be honest who says that Mr Van Buren has not accepted his nomination.'" Evidently flourishing a copy of Van Buren's acceptance letter that was publicized in the papers, Sumner snidely asked if Kinsley could read. Calista erupted. "Oh! I was so vexed." She defended him: "as for the ignorant he is wise enough & as for being dishonest any one who knows my uncle knows he is far from being so." When Sumner pounced on Lewis Cass, Hannah hit the ceiling. Calista sharply "told her to hush & let me hear." Sumner took umbrage. "He said he wished his young friend under the Chandelier would be quiet or he was willing to give up the floor to me." Calista thought, "How insulting!" She could not restrain herself from grumbling more, "& a second time he said he found it very difficult for 2 to speak at once." The mighty orator was no match for the teenaged hothead. Sarah "said she should like to have him kicked off the stand," and Calista swore "there would have been a riot" had the Whig men not been rallying in Stoughton. After the three-hour-long harangue, Calista and Caroline were crushed. "Carry" sought solace from her pastor, sobbing that "any gentleman wouldn't have spoken so." Calista turned to Lyman, who "sat & talked for a long time" about the thorny side of politics.[29]

The upcoming Taylor ball in Canton distracted the disheartened young women, who merrily babbled about their gowns two days after November 7 polling—the first time all states voted for president on the same day. They would wear "a sash scarlet across the front & back of [their] waists & a medal with the likeness of Taylor on one shoulder." Calista tried to teach Caroline the waltz, but she had two left feet. Feeling better about Taylor's prospects, she bet Carry's father "a pound of candy that Cass would not be elected." At the next day's news she whooped, "Taylor is elected Hurrah! Hurrah! Hurrah!" Frederick made good on the bet. "He put a bundle in my hand & said he believed Cass was not president," Calista giggled. "I opened it & 'twas such candy as you read of.'" Plans for the ball—now a victory dance—continued as Calista and Carry redesigned their accessories. After this fashion workshop, another waltz lesson, and a stopover at the Massapoag, where Whig caucus members exchanged "3 cheers" with the two, Carry overcame her grief. She even "made Mr Sumners speech" in the grand hall—probably a scathing parody of the bellicose orator. Samuel Noyes stopped at the Kinsleys' a few days later with his Boston *Atlas* letter nose-thumbing Sumner. "Massapoag" boasted that "the 'ignorant,' the 'dishonest' Taylor men went to the polls" to vote for "the '*ignorant*' man, and he will be found in the Representative chamber in Boston, at the next session." Calista naturally deemed the letter "*very* good." Uncle Lyman took his seat in January.[30]

On November 23, Massapoag's hall was festooned with laurel wreaths, roses, and evergreens draped from the chandelier under which Calista once fumed. Busts of Taylor and Governor Briggs oversaw the Flagg and Fales' Band playing cotillions, waltzes, and the "Tempest." "I never tore round so in my life," Calista gasped. During the Virginia reel she ripped her gown but later, good-spiritedly, sang midnight-hour Taylor songs before retiring. The next day she waltzed the hall with Hannah to imaginary strains.[31] The campaign's hardships were worth it.

Not all women celebrated Taylor's success so lavishly or so enthusiastically. Hannah Smith, who wanted Democrats out and Free-Soilers in, was glad the fuss was over. The winner hardly thrilled her; in October she had excoriated her newspaper for being "full of Taylorism." With the race over, editors would grow tired of crowing. "I hope in a week they will be satisfy'd." Persis Andrews seemed bemused that "Democrats are confounded with utter astonishment at the news." For widow Olive Worcester, tasting victory was enough. "All accounts of Taylor's election look cheering." But some women took to the streets. Elizabeth Jocelyn and her sister Frances were escorted by their father's art student to stroll New Haven's byways radiant with gaslight displays, flaming tar barrels, torchbearers, fireworks, and sparkling rockets piercing the night sky. In Bangor, Mary Poor avoided the commotion and peeked through her window for a spectacular show. "As if Nature had not done enough to illuminate the earth, the Whigs are seeing what they can do this evening," she marveled on November 19. "There is an immense torchlight procession marching about the streets, many houses are illuminated, rockets are ascending in all directions & lights & beacons of various colors & degrees are blazing all over the city." She watched "till my eyes were tired."[32] In her quiet way, she entered a public ritual.

The partying wafted into the new year for Taylor's March 5 inauguration. "There has been enough noise for a fourth of July," Mary surmised. Her thoughts turned bleak, however, as she contemplated the halfhearted Whig's ascent. "I hope Taylor will not disappoint the hopes of so many of his subjects as Tyler did," she rued. Were Whigs, she puzzled, plagued by indifference, infidelity, and, more crucially, vanity? "I have been afraid that his popularity would kill him as it did Harrison, he has been so courted & fêted wherever he has been."[33] In the next chapter, we will see how prophetic indeed she was.

10

"Such a Lukewarm Spirit"

Women Divert Their Attentions during the 1852 Campaign

On November 7, 1852, a few days after the election, twenty-one-year-old Elizabeth Dwight wrote from Boston to her older sister Ellen in London, England. Orphaned and taken in by her wealthy merchant brother-in-law, Elizabeth cherished remaining family connections, even if only epistolary ones. The sisters, who leaned Whig, shared a passion for party politics, the topic most likely to pepper their lengthy missives in the years to come. It was with some disappointment though that Elizabeth recapped the campaign's finale. Democrat "*Franklin Pierce*, my dear," she dryly wrote, "is to be our next President." What annoyed her more than the outcome was the lackadaisical voters. "I never remember such a lukewarm spirit, at the time of the Election," she remarked. "A great many people threw no votes at all, & those who voted for Scott, though they were sorry that Pierce *was* elected, would not have been glad if Scott *had* been." Mexican War hero Winfield Scott, the Whig nominee, inspired loyalty in but few partisans. His party's vaguely articulated platform sidestepped burning issues regarding slavery's extension and muzzled traditionally Whig agendas for the economy and internal improvements. While the Democrats were somewhat more candidly in favor of the Compromise of 1850, both parties engaged in issue skirting, and neither mustered enthusiasm. The mere "personality contest," as one historian dubbed it, failed to mobilize voters. Not since 1836 had there been such low turnout; throughout the rest of the century, rates would never again hit 1852's rock bottom. Although Massachusetts Whigs had turned out in respectable numbers for Zachary Taylor in 1848, nearly a third of them cast no ballot at all in 1852, while additional numbers, some die-hard Webster supporters, bolted for Pierce. One Whig scholar recently called it "the most stunning defeat in the party's history." So distraught was Elizabeth's uncle, he swore (emphatically, as her script indicates with double underlining) he would "*never throw another vote at a Presidential Contest*."[1] He would, at least, never again vote for a Whig presidential candidate. This was the last time one ran. It was a quick slide downhill from there until the party's ultimate demise.

Women seemingly heard the death knell. In the four years after Taylor's victory—itself based upon a lower national turnout than in 1844—the Whig and nonpartisan women whose voices we recovered had less to say about politics than before.[2] Democratically affiliated women remained typically diffident. The voices of more antislavery and Free-Soil women, however, made themselves heard as the slavery question came to dominate partisan warfare. But even the monumental "Compromise of 1850" legislation only activated a few pens. Whig women, the most vocal of our politicized women, had usually been reluctant to engage the slave debate. It was no different now, especially since their party was vanishing. Only a few would move on to join the rising generation eager to take up the politics of antislavery and other causes, even if there were only weak structures of parties—some dying, some being born, and some transforming—to light the way. If women politicos seemed somewhat desultory and confused, they simply mirrored the current state of politics.

Given the temporary lull in most women's political talk, it is no wonder we see so few references to the 1852 campaign. But women were probably as uninspired as the franchised about it. They focused their attentions instead on tangential events, like the death of Daniel Webster that October, shortly after losing his party's nomination. But congressional elections, California's admission, and Taylor's passing also prompted writing.

We pick up in this chapter with Taylor's March 1849 inauguration, at which we find Eliza Davis exulting in the new administration. Congressional elections after the inaugural show the power of Free-Soil, so we look at two examples that caught women's interest. We then turn to California, a widely read-about topic, and its role in shaping the compromise resolutions of 1850. Taylor's death in July saw an outpouring of commentary, followed by some outrage at the Fugitive Slave Law's enforcement in early 1851. Webster's death in October 1852 provides the chapter's finale. In mourning the man, women also marked the passing of an age, that of the Second Party System.

Taylor's Inauguration

March 5, 1849, was according to Whig sympathizer Olive Worcester a "lovely day" in Gardiner, Maine, fit to celebrate the "Inauguration of Genl Taylor to the Presidency." In Washington, the weather was dull and blustery as Eliza Davis, wife of Massachusetts Whig senator John Davis, anticipated the day's ceremonies. John, a "Committee on Arrangements" member, advised her to skip the procession carrying Taylor from his hotel to the Capitol and go directly to the Senate chamber where doors opened at 10:00 A.M. for "the ladies." By eleven, the gallery was so suffocating that three women swooned. "My seat was favorable for witnessing the intro' of the distinguished guests," Eliza wrote a friend, Nancy C. Paine, back in Worcester. Eliza waited patiently while Vice President–elect Millard Fillmore was sworn in and addressed the Senate. Simultaneously the Taylor procession, hampered by mobs of well-wishers, chugged along at snail's pace. At 12:30 P.M. Eliza finally heard the "martial music" that "announced the arrival of the President elect." Now she had to scramble to get outside near the platform erected over the flight of stairs at the East Portico where Taylor would take the oath.[3]

In a mad dash to leave, Eliza lost her friends and wandered through the corridors seeking a quick exit. A gallant senator suggested that if she "could get out of a window," she could "gain time & see the whole ceremony." She took his odd counsel seriously. "Behold your friend then, mounting a cushion seat" in front of a window and "with the alacrity of 16 instead of sixty (or thereabouts) jumping from its height to the portico below." Once outside the building, she only had to step over an iron fence to get closer to Taylor, who was giving his inaugural address. I had "as good a chance to see as if I had not entered the capitol, but had waited without," she beamed. She was right above and behind him. Perched so high, she had a panoramic view of the swarm of men and women, as many as twenty thousand, facing the Capitol. "My heart actually swelled as it looked on the living sea below." Every now and then a hurrah escaped from it, but barely carried to Eliza's lofty station. But the sudden peal of applause at the address's end set her heart racing. It was time to swear in Taylor. When Chief Justice Roger B. Taney, a Democrat, stepped forward suddenly, "it seemed as if the very air was stilled." Eliza imprinted the hushed tableau in her mind. "There stood the old gray headed man, taking the oath . . . administered by a man whose party were driven from power by the act, and every thing they covet taken from their grasp." The set piece was vindication enough for the last four years. "It was but a moment," she explained. "*The Book* was kissed, the work was done. We had a Whig President." Wild cheering broke the silence and removed any doubt that what had happened in a blink of the eye was not momentous. Eliza jumped over the fence again and sallied around to the door of the Rotunda, where she saw the horde part like the Red Sea as the procession that had ushered in the president-elect now ushered out the president. "I wish I could give you a faint idea of the sublimity of the scene," she apologized to her friend.[4] Still, it was easy to imagine.

Taylor's address was brief and sketchy. It called for nonintervention, diplomacy toward other nations, greater honesty among officeholders, and implementation of standard Whig agendas regarding the economy, manufacture, and internal improvements. Olive Worcester liked its uplifting tone. "Mr Taylor certainly promises fair & if he carries out his principals [*sic*] we certainly shall have a better order of things." But the address blithely dismissed the issue dividing his party along Northern and Southern lines in Congress: what to do with the Mexican Cession acquired after the U.S.-Mexico War.[5] Spring elections were, after all, looming, and Whig prospects looked murky indeed.

Free-Soil and Congressional Elections

Would women struggle to follow politics outside the heretofore stark Whig-Democrat division? That they would first became clear in congressional contests after Taylor's inauguration. Whigs were demolished by Free-Soilers in Connecticut's April 2 polling in 1849 because the latter strategically backed Democratic candidates for U.S. representative, hoping to overturn the Whigs' razor-thin majority in the House. In three of the four congressional districts up for grabs, all of which had previously gone Whig, Democrats won. At least one woman kept a close eye on the ins and outs. Abolitionist Hannah Hicock Smith, who, as we saw, detested the U.S.-Mexico War, was on pins and needles. On April 6 she paced in her garden, "waiting for the Post" to arrive to verify if Whigs would lose control of the state's House to the new coalition. "Free Soil are said to have carried the State," she told her diary, "but I am not anxious."[6] Such disingenuous-sounding disclaimers of enthusiasm characterized her rhetoric of diffidence. Beneath them we can discern that she full well understood the import of the Free-Soil maneuver.

Another test of women's awareness of Free-Soil's muscle occurred again in Maine's 1850 U.S. Senate election. Democrats in the state legislature, already split between the antislavery wing and conservative "Hunkers," divided further over front-runner incumbent Hannibal Hamlin, a Wilmot Proviso adherent. Persis Andrews tuned in to the fight, which lasted from May until late July. "There has been a fierce & long protracted struggle throughout the state," she affirmed before spelling out the partisan rifts: "Whigs—Democrats Wild-Cat Democrats & Free Soilers." After numerous rounds of voting in June and July resulting in Hamlin's falling short in either house, he was, she learned, "at last gratified by a bare 1. majority" in the House on July 25. The decisive member, bedridden with "typhoid fever," was literally rushed "bed and all" to the floor to cast the winning ballot. But even greater theatrics were performed in the Senate that day among Free-Soilers, who had been withholding open endorsement for Hamlin because it would have alienated his two key, conservative backers. So, upon their leader's encoded signal (he pulled out a ballot from his coat pocket), three cast for Hamlin—to Hunkers' surprise—and won the day. Andrews discerned that "ladies & all have felt an interest here." A few nearby women reveled with their neighbors, Hamlin's mother and sister. Thus, on the ground, women very much heard the death rattle of the Second Party System through incessant factioning and tenuous realignments.[7]

California and the Compromise of 1850

Increasingly, the question of what to do about the West would underpin much of the period's political turmoil, so women's interests naturally encompassed territorial issues there. California's fate became particularly pressing owing to the westward flood of fortune seekers aiming to mine gold. With its population swelling by as much as ninety thousand in 1848–49, California needed a permanent civil government to replace vestiges of military rule established during the war, so it ratified a constitution in November 1849 and awaited admittance as a state. Would it be free or slave? Its new constitution suggested the former.[8]

Not surprisingly, we find women and girls reading widely about California, for it was now on the front lines of sectional and party conflict. So commonly did the press write about it, one minister's daughter ho-hummed in March 1849, it "has become an old story." Hannah Smith was tired of hearing "The same of California" over and over by July. Still, it fascinated one rural New Hampshire clerk's twelve-year-old, who "read a good long piece about California" in April. One way to get a fresh view was through the publications—and their blurbs—of wartime California governor and explorer John Charles Frémont: *Notes of Travel in California* (1849), *Geographical Memoir Upon Upper California* (1848), and *Exploring Expedition to the Rocky Mountains, Oregon and California* (1845), which had a recent edition. A "full account . . . of Fremonts sufferings in the Rocky Mountains" kept one Plainville, Connecticut, woman connected to her prospector husband. She sent him the essay after reading it herself. Hannah Smith perused at least two of Frémont's volumes, one borrowed from a friend in January, the other, in April, probably his *Notes*.[9] These familiarized women with a figure who would soon become the nation's first Republican Party presidential candidate, but it also gave them some knowledge of the terrain on which unfolding partisan controversies would play out.

The prospect of another free state added to the Union might please supporters of the Wilmot Proviso, which called for freezing the extension of slavery, but for Hannah Smith "all the gold of California" could never "wash out" the "stain" of the U.S.-Mexico War. Obviously Southern congressmen did not want California admitted as a free state, at least not without getting something in return. So a famous—to many contemporaries, an infamous—deal was cut. In January 1850, Henry Clay put forth a series of eight resolutions that would bring California into the Union without mention of slavery, allow New Mexico and Utah to decide on slavery themselves, abolish the slave trade in the District of Columbia, and establish a stringent "fugitive slave" law regarding escaped bondsmen. Abby Stimson fastened only on one part: "That California be admitted without restriction upon the subject of slavery." Eliza Davis, however, focused on the fugitive slave law and Daniel Webster's famous "Seventh of March" Senate speech in which he denounced the Wilmot Proviso and chastised Northerners for humiliating the South by harboring runaways. He had caved into threats of secession by championing a rigorous fugitive slave act. John Davis recoiled in horror. Eliza was shocked. Her minister, Alonzo Hill, had thought Webster would act otherwise; he knew "for a fact," that Webster "wrote to a Gentleman to enquire 'how much free soil Massachusetts would bear'" in mid-February. "'He was going to make a speech and wanted it up to the mark.'" According to Hill, the "gentleman"—Hill was discrete—advised "'Mass. is ready for as much as you can put in.'" Eliza commiserated, "Judge his surprise when the speech was made." But she was certain "there is such a thing as retribution."[10] It would come during the 1852 Whig nominating convention.

The Death of Taylor

Amid heated debates about Henry Clay's proposed compromise, Annie Rotch reported to her diary on July 9 that President Zachary Taylor was "dangerously ill with dysentery." He became sick after attending in stifling heat a Fourth of July stone-laying ceremony at the Washington Monument. It was likely coronary thrombosis or severe gastroenteritis made fatal by medicine containing mercury, quinine, and opium. For Annie, his dietary "imprudence, added to the great mental excitement under which he was laboring, brought on the disease wh. he contracted in Mexico." His military exploits seemingly haunted him as much as the fighting in Congress. Taylor died as Rotch wrote. She learned of it the next day. "What a dreadful blow to the country at this time." Since she was convinced that "All parties & sects . . . were fast becoming devoted to this great & good man," she could not understand "how God should see fit to remove one who possessed the confidence & affection of the nation, & who had he lived, would have been the means of doing much good."[11] The two Whig presidents had been called heavenward early in their terms, with no apparent reason.

While several women briefly noted Taylor's passing, at least one went into great detail. Helen Warner, a Boston cooper's seventeen-year-old daughter who had been looking forward to meeting the president, was figuratively at his side, from the time of his death to Boston's obsequies a month later. Back in March, Mayor John P. Bigelow had promised her teacher he would escort "Old Rough and Ready" to the exemplary Hancock grammar school for girls during his upcoming Boston visit. When Helen heard the president was ill, the city was already preparing for him. The tenth began "pleasant[ly]," but suddenly darkened when "startling news reached the city, that President Taylor was dead." He had passed away "at half-past ten" the night before, while she was fast asleep. Even though his last words were transcribed in the Whig *Atlas*, she tucked them safely into her diary: "'I am prepared. I have endeavored to do my duty.'" After that she was transfixed by *Atlas* intelligence. She learned the city government convened on the tenth to pay their respects and plan obsequies; her journal brimmed with excerpts of Mayor Bigelow's eulogy before the Board of Aldermen. On the eighteenth she read that Faneuil Hall would be "dressed up in mourning." On August 2 she wrote extensively about obsequies in Roxbury and Charlestown and copied down the words to hymns that were sung. She watched from a friend's store window the August 13 Cambridge procession of about one thousand as it marched to church, opened "at an early hour, for the admission of ladies." She was impressed by the mottoes lining Maine Street, one including Taylor's final utterances. With Taylor's death now more than a month in the past, Helen could admit she and her friends "enjoyed" themselves "very much."[12]

Meanwhile, Boston was gearing up for the August 15 memorial procession, which Helen would witness. Twenty-six people assembled at her house for the event. She was emotionally taken with the "Funeral Car" lined in black velvet and ornamented "'with the arms of the various states in white in medallion style, surrounded by wreathes of silver.'" Twelve black horses drew it. The horse of Captain George Lincoln—the former governor's son who died at Buena Vista under Taylor's command—refused to follow the car, lying down in the muddy street as if in protest of the war that had claimed his master. "Being reluctant and inclined to repose in the gutters," he was replaced by an "animal of less fire and spirit," according to one woman present. What captured Helen's imagination most, however, was the Eleventh Ward's "ship of state," a float representing each state, featuring twenty-eight girls dressed in white and two symbolizing Virginia and Louisiana, where Taylor was born and lived respectively, in "deep mourning," or black. Helen knew the thirteen-year-old "Goddess of Liberty," Louisa Chandler, a carpenter's daughter also clad in white, who posed with her "golden-tipped wand" at the center of the others. "It was a beautiful design," Helen glowed. Girls, not unlike herself, could embody the city's deepest regard for the Union. The parade wended its way to Faneuil Hall, packed with women in their galleries for the solemn ceremony, but Helen did not join them. A few days later, she sauntered over to see its "neatly and tastefully trimmed" interiors. Silver shields inscribed with the names of war-fallen heroes, including John Rogers Vinton, Henry Clay, Jr., and George Lincoln, hung from the black and white draped pillars. That evening, she came across a poem in the *Christian Reflector* titled "The Grave of Washington" and thought of its "connexion, not only with the 'Father of our Country,' but also with him who has just left the presidential seat for that 'home from which no traveller returns.'"[13] With each word she copied into her diary, she thought of the two.

The Fugitive Slave Law

Shortly after the mourning veil for Taylor lifted, the Fugitive Slave Bill passed on September 12, 1850, in the House of Representatives, with many Northern congressmen absenting themselves. Under it Northerners could be fined and imprisoned if they helped slaves escape into free territory or did not aid marshals attempting to capture runaways. Commissioners judging each case were given ten dollars if they found the alleged runaway to be a slave and only five if they declared him or her free.[14]

Many New Englanders deemed the law a travesty, but others supported it. Some organized and attended "Union meetings" bringing together Whigs and Democrats in favor of the Fugitive Slave Bill's constitutionality and viability as one of the Compromise's "peace measures." Persis and Charles Andrews, just elected to the U.S. House as a Democrat, went to one of these events in Bath, Maine, on December 16, 1850, held for the purpose of what she called "Opposition to Nullifying Abolitionists." Hearing Maine's Democratic governor John Hubbard address "thousands . . . but no ladies" from the balcony of her hotel, she recorded she was "well pleas'd with his sensible remarks." Treated like a celebrity because of her husband's election ("I really liked the adulation, for its novelty I suppose"), she was gratified that at the event "Whigs & Democrats were hand & glove." The intraparty concord of which she dreamed was ironically only achieved as new battle lines were being dawn over federally mandated reenslavement of escaped bondsmen.[15]

In no time, the first arrest in New England was made, much to the horror of some women. On February 15, 1851, Shadrach Minkins, a Norfolk, Virginia, runaway who had been living in Boston for nine months, was seized at the Cornhill Coffee House and brought to the courthouse. Three hours after his arrest a group of African American locals rescued Minkins, who then fled to Montreal. Bells and whistles went off in Washington, D.C.—none more loudly than Webster's—and Bostonian Anna Loring was there when they were sounded. The daughter of Ellis Gray Loring, a lawyer and a founding member of the first antislavery society in 1833 in Boston, was all ears. "I look forward to hearing the debates tomorrow with great interest," the Free-Soiler wrote Ellis on the twenty-third. By that point they were in full swing. On February 17, Henry Clay submitted a resolution requesting information from President Millard Fillmore about what exactly had happened and if he thought extra legislation was needed to carry out the law. Although John Davis ferociously countered on the eighteenth, the resolution was adopted. Fillmore complied on the nineteenth (Webster authored his reply) threatening the use of federal military and naval power to enforce the law. "Only think what a time for me to be here!" Anna cried; "we shall hear plenty about it tomorrow. I am afraid it will be almost too interesting for me." On February 21, Senators hotly debated whether to consider the reply immediately in recognition of the gravity of the situation or to delay discussion with an eye toward dispensing with the matter "in the most quiet mode" possible, in the words of New Hampshire's Free-Soiler John P. Hale. During debate, he insinuated that Clay accused him of grandstanding only "when the gallery was full of ladies," which it may have been that day. Anna would join them.[16]

Helen Warner witnessed on April 3, 1851, another injustice committed under the Fugitive Slave Law, the arrest of Thomas Sims. This time the mayor and U.S. marshal commanded police to surround the courthouse, safeguarded by chains. Commissioner George T. Curtis ordered Sims to return to Savannah, Georgia. Webster, now secretary of state, personally oversaw the arrangements. "This morning," Helen wrote on April 12, "Thomas Sims was conveyed on board the brig Acorn . . . at Long Wharf, to be returned to his master." Her minister, Nathaniel Colver, was at the wharf with a throng of abolitionists (including many women) inviting "thunderbolts of

SCENE AT THE REVERE HOUSE.

FIGURE 10.1 F. E. Worcester, "Scene at the Revere House," *Gleason's Pictorial Drawing Room Companion* (May 17, 1851): 37. Courtesy of the American Antiquarian Society, Worcester, Mass.

heaven to be poured down" upon the marshal and his deputies who delivered Sims into bondage. The next day at Sunday services, she felt proud when Colver addressed a packed house including her, the usual churchgoers, and curious outsiders. "He has after choosing what seems to him the path of duty, trod it manfully," she maintained, acknowledging the editorial ridicule that greeted his "doings and sayings" regarding Sims; "I would sooner stand in his place than in the place of those who have carried this odious law into effect."[17] Helen chose her side wisely.

One politician supporting that law, Daniel Webster, shortly thereafter felt the results of judgments like Warner's when the mayor and Board of Aldermen denied him use of Faneuil Hall for an April 17 appearance because it had been off-limits to abolitionists. Fair was fair, they said. And it was politically cagey in light of the public uproar over Sims. In the face of the insult, Webster instead spoke on April 22 in front of the Revere House, where he was staying. There, he was showing signs of his decline. One woman thought his outer sickness reflected inner degeneration: "The change in his *moral* features might have convinced men of that one would think." But not all women were disgusted with Webster. News reports and an engraving in Boston's popular illustrated story paper *Gleason's Pictorial Drawing Room Companion* indicated "bouquets fell upon him from the hands of fair women" learning out from the Revere's windows (fig. 10.1).[18] "Black Dan" still had some pull.

The 1852 Nominations

Over the next year Webster would struggle unsuccessfully for one last hurrah in the 1852 presidential race. But by the time the major-party presidential nominations had been made, Webster's name was not among them. Most of our women had little to say of the less-than-thrilling candidates. Kitty Lawrence even forgot to tell her diary. "I believe I have never mentioned the nomination of the Whig and Democratic Candidates for the presidency," she yawned on July 8. Free-Soil abolitionist Louisa Loring, however, closely followed the long, nerve-wracking Whig convention, which began on June 16. "Do you know that Mr. Webster is not the Whig candidate but Gen. Scott is?" she wrote, taken aback. Although Winfield Scott was confident his inoffensive "no-platform" stance would easily win the day (the convention adopted a pro-Compromise position however), it took fifty-three rounds before he received a majority. Webster, who was anathema to many Whigs because he was so stridently pro-Compromise, attracted few delegates, but they refused to break the stalemate by shifting their votes to someone else. "His few friends made unheard of efforts for him & spent a great deal of money," she gossiped. As word of each voting round flashed in by telegraph, Louisa heard yelping and groans on State Street. "They voted at Baltimore all day & almost all night," she exclaimed; "Mr. W. had 29 & then 28 & then 29 again, the last produced great cheering." She had held her breath throughout. "I never felt so much interest in any election because just before the nomination there was reported to be a reaction in Webster's favor."[19] She was no fan, but others were.

When the vanquished Webster returned home from Washington, an estimated thirty thousand assembled in Boston on July 9 to support him in defeat and to hear him speak on Boston Common. Several women described the spectacle. Domestic servant Lorenza Berbineau ventured out in the ninety-degree heat to see Webster ushered there. The people, she said, "cheerd him most heartily & showered him with bouquets of flowers." At night, after the procession, Elizabeth Clapp could hear horses' hooves and soldiers shouting "nine cheers for D. Webster" outside her home. Louisa Loring surveyed Beacon Street, "dressed in flags & flowers with Mr W.[']s busts interspersed crowned with laurels." From her lawyer-husband's office window, where she and Garrisonian abolitionist Edmund Quincy watched the procession, Louisa detected signs of weakness and despair in Webster. "He was pulled from his seat by two men & supported standing [in] the carriage for a while. His face was demonical trying in vain to smile. It seemed to say I care not a button for this if you can do no more." Louisa, who "mourned a little over all this applause," would not give him a final moment in the sun. Her companion cracked, "'never mind it is only . . . a dead body going to its own funeral.'"[20] Quincy's words were prescient.

The Death of Daniel Webster

Between the years 1849 and 1852, a seemingly inordinate number of great statesmen died. The demise of the Second Party System was heralded by a row of tombstones. First, former president James K. Polk passed away in June 1849, followed by the "Great Nullifier," John C. Calhoun, in March 1850. Zachary Taylor, as we have seen, died four months later. In June 1852, Whig architect Henry Clay left this world, and in August Massachusetts senator Robert Rantoul Jr. suddenly expired at the nation's capital. "It will be a long time before there is another free soil senator I am afraid," Louisa Loring lamented.[21] But Daniel Webster's death that October 24 shook the nation. Whether they revered or reviled him, women responded in waves. After all, it marked a momentous transition, a New England Whig sunset before the new dawn.

The day he passed, Elizabeth Clapp recorded: "This morning Daniel Webster, the greatest man in the country died. The bells tolled, and the guns were fired for some time." Over in Charlestown, Sarah Edes, a family friend of Democratic governor George S. Boutwell, nevertheless paid homage: "Daniel Webster [died] at 23 minutes before two o'clk this morning," she scribbled, adding that the sermon she heard "this P.M. alluded most particularly to his decease." She noted her uncle brought the news to Boutwell's home. The words of a Democratic politico's daughter were appropriately terse: "Heard of Mr Websters death," while a newlywed of a Whig scion located the place of death. "Mr Webster died this morning at Marshfield," his estate just south of Boston. As the news fanned out, women in far-flung places took up their pens. Susan Tucker in Vergennes, Vermont, recorded the next day: "Heard by Telegraph that Daniel Webster died at three oclock yesterday evening. The flag hangs at half mast on the government ground." Kitty Lawrence, returning to the United States with her father Abbott—whose relationship with Webster had been rocky—after his ambassadorial stint in Britain, noted rather coldly on October 29, "We heard of Mr. Webster's death at Halifax and on that account a grand Military and Civic reception from men of all shades of political opinion was put off." The next day, Olive Worcester in Gardiner, Maine, devised a diary entry that began like a newspaper obituary: "On Sunday morning the Hon. Daniel Webster died, at Marshfield at his residence . . . in his 71st year." This Whig closed by opining, "intellectually he was the greatest man living." More than six weeks later on a vessel plying the Atlantic, Rhode Island shipmaster's wife Cynthia Congdon heard the news: "A clipper ship came up with us, passed very near spoke with her. The Northern Light from Boston fifty two days, her Captain informed us [of] the death of Daniel Webster. So one after another of our great men, are being called away from Earth," this devout nonpartisan Methodist reflected, "but I trust that others will be raised up who will fill their place, and that the affairs of our nation may be conducted with Wisdom and in peace."[22] Thus put in touch with the world for an instant, she pondered the news with civic wonder.

For those on the ground in New England, obsequies and their visual displays became a focal point. Elizabeth Dwight, who introduced this chapter, tried to convey to her sister Ellen in London what the news clips she was sending her could not: "unless you were here, you could have no idea of the effect it has produced." She began with the "Meeting of the Citizens of Boston" at Faneuil Hall on October 27 to plan the mourning ceremonies. "The room was darkened at midday, & the Hall partially lighted with gas. Healy's picture draped with black, was placed at one end of the room, so that Mr. Webster's figure seemed to stand out in the darkness." Once a testament to a living legend, George P. A. Healy's painting depicting Webster's famous 1830 reply to Hayne, in which women in the galleries are literally highlighted, had become a fitting backdrop for mourning. The silence was deafening. "The people came and went as though they were in church, the speakers were not once applauded, & the assent that was given to the resolutions, was a low deep *yea*!" What unsettled her most was how much movers and shakers were themselves moved and shaken. "The platform was covered with the respectables"—including George Ticknor, William Appleton, and George T. Curtis, who sent Thomas Sims back to slavery—"who always sit there, & every now & then, these strong men would bow their heads down on the tables before them, perfectly overcome." She observed that there was "something truly awful in seeing such a collection of people, *smitten*, as it were, with this heavy grief."[23] Bereavement muted the famed meeting hall that Webster once animated with his mighty oratory.

As the October 29 funeral approached, Boston donned mourning garb. Berbineau, the servant, on an errand the day before, saw that "they were trimming the shops with black." The next day, Elizabeth Clapp was out of school and on the scene with her friends. "As we looked down the street," she marveled, "we could see hardly anything but black and white." Elizabeth Dwight spied "scarcely a shop" on bustling Washington Street without drapery and "*fifteen* busts of Mr. Webster's set up in black recesses . . . & his pictures *everywhere*." She savored the bipartisan tribute, noting "from the Whig & Democratic Headquarters & all around the Old State [House], Flags are hung out heavily bordered with black." Sarah Edes reported to her diary not only that "abt' 20,000 people attended his funeral" but also that her late husband had manifested himself: "Delightful dream of my dear Henry last night." Personal loss and civic grieving merged. Not all women marked Webster's funeral with reverence. After telling her diary that her father attended the ceremonies, Kitty Lawrence dissed the icon: "It were better he had died long before as far as human things are concerned."[24] She was far less forgiving than Abbott.

Long after the funeral and the November 30 Boston obsequies that many of our diarists mentioned, pilgrimages to Marshfield by women were common. Mary Gardiner Davis from Brookline, Massachusetts, on March 8, 1853, took away a souvenir that yet remains in her "book of poems": a pressed leaf commemorating "Daniel Webster's Funeral Oct. 29th 1852" plucked "from a belt of trees planted by himself." Former Lowell millworker Lucy Larcom went in 1861 to take in the scene but focused on his servant Monica McCarty: "There was much that was interesting to see in the great man's home," she explained; "the two things that pleased me most were the portraits of his mother, and his black cook, or housekeeper. The latter was a fine painting, the face so full of intelligence, gratitude, and all good feelings." It was fitting that Larcom, a onetime Free-Soiler and amateur antislavery poet, should valorize the former slave.[25]

McCarty, whose freedom was purchased by Webster when she was about twenty and to whom he attributed "general genius" in the kitchen, was steadfastly at his deathbed (fig. 10.2). The legal murkiness surrounding all manumissions because of the Fugitive Slave Law, in which Webster had such a hand, forced him at his very end once again to declare her and his other servants free. McCarty, who refused to work for Franklin Pierce after Webster passed, told a subsequent employer, Newporter Eliza De Wolf Thayer, that the dying man kept repeating, "'Life! Life! Death! Death!'" McCarty recalled that "'every time he said so, it went right through me & I prayed every breath I drew, it seemed to me, that God would give him *light*.'" Thayer, a minister's wife, was moved. "What a scene," she thought. "The great statesman the giant of intellect lying there, prostrate before the last great enemy—revolving in his mind the great mystery of life—the eyes of the whole Union turned upon him . . . & here was this poor old colored woman pleading silently wrestling with God for *him*." Thayer weighed the pathos

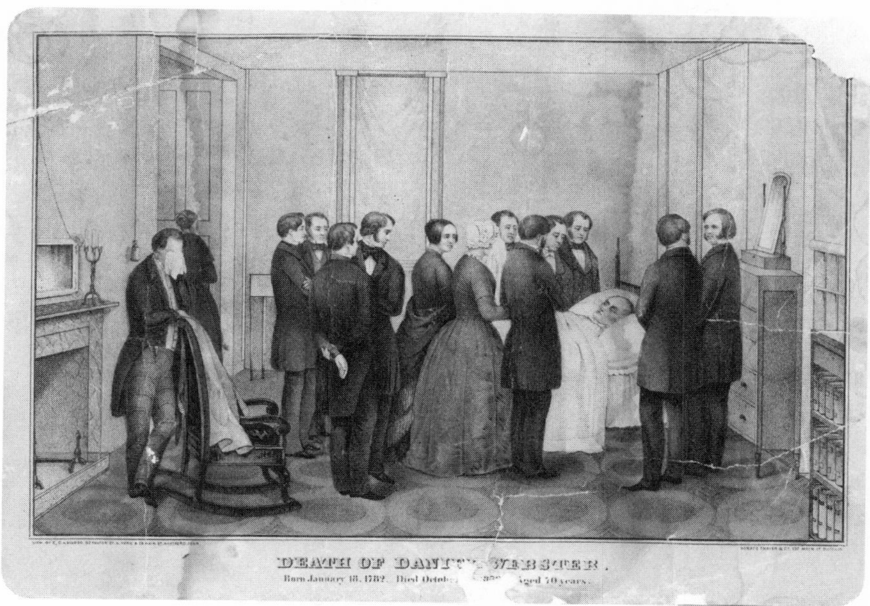

FIGURE 10.2 *The Death of Daniel Webster*, c. 1852–55 (possibly with Monica McCarty, far left). Courtesy Susan H. Douglas Political Americana Collection, Division of Rare and Manuscript Collections, Cornell University Library, Ithaca, N.Y. (2214.PR0082)

with the irony. "None noticed her—but she may have been at that moment doing a greater work than Webster had ever done—she may by the blessing of God have been the means of saving him—from everlasting death—for as she said 'God you know Mrs Thayer can work a great work in a little time.'"[26] Thayer's slyly invidious comparison between the devout Methodist McCarty and the statesman who bargained with the devil to save the Union prompts a question: what was the work done by New England women to create and sustain the Webster myth? It seems they did a great deal.

The death of Webster overshadowed the dull November 2 Election Day. Most women we located who mentioned the election lent only a brief, but sometimes suggestive, line to their diaries. Abby Stimson succinctly summed up her frustration: "Disgraceful defeat of the Whigs." Persis Andrews said it like it was: "Franklin Pierce triumphantly elected President U.S." He carried twenty-seven states while Scott took only four. If any candidly Democratic women exulted, they were not captured in our research. But Mary Baker Glover—her married name before becoming the famous Christian Science leader Mary Baker Eddy—probably crowed. Her Pierce campaign poem, printed in a Boston story paper, *The Flag of Our Union*, conceivably encouraged at least a few votes.[27]

But Whig women's voices were winding down with the party. Some of them, as we will see in the next chapter, channeled their energies into the Republican Party. Republican women's spirit was hardly "lukewarm" as they rallied behind John C. Frémont for president *and* his wife Jessie Benton Frémont, who, by many accounts, was the campaign's bright and shining star.

11

"I *Am Fremont, How Is It with You?*

Women and Sectionalism

Sarah Hurlburt, the young wife of a rural Vermont carpenter, was immersed in the 1856 campaign when she wrote on October 21 to her cousin Henry Cushman in the countryside of central Massachusetts. "Colchester is all excitement," she said of her small town. "The 'Fremonters' have built them a large cabin in the Common & we have Fremont meetings once a week." Such 1840-style "Log-Cabin" gatherings, she emphasized, "are fully attended by the *ladies*, as well as gentlemen." John C. Frémont, the Republican Party's presidential nominee, had clearly enthused her and her neighbors. Eyeing a forthcoming "great Mass Meeting," she pegged herself as a partisan. "*I* am Fremont, how is it with you? I *think* you are the same," she assumed. "I am sure you are not Buchanan," the Democratic opponent. It was a bold statement, since Cushman had recently been Massachusetts's Democratic lieutenant governor. So Hurlburt slipped in a disclaimer characteristic of politicized women's diffident rhetoric. "I do not meddle *much* with *politics* but I do feel *very much* interested in the present election."[1] The formulaic demurral erased any possible offense.

Why did she not take Cushman's Democratic partisanship for granted? Although he had a history of switching parties, more likely it was his outrage over the recent arrest of Bostonian Anthony Burns under the Fugitive Slave Act. "Slavery, being *contrary* to the *high law* of *God* as well as to the *first principles* of *Republicanism, must not be tolerated* in this *free country*," Cushman practically shouted at his diary in 1854. Hurlburt may have thought, how *could* he support the Democratic platform? It upheld the Kansas-Nebraska Act, which erased the 1820 Missouri Compromise ban on slavery above the 36° 30′ parallel and allowed settlers in those two territories, both north of that line, to determine their slave status. How could he *not* adopt the Republicans as his own? After all, they condemned slavery and its expansion, while demanding Kansas's admittance as a free state.[2]

As with the rise of the Whig Party in the mid-1830s, lines were being drawn again, now mainly over the territorial extension of slavery. Women, as before, stationed themselves alongside the divided franchise. Whereas Whigs and Democrats had previously faced off, in 1856 it was Republicans and Democrats. The old Second Party System had collapsed, and a new one had been born. Hurlburt wanted her cousin in her camp.

This chapter presents voices of women who commented upon politics between the elections of 1852 and 1856, a turbulent and confused time marked by Whiggery's last gasp, the rapid emergence and dissolution of coalitions, the Know-Nothing Party's growth, voter realignment, and the Republican Party's gestation. With all this political churning, no wonder Hurlburt imagined Cushman had been tossed to and fro. She, like most of this era's partisan women we located, felt anchored in the Republican Party.

We begin with a look at politics in 1853 and 1854 from women's vantage point at the municipal and state levels, where the Whig Party was unraveling and where local issues, like temperance reform, informed coalitions and shaped results. We then consider the intertwining of local and national politics in the public uproar over slavery and some women's private despair over the Anthony Burns case. National developments were also felt locally as parties and factions positioned themselves around the Kansas-Nebraska Act. Next we discuss how one of those parties against the act, the Know-Nothings, skyrocketed to success by pooling together a range of issues, including temperance and nativism. The sectional crisis hit home when a Southern congressman violently assaulted Massachusetts senator Charles Sumner, an act that elicited sympathy and outrage from our women. Finally, we consider the 1856 Republican nominee John C. Frémont and his political powerhouse wife Jessie, who together offered such a beacon of hope and inspiration to many beleaguered New England women that it led them to affiliate with the new Republican Party.

State and Local Elections

For roughly a year after the 1852 presidential race ended, women stayed tuned to state and local elections. Because affairs at this level were instrumental in the Whig Party's disintegration and the Second Party System's ultimate collapse, women necessarily had their fingers on the pulse of broader political change. Candidates exploited regional, state, and local issues to run their campaigns and attract voters. None was more explosive than temperance. Maine's 1851 law prohibiting liquor sales spurred similar controversial legislative initiatives in other New England states. Whigs and Democrats were internally divided over it while Free-Soilers generally were pro-temperance.[3] Another flash point had been reached with the increasing number of immigrants in the nation, especially Catholics, which sounded nativist alarms.

Women knew that the shifting coalitions these issues could spawn resulted in electoral havoc. For Whig Abby Stimson, a Providence wine dealer's elderly wife, merely recording in her diary a winner's name suggested contentiousness, as when on January 4, 1853, she entered, "Clifford made Gov. of Mass." This Whig candidate, who waffled on adopting Maine-style prohibition in Massachusetts, which was splitting his party into "dry" and "rum," had led in the November polls but fell short of victory. The decision was tossed to the state legislature. Because the Free-Soil–Democratic coalition had surrendered control of that body to Whigs, they elected Clifford that January. Often, complex stories underpin simple diary lines, like Stimson's.[4]

Other women provided more detail. One Salem woman said more about how shifting allegiances—and rum—shook up elections. On March 4, she wrote, "we" (meaning the Whigs) "are looking out for a candidate for mayor" before stating that "George Peabody, declines, Richard S. Rogers declines," and "Several others who were cald [*sic*] upon have also declined." No one wanted to tackle "the Temperance party," which would "contend strongly for a temperance man at this election." But at "Last it was decided to nominate Asahel Huntington," a well-known temperance advocate. She recorded his election on the eighth. She also wrote about delegates selected to the state "convention to revise the constitution"—a Free-Soil–Democratic coalition initiative. Temperance again reared its head in Lynn's 1854 mayoral election. A schoolteacher there noted that the town "Voted again today for Mayor. T. P. Richardson elected." Whigs came out for this "Temperance Union" candidate instead of George Foster, her "old school-master" who was, she claimed, "held up by the Whigs . . . but was not elected." One paper crowed, "It is evident the old Coalition is dead."[5] Issues trumped regular party loyalty.

The injection into early 1850s Massachusetts politics of nativist splinter parties flustered a Boston Whig printer's teenager, Elizabeth Clapp. Regular Whigs, the Young Men's League (whose nominee also ran as Whig), the Citizen's Union, and Democrats all put up candidates for mayor. On the first ballot (December 12, 1853), a regular Whig led, but without a win. He dropped out of the second round (December 27), and this time the "Union's" Jerome V. C. Smith, who also ran as a Whig, was eight votes shy of winning.

After Smith triumphed in the third round, on January 9, Clapp wrote, sarcastically, in her diary, "I am very glad of it for they have had such a fuss about choosing a mayor lately, that I am tired of it." She washed her hands of the nonsense. "To be sure I did not have anything to do with it except to hear father talk about it."[6] Nativist candidates, as we will see, would continue to roil the state.

In Maine, Persis Andrews was even more disheartened than Clapp but instead about state election stews. She followed the September 1852 gubernatorial election that yielded no majority. The regular Democratic candidate, the incumbent John Hubbard, won a plurality because new voters, plus dry Whigs and Free-Soilers, cast for him. Persis identified him as a "wool head," that is, an antislavery, pro-temperance, and Hannibal Hamlin supporter. She was aware of quickly shifting political taxonomies. The Whig candidate, William G. Crosby, also pro-temperance, lost votes of rum Whigs, who instead backed Anson G. Chandler, an opponent of the Maine prohibition law and "Wild Cat" (pro-slavery Democrat). Many other Whigs simply stayed at home. Still, the election drew a greater turnout than the state's November presidential contest. Because there was "no election," the legislature had to decide the outcome. To secure his victory, Crosby promised that if Wild Cats would vote Whig for state Senate vacancies (the winners would then vote for him, thus securing him the governorship), he would serve them up a Wild Cat U.S. senator. Crosby won. While Persis Andrews was happy her "old friend . . . Crosby is Governor of Maine," she was bewildered. "*My friends* both Whigs & Dems are gratified." She could only call them an "Odd Medley." Traditional voting patterns and party fealties were vanishing into thin air. But she was sorry that "the Wool-heads or Hamlin Dem."—meaning Hubbard supporters—"have been sacrificed." The temperance cause, however, would not be sacrificed. A liquor law even harsher than that of 1851 would pass in March 1853, intensifying party splintering. In light of it, a Limerick woman was "glad the rummies got beat at town meeting" in Baldwin, where her mother lived. If women's crusade for temperance was once untainted by partisanship, it was now fully "contaminated."[7]

Susan Tucker of Vergennes, Vermont, too, witnessed how the divisive temperance question affected campaigns—in her case, the 1853 gubernatorial race. Back in October 1852, Whigs and Free-Soilers in the legislature cooperated to pass the "Vermont Prohibitory Law," based on the stringent Maine law. Opposing the legislation were Democrats and the sizable Whig faction, the latter of whom were worried about rum Whigs bolting. But debate over the law still raged in the local lyceum. In early January, Tucker heard a lecture by temperance crusader John Pierpont on the law's constitutionality. She deferred to her dry Whig father, who found it "spirited, instructing, &

interesting." Later that month she attended another talk by the "framer of" the law "as it appeared before the Legislature." By the time September elections rolled around, the issue was still raging. Democrats, wanting to repeal the liquor law, pinned its passage on Whigs. Rum Whigs, feeling betrayed by dry members of their party, swore they would vote Loco. Free-Soilers, favoring the law, attracted dry Whig voters. Tucker was pleased that despite all the bickering, Whig G. W. "Grandy was elected as the representative for Vergennes." Predictably, though, no gubernatorial candidate received enough votes to win. In October, the legislature determined the outcome. Free-Soilers, now a sizable force there, recoiled at the idea of a Whig governorship, and so joined forces with their former temperance law foes, the Democrats, to elect John Robinson. Tucker was disappointed. "I had a fatiguing day & felt rather down hearted," she brooded on October 28. "They have elected a democratic Governor."[8] Tucker and the women who followed similar elections throughout the region fearlessly tackled these mind-spinning political concoctions, seasoned with prohibition and nativism.

All this played out against a backdrop of increasingly organized antislavery partisan activity. Even in New Hampshire, Franklin Pierce's home state, Free-Soilers tried to pick off Democrats. "I attended a Free Soil Convention at Lake Winnepiseogee" in late August 1853, Lucy Larcom told a friend, avowing that "I'm as strong as ever in the good cause!" There she met John Greenleaf Whittier, whose letter to the *National Era* explained that Pierce had exhausted "the spoils of office" for Granite State "Old Guard" Democrats, who were turning on him, opening opportunities for Free-Soilers. John P. Hale and former congressman Amos Tuck, both of whom Larcom met, spoke before three thousand listeners (with "the ladies occupying the front" seats). The high point was Hale's thundering speech against that wedge issue that was luring many Democrats and former Whigs into the Free-Soil fold, the Fugitive Slave Law. Larcom felt elevated both by the event's antislavery theme and the respectful treatment she was accorded. Having been escorted to dinner by the "Hon. Amos Tuck," she joked, "I dont know but *I* shall raise a claim to the title of 'Hon.' next."[9] She was finding an exalted place in a party close to her heart.

The Anthony Burns Case

Like temperance and nativism, the 1850 Fugitive Slave Law, which severely penalized runaway slaves and those who refused to turn them in, was a point of contention among many New Englanders, especially in Boston, where growing contempt for the Compromise of 1850 was palpable.[10] The city

FIGURE 11.1 Charlotte Forten Grimké. Photographs and Prints Division, Schomburg Center for Research in Black Culture, The New York Public Library, Astor, Lenox, and Tilden Foundations, New York.

erupted on May 24, 1854, when Anthony Burns, who had recently escaped his Virginian master, was arrested. Charlotte Forten (fig. 11.1), a sixteen-year-old African American living in nearby Salem, was incensed and disheartened.

A member of Philadelphia's boldly antislavery Forten-Purvis clan, Forten had moved to Salem in 1853 to attend the integrated Higginson Grammar School. There, she boarded with the Charles Lenox Remond family, which included noted black abolitionists who socialized with other antislavery warriors. Shortly after she arrived, she began keeping a highly literary diary considered today an important document of the antebellum free African American experience.[11] The Burns case filled her second entry.

The day after Burns was arrested upon U.S. commissioner Judge Edward Loring's warrant, Forten took up her pen. "Did not intend to write this evening, but have just heard of something which must ever rouse in the mind of every true friend of liberty feelings of deepest indignation." Burns was "arrested like a criminal in the streets . . . and is now kept strictly guarded." The level of armed control alarmed her. "A double police force is required, the military are in readiness; and all this is done to prevent a man, whom God has created in his own image, from regaining that freedom with which he, in common with every other human being, is endowed." After this reference to Genesis, she quoted poetry, as she often did, to express her feelings. In this case it was William Cowper's "The Task" (1785): "'My ear is pained / My soul is sick with every day's report / Of wrong and outrage, with which earth is filled." This blend of the biblical and poetic, enhanced by allusions to the American Revolution, marked her abolitionist rhetoric.[12]

Forten called upon friends and family to help her through the trauma. She visited her teacher Mary Shepard the next day, hoping Shepard would air her views about slavery. "She is, as I thought, thoroughly opposed to it, but does not agree with me in thinking that the churches and ministers are generally supporters of the infamous system." Forten remained adamant. "I believe it firmly." The following day at the train station, she met her father, Robert, who had intended to audit the May 26 Faneuil Hall meeting called by Boston's Vigilance Committee, devoted to thwarting the Fugitive Slave Law. Five thousand came to hear antislavery orator Wendell Phillips and Unitarian minister Theodore Parker entreat the public to rescue Burns. While Parker was rallying the masses, someone dashed in shouting that a group of African Americans—protesters from Tremont Temple—was gathering at the courthouse to storm it. Hundreds rushed out to help them. After battering down the door, two rioters burst inside, where a scuffle took place, resulting in the death of one of the marshal's deputies but not Burns's release. After that security tightened even more. Mayor Jerome Smith ordered the Boston and the Columbian artillery companies to aid the police.[13]

Although Robert had missed the event, he could see the next day that still "the excitement in Boston is very great." The rumor mill had the trial taking place on May 29. Charlotte shuddered. "We scarcely dare to think of what may be the result; there seems to be nothing too bad for those Northern tools of slavery to do." Until the decision, she "could scarcely think of anything else." Seeking solace, she read Elizabeth Barrett Browning's poem "The Runaway Slave at Pilgrim's Point" and had long chats with friends "on this all-absorbing subject." Sleep provided little refreshment.[14]

Forten traveled to Boston on May 31, several days into the proceedings. She strolled by the heavily guarded courthouse, which she described as "lawlessly converted into a prison, and filled with soldiers" who suspiciously eyed passersby through the windows. Their "air of insolent authority" made her "blood boil." Unintimidated, she proceeded with her best friend Sarah to the Melodeon, a large meeting hall, for the New England Anti-Slavery Society's annual convention. They heard abolitionist and women's rights activist Abby Kelley Foster plead with her female auditors to spur their male kin into action on Burns's behalf. While walking back to the depot afterward, Charlotte and Sarah "felt sick at heart" over the military presence, "ready at any time to prove themselves the minions of the South."[15] Violence could erupt in a moment's notice.

On June 1, Charlotte remained in Salem, minding the hair salon of a friend whose daughter was married that evening by a minister praying for Burns. Lynn's Mary Mudge noted the "Great excitement in Boston" as citizens exchanged intelligence about the proceedings and predicted the outcome. "What will that decision be?" Charlotte wondered, while blasting the absolute authority granted Loring to judge the case without a jury: "Alas! that any one should have the power to decide the right of a fellow being to himself!" She hoped for Burns's release due to insufficient evidence but realized "they will sacrifice him to propitiate the South." Although habeas corpus was suspended under the Fugitive Slave Law, as were fugitives' rights to legal counsel and self-testifying, Burns agreed to have lawyers Richard Henry Dana, Jr., and Charles Mayo Ellis defend him. Their defense did not sway the commissioner.[16]

The next day Loring made his decision. "Our worst fears are realized," Forten moaned. Burns "has been sent back to a bondage worse, a thousand times worse than death." She was horrified that the convicted man was paraded from the courthouse down to Long Wharf "surrounded by soldiers with bayonets fixed, a canon [*sic*] loaded, ready to be fired at the slightest sign." Domestic servant Lorenza Berbineau, who had recently heard Vigilance Committee members stir up the public at Tremont Temple, was likewise struck by the "company with drawn swords & a cannon loaded with balls." Protection was excessive: the National Boston Lancers, followed by companies of U.S. infantry and marines, walked ahead of Burns, who was himself surrounded by sixty volunteers and more marines. Behind them all was the formidable armed artillery and yet additional marines. Mayor Smith that day had proclaimed martial law, investing the militia's major general and the police chief with virtually unlimited power. That outraged Charlotte almost as much as Loring's decision: "these soldiers are to shoot down American citizens without mercy; and this . . . on the very soil where the Revolution of 1776 began." Taken-for-granted rights were taking a beating, as was her faith in the government. It would not be fully restored until the 1863 Emancipation Proclamation freed the slaves in the rebelling states.[17]

Kansas and Nebraska

Just before the Anthony Burns rendition hearing ended, the Kansas-Nebraska Bill was enacted, against which some New England women reacted. Upon the instigation of Southern congressmen who sought to overturn the 1820 Missouri Comprise prohibition of slavery above the 36° 30′ parallel in "northern Louisiana Territory," the bill, as presented by Senator Stephen Douglas, divided the area into two territories, Nebraska and Kansas, whose slave or free status would be determined by the people who lived there. The measure, signed into law on May 30, 1854, was vague about when or how that should happen. Northern Whig, Free-Soil, and even some Democratic reaction had been predictably negative.[18]

Some women grimly pondered the legislation. Former Lowell "mill girl" Lucy Larcom wrote a poem to expose the injustice. "I sent it to the Era at the time of the Nebraska Bill excitement—but it was not published," she later recalled. "I was in earnest . . . and really wanted to see it in print." At the Vergennes, Vermont, lyceum, Susan Tucker heard former governor Horace Eaton and state representative G. W. Grandy debate the "'Nebraska Bill'" months before its passage. Elizabeth Dwight probably sent to her sister Ellen in London a copy of Charles Sumner's February 21 Senate speech, "The Landmark of Freedom," opposing repeal of the Missouri Compromise. Later, in a letter to Elizabeth, Ellen praised Sumner's "beautiful application and extension" of a biblical phrase from Job, "'rushing on the bosses of the shield of the Almighty,'" to decry supporters' denial of the Declaration of Independence's dictum "all men are created equal." About a month after the bill's enactment, Ellen mentioned discussing "the Nebraska question" during a visit from the famous classicist George Grote. In July, Ellen told Elizabeth that she had been "studying over the set of Nebraska speeches" and called the measure "a piece of wrong-doing supported by sophistical reasoning, on the part of the South, which naturally aggravates the North."[19] Over the next two years many other New England women would voice concern over the bill's dire outcome in "Bleeding Kansas."

The Kansas Territory quickly turned into a nightmare. Because residents would decide its slave status, the proportion of pro- to antislavery voters made all the difference. Consequently, well-funded antislavery Northern emigrant aid societies sent a deluge of settlers to Kansas to vote free. Partly to counter this as territorial elections approached in March 1855, pro-slavery men streamed in over the border from Missouri to vote fraudulently. After the newly "elected" pro-slavery legislature passed outrageous legal codes, free-state advocates met at Lawrence in August to plan a constitutional convention in September that launched a "Free State party" and eventually its own constitution, one prohibiting slavery. As in the Dorr Rebellion, two governments claimed legitimacy. Most of our politicized women endorsed the Free Staters' constitution.[20]

In January 1856, President Pierce, warning of treason, refused to recognize the alternative government for which he blamed New England propagandists. When in February, he allowed the proslavery governor use of Fort Leavenworth's troops to quell unrest, Abigail Pierce exploded. "I cannot forbear to express my indignation and disgust, at the course which the President has taken with regard to Kansas," the minister's daughter wrote her sister on February 21. "I feel ashamed of my Country, and ashamed of my name"—meaning she and the President shared the same last name. Invoking the Father of the Country, she asked "What would Washington say, were he to appear in our midst? It seems almost a mockery for such people to celebrate his birthday." Certain that Kansas women were as important to the cause as men, she rejoiced that they "have shown themselves ready to aid there [*sic*] husbands in the cause of liberty and freedom."[21]

Women in New England would also help in various ways, especially when the 1856 campaign was under way. Concern for Free Kansas and partisanship against pro-slavery Democrats blurred. Eunice Cobb, a Boston Universalist minister's wife, was one of "a great number of ladies" who came out for a lecture by former Kansas governor Andrew Reeder, dismissed by President Pierce after vetoing the new pro-slavery government's bogus legislation. Cobb was certain that "No one, with a soul, could have heard him this afternoon, without saying in his heart, *Kansas must be free*!!!" Just before he spoke, newspapers reported that one delegation to the Republican National Convention would propose him for the vice presidency. Charlotte Forten claimed that a talk by Richard Henry Dana, Jr., a midwife of the Republican Party, "taught me more about Kansas than I ever knew before." Yet, as black abolitionist Charles Lenox Remond reminded her at another Kansas lecture, "Everybody has so much sympathy for the sufferers there, and so little for the poor slave, who for centuries has suffered tenfold worse miseries." Acting often as loci for Republican Party activism, societies sprang up in New England to aid the free-state settlers. In Concord, Massachusetts, an editor's wife, Harriet Robinson, and her neighbors pitched in by suspending their antislavery meetings to discuss and aid Kansas. "There have been several meetings among the Ladies lately to sew for the people of Kansas who are in want of clothing for the coming winter," she explained. "This town has contributed over two thousand dollars besides . . . over two hundred more in flannel shirts drawers, stockings &c." She and her husband gave twenty-six dollars, a hefty sum, "besides stockings and sewing, all we could spare." Anger as much as pity drove her to act. "The proslavery people seem determined to force slavery down the throats of the Kansas setlars [*sic*] but I hope they wont succeed," she seethed; "we at the east must do all we can to prevent it." It would be a short step from Kansas to Frémont, as we will see.[22]

Since some New Englanders had relatives living in the territory, it was easy to feel that the need to do something was pressing, especially after the

May 21, 1856, "Sack of Lawrence"—violent raids on the free-state settlement, by a posse with hundreds of pro-slavery Missourians. One Lawrence pioneer, Charlotte Hyde, told her Massachusetts in-laws of the fear she faced. "I know not what a day may bring forth." Night-watch shifts made her think of John Greenleaf Whittier's Frémont campaign poem, "Pass of the Sierra" (1856), about the explorer's trials. "I recalled the perfect imagery of the phrase 'Beyond their camp fire's *wall of dark*,'" a line from the poem that matched her own terror of what lurked in the shadows. For Elizabeth Pierce only divine intervention could end the suffering. "I feel as if I wanted to spend *all my spare time* in prayer for our poor degraded country."[23] Listening, learning, sewing, praying, and, ultimately, politicking—women did what they could to topple pro-slavery forces in Kansas.

The Know-Nothings

The Kansas-Nebraska Act was tied, especially in Massachusetts, to the fortunes of the American Party. Yet however much our women supported Free Kansas, almost none voiced an affiliation with the new party. This secret society of partisans—christened "Know-Nothings" by their detractors—was dedicated to sweeping out the old and tired party system, battling the "Popish threat," supporting temperance laws, and fighting against pro-slavery legislation, especially the Kansas-Nebraska Act. Many New England women might support all or any combination of these, yet the party vexed some of them.[24]

The overwhelming victory in the Massachusetts gubernatorial race of the Know-Nothings' pro-temperance, anti–Fugitive Slave Law candidate Henry J. Gardner, who won 63 percent of the votes cast on November 13, 1854, astounded some Whig-leaning women, as did the sweeping of the state legislature, which would be, with the exception of a few representatives, nativist. All Whig incumbents running for Congress were smashed by "Americans." "The 'Know Nothings' feel splendid to think they have got their Govenor [*sic*]," schoolteacher Mary Mudge winced. In Lynn, according to her, they celebrated with fire and thunder: "Burnt tar barrels fired rockets, guns; cannon &c. and illuminated." Elizabeth Dwight was even more fed up with Election Day. "Our Massachusetts politics are in such a depressing condition that I get perfectly miserable over them, whenever I think of them," she complained to her sister Ellen. "In consequence of a Coalition between the Know-Nothings & Democrats we shall probably have a gentleman . . . at the head of the Commonwealth, whose only recommendation to public notice, is that he combines the characters of *fool, liar & coxcomb*." The "coalition" she mentions refers to a wide swath of the electorate.

The Know-Nothings nabbed a majority of Free-Soilers and Democrats and a sizable portion of Whig votes, as well as ballots by newcomers. "These Coalitions are enough to drive any honest men & women to despair," she railed. She took comfort in gossip that "the Know-Nothings will kill themselves by their Candidate, & [in] *another* year will be powerless."[25] They would indeed fade, but not so quickly.

Dwight followed "the disgraceful doings of the Know-Nothings" in the months to come and sent Ellen clippings about them. Joint Free-Soil–American Party attempts in 1855 to remove Anthony Burns's judge, Edward Loring, disturbed her deeply. Although she abhorred his ruling, she valued the sanctity of an independent judiciary. It "is a phrase which we were brought up on, & this infringement of it is really a frightful warning of the lengths to which the violence of party-feeling may carry people." A measure passed by the legislature, but vetoed by the governor, preventing the simultaneous holding of a federal office and a state judgeship—for Loring, as Suffolk County probate judge, had both—infuriated her. While admitting "I, for one, am too much of an Anti Slavery woman to object," she vented to her sister, "this individual persecution makes my blood boil, for I have no manner of doubt that Judge Loring was as conscientious as the best of the Know-Nothings, & he did what he did knowing that it was the most unpopular act possible." Dwight thus stood against the many women who inundated the state legislature with anti-Loring petitions and who attended the three public hearings held in response. Dwight sent Ellen clippings about further Know-Nothing attempts to remove Loring plus ones about the party's "Grand Worshipful Instructor" Joseph Hiss, who was ejected from the state legislature after his scandalous behavior on the "Joint Special Committee on the Inspection of Nunneries and Convents." His improper remarks to some nuns and pilfering of state funds for a prostitute caused a stir.[26]

Disreputable as it was to some women, the party soon walked onto the national stage in February 1856 via the ascension of one of their own, Nathaniel P. Banks, a former Democrat, to the speakership of the U.S. House of Representatives. It was not an easy ascent for the anti-Nebraska politician. Although he was attractive to antislavery representatives, opposition was so strong that after a month he could only achieve a plurality, not a majority. Anti-Nebraska advocates were restive. By December 30, antislavery machine-shop worker Martha Osborne Barrett was fed up. "Congress has been in session four weeks—and as yet the House has not yet chosen a Speaker." Referring to the deadlock with a pro-Nebraska Democrat, she scoffed, "Slavery and liberty are having a hard struggle in our country." Although she allowed "God alone knows which will triumph," she was convinced "*right must* be victorious." Only on February 2, 1856, was Banks elected, without a single Southern vote, on the 133rd round. Charlotte Forten heard the good news on February 3 while waiting patiently for William Lloyd Garrison to speak. "Just before the lecture Mr. Innis announced the fact of Mr. [Nathaniel] Banks' election, which was received with tumultous [*sic*] applause."[27] Although Forten did not openly identify herself with a party, she was sympathetic to the emerging Republicans, who saw in Banks's speakership a signal victory.

The Caning of Charles Sumner

Forten was, after all, an admirer of Free-Soiler Charles Sumner, who helped found the Republican Party in Massachusetts. Shortly after he made waves at the September 7, 1854, Republican nominating convention in Worcester, Forten and her friends "had quite a spirited discussion on Mr. [Charles] Sumner and his party." In November 1855, she heard him speak "for the first time." She had some qualms but genuinely embraced him. "He said many excellent things, but I cannot agree with very many of his views—particularly with his reverence for the Constitution and the Union." Nevertheless, Sumner struck a chord: "he yet has a warm, true heart, and certainly he is an elegant and eloquent orator."[28] After Sumner was caned in the Senate for his famous May 1856 "Crime against Kansas" speech that unflinchingly impugned the Kansas-Nebraska Act, bitingly reproved Missourians' raid on Kansas's polls, and mercilessly assailed his pro-slavery colleagues, she revered him.

On May 22, 1856, Congressman Preston Brooks, after reading the aforementioned speech, which he deemed gravely insulting to his cousin, Senator Andrew Butler, and the state of South Carolina that they both represented, repeatedly whacked his gold-headed cane into pieces on Sumner's head as he sat in his Senate seat writing, until Sumner was blood soaked, cut to the bone, and unconscious. Abby Stimson, in her usual terse way, merely stated, "Attack upon Senator Sumner at Washington," but some New England women and girls registered anger, even trauma. "'No matter what I am doing,'" one from Massachusetts wrote him, "'I have a sort of consciousness of something black and wicked.'" Sumner's long and painful recuperation kept him confined during much of the presidential campaign season. In September, Republican Harriet Robinson regretted that "Poor Mr Sumner is disabled by the cowards blow from taking his noble part in the present contest, but let us hope that his sufferings will not have been in vain." Republicans, hoping to exploit the violent incident for campaign ends, pressured Sumner to act. He returned to Boston on November 3 to a huge procession that carried him to the State House, where Governor Gardner regaled him. Charlotte Forten hailed his enthusiastic reception. "Coming as it did from the *heart* of the people it must have been exceedingly gratifying to the noble man. I long to see him." Forten's respect for Sumner had considerably deepened. She eventually spied him, twice, at Boston's December 1856 antislavery fair. "I feasted my eyes," she glowed. "Sumner looks pale and weak but still bears the unmistakable stamp of 'nature's nobleman.'" On February 22, 1858, she wrote with "considerable trepidation, to the noble [Charles] Sumner, for his autograph." Five days later she received two packages from him, one with a signed speech extract and the other with "valuable autographs" from senators, the poet Henry Wadsworth Longfellow, and sundry duchesses and earls. "How very, very kind," she chirped. "To an entire stranger, too."[29] He had won her heart.

The Election of 1856

By the time of Sumner's caning, the campaign of 1856 was about to get under way. Already in late February, the Know-Nothings had nominated former Whig president Millard Fillmore, Taylor's successor, to run on a platform that came far short of condemning the Kansas-Nebraska Act and slavery, and thus drove Northern party members to hold their own conference. James Buchanan, a former U.S. senator and representative from Pennsylvania who had little to do with the act since he was out of the country as minister to England during the debate over and passage of the law was strategically selected by the Democrats at their convention. Their platform, retaining faith in popular sovereignty, upheld Kansas-Nebraska. John C. Frémont, the former Democrat known more for having crossed the Rocky Mountains in the 1840s than for his unsubstantial political career, became the Republicans' nominee. Their platform came out against slavery and its territorial extension. It called for Kansas's admittance as a free state.[30]

By June, women began writing about Frémont as someone other than the "Pathfinder." Frances Douglass, the young wife of a Portland crockery clerk, was thrilled on June 18 that her husband "brought the news of Col. Fremont's election for the Republican party's candidate." That evening she and some neighbors went out to "see the illuminations" that lit up the town. Eunice Cobb was "greatly interested in" John Bigelow's hot-off-the-press Frémont campaign biography that her husband brought home in July. Of course, Buchanan had his followers, but they barely left a trace in our research. One Portland Democrat, evidently sharing a roof with the opposition, "illuminated her half of the house" during a Loco torchlight procession.

But, by and large, politicized women who committed their partisanship to paper in 1856 were Republicans.[31]

By August, Log-Cabin-style razzle-dazzle had mesmerized Frémont women. Arguably, in 1856 rank-and-file Republican women came close to surpassing the mobilization of their 1840 counterparts. In some ways, they differed from their predecessors. The most active among them resembled radical Dorrites in that they spoke more often (and more overtly) at rallies and published campaign propaganda. New England women rode to rallies with male delegations and occupied carriages in daylight and torchlight processions, sometimes as representations of the states. Those embodying the South appropriately donned mourning black.[32] Since 1840, some women had become even more conspicuous campaigners.

First lady–hopeful Jessie Benton Frémont was as much the star as her husband (fig. 11.2). Her hands-on involvement in the campaign, contributions to Bigelow's biography of her husband, and relation to the famous former senator Thomas Hart Benton, her father, all contributed to her magnetism. Her strained relationship with the Democratic paterfamilias over her elopement, partisan issues, and, of course, the campaign probably resonated with women politically at odds with their own kin. Her maverick spirit was ever enlivening rallies. On August 7, Harriet Robinson went to the "Freemont Mass meeting" in Fitchburg, Massachusetts, attended by ten thousand, who gathered for speeches, a procession, and a picnic by which "the ladies of Fitchburg not only supplied the friends of Jessie" but "thousands of John's friends," too. Jessie's "friends" came first in the hearts and minds of those who dished up the snacks. One Salem Normal School student who attended the "Great Fremont Meeting at Manchester Mass." in September probably heard the "rousing cheers for John and Jessie" drowning out the rain. Eunice Cobb would have seen the Jessie tableau, a portrait surrounded by wreaths and cupids, aloft in the huge October 29 Boston torchlight procession. Never before had women witnessed such public endorsement of a potential first lady. In her honor, Martha Barrett's nephew was christened "*Jesse Fremont*," a gender-neutral name. One woman even reported hearsay that Jessie had "received the nomination of her husband" with the words, "'I am perfectly satisfied—his nomination by such a party, at such a crisis, is the greatest honor he could arrive at.'" She supposedly "then ran to the Piano, and sung, 'wh'all be king but Charlie?'" The story's veracity matters less than its retelling as evidence of New England Republican women's fervor over Jessie.[33]

Eighteen-forty-style spunk was making an impact on girls as well as women. "You dont know what great Fremont excitement we are having here, in which all our family partake," a minister's wife wrote to her sister from

FIGURE 11.2 "John and Jessie" Frémont 1856 campaign ribbon. © David J. & Janice L. Frent Collection, CORBIS, Seattle.

Providence in August. Having been back to Massachusetts to visit her mother, she vouched for equivalent Frémont frenzy there, despite a show of third-party following. "My girls are very indignant at the prevalence of *Fillmorism* in Brookline and say 'how can we leave such free atmosphere as this,'" meaning Providence, "'for such a place?'" Youngsters were well aware of partisan divides. Girls too young to remember 1840 were as caught up in the 1856 election as those old enough to recall. Apparently, fourteen-year-old Agnes Poor, who, as we have seen, was gung ho for Henry Clay in 1844, still clung to his all-but-defunct party. "Tell Agnes," the girl's aunt wrote to her mother, "even the *strait Whig* says, if he had a vote, he should give it for Fremont." Girls could be every bit as passionate as women. At one Sandwich, New Hampshire, procession, a stonemason's wife was amused that "the girl that stood next to me kept crying 'Hurrah for Fremont' 'Hurrah for Fremont' and waving her handkerchief." She also caught the marchers' attention. They "stopped and cheered us," the writer blushed. East Greenwich, Rhode Island, teens rehearsed for adult civic participation in campaigns by joining clubs at their school, where Millard Fillmore partisans were aggressive recruiters. Mary Congdon, a thirteen-year-old sea captain's daughter, was lured on October 23 into one at which her classmate Julia Pierce was elected president. There, Mary and a friend were enlisted to speak at the next get-together. She began drafting a speech that evening, but two days later she demurred that "mamma does not think it best for me" and ditched the effort. Whether Cynthia Congdon thought speechifying was off-limits for girls or only on Fillmore's behalf is unclear. The Fillmore girls also tried to snare fifteen-year-old Mary Dawley, the granddaughter of a miller, who was at the meeting with Congdon. Dawley was curious about all things partisan—the town's Frémont meeting or the post office's new Buchanan flag. She went away from a subsequent gathering with skepticism, however. Dawley granted, "it was very interesting, but I was not convinced that I was wrong," meaning she was right about the Republicans. She followed up on October 29. "We (the Fremont girls) met at the school-room this evening from 6 to 7 and joined the Hillside Fremont Club." When Election Day came round, Dawley marked it in her journal.[34]

Of course, girls and women could express their devotion to Frémont without going to clubs or spectacular events. They could honor him in letters and diaries. Mostly, they fretted because so much was at stake in this election—the extension or containment of slavery and, indeed, the fate of the Union itself. A minister's wife confided in late October, "I tremble when I think of the future if we have not a Republican President." To her it would be devastating. "If it were not for my faith in an overruling Providence," she wept, "my heart would die within me." Harriet Robinson also feared the worst: "if Freemont [*sic*] is not elected what will become of us, the slaves and the Kansas people?" She answered herself, "I shall think the end is near."[35] To countless other New Englanders, such an outcome would, indeed, be apocalyptic.

On November 4 Frémont, who took every New England state, nonetheless lost to Democrat James Buchanan, 114 to 174 in the Electoral College, with Fillmore getting the remaining eight. Most Republican women were dumbfounded. Frances Jocelyn in New Haven shrieked, "Buchanan is elected President!!!" One New Hampshire woman could only tersely muster, "The Buchananites firing cannons." Harriet Robinson snorted, "slavery reigns there is nothing to be said." Only Lucy Larcom kept up her spirits. "The agony is over, but the end is not yet," she soothed her doomsayer friend. "I feel as if a great triumph had been achieved." Indeed, it was remarkable that the fledgling party did so well. It had proven itself, in conquering the Northeast and vanquishing the American Party, to be the Democrats' major rival. And although it has taken some sharp twists and turns along the way, it would remain so until the present day.[36]

Larcom prophesied that Frémont would "occupy the White House yet."[37] Although she was wrong, a Republican, Abraham Lincoln, would win the presidency in 1860. In the next chapter we will look at women's continuing support of the party, their fight against pro-slavery forces, and their horror at the disintegration of the Union that led to the Civil War.

12

"I Read the Papers as Hard as I Can"

Women Face the Nightmare of Civil War

By December 1860, Elizabeth Dwight Cabot of Brookline, Massachusetts, was feeling lonely for her sister Ellen in London (fig. 12.1). Elizabeth had dreamed of setting up a vacation home by the seashore for her sister's anticipated visit, but with recent reports about economic "panic," "depreciated paper currency," and "scarcity of specie," she wondered if she could afford the rent. Making matters worse, South Carolina, which had been threatening to leave the Union for decades, was now poised to do so in the wake of Abraham Lincoln's November 1860 election. "If Secession comes," she wrote Ellen, "I am afraid we may all be too poor for any extra expenses." She was not optimistic about the state of the Union, either. "The Secession of some of the States seems inevitable & the only question is how many." She tried in vain to understand their position "that Slavery is a divine institution & that we are '*Atheistic*' in our view of it." She puzzled, "I can't realize it though I read the papers as hard as I can."[1] There was simply no justification for slavery, even if, by opposing it, slave states might leave the Union.

Ten days after her letter, South Carolina seceded from the Union, followed by five more Southern states in January 1861. Ellen was mortified. She wrote back, "we have become the Dis–United States;— . . . our history under this great constitution, is over,—just 70 years from Washington to Buchanan." The republic was falling apart. "[T]o live to see one's own country pointed at as a ruin . . . ,—to see her sink to the rear among nations, who was the greatest of them all," was more than she could bear.[2] Unlike Elizabeth, Ellen was willing to compromise on slavery to preserve the Union, even if by force.

Although the two sisters were mutually apprehensive about the onset of

FIGURE 12.1 Elizabeth Dwight Cabot and Ellen Twisleton, c. 1846–50. Courtesy of The Schlesinger Library, Radcliffe Institute, Harvard University, Cambridge, Mass.

war, the partisan lenses through which they tried to understand it would differ so much that they, at times, in their extensive transatlantic correspondence, would cease "political talk" altogether. The Civil War in the nation, which broke out in April 1861, threatened to have its private counterpart in their interpersonal conflict—at times almost to the point of rupture. For both women were passionately uncompromising about their divergent politics, even though they grew up in a household dominated by a Boston Whig politician, a merchant who died suddenly in 1849 leaving them orphaned. They thus presumably began with a shared partisan orientation. Elizabeth had closely followed the political evolution of the 1850s that led to the Republican Party's formation and embraced the new party with a relish. By contrast, Ellen had left the United States for England in 1852 when she married Edward Twisleton, a Liberal politician. Her political sensibility developed outside of the partisan ferment of the 1850s and so remained essentially that of a Whig circa 1852, the year of Daniel Webster's death and, arguably, that of the Whig Party as a national force. Like him and, ironically, like many Northern Democrats in 1860, such as Persis Sibley Andrews, Ellen put a premium on saving the Union, even at the cost of unpalatable measures to keep it together, like the Compromise of 1850, and bemoaned the potential violence ensuing over the nation's breakup. Like Rip Van Winkle returning to his Hudson Valley village on voting day after the Revolutionary War had transformed it, Ellen had difficulty understanding the new political idioms, in her case those of Republicanism.[3]

Comparing Elizabeth's and Ellen's political disagreement provides a way of marking the distance that some partisan women in New England had come from the days most of them strongly objected to the Mexican War. Now most Republican women supported aggressive military action, not just against another nation, but against a region within the United States. The scale of conflict and the extent of the resulting loss of life would far, far exceed anything previously imagined, yet nary a female voice advocating peace short of victory could be heard in Republican ranks. A sea change had taken place.

This chapter examines the nature of that change, not only through the two sisters' pained colloquy over the war, but also by summoning a host of other women, of varying sorts, who give their own insights into the shifting circumstances underpinning their partisanship. Throughout we compare their take on key issues of the years 1857 to 1861—including John Brown's raid on Harpers Ferry, the 1860 election, and secession. The chapter ends with a peek into the war years to plumb the fate of women's partisanship in light of the patriotic imperative. We begin, however, by listening to what these New England women were thinking about during the transition to James Buchanan's administration and its earliest years, as war clouds were just forming.

The Early Buchanan Years, 1857–58

Compared with the start of previous presidencies since 1840, except maybe Franklin Pierce's, Democrat James Buchanan's March 1857 inauguration hardly impressed New England women. One from Meriden, Connecticut, merely registered it, while a Hartford antislavery advocate mentioned "a long procession escorted James Buchanan to the Capitol where he took the constitutional oath." A Framingham, Massachusetts, student was skeptical of his inaugural address: it had "much that is wise and some that savors too strong of the worst principles of the democratic party"—in other words, that popular sovereignty regarding slavery in the territories would prevail and that federal protection of slave ownership would be guaranteed.[4] Hers was a common Republican view of unfolding events.

Perhaps the most important of these was one that would keenly alter many women's lives and would set the course for future Republican Party electoral victories in the North: the Panic of 1857, which led to a sustained period of economic contraction. Between October 1855 and October 1858, Elizabeth Cabot spent much of her time in Europe, but she was home briefly for her wedding just as economic panic struck. She had long been living comfortably in Boston with her merchant brother-in-law and her sister. But in September 1857, her life suddenly changed. "Charles H. Mills and Co. have failed," she sadly chronicled. The downturn that ate up 90 percent of Charles's (and, therefore, Elizabeth's) fortune began in August with the collapse of the Ohio Life Insurance and Trust Company. By September, other banks were dropping like flies. "My wedding dress is not made and will not be," she divulged and asked Ellen to find the "wisest and cheapest" housing for her and her husband James Elliot Cabot's European honeymoon. "If we are not prosperous people we are, at least, loving," she sighed. Other New England women shuddered at the Panic's arrival. Abby Stimson found that "Banks suspended specie paymt," and a Bostonian beheld "every day new failures, . . . such a state of things as has not been known since 1837." A Hartford resident counted "2,705" bankruptcies by January's end. One staunch Republican feared for her party press's life. The economy would not fully recover until mid-1860, only to dip again with secession threats.[5]

Buchanan and his party naturally would be blamed for the financial convulsion but also for not resolving the looming sectional crisis or even tamping down increasingly tense debates over slavery. New England women engaged these partisan controversies by attending Republican meetings and balls, antislavery fairs, sewing societies, and lectures, reading relevant news and books, and even by arguing among themselves. One Maine student at a Delaware academy up in arms over the slavery issue witnessed a scuffle between her music teacher and a classmate: "Miss Boylan is a whig—and they are growing quite warm." Even normally diffident women like Charlotte Forten were spurred to go public. She penned a sly "Parody on 'Red, White and Blue'" that was sung at an 1858 black abolitionist festival commemorating Boston Massacre martyr Crispus Attucks. At this time, women noted orators such as George W. Curtis, Gerrit Smith, and Wendell Phillips who were merging women's rights and antislavery. Charlotte Forten described Curtis's "Fair Play for Women" as being "as much Anti-Slavery as Woman's Rights." The growing awareness of first-wave feminism caught some off guard, though. "'Ladies dont vote,'" Mary Poor's niece declared. "'God would not make them do such a hard thing, would he Auntie?'"[6] Children parroted backward-looking adults who may have seen voting, in the tumultuous 1850s with its new parties, as particularly onerous.

The Approach of War

Indeed, in the late 1850s some women simply navigated the chaos to avoid storms. For example, when Elizabeth Cabot returned to Massachusetts from Europe in October 1858, she did not immediately enter the fray of U.S. politics. She took up German and settled into some good books that she wrote about to Ellen. Martin Luther's *Psalter* she found "very refreshing as I am sure not to come upon a Mephistopheles, or a mortgage to make me miserable."[7] The Panic yet menaced her security.

Elizabeth could not long suppress the political impulse, however. Soon she was sending Ellen news clippings about speeches, including one by Democrat Stephen A. Douglas, "a good statement of the views & present position of the majority of the Democratic party," meaning the Northern antislavery faction. But Elizabeth, albeit with a decided slant, gave Ellen both sides of the slavery argument, perhaps suspecting that their father's "Cotton Whiggery" remained strong in her. She sent a speech by Republican senator William Henry Seward of New York and one by Democratic senator James Henry Hammond of South Carolina. The former she predicted "no doubt has an eye on the next election"—he did—while she dispatched the latter with: "The condition of his mind is really amusing."[8] Ellen in return mailed English papers and wrote about international affairs.

Elizabeth was protective of her sister, knowing how embarrassed she could get amid her circles in England over U.S. controversies. Like Harriett Low, Ellen, a representative American in a foreign land, felt the eyes of all Englishmen and women upon her. As we will see, to a certain extent they were. Her husband, Edward Twisleton, noted for being on more government commissions than anyone else of his day, was Lord Saye and Sele's brother, and a good friend of Thomas Carlyle and sundry lords, duchesses, and ladies.[9] Ellen blanched under their aristocratic scrutiny as she found herself called upon to account for American affairs.

Aware of Ellen's dilemma, Elizabeth took steps to shield her sister from some bad domestic news generated by Buchanan's cronies. When word broke of Democratic representative Daniel E. Sickles's April 1859 murder trial for killing his wife's lover, U.S. district attorney Philip Barton Key, she suppressed it. Little could she know it was splattered on London's front pages. Fleet Street publishers had reason to take note: while serving James Buchanan as secretary of legation in England, Sickles had caused a stir by bringing his mistress with him. Ellen confronted Elizabeth, who was sorry for the omission. "I knew you would suffer from it," she explained in April and then came clean. "My dear, I haven't a rag of comfort about the Sickles fight," she sheepishly replied. "It is the worst disgraceful thing that has happened yet in Washington." All Elizabeth could do was to send a hymn to assuage her.[10]

Ellen had other woes alienating her from society. The same month, Edward lost his bid for Parliament, another insufferable humiliation she admitted made her green with "envy of the more fortunate." Ellen's aloof coteries were becoming grating. Elizabeth sympathized. "I agree with you through every pore of my mind and body about an aristocratic form of society," she soothed Ellen; "It seems to me neither natural nor Christian." Apparently, Ellen's husband upheld the peerage. "I love Edward very much," Elizabeth replied, "and I wish I didn't disagree with him."[11] Like Harriet Low, Elizabeth was too much a republican to tolerate titles.

Yet hints of a vestigial Websterian Whiggery that would divide Ellen from her sister's brand of U.S. Republicanism soon emerged. Referring to a sometime Cotton Whig who resisted the Republican surge, Elizabeth wrote back to Ellen, "I am sorry I didn't read Mr Everett's speech, since you liked it." She meant she regretted not sharing the experience of it with her and nothing else about it. "I am so sick of him, that I never think of reading what he says these days." By dispensing with this tersely, she left it ambiguous whether it was overexposure that put her off or that he repeatedly disappointed her with his conservative stances. Despite receiving such subtle deflections, Ellen persisted in taking up politically charged topics. She brought up Charles Sumner, who was sojourning in Europe in 1859. His condemnation of the South, with which England traded, perturbed one of Ellen's friends, who feared war would be the logical outcome of Sumner's agitation. Elizabeth tried to mollify Ellen: "We think it very likely the North & South struggle will work itself off by degrees . . . without any great crisis." Elizabeth warned her, "it may be a slow fight," but trusted it would deploy "more words than swords for weapons."[12] Weapons, however, would ultimately prevail, which Elizabeth may have suspected by not taking "swords" off the table. She avoided disclosing too openly her dawning belief in the necessity and righteousness of force.

By early 1860, Ellen was questioning the Northern Republican position. She even suggested antislavery advocates were "'doing evil.'" Elizabeth kept her cool and responded, "I don't think we are '*doing* evil,' only resisting evil, in opposing the *extension* of slavery, & that is what makes the South so angry." Ellen also let loose about John Brown, who in October 1859 had raided the United States Armory and Arsenal at Harpers Ferry, Virginia, to arm and free slaves. Elizabeth was not so quick to condemn him. "Also I think John Brown *did* very wrong, but I think he did a wrong thing in the right direction & that his courage will help men of weaker conscience, tho' perhaps better judgements, towards the right." The tide in New England was against Ellen, for many Northern women called Brown a hero, even though he was found guilty of treason.[13]

With Brown, a less than full and immediate condemnation of violence, even embrace of it, had entered Republican women's discourse. "The Harper's Ferry affair has aroused the public mind as it seldom [has] been aroused," the factory worker Martha Barrett resounded. "A deep sympathy extends through the whole north" while "The South is frightened as well may be." For her it was "the beginning of the end" of slavery. "It may be by the shedding of rivers of blood," she forewarned, praying "God grant that it be not so." For others, Brown represented passion unleashed. "'How I love that man!'" Mary Poor gushed. "'I don't blame Brown for fighting. When I feel mad, real mad. . . . I want to fight too and pull somebody's hair.'" Just before Brown was hung on December 2, an astonished Lucy Larcom recorded the fact with an exclamation point and wondered, "Do we live in Christendom?" With outrage at the execution later that month of Brown's followers and scorn for Southerners' "fiery speeches threatening dissolution of the Union," Barrett adopted the slogan "Let them storm." She later attended a benefit meeting for Brown's family where she heard Emerson, Wendell Phillips, and James Freeman Clarke sanctify the martyr. His legacy lived on at Elizabeth Dwight Sedgwick's school in Lenox, Massachusetts, where student Ellen Wright hung a portrait of Brown much to her roommate's horror. "It creates quite an excitement," she proudly informed her mother. "Abby Teackle . . . hopes it wont make her wicked to see that dreadful man—& we join her in her ardent desire."[14] Ellen had zero tolerance for issue-waffling classmates. Brown's martyrdom had galvanized belligerence.

By the time Elizabeth wrote again in April 1860 about the bungled arrest and release of Franklin B. Sanborn, one of the "Secret Six" backing Brown, and about the Senate's "Mason Committee" formed to investigate the Harpers Ferry raid, Ellen's health was sinking in seeming concert with Whiggish unionism's dying gasps. It is unclear what ailed her, but she endured intense bouts of pain, mental disorientation, depression, and weakness. She had long lost the strength even to clip newspapers and had Edward do it for her. Elizabeth insisted she "write *very short* letters," assuring her, "We shall all understand it." Despite her frailty, Ellen broached ever more divisive topics. She asked about Republicans' purportedly wild charges in the *Tribune* of Democratic bribery in the March Rhode Island elections. Ellen was probably confusing Rhode Island with Connecticut, about which similar reports circulated. The Democratic *New York Herald* ballyhooed the rumors to associate Republicans with extremism.[15] Ellen bought into them hook, line, and sinker, suggesting her readiness to think ill of the new party. She would eventually openly repudiate it.

The 1860 Election

In May 1860, Abraham Lincoln and Hannibal Hamlin were nominated as the Republican candidates for president and vice president. Elizabeth gave Ellen a thumbnail biography, painting Lincoln as "a rough customer, but a very upright & straight-forward one; somewhat of the General Jackson order." Even her husband Elliot could not vouch for his grace. "The Boston Courier . . . calls him 'a tall, course, illiterate man' wh. I dare say may be correct." Ellen was evidently displeased with Elizabeth's description—another stab at U.S. dignity. Still, Elizabeth could not help but make fun of the vice presidential nominee's brothers' names: "Africa, Asia, America, & Europe" Hamlin. She teased, "you have a great deal to be thankful for that this is only Hannibal." It was a way of creating some humorous space for the two sisters to share. Elizabeth confessed to Ellen her uncertainty of Lincoln's election, possibly recognizing Ellen's conservative unionism. "I am firm in the faith that the Democrats will yet unite on someone & carry the day, but I hope I am mistaken." She was wrong, of course. The party would split on North-and-South lines at its June Baltimore convention and eventually nominate two candidates, Stephen Douglas and John C. Breckinridge.[16]

As the campaign began political talk lessened between Elizabeth and Ellen owing to the latter's poor health, her husband's political career moves, and perhaps the fact that discussing candidates would leach out the two sisters' differences too much. But other women were worked up about the upcoming contest. Most of the activity, as represented in our material, was Republican. Mary Poor, now a New York transplant, "walked out to see the Republican ratification meeting" in June at the Cooper Institute. The next month in Kingston, Massachusetts, a ship carpenter's wife took note of Republican "wide awake Club" speech making in a local shop. One Lynn, Massachusetts, schoolteacher, wishing she could engage in forensic debate—she even proclaimed, "*I wish I were* a *Man*!"—campaigned in conventionally gendered ways. Until Election Day she wore a medal bearing an ambrotype of Lincoln and Hamlin. Much more problematic was partisanship for Ellen Wright, whose classmates were mainly conservative. Bel Edwards, she grumbled, "is the only Republican except ourselves, and we get *thrashed*!" Worse still was the Southern presence. "There is *Tellulah* Law, from New Orleans, whose father has slaves, and who is a lady like, pale goose, and Minnie Oglesby from St. Louis, who is a lovely looking creature, but cant endure any one who is *Jno.* [i.e., *John*] *Brown* or Anti S.[lavery]!"[17]

Beyond these Republican voices were others less stridently partisan. One would think Sarah P. E. Hale favored the Constitutional Union Party because her brother Edward Everett was its vice presidential nominee, but she would reveal to one of his sons the January after the election that she "was too staunch a Republican to wish even the [John] Bell and Everett ticket to prevail." Yet she left open whether she "might have felt differently" if her brother had headed the ticket—she viewed the number two slot as an "insult." Any sympathy she had for the reactionary party led by ex-Whigs and former Know-Nothings and simplistically standing for the Union's preservation may have been purely on her brother's behalf. During election season, she recorded in her diary without commentary Boston's competing Republican "Wide Awakers" and Union torchlight processions, and that the "election [is] going on spiritedly." Bostonian Caroline Curtis, whose husband reveled in the Whig glory days, may have also simply tolerated his "Bell & Everett" activities, for she generally took no note of the party.[18]

Circumspection characterized some Democratic women, too. Even before her husband's death in 1852 Persis Andrews had been gravitating toward the Democratic Party. As her former Whig Party faded, she had scarcely anywhere else to go. She remained in the Democratic fold when she married another politico in 1855, Alvah Black, her husband's sometime business partner. In early 1860 he was away from Paris Hill in Augusta serving as a Maine representative and later that year would be renominated for office. He would campaign actively for Douglas, gubernatorial nominee Ephraim K. Smart, and himself. Given the momentousness of the election, however, Persis did not reflect as much on the times as she did in days of yore, but rather acted as chronicler of partisan events. For example, on July 1, she reported, "Mr. Black went to Portland Wednesday & returned Friday. State Convention to nominate Democratic candidates for Governor." Yet she could also describe in a similarly straightforward manner the opposition's doings, as on July 15: "Tuesday was the Great Republican Mass Meeting in Paris-Hill. . . . The meeting was held under the shade of the elms in front of the old Hamlin Mansion. Israel Washburn spoke.—Han. Hamlin," the gubernatorial and vice presidential nominees. "There were four Bands present & a 'Wide awake Club' from Portland who sang songs." Only in December 1860 did she reveal a deliberate course of restrictive diary keeping: "I do not often write of State or National affairs, in my book." The Union's imminent shattering gave her leave to do so, however.[19] Because the Republican vice presidential candidate was the town's favorite son, there may have been practical reasons to censor her thoughts—to keep them away from prying eyes.

Still, her partisanship occasionally appeared. She "was much disappointed in not being able" to attend a Democratic mass meeting at Wheeler Island near Dixfield where her daughter Lotte had been born. The now-grown girl had gone with her stepfather, who presided and made a speech. Clearly, women were still welcome at the Democratic gatherings. When a similar event took place in Paris Hill about a week before, she exulted, "They have a splendid Douglas Flag suspended over the street by a chord [*sic*] reaching from the B. Church to Bate's." In the same diary entry she displays some of her old punditry: "Mr. Black is again nominated for the Senate, but there is very little expectation that Democrats will elect in this state this year—tho' they fully expect to make some gain. Mr. Black is very popular, & will concentrate the whole vote of his party. Therefore his partisans wo'd not release him from this nomination." Even though she used "they" instead of "we," an entry from the eve of the September state election hints that she may have been campaigning. "I have the past week washed, ironed, baked in the brick oven—had a dressmaker one day—went to a political discussion six miles off one eve[g]." Her efforts were in vain, as she tersely conceded at the end of the month: "Election is over & the Republicans carried almost everything."[20]

Down in Massachusetts, when balloting day in the November presidential contest drew near, Elizabeth Cabot kept her epistolary tone with Ellen upbeat. "Tomorrow settles the Election & we Republicans are very confident of success," she beamed. She was hardly being disingenuous. Fall elections in Pennsylvania, Ohio, and Indiana showed the party's strength. Still, she had to admit, "There is 'no end' of talk of disunion at the South." Southern newspapers were spewing out threats of secession if Lincoln was elected, and South Carolina's governor echoed them the day before election. But she like many other Republicans dismissed it: "wise folks say it is all bluster & that a baby might as well say it would separate from its mother since the South would simply starve & go naked without the North."[21] It was wishful thinking.

Secession

On November 6, in an election of unprecedented turnout, Lincoln took all of the North except New Jersey and won decisively with 180 of 303 electoral votes, albeit with only 40 percent of popular vote nationwide. He garnered

62 percent of the vote in New England. His victory would rally Southerners to sever ties with the Union. Elizabeth was reluctant to ruffle Ellen even though South Carolina's legislature had, in response, unanimously voted to hold an election for delegates to a secession convention and Georgia's governor had asked the state's legislature to consider immediate secession. "It is difficult to see how South Carolina can secede alone, and no other State but Georgia seems to sympathize with her," she consoled Ellen. "So we wait and don't feel particularly serious." She commended Lincoln "for holding his tongue so steadily & making no further declarations of policy" but castigated Buchanan, now the lame-duck president, for helping "the mischief as far as possible"—perhaps referring to his easy dismissal of his general-in-chief of the army's pleas to garrison Southern federal forts, which would be claimed by seceding states as their own.[22] Still, she was not apprehensive.

Other women felt calm before the storm too. Elizabeth's mother-in-law, who had lived through the 1832–33 nullification crisis, put forward that "South Carolina behaved much worse then." One Down-Easter teaching in Delaware, a border state, assured her parents, "Since election all is very quiet here." In Lenox, Massachusetts, Ellen Wright listened placidly to her teacher read aloud Southern secession speeches "so we know a little." She was unflappable, like Lucy Larcom, who truly hankered for a fight. "I wish they would let S. Carolina Secede, just to see what they would do," she chortled. "What kind of a muss they would get themselves into. . . . I dont see any harm in letting them split off and live in their own unprincipled way."[23] By the end of November, Elizabeth would agree with her.

The only thing that truly worried Elizabeth about secession was the effect it would have on her pocketbook. Indeed, the New York stock market was sluggish and banks, North and South, contracted credit or folded altogether. "The state of the country is very alarming now," Persis Black née Sibley observed in December 1860: "Business at a standstill—thousands out of employment & anxiety everywhere. Over *here* many are afflicted by the panic." Still, many Republican women saw it as an occasion for necessary sacrifice. "I shan't complain if secession comes," Elizabeth wrote Ellen, "but shall peaceably try to make $2000 take the place of $6000 which would be the practical working of it on our incomes." To her, appeasing the South was no longer an option. "Altogether I feel that the Southerners have a great many excuses & I should rather bear with them if it is practicable without compromising our consciences any farther but I feel so doubtful whether this is possible." Choosing sides was easy. "It is partly the fault of the North which for years never protested against slavery but allowed it peaceably because we wanted the Cotton." Mary Poor would have concurred. "We ought to submit to privation & trouble if out of them is to come freedom to the oppressed."[24] Tightened belts would be a small price to pay.

By this point Ellen's depression was so great that despite the shrinking economy, she determined to visit her sister, her rock of sanity. Her letters betray an increasing alienation from her husband, a loss of control over her emotional state, and a withdrawal from much of society. Even favorite papers no longer offered solace; she was "astonished . . . to see a *civil* article in the *Saturday* [*Review*] about *America*." Elizabeth did her best to prop up Ellen, explaining that her moodiness was rational, a natural reaction to having moved to a foreign country. She urged her to occupy her mind with painting. But also, Elizabeth was short on money, and as much as she wanted to take in Ellen, she gently broke it to her that it would be impossible.[25] It would take a while for Ellen to receive the dismal news, but from there on in, tensions mounted between the two as the country itself was dividing.

On December 20, 1860, South Carolina seceded from the Union. "National matters are in a most deplorable condition" was Persis Black's take. Writing from her Democratic viewpoint with a tinge of an old Whig's valorization of "disinterestedness," she blamed everyone for their selfishness: "The whole nation—as one man—is now devoted to national matters." She saw that "Its perpetuity as a United Country is threatened, by internal broils." She bemoaned the loss of a compromising spirit: "Criminations & recriminations between different sections North & South are wafted on every breeze, & a defiant tone largely prevails." She could only put down her pen in disgust. "But these are not things for me to record," she ended, for "every paper in the land is full of the transpiring record," before paraphrasing biblical verses of resignation. "God who doeth all things well can make the wrath of man to praise him" (Mark 7:37, Psalms 76:10).[26]

Regarding South Carolina's secession, Elizabeth was not astounded. She had seen it coming. But she was convinced now that other states would follow, "since there is no hope that they will be satisfied with anything less than protection of Slavery." Florida, Mississippi, Alabama, Georgia, and Louisiana all broke away before January's end. In February, with Texas now counted in, the constitution for the Confederate States of America was drawn up. At this point Elizabeth was developing a mind-set independent from that of her husband Elliot, who thought South Carolina's departure would be the first and last. "I 'lean up' against him of course," she made clear to Ellen.[27] She was careful to downplay any intimations of quarreling. Elizabeth's independent thinking was carrying the weight of prediction. It would serve her through four years of war.

Ellen, feeling well enough to write a lengthy letter on January 3, 1861, lashed out at Elizabeth. Perhaps she was disappointed about the expected visit. Perhaps she was being pressed by her upper-crust companions to explain why the North was letting the South go. She had certainly fought with one who called Northerners "'cowards & mercenaries'" and caved before another who deemed the federal government "'but a name and a sham.'" In any case, she expressed her anger over South Carolina's action and her bewilderment over Elizabeth's seemingly flippant reaction. Ellen imagined her sister and brother-in-law were more afraid the government would appease secessionists than let them leave. She called it irresponsible. "I am perfectly *enraged* by the sort of callousness, almost amounting to indifference, that both papers and letters from the North seem to show." She wanted to keep the Union together at any cost and wondered why the North let things go so far. "If we are to fight, why not to prevent secession, instead of to aggravate it?" From Ellen's perspective, her country was setting a bad example to the rest of the world. It was not living up to its glory. "Once disunited, we shall never regain the place among nations we have lost," she argued, "& even if we get over this crisis without disunion, which now seems impossible, fifty years would not restore the confidence in our government, in its permanence & power, nor give it back its prestige." She then lost all composure and blasted Elizabeth. "If you *realize* this all . . . , & don't regret it more than it *seems* you do—I don't know what to make of it & you!"[28] It was yet another point of shame for Ellen.

Elizabeth uncharacteristically shot back on January 21, 1861. "I feel very sorry at all you & Edward are going through about the Union & I don't wonder in the least that you are puzzled at our calmness," she began her retort. "In the first place you must remember that we think very little, almost nothing, of our 'prestige' & our effect upon other nations." In other words, Ellen was obsessed with appearances. "We live far away from Europe . . . & too much absorbed in our own busy active lives to think about what other people are thinking about us." Elizabeth was obliquely suggesting her sister should "get a life." But she had more to spill out. "We," she wrote, referring to Northern citizens, as opposed to a certain expatriate and her aristocratic circle, "believe that self-government is going to go on & thrive in spite of the breaking up of the Union & we have a profound conviction that if the Union has not strength enough to hold together without what we consider concessions of principle on the part of the North, it had better be dissolved." Elizabeth wound down somewhat patronizingly. "Now can you understand that philosophy at all[?]" she spat.[29]

Ellen and Elizabeth were not the only ones with frazzled nerves. Persis Black forecast a bleak future. "What the year we have just entered upon, has in store for our beloved Country is of course unknown, but the most disastrous consequences are to be apprehended." Referring to the White House's long-overdue recognition of the crisis by recommending a day of solemnity, she noted, "The National Fast was had by Proclamation of President Buchanan on Friday last . . . [and] was generally kept in this state, & through New England." In Lenox, Massachusetts, Ellen Wright's classmates were unraveling. One girl "anxiously" wondering "as to the probability of war" was having visions of violence on home ground. And the Southern students were becoming "exceedingly *touchy*." The Republican speeches her teacher read aloud after classes "excite them to the last degree," Ellen smirked. "Minnie Oglesby grows flushed, & thinks Northerners are so detestable!" While Southerners in the North faced growing reprobation, New Englanders in the South did too. "The difficulty with you at the North is that you only read *one side*," Annie Middleton scolded her mother in Rhode Island. The South Carolinian ex-slaveholder's wife referred her to speeches by Virginia senator Robert M. T. Hunter. "I believe that the *moral emancipation* of the colored race and the physical emancipation of the white race will be furthered by the present movement of the South," she wrote defiantly. So distracting was the crisis that any conflict, even such a nonpolitical one as disgruntled members bolting their reading club, could raise allusions to the secession movement.[30]

Meanwhile, the Cabot-Twisleton secession played out. Elizabeth apparently never apologized for taking Ellen to task. But she did soften her tone as she faithfully maintained correspondence. "I wish I could comfort you about your country in the least, but I am afraid not," she regretted. "Don't you see that we *can't* . . . compromise about slavery, no matter how much we may want to save the Union?" Unsurprisingly, she deplored Senator John J. Crittenden's plan calling for extension of the Missouri Compromise line westward in exchange for repeal of states' "personal liberty laws," which subjected slaveholders' claims to fugitives to rigorous legal procedures. She had faith a Republican administration would save the day. "Lincoln once in," she asserted, with the inauguration still about six weeks away, "will set things straight." She was confident "an honest man must do better than such an old liar & coward as Buchanan."[31] To her mind, slavery-tolerant Democrats had made a mess of things.

By now the two sisters knew they were hopelessly at odds. In February letters, written on the same day, both acknowledged the rift. Ellen sobbed, "I feel as if another *open door* was '*shut*'—& fear, a little, that so many changes, & so much time, must quite separate us, & that . . . old Lizzie & Ellen are destined to meet no more!" Elizabeth coldly indicted Ellen: "I am afraid we cannot count you among Republicans." Ellen's departure from the party line was freezing out political comment by Elizabeth.[32]

She hardly mentioned Lincoln's inauguration on March 4, a significant event that registered in several of our women's letters and diaries. Mary Poor, reporting to her sister that her husband "liked the President's inaugural very well," reflected that "Perhaps honest old Abe is 'all our fancy painted im,' & will steer the ship of state safely through all breakers." After Ellen Wright heard her schoolmistress read the inaugural address, she spoke about "Abraham—He seems like a firm, courageous man, which is a relief isn't it? after the imbecile Grandpapa, from whom we are just delivered." Lucy Larcom pondered in her diary, "Yesterday was the inauguration: we have a President, a country: and we are 'the Union' still, and shall so remain, our President thinks. But I doubt whether the pride of slavery will ever bow to simple freedom, as it must, if the self-constituted aliens return. There is a strange new chapter in the world's history unfolding to-day; we have not half read it yet." To a friend, she intimated "How glad I am in our own new president: a real, live man, *isn't* he?" By contrast, Elizabeth Cabot mustered only a few words on his address. "*Do* like Mr Lincoln's message," she entreated Ellen, "for we all like it to the utmost." If Ellen could not regard the Republicans, she could at least respect her sister's wishes.[33]

Ellen did. She read the address and found it appealing. Nationwide reaction varied tremendously, but Ellen evidently appreciated its firm, yet conciliatory, tone. Lincoln vowed not to interfere with slavery where it was established but declared secession illegal. What was important to Ellen was that he promised to enforce federal law and retain federal property in states that secede. It made the United States look strong internationally. But when Major Robert Anderson asked Lincoln to send provisions to Fort Sumter, the new president long deliberated, because such action would provoke South Carolina into war. Ellen balked. "Any gratification we may have felt at Lincoln's Inaugural, was speedily quashed, by news of the intended evacuation of Fort Sumter." She was exasperated. "It must give a shabby & defeated appearance to the new administration." After all, some of her friends thought Lincoln's inaugural was "childish." Ellen thought he was practically admitting it now by even considering relinquishing the fort. She buckled beneath the chiding. "I . . . have 'shut up,' myself, & declined to talk on the subject," she told Elizabeth. "The American view is too different from the English, & I cannot decide between the two." The Britons' very different lens would indeed color debate over recognition of the Confederacy and, with it, possible intervention.[34]

Fort Sumter

The Confederate firing upon Fort Sumter on April 12 and its capitulation two days later sent a shock wave through women's diaries. Sarah P. E. Hale from her perch as a newspaperman's wife got the scoop almost immediately. "Telegraphic news today that war at the South is begun," she began her

April 13 diary entry. "The government fort Sumter at Charleston has been attacked and destroyed, the American flag lowered, and the officers taken prisoners, and sent to New York." The next day, Sarah Browne in Salem registered in her diary, "At noon—the news from the South created great excitement." Soon conflicting news stories flummoxed her. "The reports yesterday from the South cause us to seize with anxiety the morning's paper," she wrote. "None of the accounts seem reliable." The wife of a former Bell-and-Everett supporter scribbled that her husband "Charles brought out accounts of great excitement in town—the streets full of troops, assembling from the country to start for Washington." That same day, another stunned woman on Boston's South Shore entered, "NE rain storm. Standish Guards left Plymouth for the seat of War." In the storm, literal and figurative, Lucy Larcom discerned a silver lining on April 14: "Though the clouds of this morning have cleared away into brightness, it seems as if we could feel the thunder of those deadly echoes passing to and from Fort Sumter." Yet she felt the divine hand: "He will uphold the government which has so long been trying to avert bloodshed." Persis Black was not so sanguine, as she reflected in her diary a week later. "War! Civil War has been precipitated!" she screeched. "Even the Capitol of our Country is threatened! Armies of our countrymen are now hastening from the North & the South to meet each other upon the fields of Battle." For her, it was the Whig-cum-Democrat nightmare of national dissolution come true. "Brother to meet brother in deadly slaughter—to destroy the *Union*—Our Glorious Union."[35]

Given this broad reaction, it is not surprising that Elizabeth broke her silence on politics on April 15, the day after Major Anderson surrendered Sumter. Perhaps she had hoped that Ellen was coming around. Perhaps the tension of scattering a word here and there about momentous happenings was becoming intolerable. But she burst forth in a long summary of events. The surrender is "the only thing that any one can think of in these parts today," she excitedly wrote Ellen. She could not understand why the fleet Lincoln had ordered in to provision the fort "stood by there without even an effort to sustain or reinforce Anderson." Yet she was pleased with Lincoln's proclamation that day asking states to raise seventy-five thousand militiamen. It was enough to "revive the confidence his inaugural gave me in him, which the silence of the last month & the constant reports that Sumter was to be evacuated have rather weakened."[36] Here the two sisters agreed.

Elizabeth, with her unflagging convictions, willingness to grant Ellen some ground, or perhaps patience with her sister's provocations, finally won the day. Or did she? After all, it was Ellen who earlier had advocated applying force to keep the Union together and who criticized Elizabeth and the Republicans for not doing enough. Paradoxically, circumstances had changed, as had Republicans, but perhaps Ellen had not. Not surprisingly, she wrote, on May 11, "we think this up-rising of the free States magnificent, & most necessary & just & hope & pray with all our hearts that treason may be thoroughly chastised." Yet Ellen did change in repudiating English opinion and embracing the Cause. She sensed more than ever she dwelled "in the midst of a foreign people," and she sent Elizabeth London *Times* articles to prove it. "But for the first time in my life, I don't care a pin," she announced, "& . . . both Houses of Parliament wouldn't effect either my opinions or feelings in the least." Scorning her own tendency to conform to those around her, she disclosed, "I am not often blessed with such *complete conviction*," adding, "I wish I were, because life would then be perfect peace."[37] Ironically, war had instilled inner tranquillity.

Elizabeth was delighted with Ellen's letter. She called it "the best thing that has happened this year" because "your sympathy about the war was all I needed to complete my own pride & satisfaction." Most of all she was happy that "now that we have you & Edward to agree with us we are a close company again." It took the violence of a war to bridge the sisters' partisan differences.[38]

After the reunion, Elizabeth responded with copious but largely unrequited political letter writing on Ellen's entreaty "Please to write all you care about politics." Ellen explained, "next to the health of my own people, nothing is to be compared to that in interest." As she grew more and more ill, however, her letters grew shorter and shorter; some were only two pages long. One, she owned, was "full of unwritten and unspoken things." At times, Edward took up the pen for her. She managed to scratch out a few long letters in June, November, and December about the protective Morrill Tariff, decried by the British for raising the price of their exports to the United States, and the "*Trent* Affair"—the Northern seizure and imprisonment of two Confederate envoys on their way to England on the mail packet *Trent*, which caused an uproar there, and even threat of reprisal. "I have a *deadly fear* & the first time I had any, of war with England," Ellen cringed. "It is at least a mercy that the President did not commit himself by his message" to saber rattling, she exclaimed, adding she was hoping for "peace & concession." Soon the envoys were released, occasioning Elizabeth to write on December 30, "I trust, beloved, the news of the surrender [of them] by our government . . . will comfort you." Although it turned to naught, the incident apparently precipitated Ellen's decline. After that she found corresponding difficult and then impossible. She died less than five months later, happy in her sister's and her beloved country's confidence.[39]

For other women, the martial spirit was quick to take hold. As early as January 1861, a New England schoolteacher in New York City reported that her school's proprietor "drilled the young ladies in marching, so that they did it beautifully." According to her, "They ended electing him Colonel, giving him three cheers, and three working cheers for the Union." The wife of a battlefield surgeon signed off a letter to him with, "We are all well & think only of you & the army." Some women waxed hungry for increased militarization. "I do wish the President would issue orders for more men," one Cape Codder complained to her husband before faulting the army high command for not being tough enough: "True, our Generals don't all seem to be of the right stamp." Other women followed the course of hostilities. "I traced out the ocean path, for our iron-clads," Sarah Browne told her husband, and remarked of news accounts of a positive reception in Cape Town, South Africa, accorded the pirate ship *Alabama* for preying on Northern shipping: "they are enough to put *spirit-fire* into an automaton." A schoolgirl promised her mother, "I am going to have my photograph taken in my military dress (as I cannot call it a uniform exactly)."[40] For these women, so unlike those who had stood steadfast against hostilities with Mexico in the 1840s, war had become the rage.

The Civil War

As women entered the maelstrom of war, boundaries surrounding their partisan politics became blurred by claims upon their patriotism and humanitarianism. Such claims goaded them into direct public action or private collective endeavors for the Cause. There was an abiding sense that women could no longer justifiably remain ensconced in the quiet rhythms of their daily lives. Mary Poor chided her sex in 1861 via an invidious comparison with the founding mothers: "Female heroism of the present day does not seem to equal that of seventy-six." Perhaps as a response, she avidly participated in Sanitation Fairs and encouraged her daughters to labor tirelessly for the Cause, as did an army of women war-relief volunteers.[41]

Yet neither support for the war nor for the Republican Party can be ascertained from specific women's work to aid soldiers. Persis Black, for example, noted in November 1861 that "The ladies here have been getting ready boxes to send to the soldiers, sick & wounded. All give liberally. I send two bushels of bundles of old linen & cotton, & it was no small task to cleanse them nicely & get them ready." She affirmed, "I have done my share." Nevertheless, it was a war she thought could have been prevented. "Might not this war have been spared?" she asked. "Where are the peacemakers? Everybody is for war. We need to have peace societies." As we have seen, after the death of her first husband she married another Democratic politician, who frequently lost his bids for state office because, according to her, "Democrats are greatly in the minority." So was her participation in war relief part of a deft political move to allay suspicions that Democrats lacked sufficient patriotism? After all, she reported in late 1863 on her town's "abolitionist" school committee refusing a teaching position to a Democrat who had "skedaddled to Canada two years ago" to elude military service. She called the committee decision "Political tyranny entirely."[42] Or did she work in war relief because she thought the soldiers victims of their government's malfeasance in fighting instead of negotiating? Or both?

However, when a woman like Elizabeth Cabot saw the war through the lens of her strident Republicanism, as seen earlier in this chapter, the partisanship is clear. When in August 1861 she began a paragraph with "Politics look much the same," she immediately presented developments in military leadership, as if they were equated. "A few arrests [of alleged spies and traitors], & [General George] McClellan's improved discipline in Washington are the hopeful signs which we build upon." When the soon-to-be-former Army of the Potomac's commander took on the Democratic mantle in 1864 to vie against Lincoln for the presidency, she also applied the word "politics" in a letter to her late sister's widower. She summoned the rhetoric of diffidence—"It is rather absurd to me, however, to write politics to you, who know so much more even about ours than I do"—after launching into her analysis. "McClellan's name is a strong one, even with sensible people & our hope lies in the division of the Democratic party, which seems almost certain to take place." Ever the partisan, she was "afraid" that the "political condition will give way, & the Republicans be defeated."[43] For her, at least, war talk remained political talk.

Probably the 1864 election provides the best opportunity to plumb women's partisanship apart from their public volunteer service. Aside from Elizabeth Cabot, however, most of them act as record keepers and reporters, not pundits. One Bostonian announced to her diary on August 31 that "McClellen is the Democratic candidate for president" and thereafter carefully tracked her husband's attendance at party meetings. The ever-taciturn Abby Stimson began keeping more detailed records, including an extensive account of Lincoln's speech at the Baltimore Sanitary Fair in April. In November she chronicled a "Grand mass meeting of supporters of Lincoln & Johnson," and wielded her pen, after Election Day, to inscribe every state voting the Republican ticket—all but three in the Union—or not. A Salem abolitionist told her husband that their eleven-year-old son was in a Lincoln procession in which Democrats threatened to choke him.[44] It is as if most women were too busy with all the war-related public activities to give any extensive commentary upon the election. There were so many competing pulls on one's time.

In early September 1862, Elizabeth Cabot pondered how best to give her energy and resources to the Cause. "My mind is dreadfully racked between the San[itary] Com[mmision] & the Negroes as they both seem to need every cent we can raise." The alarm about the latter was raised by Hannah Jackson Cabot, who had, as a young woman in chapter 4, struggled to wrest political news from papers about the Panic of 1837. Hannah was now, according to Elizabeth, "overflowing with the sorrows of the Negroes at Port-Royal & feeling that we had done nothing for them." The Port Royal Experiment to which Hannah referred was an attempt to settle freedpeople on their former masters' estates and to educate them. Among the small southward stream of teachers destined to take part in the experiment was Charlotte Forten. Just after sunset on October 28, 1862, she rode in a carriage to her teaching assignment "in the very heart of rebeldom" on St. Helena Island in South Carolina. As her party glided along, she wrote, "We were in a jubilant state of mind and sang 'John Brown' with a will as we drove through the pines and palmettos." A little over a week later she taught her new charges the song celebrating the martyr of Harpers Ferry, and it played a central role in a subsequent Thanksgiving celebration. Forten sent her account of the event to the *Liberator*, where it was published, to much acclaim. Of the freedpeople's rendition of the song, she cackled, "I wish their old 'secesh' masters, powerless to harm them, could hear their former chattels singing the praises of the brave old man who died for their sake!" Sarah Browne's husband, a U.S. Treasury official operating in the area, met Forten and described her as "a very interesting young woman formerly a teacher in Salem," their hometown. He, too, later summoned in a February 1865 letter to his family the "John Brown" tune, but quoting Julia Ward Howe's famous lyrics, "Mine eyes have seen the glory of the coming of the Lord," and adding his own words: "'mine eyes have seen' *the downfall of Charleston the accursed city*." Later, though, when he hinted at conciliation with the vanquished Southerners, his wife reminded him, true to John Brown's memory, of episodes of Confederate abuse of Union prisoners: "Think of the fiendish revelations of Andersonville—even of Wilmington! Are we not merciful if we but grant *life*?"[45] Many lives would yet be lost between the fall of Charleston and the final surrender of the Confederacy at Appomattox on April 9, 1865.

The denouement involved taking of life, indeed, but it included that of the president, shot April 14, dying early the next day. Sarah Browne reported to her husband that "The first telegrams . . . froze the blood of the nation." "The day it happened was frightful," one of Sarah P. E. Hale's daughters attested to a brother, as she described "the silence, the gloomy stillness such an event cast over everything." The nineteen-year-old daughter of Sarah Watson, who opened chapter 2, also inscribed in her diary that her family heard the news via telegram. On April 19 she gave a vibrant account of Boston bedecked in mourning with echoes of the previous decade's Daniel Webster obsequies: "All stores theaters &c were closed & all [business] stopped. Every building was draped with black & white." Her family, attuned to the occasion's symbolism, grafted funerary accents onto their patriotic display: "Our flag has been draped with black since Saturday but today we hung the evergreen arch with black & white & hung black & white from the windows." She attended a memorial service at noon and reported, "This evening Rosa & I went down to a meeting at City hall" in Cambridge, where she and her sister heard speeches. Taken in by the civic pageantry, while enraged by the murder that prompted it, the two sisters then took revenge against a family they "suspect[ed] of having rather southern feeling" because "they haven't put any black on their house & have never had out a flag." In memory of the fallen President, "We tied black crape to their gatepost, [pinned] two festoons of black & white [on] their front window & stuck a little 6 inch flag half mast & tied with black crape in the view on their piazza." Proud of this richly symbolic act of patriotic vandalism, she polished off her diary entry by musing, "I wonder if they will take the hint."[46]

Certainly, the drums of war had roused many New England women to embrace the Cause passionately, even to be willing to follow, in their own varied ways, in the transgressive footsteps of John Brown. Certainly, too, the war licensed their greater public presence and fueled their identification with the nation and, if they were so disposed, with its ruling party.[47] But when the fog of war would clear, what would remain of their partisanship? To this, we next turn.

Epilogue

The din of civil war intervenes between us today and the voices of political women we have heard throughout these pages. The civic obligation shouldered by a few million men to lay their lives on the line in combat to defend their nation spectacularly advertised another impassable division, besides suffrage, between men and women. About 10 percent of the New England population would serve, which meant just over half of the men between forty-five and eighteen in a state like Vermont. The somewhat honorific, underutilized local militia structure had given way almost overnight to an intensive national militarization and mobilization reaching down into the region. The militarization reconfigured the civic landscape to foreground women's affiliative roles as mothers, wives, sweethearts, daughters, nurses, teachers, and, generally, all-purpose angels serving men who served in uniform for the Cause. The wartime reconfiguration provided, however, new openings for the scope of what women were allowed to do. Nurses began to professionalize, women became office workers in unprecedented numbers, while some others had to take charge of farms or family businesses. Overall female workforce participation increased. Above all, partisanship—albeit morphed into patriotism—continued, especially in areas where Peace Democrats ran close campaigns against Republicans, as in the Connecticut gubernatorial race in April 1863. That contest's outcome in favor of the Republicans has been attributed to the oratorical campaigning skills of working-class teenager Anna Dickinson, who eight months later would become the first woman to speak before Congress. Yet there was a sense that such activity by women, however much it might have grown out of antebellum politicization, was part of a wartime exception to "normal" conditions. Hence, woman suffrage's postbellum failure is not surprising.[1]

The length of the woman suffrage struggle prompts the question: if women were "ready" for enfranchisement before the war, why did it take until 1920 for them to get the vote nationally via the Nineteenth Amendment? The matter is more puzzling because progress to the vote was far from steady. Meanwhile, generations of women activists organized, not just for suffrage, but in a wide range of interest groups, perhaps the most notable being the Woman's Christian Temperance Union. Workingwomen, too, were organizing, both in and out of trade unions, and middle-class women, some of whom were now college educated, continued to enter the professions. Moreover, a range of women became officeholders in government. Women seemed more ready for the vote than ever, so what was the problem?[2]

Some possible answers can be found in general trends. There was a post-Reconstruction recoil from exercise of federal power in pursuit of social ends (apart from the extension of veterans' pensions), a conservatism that made it unlikely that there would be constitutional redress. After all, forty-three years would pass between the adoption of the Fifteenth and Sixteenth Amendments. Legislatively, the period saw the emergence of a women's maternalist protective discourse that highlighted sexual difference, thus undermining the equality argument ever implicit in woman suffrage. At the same time, the federal courts drifted rightward, making any judicial extension of the Fourteenth Amendment to encompass women's voting rights unlikely. Above all, within this discouraging landscape, woman suffrage became a wedge issue. It came to symbolize much more than female enfranchisement: it carried the added burdens of seeming to challenge prevailing maternalist discourses, stoke mounting masculine anxieties, and contradict current social-Darwinian gender essentialism that put a new "scientific" face on ages-old misogyny. And, as the United States once again militarized beginning in the 1890s to conduct imperial ventures abroad, an aggressive remasculinization of the nation's political culture occurred at home.[3]

Yet women in New England remained partisan. A Republican politician's wife described to her son her sister's excitement, measured by her neglect of a beloved pet, over an 1871 Maine gubernatorial election: "Aunt C has forgotten 'Pie,' and the dog is as a shadow which flitteth away, so overwhelming is her interest in the election to-morrow." The woman added, "I am immensely interested," too. That same year, a Lowell wife with a newborn told her husband, "We are all quite excited over the coming election." Such responses continued throughout the rest of the century. "We are very much interested in politics," a woman declared in 1884 before announcing her support for the Democratic presidential candidate: "I should vote for [Grover]

Cleveland if I could vote at all." There remained traces of antebellum campaign mania. During the same presidential contest pitting Cleveland against James G. Blaine, a college student wrote to her Republican father to "send me a dozen Blaine and Logan badges, such as Marshals pin on the lapels of their coats," before describing her attendance at a "Republican torchlight procession." She also reported on a mock election at her school: "before the voting, speeches are to be made in favor of all the candidates. Miss Flint and I are to speak in favor of Blaine." And women still acted as pulse takers of politics: "Not since the Civil War has there been so widespread patriotic enthusiasm," a seventy-eight-year-old told her diary in 1896, "so clear an estimate of what is at stake in the election of the next President of this great nation." After the ballots were cast, another woman opined, "McKinley's election is a good thing . . . and will put all manner of 'spunk' and pluck into every body." Even Helen Keller could proclaim "I am deeply interested in politics" in a 1901 letter to a politician; "I like to have the papers read to me, and I try to understand the great questions of the day."[4] Women's campaign talk continued on, unabated.

So, despite blockages to suffrage, women kept on talking politics. Apparently they did so whether or not they were suffragists. And there were suffragists, some quite prominent, who eschewed partisanship.[5] This suggests that the relationship between the suffrage crusade and voicing partisanship is complex. The two may represent distinct, if occasionally overlapping, streams in American women's civic history. That politicization does not necessarily lead to suffrage advocacy problematizes that history by casting women as highly informed nonvoters. From a modern perspective, these women may seem open to the charge that they were accommodating themselves to a system that deprived them of civil rights, making them complicit in their own oppression. Certainly, suffragists seem more attractive role models today than these partisan nonvoters. However, by the lights of their own time, our antebellum women can be viewed as simply pragmatic, seeing the hand that was dealt to them and playing it out as best they could. But what did those cards, when laid on the table, mean for women's civic future?

Most obviously, antebellum women's partisanship set the stage for their recruitment in formal party-sponsored auxiliary organizations. With the country up for electoral grabs in the two decades after 1876, as during the competitive 1840s, women worked within the two mainstream parties to make a difference. In 1888 Democrats launched all-women antitariff Frances Cleveland Influence Clubs, named after the first lady. Republicans responded with pro-tariff "Carrie Harrison Clubs," after Benjamin Harrison's wife; these were most active in the hotly contended Midwest, not solidly Republican New England. The GOP soon went further with the National Women's

Republican Association it bankrolled, with which it coordinated educational campaign activities. By the turn of the century the mainstream parties had come to expect women's involvement as a given.[6] It is difficult to see how this gradual acceptance and reliance could have occurred as easily without the precedent of antebellum women pioneers in the partisan arena.

Another impact of these women is less direct and more diffusely cultural. The late nineteenth century saw a mythologization of New England in U.S. print media. It fused nostalgia with celebration of Yankee stock, depicted as unostentatious and intrepid hard workers in small towns. An expression of the colonial revival, it was obviously critical of the increasing diversity due to immigration (the newer workers were presumably lazier than old stock) but also of the newly superwealthy and well-to-do parvenus lacking appropriate Yankee pedigrees and enculturation. This cultural discourse featured several species of New England womanhood, opinionated yet reserved, grounded but elevated, worldly and a bit otherworldly, flinty but gracious, parsimonious but generous, spry yet maternal, and feisty yet well-manneredly aloof. Many are portrayed as "spinsters" or "old maids." Even if these archetypal women are not represented as talking politics, they come off as if they could.[7]

And sometimes they do. In Rose Terry Cooke's 1884 short piece "Miss Dorcas's Opinion," the widowed "Mrs. Morgan" circulates a petition to the state legislature to permit women to vote. She visits Miss Dorcas, a single woman Cooke describes as true to the Yankee stereotype:

> tall, lean, straight as a dart, with a keen, sensible face and cool gray eyes; her steel gray hair was knotted tightly at the back of her head, and every item of her dress gave the idea of perfect neatness and strict economy. She lived by herself in this small red house . . . , did a little millinery, tailoring now and then, and at other times plain sewing; she had some money, but being at once thrifty and generous she worked hard always, and let the two thousand dollars her father left her accumulate for her old age, rendering her independent and fearless.

Mrs. Morgan explains, "it's a p'tition for womenfolks to get their rights . . . I b'lieve this is about votin', specially." Miss Dorcas, assuming partisan armor, says she would not want to go to the legislature, because it is filled with "swearin', drinkin', low-lived Dimmicrats." Mrs. Morgan bristles at what she takes to be a stab at her late husband: "I do'no' as you need to throw it into my face that Hiram was a Dimmicrat, and consequently I b'long to that p'litical persuasion myself." A long argument follows that Cooke loads against the petitioner by having Dorcas let loose a disquisition on the sorry state of politics, which shows she knows quite a bit about the parties. Cooke concludes, "So Mrs. Morgan went home with Miss Dorcas's opinion instead of her signature; but is not, in these days, so unusual and so positive an opinion worth preservation and record?" She adds, "Being in full agreement with Miss Dorcas *I* have thought so."[8] By bringing herself in at the end, Cooke defines the boundaries of political but nonvoting New England womanhood and places herself firmly within them, inviting her female readers to join her there.

One can imagine characters like the ones Cooke sketches in real life, certainly less caricatured, influencing through the example of their political talk subsequent generations. This could be as subtle as recounting hearing a politician's speech at a public event. WCTU founder-to-be Frances Willard was just over twenty-one in 1860 when she wrote in her diary, "My landlady has been telling me about Bunker Hill and the dedication of the monument by Daniel Webster when Lafayette was present, and the wonderful address delivered by the greatest orator of his time." In a few words, the woman connected Willard to the memory of the Revolution and Webster's 1825 speech, in which he famously rededicated the Republic to economic development. An inspired Willard reflected, presciently, "I wish I had seen something of the world, and I think I shall some day." She would go on, after the Civil War, to become herself a speaker celebrated for her eloquence.[9]

Other influences came, not through chance encounters, but down through families. For example, Sarah Hildreth Butler had been in the public eye as a renowned actress when she married in 1844 Lowell Democratic politician Benjamin Franklin Butler. She quickly took on the role of political partner, like Eliza Davis a generation earlier. Her husband recollected, "I had an advantage [of] . . . having an adviser, faithful and true, clear-headed, conscientious, and conservative whose conclusions could always be trusted." Beyond military tactics, which he kept within his staff, "all that she agreed to was right and for the best." Their daughter Blanche already voiced interest in public affairs when still only fourteen in 1861, just as war erupted. In a letter marked "strictly private," she wrote: "Dear Mother: Why are you so anxious about this war, it was destined to be from the first settlement of this New World. . . . The Southerners are sure to be overcome at last." She then insisted upon having her say: "Do not make fun of this and say how foolish it is in Blanche to try to write what she is not old enough to comprehend, for although I may have not expressed my thoughts very clearly (for that would be impossible) still overlook all the mistakes and take the will for the deed." Perhaps not surprisingly, she later married a Maine politician, Adelbert Ames, and became an ardent partisan wife, politically coordinating his activities as Reconstruction governor of Mississippi with local politics in Massachusetts. After a long political analysis in a letter she sent him from Lowell on the eve of the 1873 elections, she took his reaction into account, as she did her mother's so many years before. "So, Dearie, you *must not give it more consideration than it deserves*," is her concluding advice, to which she immediately adds, perhaps aware of the apparent overreaching condescension of the last statement, "I think I can see you smile. Ah-well! If I were a member of the Legislature, and no wiser, my opinion would amount to something, because it would be an earnest [expression] of my vote. Ergo, women should hold office and vote. Then their husbands could not afford to smile, and would have to display a proper spirit and keep in good subjection." Woman suffrage, which she fancifully references, would become for her own daughter Blanche, born in 1878, a more serious cause. The younger Blanche was a Smith College graduate, member of the Massachusetts Woman Suffrage Association, president of the Massachusetts Birth Control League, and a well-known cartoonist advocating woman suffrage.[10] In short, the intergenerational chain of political women remained unbroken, but would it have been as strong without Sarah Hildreth Butler's nonvoting partisanship at the head?

Such lineages of politicization among descendants of the women who talk politics in these pages are common. The daughter of Harriett Low, whose story was the focus of chapter 1, Mary Hillard Loines, became in 1869 the secretary of the newly founded Brooklyn Equal Rights Association and would remain devoted to suffrage, consumers' rights, and prison reform until near the end of her long life. In the early 1820s, Sarah P. E. Hale rocked her daughter Lucretia's cradle while, as discussed in chapter 8, "Webster and Justice Story dictated to her the speeches that were to appear in her husband's paper." In 1843 Sarah reported on her twenty-two-year-old's Independence Day obsession: "Lucretia, as she always insists on doing, read to them [her young brothers] the Declaration—they winced under its length." In December 1874, the daughter, now at fifty-four a celebrated educator and prolific author, would become one of the first six women elected, after a year-long controversy over whether "ladies" could be seated, to Boston's School Committee. Ellen Wright, who played a central role in chapter 12, already had a strong suffrage streak from her mother Martha Coffin Wright, one of the organizers of the 1848 Seneca Falls Women's Rights Convention. Ellen would pick up the torch as an activist in the National American Woman Suffrage Association, in which she was, for example, a Massachusetts delegate at its 1898 convention. Her own daughter Eleanor would be an organizing agent on the group's payroll and would make an appearance, to cheers, at the 1912 New York Progressive Party state convention, reported under the *New York Times* headline "Women Rule Moose State Convention."[11] In short, the influence of the voices without votes we have reinvoked in these pages could be heard down through the generations, even if as hushed echoes of past lives remembered.

Although cherished in family members' recollections, these politicized women were not as enduring in collective memory. One can only ask, why not? One reason is that families tend to remember selectively and forget strategically, especially in deciding how to preserve and present memories betokened in personal documents. For antebellum partisan women, many preservation decisions took place during later heated debates over suffrage, and some families apparently did not want their forebears to contribute to it, via precedents, by their earlier partisan actions.[12]

Take, for example, Richard Cabot's privately printed 1905 edition of his mother Elizabeth Dwight Cabot's voluminous correspondence with her London-based sister, which we encountered in chapter 12. For November 1854, there are only two excerpts of letters. In the November 6 one, she presents a warmly humorous character sketch of a sewing-obsessed and cleanliness-lacking aunt. In the November 21 one, she undertakes a contortion of apology for an unspecified affront in a prior letter: "I ought to be able to work and watch and pray and leave the end in God's hands." Together, the letters cast Elizabeth as strongly family oriented, careful of avoiding offense, and devoutly pious for her transgressions. Among the manuscript letters we read in the archives, however, there is one from November 13 intervening between these two, and having been written after the November elections, it happens to brim with politics, as we discussed in chapter 11. In the letter, we learn, in turn, that one woman in the household reads the *London Times* about the Crimean War and forms an opinion about it; Elizabeth objects to *Punch*'s caricatures of Lord Aberdeen as an "old nurse" because "I sympathize deeply with [his] delay"; she speaks of diplomatic maneuvering between Prussia and the czar to end the war; she "passed . . . the whole of Saturday evening in reading the Newspapers"; and, above all, she is upset enough by the recent election to expound at fascinating length upon the woes of coalitional politics between Democrats and Know-Nothings. The letter shows that this woman is well informed and deeply engaged in politics at home and abroad—at odds with the printed version of what the compiler calls the "most characteristic phases of a full and varied life."[13] Apparently, her thinking about midcentury party politics was not, for her son, characteristic.

The Cabot example suggests the nervousness that many remembrancers experienced in confronting and representing New England women's partisanship. Many chose not to represent it at all. There are no statues of female partisan nonvoters, no annals of their deeds, and few published excerpts of their writing. Early suffragist historians overlooked them, as did the pots-and-pans school of social history and a handful of late nineteenth-century collective biographers of American women. Some representational problems emerge from original lack of reportage, as in the case of the Quincy Female Pic Nic during the Log-Cabin Campaign, discussed in chapter 5, which probably was up to that time the nation's largest partisan gathering entirely organized by women at which men and women spoke to auditors of both sexes. The Quincy paper reported on it, and it was given passing notice in the Boston papers (Democratic editors pounced on it as evidence of the feminization of Whiggery), but the story simply did not have legs, and so it vanished from history. One cannot even recover accounts in the papers of the principal speakers on that occasion.[14] The nervousness seems to have affected them, too.

Could the standing practices of representing civic politics, let alone party competition, accommodate the presence and voices of women? Perhaps only partially: women could be shown collectively (and usually anonymously) as part of masses and as "the fair." They could be spoken of generally, seldom specifically. In news columns, a short unattributed phrase from a politicized woman might be quoted, rarely. A common view was that antebellum women in politics, particularly Whigs, followed in the footsteps of their New England Revolutionary predecessors. It was nothing new, and it indicated a similar temporary crisis situation to which women had to respond. By contrast, the few representational practices common in those days that could capture thinking and speaking partisan women as actors depicted them negatively as "Fanny Wrightists" or feminist extremists. Yet the parties came to rely too much on women to subject them broadly to such charges when they acted as partisans. Only the "brash" few were targeted, usually, as examples. Consequently, partisan women's presence was represented only in the most abbreviated form, while their voices were stifled.[15]

This restricted scope for representing women's politicization in public discourse makes it all the more remarkable that the antebellum New Englanders whose "private" voices we have heard here were able, in their letters and diaries, to represent themselves and the partisan activities of other women around them at all, let alone so well, and often so eloquently. With few positive models in print, women had to invent a civic self-representation on the page. Often this meant simply adopting partisan discourse in newspapers to private discursive spaces through personalization of content, often, in the process, slyly evading the issue of appropriate gender style. This is to say that, technically, when the language they use is closely scrutinized, we can see they wrote politically not unlike men. However, the gendered position from which they wrote, that is, sex-based disfranchisement, casts their political utterances hitting the page as, in themselves, arguments for a shared civic participation without respect of gender. The rhetoric of diffidence—for example, "I take too much interest in Legislation for a lady"—they occasionally employed in their political writing was one means of acknowledging their subversion of a sex-segregated polity.[16] That rhetoric also licensed them to write politically.

Why did they not just think and act politically without writing about it and, by so doing, avoid having to invent a civic projection? The genres in which they chose to write suggest some answers. In an age of romantic self-disclosure within moral frameworks, both letters and diaries had to be "faithful" representations of the self. The result was a kind of moral mimesis, a written reflection not of the life lived but of the life as it should be lived. Diarists in particular rhetorically weighed their good and bad behavior, but, less directly, so did correspondents in deeming their political sayings and doings worthy of conveying to addressees.[17] Clearly, the women who wrote letters and diaries usually mapped their politicization on the side of good, and hence were eager to accept the discursive challenge of faithfully reporting their partisan thinking and other activities. From their tone, such reports only reflected well upon their authors.

The need to record the political in one's life faithfully had consequences insofar as public concerns intruded upon the stream of private correspondence and diary keeping, making it and the women who produced it more political than they might otherwise have been. After all, as modern composition theorists maintain, through developing a discursive voice, "writers come to know themselves and share themselves with others."[18] This self-construction and sharing implies a contagion effect among our women: the more women wrote about politics, the more they, through their example, encouraged other women to become political.

As this book has shown, writing was only one partisan act, albeit one that could uniquely convey reports of other types of politicking. We can only imagine the scope of partisanship escaping these women's letters and diaries. The politics on the manuscript page surely only dimly reflect the partisanship in their hearts and minds that led them to take to the streets, canvass among neighbors, labor at events, and otherwise advocate for candidates, parties, and policies. In a way, then, the voices we have heard in these pages represent this now-silent army of partisans. Voices without votes they may have been, but these writers, like the woman economic-policy pundit we quoted in the introduction, "said their say." They spoke for the voiceless, too, and, in so doing, perhaps they "voted," after all.[19] The political history of antebellum New England would not be the same without them.

Abbreviations

Historical sources referenced in this book are, for purposes of documentation, divided into three categories: *personal names*, abbreviated as two or more roman characters (e.g., AA); *periodicals*, abbreviated as two or more italic characters (e.g., *BCW*); *archives and databases*, abbreviated as two or more bold characters (e.g., **AAS**).

Personal Names

AA	Adelbert Ames
ACS	Abby Clarke Stimson
ADWM	Annie De Wolf Middleton
AGB	Albert Gallatin Browne, Sr.
AgP	Agnes Paine
AHE	Alexander Hill Everett
AL	Annie Lawrence (Rotch)
AM	Aurilla Ann Moffitt
AMNL	Abigail M. N. Lummis
AnL	Anna Loring
AnP	Ann Parlin
AP	Abigail Pierce
BBA	Blanche Butler Ames
CAW	Caleb A. Wall
CB	Calista Billings
CBE	Charlotte Brooks Everett
CC	Cynthia Congdon
CGCC	Caroline Gardiner Carey Curtis
CH	Clarissa Harrington
ChC	Charles Clement
CP	Charlotte Pettibone
CR	Charlotte Rantoul
CRW	Catherine R. Williams
CSB	Cyrus S. Brown
DFC	Daniel F. Child

EAC	Elizabeth Atherton Clapp
EC	Elizabeth Clement
ED	Eliza Bancroft Davis
EDC	Elizabeth Dwight (Cabot)
EdE	Edward Everett
EE	Elizabeth Edwards
EEH	Edward Everett Hale
EEPB	Elizabeth Ellis Prescott Betton
EGL	Ellis Gray Loring
EJ	Elizabeth Jocelyn (Cleaveland)
EK	Electa Kimberly
EnC	Eunice Cobb
EO	Emmeline Augusta Ober
EP	Elizabeth Pierce
ET	Ellen Dwight Twisleton
EWG	Ellen Wright (Garrison)
FD	Frances Small Douglass
FJ	Frances Jocelyn
FM	Frances Merritt
GB	George Bancroft
HFC	Harriot F. Curtis
HHR	Harriet Hanson Robinson
HHS	Hannah Hicock Smith
HL	Harriett Low
HLJC	Hannah Lowell Jackson (Cabot)
HP	Henry Varnum Poor
HPr	Harriet Prescott
HW	Helen Warner
HWC	Henry Wyles Cushman
JC	John Congdon
JD	John Davis
JnP	John Pierce
JP	John Park
KBL	Katherine Bigelow Lawrence
KL	Kitty Lawrence (i.e., Katherine Bigelow Lawrence, Jr.)
LB	Lucretia Bancroft, Jr.
LCB	Lucretia Chandler Bancroft
LE	Lucretia Anne Peabody Everett
LGL	Louisa Gilman Loring
LH	Lucy Pierce (Hedge)
LL	Lucy Larcom
LLN	Levi Lincoln Newton
LLW	Louisa Lee Waterhouse
LPH	Louisa Park Hall

LTP	Lucy Tappan Pierce
LzB	Lorenza Berbineau
MAB	Mary A. Byrum
MAW	Mary Avery White
MB	Mary Brown
MC	Maria Chase
MCM	Mary Crowninshield Mifflin
MCS	Mary Caroline Sweetser
MCW	Martha Coffin Wright
MDC	Mary D. Child
MF	Mary Fiske
MH	Mary Hall
ML	Mary Low
MM	Mary Mudge
MOB	Martha Osborne Barrett
MP	Mary Pierce (Poor)
NB	Nellie Browne
NBD	Nancy Bartlett Drew
NCP	Nancy C. Paine
NHJ	Nathan Hale, Jr.
NHS	Nathan Hale, Sr.
OW	Olive Gay Worcester
PC	Phebe Beede Clark
PSA	Persis Sibley Andrews (Black)
RR	Robert Rantoul, Sr.
RS	Rebekah Scott Dean Salisbury
SB	Sarah Smith (Cox) Browne
SBE	Sarah B. Eaton
SBn	Sarah Brown
SCH	Sarah Cushman Hurlburt
SEH	Sarah Everett Hale, Jr.
SEW	Sarah Elizabeth Wall
SH	Sarah P. E. Hale
SHB	Sarah Hildreth Butler
SJ	Sarah Jocelyn
SJR	Sarah Jackson Russell
SL	Seth Low
SLE	Sarah L. Edes
SP	Sophia Peabody
SS	Stephen Salisbury II
ST	Susan Tucker
SuH	Susan Hale
SuJ	Susan Johnson
SWD	Sarah Watson Dana

TWD	Thomas W. Dorr
WSR	William Stevens Robinson

Periodicals

AM	*American Mercury*
BA	*Boston Atlas*
BC	*Boston Courier*
BCW	*Berkshire County Whig*
BDA	*Boston Daily Atlas*
BDAv	*Boston Daily Advertiser*
BDET	*Boston Daily Evening Transcript*
BDW	*Bangor Daily Whig and Courier*
BG	*Barre Gazette*
BJ	*Berkshire Journal*
BMP	*Boston Morning Post*
BP	*Barre Patriot*
BS	*Baltimore Sun*
BSD	*Bay State Democrat*
CC	*Connecticut Courant*
CM	*Connecticut Mirror*
CONST	Middletown, Conn., *Constitution*
CP	*Cherokee Phoenix*
DG	*Daily Globe*
DGSA	*Dover Gazette and Strafford Advertiser*
DNI	*Daily National Intelligencer*
DOS	*Daily Ohio Statesman*
DVR	*Dedham Village Register*
DVRNCA	*Dedham Village Register and Norfolk County Advertiser*
EFA	*Emancipator and Free American*
EM	*Emancipator*
ER	*Emancipator and Republican*
FC	*Farmer's Cabinet*
GPDRC	*Gleason's Pictorial Drawing Room Companion*
HDC	*Hartford Daily Courant*
HG	*Haverhill Gazette*
LC	*Log Cabin*
MN	New London *Morning News*
MS	*Massachusetts Spy*
NBM	*New-Bedford Mercury*
NHG	*New-Hampshire Gazette*
NHP	*New-Hampshire Patriot*
NHPSG	*New-Hampshire Patriot and State Gazette*

NHS	*New Hampshire Sentinel*
NHSSJ	*New-Hampshire Statesman and State Journal*
NM	*Newport Mercury*
NYH	*New York Herald*
NYS	*New York Spectator*
NYT	*New York Times*
OS	*Ohio Statesman*
PI	*Philadelphia Inquirer*
PJLP	*Portsmouth Journal of Literature and Politics*
PP	*Providence Patriot*
QP	*Quincy Patriot*
RIA	*Rhode-Island American*
RIR	*Rhode Island Republican*
SG	*Salem Gazette*
SP	*Southern Patriot*
SUN	Pittsfield *Sun*
VG	*Vermont Gazette*
WAG	*Worcester Aegis and Gazette*
WE	*Weekly Eagle*
WH	*Weekly Herald*

Archives and Databases

Manuscript collections are cited first by collection name and then by archive name. Thus, **JDP-AAS** refers to the John Davis Papers located at the American Antiquarian Society, Worcester, Mass.

AAS	Courtesy American Antiquarian Society, Worcester, Mass.
CFP	Cheever Family Papers
JDP	John Davis Papers
NFP	Newton Family Papers
PFP	Park Family Papers
SFP	Salisbury Family Papers
WFP	Wall Family Papers
AHTL	Andover-Harvard Theological Library, Harvard Divinity School, Harvard University, Cambridge, Mass.
ALPL	Abraham Lincoln Presidential Library, Springfield, Ill.
ANB	*American National Biography Online*, http://www.anb.org/
BD	United States Department of Veterans Affairs, *Bivouac of the Dead*, http://www.cem.va.gov/cem/hist/bivouac.asp
BDUSC	Biographical Directory of the United States Congress, http://bioguide.congress.gov
BHS	Beverly Historical Society and Museum, Beverly, Mass.

EC	Endicott Collection
RC	Rantoul Collection
BPL	Courtesy of the Trustees of the Boston Public Library/Rare Books
BUL	Manuscripts Division, Brown University Library, Providence
SRC	Sidney S. Rider Collection, John Hay Library
CD	*Congressional Debates*, http://lcweb2.loc.gov/ammem/amlaw/lwrd.html
Census	U.S. Federal Census, Population Schedules, Sixth-eighth Census, 1840, 1850, 1860, via *Ancestry.com*
CG	*Congressional Globe*, http://lcweb2.loc.gov/ammem/amlaw/lwcg.html
CHS	Connecticut Historical Society, Hartford
JFP	Jocelyn Family Papers
CSL	Connecticut State Library, Hartford
CU	Division of Rare and Manuscript Collections, Cornell University Library, Ithaca, N.Y.
GBP	George Bancroft Papers (#1262)
DJQA	*Diaries of John Quincy Adams: A Digital Collection*, http://www.masshist.org/jqadiaries
GWD	Rick Stattler, *A Guide to Women's Diaries* . . . [at **RIHS**], http://www.rihs.org/mssinv/WomenGuide.htm
HCB	*Historical Census Browser*, University of Virginia Library, http://fisher.lib.virginia.edu/collections/stats/histcensus/php/county.php
HL	By permission of the Houghton Library, Harvard University, Cambridge, Mass.
PTF	Papers of the Twisleton-Dwight-Parkman-Vaughn Families (MS Am 2197)
HM	*Historical Marker Database*, http://www.hmdb.org/
LC	Library of Congress, Washington, D.C.
CCP	Caleb Cushing Papers
LHS	Quotes from the collection of the Lexington, Massachusetts, Historical Society, Lexington, Mass.
LyHS	Lynn Historical Society, Lynn, Mass.
MBEL	Mary Baker Eddy Library for the Betterment of Humanity, Boston
MCUS	Greg Hlatky, *Membership of the Congresses of the United States*, http://borzoiblog.com/Congress.htm/
MeHS	Collections of the Maine Historical Society, Portland
BFP	Brown Family Papers
MHS	Massachusetts Historical Society, Boston
ALP	Amos Lawrence Papers
CFP	Cary Family Papers, III
DCD	David Clapp Diaries and Account Book
DFCP	D. F. Child Papers
DFP	Dabney Family Papers (microfilm edition: *Dabney Family Papers,*

1716–1900, 2 reels) (Boston: Massachusetts Historical Society, 1993)

FCLP Francis Cabot Lowell Papers, 1788–1966
LFP Lamb Family Papers
LLWJ L. L. Waterhouse Journal
RLFP Rotch-Lawrence Family Papers

MS Mystic Seaport, G. W. Blunt White Library, Mystic, Conn.

NEHGS New England Historic Genealogical Society, Boston
CC Cushman Collection (Spec. Col. 11 C 7)

NHHS New Hampshire Historical Society, Tuck Library, Concord, N.H.

NYSL New York State Library, Albany, N.Y.

OCHS Old Colony Historical Society, Taunton, Mass.

PEM Phillips Library, Peabody Essex Museum, Salem, Mass.
BFL Elizabeth Ellis (Prescott) Betton Family Letters

PG *Political Graveyard*, http://www.politicalgraveyard.com

RH *Roll of Honor-U.S. Casualties of the Battle of Churubusco and Contreras*, http://www.dmwv.org/honoring/chucon2.htm

RIHS Rhode Island Historical Society, Providence
CFP Congdon Family Papers (MSS 363)
DFP Diman Family Papers (MSS 386)

SCHS South Carolina Historical Society, Charleston
DWFP De Wolf-Middleton Family Papers (1075.01)

SL Schlesinger Library, Radcliffe Institute (Harvard University), Cambridge, Mass.
AFP Almy Family Papers
BroFP Browne Family Papers
CFP Cabot Family Papers
DFP Dana Family Papers
FMQP Frances Merritt Quick Papers
HC Hooker Collection
LFP Ellis Gray Loring Family Papers
PFP Poor Family Papers
RSP Robinson-Shattuck Papers
SFP Swanton Family Papers

SPCRD *Seamen's Protection Certificate Register Database*, MS, http://library.mysticseaport.org/initiative/protectionindex.cfm

SSC The Sophia Smith Collection, Smith College, Northampton, Mass.
BFP Bodman Family Papers
GFP Garrison Family Papers
HFP Hale Family Papers
PFP Peabody Family Papers, Munroe Collection

THSN *Thompson Historical Society Newsletter*, http://thompsonhistorical.org/Newsletters.htm

URI University of Rhode Island, Kingston

SHC	Susan Hale Collection
UVL	Special Collections, University of Virginia Library, Charlottesville
VHS	Vermont Historical Society, Barre, Vt.
CFP	Clement Family Papers (Doc 187)
WCFP	Chamberlain Family Papers (Doc 73, Size C)
YU	Yale University, New Haven, Conn.

Notes

Introduction

1. ED to JD, Feb. 6, 1833, **JDP-AAS**; HL, June 7, 1833, Diary, in Hodges and Hummel, *Lights and Shadows*, 563; SWD, Apr. 7, 1834, Diary, **DFP-SL**; HLJC to SJR, May 18, 1837, **AFP-SL**; MP to JnP and LTP, Sept. 7, 1838, in Aug. 31, 1838, and Sept. 10, 1838, in Sept. 8, 1838, **PFP-SL.** Note that these latter two (and many letters below) are so-called diary letters with dated entries beneath a header date that can be earlier (i.e., when the letter was started) than specific entries.

2. RS to SS, Feb. 20, 1840, **SFP-AAS.** LLW, Feb. 14, 1840, Journal, **LLWJ-MHS.** LB to GB, July 2, 1840, **GBP-CU**. CH, Oct. 15, 1840, Journal, **LHS**. MP to HP, Nov. 9, 1840, **PFP-SL.** PSA, Feb. 11, 1841, Diary, **MeHS**. HHS, Sept. 2, 1846, Diary, **CSL**. HFC to WSR, Aug. 10, [1847?], **RSP-SL.** CB, Sept. 4, 1848, Diary, **SL.**

3. PSA, May 5, 1850, **MeHS**. C[harlotte] D[e Wolf?] to ADWM, Feb. 11, 1851, **DWFP-SCHS**. EDC to ET, Nov. 13, 1854, **CFP-SL.** SCH to HWC, Oct. 21, 1856, **CC-NEHGS**. EDC to ET, Nov. 19, 1860, **CFP-SL.** MP to LH, Dec. 30, 1860, **PFP-SL.**

4. While we acknowledge that including women expands the "political" (see Flammang, *Women's Political Voice*), we focus on women and mainstream political parties because in "coming to voice" over partisan politics these women resisted the sociocultural consequences of disfranchisement and partial citizenship. On coming to voice, see hooks's "'When I Was a Young Soldier'"; Miller and Bridwell-Bowles, "Introduction" to their *Rhetorical Women*, 9–10.

5. Hart, *Campaign Talk*. Cf. the Habermasian approach in Kelley, *Learning*.

6. Kerber, *No Constitutional Right*; Isenberg, *Sex and Citizenship*. On women as political actors, see Coryell, "Superseding."

7. Zboray and Zboray, "Is It a Diary?"

8. Information on the nature and extent of the material can be found in Zboray and Zboray, *Everyday Ideas*, xix–xxv, 299–304; and Zboray and Zboray, "Transcendentalism," 312–18. Our total number of women is slightly higher for this project because we added in a few new ones since the reading project was completed.

9. We discuss representativeness in *Everyday Ideas*, xx–xxii, and 301–2. While we did include proportionally more African Americans than in the general population, our restrictive partisan-based definition of politics resulted in only a few black voices in these pages.

10. For a list, see Zboray and Zboray, *Everyday Ideas*, 399–400. Idem, "Political News"; idem, "Whig Women."

11. Zboray and Zboray, *Literary Dollars* and *Everyday Ideas*.

12. The database was derived from the one described in Zboray and Zboray, *Everyday Ideas*, 303n27, with, for this project, two "logical" fields (i.e., yes or no) added to code each line of text for references to politics or newspapers, respectively.

13. Altschuler and Blumin, *Rude Republic*, 146, 143. Pierson, "'Prairies'"; Neely, *Boundaries*. See Watson, "Humbug? Bah!" and other rejoinders in the Dec. 1997 issue of *Journal of American History* (886–903); Gienapp, "Politics."

14. On rhetorical alternatives available, see Gaillet and Tasker, "Recovering." N. Johnson, *Gender*, 1–76.

15. RS to SS, Feb. 25, 1840, **SFP-AAS**. Huspek and Kendall, "On Withholding."

16. Almond and Verba, *Civic Culture*. R. Wilson, "Many Voices." Gienapp, "Politics," esp. 16–17.

17. Zuckerman and others, "Deference." Willingham, "Deference."

18. See, for example, Nash, *Urban Crucible*.

19. Travers, *Celebrating*.

20. Dublin, *Women*, 93–95.

21. Crocker, *Magic*; Saxton, *Rise and Fall*, pt. 1.

22. Kohl, *Politics*; Howe, *Political Culture*. Formisano, "Invention."

23. Gilmore, "Elementary Literacy." Adult women's regional literacy rate in 1850 was 97.93 percent; **HCB**, 1850 schedules. On seminaries, see Kelley, *Learning*, chaps. 1–3.

24. K. Hansen, *Very Social Time*. Ray, "What Hath"; idem, *Lyceum*.

25. These women represent the first in the "two-step flow" of information from media to the masses (Mattelart and Mattelart, *Theories,* 34). Popkin, *Reasoning Voter,* 46–47.

26. R. Brown, *Knowledge*, 245–67.

27. Zaeske, "Promiscuous Audience."

28. Grimsted, *American Mobbing*, 3–9, 188–89.

29. On women speaking in public, see Campbell, *Man*; Mattingly, *Appropriat[ing] Dress*; Browne, *Angelina Grimké*.

30. For examples of secondhand awareness, see SBE, Mar. 18, June 15, 1843, Diary, **RIHS**. SH to EdE, May 31, 1844, **HFP-SSC**. Mehetable May (Dawes) Goddard to Lucretia Dawes, Jan. 3, 1843, May-Goddard Family Papers, **SL**. PSA, Mar. 11, 1841, Diary, **MeHS**. CRW, quoted in Graham, "Female Politician," 237. SCH to HWC, Oct. 21, 1856. Emily Dickinson to Mrs. A. P. Strong, Feb. 23, 1845, in Dickinson, *Letters*, 4. PSA, Mar. 4, 1841, Diary.

31. Zelizer, "Beyond," 346–52.

32. Some like Scott and Scott, *One Half*, continued to be concerned with women's civic history (7).

33. Kerber, *Women*. Kann, *Gendering*.

34. Cott, *Bonds*, xiii-xv; cf. Welter, "Cult"; Kraditor, "Introduction"; Smith-Rosenberg, "Female World." See, however, Kerber, "Separate Spheres."

35. Examples include Ginzberg, *Women*; Hewitt, *Women's Activism*; Epstein, *Politics*. Hewitt's scheme of benevolent, perfectionist, and ultraist accommodates a range of positions within reform. More recent work, like Zaeske's *Signatures*, emphasizes the politics in reform.

36. Tilly and Gurin, *Women*, 9–10.

37. Branson, *Fiery Frenchified Dames*; Zagarri, *Revolutionary Backlash*, chaps. 4 and 5. On "the flux and uncertainty concerning gender roles and sexual norms in post-Revolutionary America," see Cohen, "Introduction," 21–28 (quote on 28).

38. For examples, see Allgor, *Parlor Politics*; Gelles, *Abigail and John*; Denton, *Passion*; Coryell, *Neither Heroine*.

39. Gunderson, *Log-Cabin*, 4, with his main treatment of Whig women on 135–39; for a similar view, see Dinkin, *Before Equal Suffrage*, 31–34. McGerr, "Political Style," 867; Ryan, *Women*, 136–37; P. Baker, "Midlife Crisis," 164.

40. Kincheloe, "Transcending Role Restrictions." DeFiore, "Come"; Varon, "Tippecanoe"; see also her *We Mean*. Research on Southern women would continue, e.g., Olsen, "Wise Allotment"; Sacher, "Ladies." Zboray and Zboray, "Political News," 3, and "Whig Women," 314. On Dorrite women, see Graham, "Female Politician"; and Formisano, "Role."

41. On the gender politics of penmanship, see Thornton, *Handwriting*, 43–71. On lack of privacy, see Zboray and Zboray, *Everyday Ideas*, 13–16, 23–24. Putala, *Reading*; Gring-Pemble, "Writing Themselves."

42. Zaeske, "Unveiling Esther," 208–15. Kerber, *No Constitutional Right*, chap. 1.

43. Campbell, *Man*, 1:12. Nystrand and Duffy, *Rhetoric*.

44. Powell, "Association"; Carlson, "Limitations," 310.

45. Brummett, "Theory." Cf. Moulton, "Paradigm," on the *elenchus* in the Socratic dialectic, 12–13.

46. Austin, *How to Do*.

47. P. Baker, "Midlife Crisis," 164. Cf. Ginzberg, *Women*, 109–32, on ultraists turning partisan.

48. Motz, "Folk Expression."

49. On negative images of politicized women, see Zboray and Zboray, "Gender Slurs."

Part I. The Rise of the Second Party System

1. Zboray and Zboray, "Gender Slurs," quote 413. Pugh, *Sons*; quote, Formisano, "New," 682n36; Pierson, *Free Hearts*, 4, 6–7, 19, chap. 4. Howe, *Political Culture*, 222; quote, Basch, "Marriage," 917. Zboray and Zboray, "Gender Slurs," 415–16, 416n4.

Chapter 1. Harriett Low and the "Reign" of "King Andrew" Jackson

1. HL to SL and ML, Apr. 13, 1830, in Loines, *China*, 36. Watson, *Liberty*, 95–115; Remini, *Andrew Jackson . . . Freedom,* 148–217. Most of HL's letters home no longer exist; see Hillard, *My Mother's Journal*, vi. Throughout this book, we usually denote our women by their first names once they have been introduced with their full names. We do this for two reasons. It accords with the immediacy and intimacy of personal letters and diaries. First names are also useful in discussing people sharing the same last name to distinguish between them. On HL's presence in Macao, see Lamas, *Everything*; Taketani, *U.S. Women Writers*, chap. 4, 93–124.

2. Zuckerman and others, "Deference." Elkins and McKitrick, *Age*. Wilentz, *Rise*. Cott, *Bonds*.

3. See, for example, HL to SL, Aug. 31, [1828?], in Loines, "Hard Cash," 254–55; HL to SL, Mar. 16, 1829, HL to SL and ML, Sept. 5, 15, 1829, HL to Mary Ann Low, Sept. 15, 1829, in Loines, *China,* 19, 22–30. Hodges, introduction, in Hodges and Hummel, *Lights and Shadows* (hereafter, *L&S*), 2–3. Augur, *Tall Ships*, 21–23, 84, 86–87. Watson, *Liberty*, esp. 10–11, chap. 3.

4. Loines's introduction to chap. 3, *China*, 17. On Eliza Wetmore Ward, see *L&S*, 375–76n73. ML was paying bills to Ward in 1828; ML to SL, Aug. 31, 1828, in Loines, "Hard Cash," 253. Kerber, *Women*; Kelley, *Learning*. Hodges, introduction, *L&S*, 3.

5. May 28, 30, June 3, 6, 9, 8, 10, 13, 1829, in *L&S*, 20, 21, 23–27, and, on Ammidon, see *L&S*, 368n3. Travers, *Celebrating*.

6. June 13, 15, 16, 24, 1829, in *L&S,* 27, 28, 29, 32. Watson, *Liberty*, 91–92. Horward, "American Press"; Kennett, "Le Culte."

7. July 4, 1829, in *L&S*, 34.

8. July 6, 20, 1829, in *L&S*, 35, 39.

9. July 21, 22, 29, Aug. 13, 19, 26, 30, 1829, in *L&S*, 39–40, 43, 47, 49, 52, 54.

10. Coates, *Macao*, 46–47, 63; Dennett, *Americans*, 46; de Pina-Cabral, *Between China*, 8.

11. Mar. 6 and 15, 1830, in *L&S*, 111, 118.

12. This may be Benjamin B. Swasey of Salem, Massachusetts. **SPCRD**; and the 1850 **Census** schedules. HL to SL and ML, Apr. 13, 1830, in Loines, *China*, 36.

13. June 7, Aug. 3, Apr. 14, 1830, Jan. 8, 1831, in *L&S*, 156, 177–78, 139, 194–95.

14. Hodges, introduction, 6–7. Augur, *Tall Ships*, 35, 49–55. Loines, *China*, 304. Fragments of HL's letters to unidentified recipients: Nov. 6, [1830], Jan. 25, [1831], Jan. 8, 1831, in *L&S*, 190–96. Aug. 22, 1830, and HL to [?], Mar. 3, 1831, in *L&S*, 183, 199. May 18, 1831, in *L&S*, 227–28; on the charter renewal, see HL to Family, July 28 in July 20, 1830 [i.e., 1831?], in Loines, *China*, 39. Dennett, *Americans*, 51–52, 55, 92–93.

15. Watson, *Liberty*, 125. Remini, *Andrew Jackson . . . Freedom*, 315–16. Sept. 6, 1831, in *L&S*, 260. Marszalek, *Petticoat*, 162–63.

16. *L&S*, 400n104, 381n113. Oct. 28, Nov. 3, 1831, Mar. 30, 1832, in *L&S*, 276,

278, 305. Marszalek, *Petticoat,* 157–58, 179, 238–39, 163. Coverage continued into the summer; Remini, *Andrew Jackson . . . Freedom*, 320–21.

17. Remini, *Andrew Jackson . . . Democracy*, chap. 1. June 29, July 4, 1832, in *L&S*, 354, 356. Loines, "Hard Cash," 246–48. Marszalek, *Petticoat*, 91. Remini, *Andrew Jackson . . . Freedom*, 248–50, 144–47, 3, 250. VanVugt, *Britain.*

18. June 8, 1832, Feb. 21, 27, Mar. 13, Apr. 7, 1833, in *L&S*, 342–43, 512, 516, 521, 533. See also HL to Mary Ann Low, Dec, 16, 1832, in Loines, *China*, 308–9.

19. May 4, 1833, *L&S*, 545–46. Remini, *Andrew Jackson . . . Democracy*, 11–14; Watson, *Liberty*, 126–28.

20. May 4, 1833, in *L&S,* 546.

21. May 21, June 7, 1833, in *L&S,* 554, 562. On Livingston, see *L&S*, 803n35; Watson, *Liberty*, 127–29.

22. July 4, 1833, in *L&S*, 577. HL to SL and ML, Summer 1833, in Loines, *China*, 52.

23. July 17, 1833, in *L&S*, 586. Watson, *Liberty*, 149; Remini, *Andrew Jackson . . . Democracy*, 137.

24. Aug. 11, 1833, Mar. 30, 1834, in *L&S*, 603, 723–27.

25. Watson, *Liberty*, 154–59. Jan. 1, June 8, 1834, in *L&S*, 682, 755–56. Remini, *Andrew Jackson . . . Democracy,* 112–13, chaps. 5 and 6, esp. 80, 100. Robotti, *Chronicles*, 59. Temin, "Economic Consequences," absolves Jackson's policies. SL to Abbot Low, circa May 1837, quoted in Augur, *Tall Ships*, 87.

26. Sept. 21, 1834, and Aug. 1, 1832, in *L&S*, 789, 421. Hodges, introduction, 1–2, 14–15, quote on 1. Abiel Abbot Low to HL, Apr. 17, 1839; William Henry Low to HL, Feb. 9, 1841; HL to Edward A. Low, July 5, 1846-all in Loines, *China*, 68–72, 84–87, 251.

Chapter 2. Women at the Birth of the Second Party System

1. SWD, Apr. 7, 11, 1834, and all entries below, Diary, **DFP-SL**. Eaton, *Henry Clay*, 112–13. Holt, *Rise and Fall*, 20, 25–28, 34; 39. *CC*, Apr. 14, 1834. Van Deusen, "Whig Party," 336–37.

2. ED to John Davis, Jr., and Horace Davis, Dec. 9, 1835, **JDP-AAS**.

3. LE to SH, Sept. 19, 1828; Jan. 10, Mar. 4, 1829, and all Hale Family letters below, **HFP-SSC**. EP, Mar. 4, 1829, Journal; this and subsequent cites to documents by her in **PFP-SL**.

4. Remini, *Andrew Jackson . . . Indian Wars*, 233–39. Hershberger, "Mobilizing Women." Portnoy, *Their Right*, 1, 64–65, 58.

5. EP, Apr. [n.d.], 1825, entry under Jan. 11, 1829, Notebook. EP, Mar. 19, July 1, 1829, Journal. *CP*, Mar. 11, 1829, 4, col. 1A.

6. EP, Dec. 11, 1829, Journal. **CD** 21: appendix, 3–19 (1829). Remini, *Andrew Jackson . . . Indian Wars*, 231–33.

7. Clark may have taught Indians in Narragansett, R.I., in 1823; see *NBM*, Oct. 10, 1823. EP, Jan. 7, 1830, Journal. Beecher, *Educational Reminiscences*, 62–69.

EP lived near Hartford, where the "Circular" was written. Hershberger, "Mobilizing Women," 25–26. Zaeske, "Unveiling Esther."

8. EP, Jan. 12, 23, 26, Mar. 11, 1830, Journal, Jan. 30, 1830, Notebook. The Anti-Masons, an anti-Jackson party, also called for Sabbatarian reform; see Holt, *Rise and Fall*, 13. Remini, *Andrew Jackson . . . Indian Wars*, 233–34.

9. EP, June 16, Dec. 6, 16, 23, 1830, Feb. 11, 1831, Journal.

10. Remini, *Andrew Jackson . . . Indian Wars*, 247–50, chap. 15. Gabriel, *Elias Boudinot*, 132. ED to JD, Mar. 8, 1832, and all their letters below, **JDP-AAS**. LPH to Agnes Park, Apr. 29, 1832, **PFP-AAS**.

11. Holt, *Rise and Fall*, 16–17. Prescott, *Prescott Memorial*, 70–71. J. Chris Arndt, "Holmes, John," **ANB**. **CD**: 21/1: 385–96. HPr to EEPB, July 23, June 29, 1830, and all her letters below, **BFL-PEM**. *CM*, Jan. 2, 1830. ED to JD, Feb. 6, 1833. SP to MC, Mar. 22 and June 24, 1834, and all their letters below, **PFP-SSC**. Temin, "Economic Consequences."

12. Bulkley, "Robert Rantoul," 115–16, 115–16n9, 179–83; Darling, *Political Changes*, 195–97; Jane Woodbury Rantoul to CR, [received June 13, 1836], **EC-BHS**. Baldwin, Mar. 7, 1834, *Diary*, 280. LLW, July 12, 1839, Journal, **LLWJ-MHS**.

13. MH, June 28, 1833, and all entries below, Diary, **NHHS**. See also Mary Ann Tucker Chandler, June 1833, [8], Diary, **NHHS**. Almira Marshall Woods, Mar. 17, 1831, Diary, Alvah Woods Family Papers (MSS 816), **RIHS**. Clapp, "'Virago-Errant.'"

14. SH to AHE, Feb. 14, 1836; CBE to SH, Jan. 6, 1832. HPr to EEPB, Mar. 24, 1835. ED to JD, May 11, 1832. SWD, Apr. 7, 11, 1834. SP to MC, Jan. 6, Feb. 1, 1829. EP, July 1, 1829, Journal; SH to EdE, Jan. 14, 1829, Feb. 2, 1830. Webster's second "Reply" was published in *DNI*, Feb. 23, 25, and 27, 1830; see Bartlett, "Daniel Webster," 504. HPr to EEPB, Oct. 1, 1834, and Oct. 9, 1830, Mar. 24, 1835. Remini, *Webster*, 337–39, 428–36. Holt, *Rise and Fall*, 40–41. MP to JnP and LTP, July 15 in July 5, 1836, **PFP-SL**.

15. CBE to SH, Jan. 6, 1832. SP to MC, June 24, 1834. Holt, *Rise and Fall*, 21–23.

16. Hansen, "Boston." Jeffrey, *Great*. Zaeske, *Signatures*; Van Broekhoven, *Devotion*. On the national response, see Repousis, "'Cause,'" and E. Earle, "American Interest." *DVRNCA*, Mar. 27 and May 8, 1828. *NM*, Mar. 29, 1828. On New York, see *VG*, Mar. 11, 1828. *NM*, Mar. 29, 1828. *BC*, Mar. 20, 1828. SH to EdE, Mar. 24, 1828.

17. Martin, "Women Fought." [S. Hale], "Worth." "Dearborn, Henry Alexander Scammell," **BDUSC**. Sarah Josepha Hale to Henry A. S. Dearborn, Feb. 24, 1830, Grenville H. Norcross Autograph Collection, **MHS**. Purcell, *Sealed*, 197. *BDAV*, July 3, 1823. "To the Women," 173. *NHS*, Mar. 26, 1830. *SUN*, May 6, 1830. *BJ*, May 13, 1830; *NHP*, May 17, 1830. Laura M. Davis to OW, July 25, 1830, typed transcript, **SFP-SL**. *RIA*, May 25, 1830. SH to EdE, Aug. 10, 1835.

18. Varon, *We Mean* (71–75), discusses the lack of female campaigning before

1840. EP, June 7, 1828, Journal. *DVR*, May 8, 1828. SP to MC, Jan. 6, 1829. HPr to EEPB, Feb. 15, 1830. *NHP*, Feb. 1, 1830. Upham, Hill, and Barton, *Report*.

19. ED to JD, May 11, 1832, Jan. 16, 1833.

20. HPr to EEPB, Apr. 8, Oct. 1, 1834 [1835?], Aug. 15, 1836.

21. Plumstead, *Wall*, 6–15. See EP, June 7, 1828, Journal. *PJLP*, June 4, 1831; *NHS*, June 10, 1831. *NHG*, June 7, 1831. MH, June 2, 1831, June 7, 1832, June 6, 1833, June 2, 1836. *PJLP*, June 25, 1831. *NHP*, June 11, 1832. Cyrus Bradley, June 14, 1833, Diary, **NHHS**. Samantha Barrett, May 7, 1828, and May 6, 1829, Journal, **CHS**. *AM*, May 12, 1829. Stavely and Fitzgerald, *America's Founding*, 253–56.

22. Travers, *Celebrating*. Dublin, "Women." MH, July 4, 1834.

23. EP, July 4, 1829, Journal. *NHG*, Nov. 11, 1828. HPr to EEPB, July 4, 1829.

24. ED to JD, June 11, [1836?].

Chapter 3. Eliza Davis as Political Wife

1. ED to JD, June 11, [1836?], and all letters between the two below, **JDP-AAS**. LCB to GB, Feb. 12, 1836, **GBP-CU**. Henry Clay supposedly named her "the foremost woman at Washington"; see *MS*, Jan. 26, 1872.

2. ED to GB, Feb. 12, 1826, **GBP-CU**. On Whig traits, see Kohl, *Politics*; Howe, *Political Culture* and "Evangelical Movement"; Ashworth, *Agrarians*.

3. On the power of political kin, see Allgor, *Parlor Politics*; Varon, *We Mean*, 88–93, 105–7; Jabour, *Marriage*; Rohrs, "'Public Attention,'" 112–17, 120, 122–23. Chase, "Worcester," 626.

4. ED is featured in Lawes, *Women*, 52, 97, 103, 110; Formisano, *Transformation*, 459n5. See also "John Chandler Bancroft Davis," 13–17; *MS*, Jan. 26, 1872; *WAG*, Jan. 27, 1872. Chase, "Worcester," 626. On JD, see Lincoln, *History*, 207–8; Handlin, *George Bancroft*, 20, 109, 118–19, 124–25, 244; Formisano, *Transformation*, 212–13, 215–16, 253–54, 271, 276, 301, 437n58, 471n6.

5. Lincoln, *History*, 166–69. Chase, "Worcester," 566–67, 626. Aaron Bancroft, "Memoranda designed for the inspection of my Wife & my children Worcester, June 1826," **GBP-CU**. LCB to GB, Jan. 3, 1827, **GBP-CU**. ED to GB, Feb. 28, 1819, **GBP-CU**.

6. There are few extant letters by ED between 1825 and 1829. JD to GB, Jan. 29, 1826, **GBP-CU**. See, for example, JD to ED, Dec. 8, 10, 26, 1825, Jan. 3, 13, Feb. 12, Mar. 8, 1826. JD to ED, Dec. 14, 1825, Jan. 9, 1826. On the speech, see **CD**, 2:912–25, 927–39 (1826). JD to ED, Jan. 2, 21, Feb. 5, 1826.

7. JD to ED, Feb. 13, 1826. LCB to GB, Jan. 26, 1833, **GBP-CU**.

8. Lawes, *Women*, 110. ED to JD, Dec. 20, 1829. JD to ED, Dec. 23, 1829, Feb. 8, 1830.

9. JD to ED, Apr. 20, Jan. 26, Mar. 31, 1830. **CD**, 6:683–86 (1830); 6:58–80 (1830).

10. JD to ED, Feb. 23, Dec. 12, 1831. Watson, *Liberty*, 122–23. **CD**, 8:1424 (1831). *SG*, Oct. 29, 1830.

11. ED to JD, Jan. 15, Mar. 23, 1832. Webster, "Character." *SG*, Oct. 25, 1833. **CD**, 8:1484–85 (1832).

12. **CD**, 7:873–84 (1830). ED to JD, Mar. 8, 1832. **CD**, 8:257–96 (1832). *SG*, Oct. 25, 1833.

13. Reed, "Battleground," 80–82. Holt, *Rise and Fall*, 13, and on National Republican ineffectualness in attracting Anti-Masons, 12–15. ED to JD, May 11, 1832. Silbey, *Martin Van Buren*, 82.

14. Lincoln, *History*, 311. George Folsom spoke for Everett, stuck in Washington; Baldwin, July 4, 1832, *Diary*, 188. ED to JD, June [1832].

15. Watson, *Liberty*, 126–29. ED to JD, Feb. 6, 10, 1833.

16. ED to JD, May 1, June 20, 1832, Jan. 16, 1833. **CD**, 9:1811 (1833).

17. LCB to GB, Mar. 24, 1833, **GBP-CU**. ED to JD, Mar. 8, 1832. *SG*, Mar. 27, 1832. *HG*, July 14, 1832, Oct. 5, 1833.

18. ED to JD, postmarked Dec. 14, 1832, Jan. 16, Feb. 10, 17, Mar. 3, 1833. *NBM*, Mar. 1, 1833. Baldwin, Oct. 2, 1833, *Diary*, 235. *SUN*, Mar. 14, 1833. JD to GB, Dec. 25, 1833, **GBP-CU**. One newspaper reported in January 1833 that JD declined congressional reelection; *SG*, Jan. 18, 1833. According to Baldwin, Oct. 2, 1833, *Diary*, 235, JD "accepted with sincere regret."

19. *SG*, Oct. 4, 1833. Baldwin, Oct. 2, 1833, Jan. 21, *Diary*, 235, 265. *SUN*, Apr. 18, 1833. See JD to GB, Dec. 25, 1833, **GBP-CU**. *SG*, Nov. 26, Dec. 27, 1833. ED to JD, Dec. 17, 1833. *SG*, Dec. 27, 1833. Formisano, *Transformation*, 212–13, 216. **MCUS**. *SG*, Feb. 4, 21, 1834. *MS*, Jan. 26, 1872. She hosted at least one party; see Baldwin, Mar. 13, 1834, *Diary*, 282.

20. *SG*, Jan. 30, 1835. ED to LCB, Dec. 8, 25, 1835, **JDP-AAS**; ED to her sons, Feb. 15, 1836; ED to NCP, Mar. 10, 1836, all **JDP-AAS**.

21. ED to her sons, Dec. 9, 1835, **JDP-AAS**. ED to GB, Feb. 23, 1836, **GBP-CU**. "M" [Matthew Livingston Davis] to "Madame" [ED], June 6, 1836, **JDP-AAS**; the letter's internal evidence suggests Davis. Pasley, "Minnows," 635–36. ED to JD, June 11, [1836?].

22. ED to JD, Apr. 3, [1836?]. Handlin, *George Bancroft*, cf. 158; see also 125, 159–60. ED to JD, June 11, [1836?]. JD to GB, Apr. 17, 1836, **GBP-CU**.

23. LB to GB, Sept. 20, 1836, **GBP-CU**.

24. ED to JD, Dec. 15, 1836, Jan. 8, 1837. He sent other women pamphlets; Belohlavek, *Broken Glass*, 60–61. Lincoln, *History*.

25. ED to JD, Dec. 15, 1836, Jan. 20, 1837. Silbey, *Martin Van Buren*, 113. Holt, *Rise and Fall*, 60. Watson, *Liberty*, 156–57, 165. **CD**, 13:504 (1837). **CD**, 13:453–55 (1837).

26. Silbey, *Martin Van Buren*, 114–17, 119–24. M. Wilson, *Presidency*, chap 3.

27. ED to JD, Sept. 30, 1837. Niven, *John C. Calhoun*, 229–33. C. Wilson, *Papers*, 306.

28. M. Wilson, *Presidency*, 41. Silbey, *Martin Van Buren*, 131–33. J. Earle, *Jacksonian Antislavery*, 42–47. ED to NCP, Jan. 17, 1838.

29. **CG**, 25/2/202 (1838). ED to JD, Apr. 20, May 13, 1838. Lincoln, *History*, 201, 367.

30. ED to JD, Jan. 13, Feb. 3, 1839. By 1838, there were thirty-two antislavery societies in Worcester County; Laurie, *Beyond Garrison*, 22; Brooke, *Heart*, 353–68. LCB to GB and Elizabeth Bliss Bancroft, Dec. 24, 1838, **GBP-CU**. **CG**, 25/3/40–41 (1838). **CG**, 25/3/60 (1838). Raikes, *City*, 131–32.

31. ED to JD, Feb. 3, 1839.

32. ED to JD, Feb. 20, 1839, Jan 1, 1840. LB to GB, Sept. 8, 1839, **GBP-CU**.

Chapter 4. Women's Political Polarization during the Van Buren Administration

1. Handlin, *George Bancroft*, 157. On similar attacks upon Van Buren, see Silbey, *Martin Van Buren*, 103–4. LB to GB, Dec. 21, 1836, **GBP-CU**.

2. Handlin, *George Bancroft*, 139, 141–43, 157, 159; Formisano, *Transformation*, 216, chap. 10. LB to GB, Dec. 21, 1836, Nov. 19, 1834, **GBP-CU**.

3. On the gradual, growing interest in national elections from 1828 to 1840, see Formisano, *Transformation*, 17. Holt, *Rise and Fall*, ix, 110. Formisano, *Transformation*, 262. On 1836, see M. Wilson, *Presidency*, 18; Silbey, *Martin Van Buren*, 105.

4. Holt, *Rise and Fall*, 71–76.

5. Ibid., 71–78. Templin, "Panic Fiction."

6. LCB to GB, Nov. 20, 1833, and May 10, 1837, **GBP-CU**. M. Wilson, *Presidency*, 43. Temin, *Jacksonian Economy*, chaps. 4 and 5. Handlin, *George Bancroft*, 122, 170. *BDET*, May 17, 1837. Schlesinger, *Age*, 223–24; Darling, *Political Changes*, 203. Putnam, *Memoir*, 150–53. M. Wilson, *Presidency*, 57. HLJC to SJR, May 18, 1837, **AFP-SL**.

7. Holt, *Rise and Fall*, 76–77; Silbey, *Martin Van Buren*, 140–41. *SG*, Oct. 20, 1837. LCB to GB, Nov. 12, 1837, **GBP-CU**. SH to EdE, Dec. 11, 1837, **HFP-SSC**. *NBM*, Dec. 15, 1837. Cockrell, *Demons*, 113–14.

8. KBL to AL, Nov. 6, 23, 24, and 28, 1837, and subsequent correspondence from KBL to AL below, **LFP-MHS**. *SG*, Nov. 10, 1837, Nov. 21, 1837; *SUN*, Nov. 23, 1837. For this and the next two paragraphs, see Zboray and Zboray, "Whig Women," 305–7.

9. KBL to AL, Dec. 21, 1837, Jan. 1, 4, 22, 24, Feb. 10, 28, July 24, 1838. *SUN*, Dec. 21, 1837. Pasley, "Minnows," 632–50. *SG*, July 27, 1838. AL to KBL, Mar. 8, Apr.1, 8, 1838, **RLFP-MHS**. AL to Abbott Lawrence, Mar. 11, 1838, **RLFP-MHS**.

10. KBL to AL, Nov. 14, 1838. Hampel, *Temperance*, 57, 82. *NBM*, Nov. 29, 1838; *SG*, Nov. 16, 1838.

11. Bulkley, "Robert Rantoul," 115–16, 115–16n9, 212, 212n38, 228–32. CR to "Friends," Oct. 3, 1838, **EC-BHS**.

12. CR to RR, Oct. 18, 1838, **RC-BHS**; CR to "Dear People," Oct. 22, 1838, **EC-BHS**. CR to "Friends," Oct. 3, 1838.

13. Bulkley, "Robert Rantoul," 229–36. *NBM*, Oct. 12, 1838. CR to RR, Oct. 29, 1838, **RC-BHS**. CR to RR, Oct. 16, 1838, **RC-BHS**. Zboray and Zboray, *Literary Dollars*, 26.

14. Darling, *Political Changes*, 235; Bulkley, "Robert Rantoul," 235. *ER*, Nov. 1, 1838. McKivigan, *Abolitionist Movement*, ix; Laurie, *Beyond Garrison*, 41–45; Mitchell, *Antislavery Politics*, 12. CR to Hannah Rantoul, Nov. 5, 1838, **EC-BHS**.

15. McGovern, *Yankee Family*, 56–58. For this and the next two paragraphs, see Zboray and Zboray, "Whig Women," 295–97.

16. MP to JnP and LTP, Sept. 7 in Aug. 31, 1838, May 16 in May 14, 1838, and all subsequent letters among these three, **PFP-SL**.

17. MP to JnP and LTP, Sept. 10, 1838, in Sept. 8, 1838. *NHG*, Oct. 2, 1838. *BDW*, Sept. 10, 1838. For earlier tricks see A. Taylor, "'Art,'" 1388–89.

18. MP to JnP and LTP, Sept. 11, 12, 1838, in Sept. 8, 1838; Sept. 16 in Sept. 14, 1838.

19. Formisano, *Transformation*, 263–64, quote, 264. Darling, *Political Changes*, 240–41. *NBM*, Nov. 15, 1839. *HG*, Dec. 27, 1839. *NBM*, Jan. 17, 1840. ED to JD, Jan. 1, 1840, and letters between them below, **JDP-AAS**. LB to GB, Nov. 21, 1839, **GBP-CU**.

20. Darling, *Political Changes*, 251–59. LLW, Feb. 14, 1840, Journal, **LLWJ-MHS**.

21. AL, Dec. 21, 1838, Apr. 1, Aug. 1, 1839, Diary, **LFP-MHS**. Lynch, *Epoch*, 2:428–36. Philena Hawks Bodman to Silas and Rebecca Hawks, July 8, 1839, **BFP-SSC**. For this and the next paragraph, see Zboray and Zboray, "Whig Women," 307–8.

22. AL, Nov. 23 and 27, 1839, Jan. 3, 9, 1840, Diary. Gelles, *Abigail Adams*.

23. Smith appears in Jeffrey, *Great*, 47, 3, 6, and Zaeske, *Signatures*, 47. Gienapp, "Abolitionism," 24, 32. MP to JnP and LTP, Jan. 25, 1837, Aug. 6 in July 31, 1837. Blanchard, "Politics."

24. SB, Dec. 1839, Account Book, **BroFP-SL**. *ER*, Dec. 5, 1839. AMNL, Jan. 2, 1839, Pocket Memorandum, **PEM**. Gordon, *Bazaars*, 10, 38, 42–46, 52–57.

25. Jeffrey, *Great*, 27–28. MP to JnP and LTP, Jan. 25, 1837, Aug. 6 in July 31, 1837. For a lecture goer, see Mary Gardner Lowell, June 25, 1837, Diary, **FCLP-MHS**.

26. Elizabeth Fuller to Elizabeth B. Cheever, [Feb. 1837], **CFP-AAS**. SJ, Mar. 3, 1839, Diary, **JFP-CHS**. EJ, Sept. 23, 1839, Diary, **JFP-CHS**. Jones, *Mutiny*. Elizabeth B. Cheever to Henry T. Cheever, Dec. 4, 1837, **CFP-AAS**. Simon, *Freedom's Champion*.

27. M. Wilson, *Presidency*, 164, 167; Jones, "Anglophobia," 532. Sprague, *North Eastern Boundary*, 59–61, Fairfield quote on 59. Le Duc, "Maine Frontier," 30–32.

28. See Le Duc, "Maine Frontier," 30. Jones, "Anglophobia," 530, 528; Silbey, *Martin Van Buren*, 127–28. M. Wilson, *Presidency*, 166–67.

29. Jones, "Anglophobia," 524. MP to JnP and LTP, Feb. 6 and 16, 1839, in Jan. 31, 1839.

30. *BDW*, Feb. 18, 1839. Sprague, *North Eastern Boundary*, 61. Jones, "Anglo-

phobia," 524. M. Wilson, *Presidency*, 166. MP to JnP and LTP, Feb. 17, 18, in Jan. 31, 1839. McGovern, *Yankee Family*, 58. See General Orders no. 5 and 6, in Maine Council, *Aroostook*, 7–8, 40. Uviller and Merkel, *Militia*, 113–14. All states allowed replacements; see Mahon, *History*, 52–53.

31. General Order no. 5, in Maine Council, *Aroostook*, 7. MP to JnP and LTP, Feb. 18, 20, 1839, in Jan. 31, 1839, Mar. 1, 1839.

32. General Order no. 7, in Maine Council, *Aroostook*, 8; Jones, "Anglophobia," 525; Sprague, *North Eastern Boundary*, 64–65. "Constitution," 182. Maine Council, *Aroostook*, 29, 33–34, 46, 64. HPr to Mary Prescott Delesdesnier, Mar. 3, 1839, **BFL-PEM**.

33. EJ, Feb. 25, Mar. 1, 1839, Diary, **JFP-CHS**. SJ, Mar. 12, 1839, Diary, **JFP-CHS**. MP to JnP and LTP, Mar. 1, 1839.

34. Caroline Haynes, Mar. 9, 1839, added entry in William Durkee Williamson, Album and Diary (ms.Am.164), **BPL**. *SUN*, Apr. 4, 1839. M. Wilson, *Presidency*, 166–68. Jones, "Anglophobia," 534.

35. LH to JnP and LTP, Mar. 30, 1839, in MP to JnP and LTP, Mar. 20, 1839. Jones, "Anglophopbia," 520–21.

36. Maine Council, *Aroostook*, 40, 22. MP to JnP and LTP, Apr. 15, 1839.

Chapter 5. Women and Mass Politics in the 1840 Campaign

1. MP to HP, Sept. 6, 1840, and all their letters below, **PFP-SL**. *BA*, Sept. 2, 5, Oct. 27, 1840; *BMP*, Sept. 1, 5, 10, Oct. 2, 10, 1840. This chapter contains scattered passages from Zboray and Zboray, "Whig Women" (© 1997 Society for Historians of the Early American Republic), which are reprinted by permission of the University of Pennsylvania Press.

2. Gunderson, *Log-Cabin*, 8, 73, 121, 127, 134–39; Formisano, *Transformation*, 262–67; Peterson, *Presidencies*, 29–30; Goebel, *William Henry Harrison*, 348–65. Kincheloe, "Transcending Role Restrictions," 158–69; Varon, "'Ladies'"; idem, "Tippecanoe," passim, esp. 518–19; DeFiore, "Come"; Formisano, "New"; Chambers, "Election of 1840." Fischer, *Tippecanoe*, 29–48; Melder, *Hail*, 75–90. RS, July 1, Account Book, **SFP-AAS**. LLN, July 23, 1840, Diary, **NFP-AAS**. Sarah K. (Batchelder) Fuller Notebook, [c. 1840] 1842, **BPL**.

3. Handlin, *George Bancroft*, 168, 176–77. Zboray and Zboray, "Gender Slurs," 413–33.

4. Ryan, *Cradle*; Boylan, "Women and Politics"; Carwardine, "Evangelicals"; Howe, "Evangelical Movement." On "Whiggery, religion, and women," see Formisano, "New," 681–82n36. Verba, "Women," 567. On the ethnocultural, see Feller, "Politics"; Formisano, *Transformation*, 278–301. On party loyalty, see Silbey, *Partisan Imperative*, and J. Baker, *Affairs*. Cf. Shover, "Another Look." On "multicausality," see Formisano, "New," 672, and on synthetic consensus, see Feller, "Politics," 154–61. On "rational" issue-oriented voters, see Holt, "Election of 1840."

5. For views on women's limited involvement, see Gunderson, *Log-Cabin*, 4,

137–39; Ryan, *Women*, 135–37; Goebel, *William Henry Harrison*, 353; McGerr, "Political Style."

6. *QP*, July 18, 1840. ED to JD, Jan. 1, 1840, and all letters between them below, **JDP-AAS**. Shover, "Another Look," esp. 551–55.

7. ED to JD, Feb. 12, 1840. *BG*, Feb. 21, 1840.

8. M. Wilson, *Presidency*, 138. Harrison was pro-Bank; Gilbert, "Banks and Politics." Hammond, "Jackson, Biddle." It was state chartered in February 1836; Catterall, *Second Bank*, 372. ED to JD, Feb. 12, 1840. *BS*, Feb. 3, 5, 1840; *Madisonian for the Country*, Washington, D.C., Feb. 4, 1840; *NHG*, Feb. 11, 1840; *RIR*, Feb. 12, 1840. Holt, *Rise and Fall*, 66.

9. ED to JD, Feb. 12, 1840. Her insightful analysis accurately predicted the Democratic Party's largely reactive Log-Cabin Campaign, as described in Chambers, "Election of 1840," and Troy, *See How They Ran*, 21–30. On GB's party vision, see J. Baker, *Affairs*, esp. 120–40. Formisano, *Transformation*, 263.

10. ED to JD Feb. 15, 1840.

11. ED to JD, Feb. 15, 1840. **CG**, 26/1/Appendix: 157–61 (1840). See, for example, *NBM*, Feb. 21, 1840; *HG*, Mar. 6, 1840; Mar. 7, 1840, letter in *NBM*, Mar. 13, 1840.

12. RS to SS, Feb. 20, 25, 1840, **SFP-AAS**.

13. This may be Charles Warren, who advised Elizabeth Bliss not to marry Bancroft; ED to JD, May 13, 1838, Mar. 5, 1840. Lincoln, *History*, 387.

14. ED to JD, Mar. 8, 1840.

15. *SUN*, Mar. 26, 1840; *NBM*, Mar. 13 and 7, 1840. The exchange appeared in **CG**, 26/1/Appendix: 129–37, 157–61, 230–32, 244–47, 335–40. On Walker, see ibid., 137–40 (1840). The speech and replies were published in several pamphlet editions. ED to JD, Mar. 15, 1840. Eliza probably referred to "Correspondence . . . Washington March 7th, 1840," *BMP*, Mar. 12, 1840. JD to ED, Mar. 18, 1840.

16. ED to JD, Mar. 22 [i.e., 21], 1840.

17. ED to JD, Mar. 28, Apr. 5, 1840. LLW, Apr. 19, 1840, Journal, **LLWJ-MHS**. Gideon Welles to GB, Apr. 7, 1840, George Bancroft Papers, **MHS**. Klein, *President James Buchanan*, 133–34.

18. ED to JD, May 14, 1840.

19. ED to JD, June 6 [i.e., 5], 10, 1840.

20. ED to JD, June 10, 13 [i.e., 12], 14, 1840. *NBM*, Mar. 6, June 5, 1840; *BG*, June 19, 1840.

21. ED to JD, July [i.e., June] 18, 1840.

22. Ibid. *HG*, June 20, 1840. LLN, June 17, 1840, Diary. *PJLP*, June 20, 1840. *BA*, June 17, 18, 19, 1840; *MS*, June 24, 1840. Formisano, *Transformation*, 264, estimates the number of conventioneers at 10,000–20,000. **HCB**, 1840. EE to RS, June 19, 1840, **SFP-AAS**. SEH to NHJ, June 18, 1840, **HFP-SSC**.

23. ED to JD, July [i.e., June] 18, 1840. *HG*, June 20, 1840; EE to RS, June 19, 1840.

24. ED to JD, July [i.e., June] 18, 1840. SEH to NHJ, June 18, 1840, **HFP-SSC**.

25. JD to ED, June 22, 1840. Zboray and Zboray, "Gender Slurs," 429. *BMP*, Sept. 3, 9, 1840; *BSD*, Aug. 5, 1840.

26. ED to JD, July [i.e., June] 18, 1840.

27. MP to HP, Mar. 30, Apr. 11, June 30, 1840.

28. MP to HP, July 12, 1840; HP to MP, Aug. 16, 1840.

29. AM, July 4, 1840, Diary, **OCHS**. MF, July 4, 1840, Diary, **LHS**. *NBM*, July 10, 1840. LLN, July 4, 1840, Diary. LB to GB, July 2, 1840, **GBP-CU**. ED to JD, July 6, 1840.

30. *QP*, July 11, 18, 1840. **DJQA**, Aug. 15, 1840. Names and occupations are based on *QP*, July 25, 1840, and the 1850 **Census**. *QP*, July 25, Aug. 8 and 15, 1840.

31. *QP*, Sept. 5, 12, 1840. *BDA*, Sept. 5, 1840. MP to HP, Sept. 6, 1840; HP to MP, Sept. 13, 1840. *BA*, Oct. 27, Sept. 5, 1840.

32. MP to HP, Sept. 11, 19, 1840. Darling, *Political Changes*, 262.

33. MP to HP, Sept. 19, 1840. On reading rooms, see AHE, Dec. 23, 1838, to Mar. 3, 1839, Diary, **HFP-SSC**.

34. HP to MP, Nov. 1, 1840; MP to HP, Nov. 9, 1840. Watson, *Liberty*, 222. For similar stories, see *BMP*, Sept. 8, 1840; Gunderson, *Log-Cabin*, 139. Kohl, *Politics*, 3–18.

35. MP to HP, Nov. 9, 1840.

36. AL, Feb. 6, 9, 12, 16, 22, 24, 26, Apr. 19, 1840, Diary, **LFP-MHS**. Hoffman's speech appeared in *DNI*, Feb. 28, 1840.

37. *BS*, May 5, 1840. M. Wilson, *Presidency,* 202. AL, May 4, 1840, Diary. RS to SS, May 6, 1840, **SFP-AAS**; *HG*, May 9, 1840. Gunderson, *Log-Cabin*, 2.

38. *BS*, June 24, 1840. AL, May 30, June 17, 27, 1840, Diary.

39. *HG*, Sept. 5, 1840. AL, Sept. 9, 10, 1840, Diary. AM, Sept. 10, 1840, Diary, **OCHS**. On the number in light of other meetings, see Chambers, "Election of 1840," 1:679.

40. Thornton, *Cultivating Gentlemen*; AL, Sept. 10–11, 1840, Diary.

41. On the revolutionary legacy, see Howe, *Political Culture*, 90–91; Kruman, "Second American Party System."

42. R. Frothingham, *History*, 337–55; Packard, *History*, 7–32. *BDA*, Sept. 12, 16, 1840. *BMP*, July 24, 28, 29, Aug. 5, Sept. 9, 14, 15, Oct. 1, 20, 1840. *BC*, Aug. 13, Oct. 26, 1840. For Hale quote, see W. Taylor, *Cavalier*, 141. Zboray and Zboray, "Political News," 5–6; AL, Sept. 11, 1840, Diary.

43. AL, Sept. 16, 1840, Diary. Guest, *Fanny Elssler*, 170; Banner, *American Beauty*, 63–64. Moore, "Ballet Slippers." *BMP*, July 31, Aug. 24, 29, Sept. 3, 7, 8, 29, Oct. 2, 6, 1840. SH to CBE, Oct. 5, 1840, **HFP-SSC**. Zboray and Zboray, "Gender Slurs," 431–32. Caleb Cushing to "Dear Sir," Sept. 19, 1840, **CCP-LC**.

44. [KBL?] to [AL,] n.d., [late summer], 1840, **LFP-MHS**. SEW to CAW, Aug. 19, 1840, **WFP-AAS**. LLN, July 30, 1840, Diary. EC to ChC, Sept. 1, 1840, **CFP-VHS**. SJ, Oct. 9, [i.e., 8] 1840, Diary, **JFP-CHS**. LTP to LH, Nov. 6 in Oct. 29, 1840, **PFP-SL**. For New Hampshire and Connecticut, see *PJLP*, Sept. 5, 1840; *CC,* Oct. 24, 1840; for Rhode Island, see Formisano, "Role," 91.

45. CH, Oct. 9, 15, 17, 27, 1840, Journal, **LHS**.

46. SH to CBE, Oct. 5, 1840, **HFP-SSC**. Amos Lawrence to Amos A. Lawrence, Sept. 19, 1840, **ALP-MHS**. Fanny Calderon de la Barca to AL, July 4, 1840, **RLFP-MHS**, is full of politics. AL, Sept. 19, 1840, Diary. The letter from Abbott Lawrence to Philip Marett, Sept. 19, 1840, **RLFP-MHS**, is clearly in her hand. Hill, *Memoir*, 58–59.

47. AL, Sept. 19, Oct. 13, 1840, Diary.

48. Gunderson, *Log-Cabin*, 253; *BS*, Oct. 24, 1840. SJ, Nov. 3, 5, [i.e., 2, 4] 1840, Diary, **JFP-CHS**. CH, Nov. 9, 1840, Journal, **LHS**. SH to EdE, Nov. 30, 1840, **HFP-SSC**. Holt, "Election of 1840"; idem, *Rise and Fall*, 89–90, 111–12.

49. AL, Jan. 29, 1841, Diary.

50. SH to EdE, Nov. 30, 1840, **HFP-SSC**. SJ, Nov. 13 [i.e., 12], 1840, Diary. AL, Nov. 22, 24, 1840, Diary. MP to HP, Dec. 27, 1840. Howe, *Political Culture*, 50–54.

51. SH to EdE, Nov. 30, 1840.

Chapter 6. Persis Sibley Andrews and the Politics of Covert Partisanship

1. PSA, Mar. 4, 1841, and all her quotes below, unless otherwise stated, Diary, courtesy of **MeHS**.

2. **BDUSC**; "Andrews, Charles," **PG**.

3. Monroe, *Republican Vision*; Watson, *Liberty*, 226–30; Chitwood, *John Tyler*. Holt, *Rise and Fall*, chap. 6, esp. 123–24, 127–28, 137, 140, 147, 149–50.

4. Crapol, *John Tyler*.

5. PSA, Jan. 1, 13, 1841, Oct. 22, 1844. PSA, Jan. 1, 1842, Diary, **DFP-MHS**. Lystra, *Searching*, 158–65.

6. PSA, Jan. 1, 6, 13, 18, and 31, Feb. 2, 1841. *SG*, Jan. 1, 1841. *NHG*, Jan. 19, 1841. *NHPSG*, Jan. 15, 1841.

7. PSA, Feb. 7, 8, 9, 10, 1841.

8. *LC*, Feb. 20, 1841. PSA, Feb. 9, 1841.

9. PSA, Feb. 9–10, 1841. *LC*, Feb. 20, 1841.

10. PSA, Feb. 11, 1841.

11. PSA, Feb. 25, Mar. 11–13, 16, Apr. 1, 1841. Peterson, *Presidencies*, 35–36.

12. PSA, Mar. 14, Apr. 4, 28, 1841. Zboray and Zboray, *Everyday Ideas*, 79–85. PSA, Jan. 1, 1842, **DFP-MHS**.

13. Peterson, *Presidencies*, 34–41. PSA, Apr. 8, 1841.

14. CC, Apr. 7, 1841, Journal, **RIHS**; see also SuJ, Apr. 7, 1841, Diary, **LHS**, and CH, Apr. 8, 1841, **LHS**. Fanny Dean (Kingman) Holmes, Apr. 11, 1841, Notebook, **SL**; see also Jane E. Shedd to Elizabeth Chamberlain, Apr. 13, 1841, **WCFP-VHS**. SJ, Apr. 17, 1841, Diary, **JFP-CHS**. CP, Apr. 23, 1841, Diary, **CHS**. KBL to AL, Apr. 11, 1841, **LFP-MHS**. SH to CBE, Apr. 24, 1841, **HFP-SSC**; *BDA*, Apr. 12, 1841; *SG*, Apr. 16, 1841. *HG*, Apr. 24, 1841.

15. PSA, May 1, 8, 14, 22, 26, 29, 31, July 3, Aug. 4, 1841. On fast day, see OW, May 14, 1841, Journal, **SFP-SL**; SuJ, May 14, 1841, Journal, **LHS**.

16. PSA, July 29, Aug. 7, 14, 18, Sept. 14, 1841. Chitwood, *John Tyler*, 226–51; Holt, *Rise and Fall*, 129–35; Watson, *Liberty*, 228.

17. PSA, Nov. 15, June 2, Sept. 13, 1841. Holt, *Rise and Fall*, 139.

18. PSA, Sept. 29, 1841, June 10, 1843.

19. PSA, Oct. 15, 16, 23, Nov. 9, 15, 18, Dec. 13, 1841. **CG**, 27/2/3–7 (1841). Chitwood, *John Tyler*, 291–93. Seager, *Tyler Too*, 164.

20. PSA, Dec. 31, 1841. PSA, Jan. 2, 6, 7, 1842, Diary, **DFP-MHS**.

21. PSA, Jan. 9, 11, 1842, **DFP-MHS**.

22. PSA, Apr. 2, Oct. 18, 1842, **DFP-MHS**.

23. PSA, Jan. 1, 14, 21, Oct. 8, 1843.

24. PSA, Jan. 1, 8, Mar. 3, 12, Apr. 9, 15, 22, 1843. Zboray and Zboray, *Everyday Ideas*, 136–37.

25. *BDA*, Mar. 28, 1843; *SP*, Oct. 20, 1843. *BDW*, Dec. 19, 1843. PSA, Mar. 25, June 4, 1843.

26. PSA, June 10, Aug. 19, 1843.

27. PSA, June 17, 25, Aug. 19, Sept. 10, 21, Nov. 19, Dec. 10, 1843.

28. PSA, Sept. 11, 1843. Pierson, *Free Hearts*, 25. *SUN*, Sept. 28, 1843. *BDW*, Oct. 26, 1843; *EFA*, Sept. 21, 1843; *NHP*, Sept. 21, 1843.

29. PSA, Sept. 23, 1843.

30. *BDW*, Oct. 18, 1843. PSA, Nov. 19, Oct. 8, 19, Nov. 5, 1843.

31. PSA, Nov. 19, 1843. *BDA*, Dec. 15, 1843.

32. PSA, Dec. 16, 1843.

33. PSA, Jan. 1, 12, 1845, June 2, 1844.

34. PSA, Jan. 1, 12, 27, Feb. 15, Mar.1, 31, Apr. 15, May 19, 1844.

35. PSA, Sept. 16, 1843, June 2, 22, July 8, 19, 1844. Holt, *Rise and Fall*, 164. Leonard, *James K. Polk*, 34–39. Hatch, *Maine*, 598.

36. PSA, Aug. 7, 11, 28, 30, Sept. 7, 1844.

37. PSA, Sept. 15, 1844.

38. PSA, Oct. 19, 22, 1844, Jan. 1, 1841. *HG*, Oct. 10, 1840.

39. PSA, Nov. 10, 1844.

40. PSA, Sept. 27, Nov. 24, Dec. 31, 1845, June 22, 1846.

41. PSA, May 5, Sept. 15, 1850; Nov. 24, 1851; Jan. 4, Feb. 8, May 9, 1852.

Chapter 7. Women Encounter Radical Democracy in the Dorr Rebellion

1. *SP*, Apr. 26, 1842. Mowry, *Dorr War*, 175–76. Chitwood, *John Tyler*, 327. Gettleman, *Dorr Rebellion*, 109–17; Dennison, *Dorr War*, 72, 84. Lawson, *American State Trials*, 28. AM, May 16, 1842, and all her cites below, Journal, courtesy **OCHS**.

2. Formisano, "Role," 91–96; Gettleman, *Dorr Rebellion*, 168n111; Schantz, *Piety*, 67, 195–96, 206–13, 229, 250. Graham, "Female Politician," chap. 1.

3. Graham, "Female Politician," 35, 237 (quote). Dennison, *Dorr War*, 20–22.

4. AM, Apr. 17, 1841. *NM*, Apr. 17, 1841. Gettleman, *Dorr Rebellion*, 39.

5. Gettleman, *Dorr Rebellion*, 33, 34, 7, 35n11, 38–39. Formisano, "Role," 91; Dennison, *Dorr War*, 30, 36; Graham "Female Politician," 5. Sterne, *Ballots*, 14. Holt, *Rise and Fall*, 112.

6. Sterne, *Ballots*, 14–15; Gettleman, *Dorr Rebellion*, 3–7, 18–20, 21–22, 25–30. *PP*, Feb. 22, 1834, Mar. 1, 1834. *NM*, May 10, July 5, Aug. 16, 30, Sept. 6, 20, 1834. *RIR*, Nov. 19, 1834.

7. Gettleman, *Dorr Rebellion*, 34–40. AM, July 5, 1841.

8. Gettleman, *Dorr Rebellion*, 40–46, 60–62.

9. Gettleman, *Dorr Rebellion*, 53–54, 63, 242.

10. Sterne, *Ballots*, 14. Formisano, *People*, 166–67. Gettleman, *Dorr Rebellion*, 9, 146. AM, Mar. 24, 1842. Silverman, *Lightning Man*, 337.

11. Gettleman, *Dorr Rebellion*, 82–84, 90–93.

12. *NYS*, Apr. 9, 13, 1842. Gettleman, *Dorr Rebellion*, 95–96.

13. See LLN, Apr. 22, 1842, Diary, **NFP-AAS**. JP, Apr. 11, 12, 13, 16, 19, 1842, Diary (ms.1.Am.1352), **BPL** (hereafter all JP quotations and references are from the Diary, courtesy of **BPL**).

14. Graham, "Female Politician," 211. Mowry, *Dorr War*, 151–54. Gettleman, *Dorr Rebellion*, 101–3. JP, May 2, 3, 4, 1842. AM, May 3, 1842.

15. Mowry, *Dorr War*, 160–63, 168–71, 178; Gettleman, *Dorr Rebellion*, 108, 114, 116. Dennison, *Dorr War*, 81. JP, May 14, 1842.

16. Gettleman, *Dorr Rebellion*, 118; Mowry, *Dorr War*, 176–78, 181–82. AM, May 18, 1842. Dennison, *Dorr War*, 84. *BDA*, May 19, 1842. Lawson, *American State Trials*, 2:28–29.

17. Mowry, *Dorr War*, 184–88. Gettleman, *Dorr Rebellion*, 120–22. Lawson, *American State Trials*, 2:28–29. CRW, "Recollections of the Life and Conversation of Thomas W. Dorr, First Governor of Rhode Island under the People's Constitution," 24–25, **SRC-BUL**.

18. AM, May 18, 1842. Dennison, *Dorr War*, 88, 90. AM, May 20, 1842. Nicholas Power to TWD, June 12, 1842-this and all subsequent letters to TWD, **SRC-BUL.**

19. MAW, May 21, 1842, Diary, **AAS**. Dennison, *Dorr War*, 87–88; Gettleman, *Dorr Rebellion*, 128, 130. Carter and Holmes, *Genealogical Record*, 64–65.

20. Dennison, *Dorr War*, 87, 88, 92, 218n13, 14; Gettleman, *Dorr Rebellion*, 131–32. JP, June 4, 1842. AM, June 18, 1842.

21. Mowry, *Dorr War*, 210. *BCW*, June 30, 1842. *NM*, July 2, 1842. LPH to JP, June 24, 1842, in JP, June 26, 1842 (hereafter LPH to JP).

22. LPH to JP. *NM*, July 2, 1842. Van Broekhoven, *Devotion*, 46; Schantz, *Piety*, 160, 198, 213, 216.

23. LPH to JP. *SUN*, June 30, 1842. *BDA*, June 27, 1842. Van Broekhoven, *Devotion*, 40–41.

24. LPH to JP. *NM*, June 25, 1842.

25. LPH to JP. Dennison, *Dorr War*, 93–94. JP, June 25, 1842.

26. Dennison, *Dorr War*, 92; Gettleman, *Dorr Rebellion*, 135. Mary A. Anthony

to TWD, Aug. 21, 1842. AM, June 25, 26, 30, 1842. Mowry, *Dorr War*, 213, 223–24.

27. Mowry, *Dorr War*, 214–19. AM, June 27, 29, July 2, 1842. LLN, June 30, 1842. Gettleman, *Dorr Rebellion*, 141. *NM*, July 2, 1842. *SUN*, July 7, 1842. CRW to TWD, Oct. 9, 1842.

28. MAW, July 2, 4, 22, Aug. 13, Nov. 25, Dec. 26, 1842, Feb. 7, Mar. 18, 1843, Diary. **THSN** (Winter 2003): 4. Graham, "Female Politician," 22.

29. CRW to TWD, Oct. 9, 1842; Suffrage Ladies of Providence to TWD, Aug. 20, 1842; Franklin Croley to TWD, Aug. 20, 1842. Graham, "Female Politician," 29–35, 231. CRW, "Recollections," 10–11. Formisano, "Role," 94–95; idem, *People*, 174–76.

30. Almira Howard to TWD, Aug. 16, 1842; E. Taylor to TWD, Sept. 4 1842; Graham, "Female Politician," 34. AnP to TWD, Sept. 4, 1842; CRW to TWD, Sept. 6, Oct. 9, 1842; Mary J. Campbell to TWD, Oct. 8, 1842.

31. CRW to TWD, Nov. 2, 1842; Sam Ashley to TWD, Oct. 12, 1842. Darling, *Political Changes*, 284–87. *BS*, Aug. 8, 1842. *NHPSG,* Aug. 11, 1842. *BS*, Aug. 9, 1842. *DGSA*, Aug. 13, 1842. *BDA*, Aug. 9, 1842.

32. *BG*, Aug. 26, Sept. 2, 16, 1842. *BS,* Sept. 3, 1842. *SUN*, Sept. 15, Oct. 6, 1842; *NHPSG*, Sept. 22, Oct. 6, 1842. James Buchanan to P. W. Ferris, Aug. 22, 1842, in *SUN*, Sept. 15, 1842. *BDA*, Oct. 20, 22, Sept. 2, May 31, Nov. 1, Sept. 24, Nov. 12, 1842. *EM*, Sept. 22, 1842. Graham, "Female Politician," 118–221. *Pennsylvania Inquirer and National Gazette*, Sept. 2, 1842. *NYS*, Sept. 3, 1842. AnP to TWD, Sept. 4, 1842. *OS*, Sept. 12, 1842. CRW to TWD, Nov. 2, 1842; Abby Lord to TWD, Oct. 2, 1842. Darling, *Political Changes*, 287. Formisano, *People*, 173.

33. Graham, "Female Politician," 208–23, 280–86, 209–11. Ashley to TWD. Formisano, *People*, 175–76. AnP to TWD, Nov. 6, 1842. *NYH*, Nov. 5, 1842; *NHPSG*, Nov. 10, Oct. 27, 1842. *OS*, Dec. 19, 1842; *BDA*, Dec. 9, 1842. CRW to TWD, Nov. 2, 1842. The Nashua picnic was canceled; see *FC*, Nov. 4, 1842.

34. Mowry, *Dorr War*, 286–87, Darling, *Political Changes*, 289–93. AnP to TWD, Nov. 6, 1842. CRW to TWD, Dec. 28, Nov. 2, 1842; Holt, *Rise and Fall*, 157.

35. Gettleman, *Dorr Rebellion*, 145–51, 160–61n79, 158–59. "Dorrite Suffrage Meeting," broadside in Graham, "Female Politician," 139; see also 63, 163, 244. CRW, "Recollections," 23; CRW to TWD, Nov. 27, Dec. 28, 1842, Mar. 11, Apr. 13, 22, 1843. *NHPSG*, Oct. 5, 1843. Field, *State*, 350. *DOS*, Apr. 12, 1843. *SUN*, Apr. 13, 1843.

36. *NM*, July 1, 1843. Burke, *Rhode Island*, 836–38, 1068–70, 316. *OS*, Oct. 18, 1843. CRW, "Recollections," 48–50. Graham, "Female Politician," 254–59.

37. *BDA*, Aug. 31, 1843. Gettleman, *Dorr Rebellion*, 159–61; Mowry, *Dorr War*, 241–43. Ida Russell to TWD, Apr. 24, 1844. Sophie L. Little to TWD, Apr. 24, 1844. Graham, "Female Politician," 63–64, 162, 94. Hudson, *Journalism*, 345. *NYH*, Feb. 9, 1844. Green, *Might*, 13–26.

38. Mowry, *Dorr War*, 253, 243. CRW, "Recollections," 27. *NHP*, July 18, 1844.

Graham, "Female Politician," 261–63, 289–93. Gettleman, *Dorr Rebellion*, 167–68. *NHP*, Aug. 22, 1844.

39. *NHP*, Sept. 12, 1844. JP, Aug. 31, Sept. 4, Nov. 13, 1844. *WH*, Sept. 7, 1844. *SUN*, Sept. 12, 26, 1844. *BS*, Sept. 10, 1844. *NHP*, Sept. 12, 30, 1844. *NHG*, Sept. 10, 1844. *BDA*, Sept. 10, Oct. 19, Sept. 30, 1844. *Boston Times,* Nov. 4, 1844; *Boston Statesman*, July 13, 1844.

40. Holt, *Rise and Fall*, 194, 197. Steffens, *Struggle*, 124–26. On Connecticut, *NYH*, July 11, 1844; on Maine, *NHP*, Aug. 29, 1844; on New Hampshire, *NHP*, Oct. 17, 24, 1844; "A Farmer," letter to editor, *DGSA*, July 27, 1844. On another state's 1844 appeals to Democratic women, see DeFiore, "Come," 198–99, 203–7; and Varon, *We Mean*, 87.

41. JC, Dec. 4, 1844, Feb. 2, Nov. 7, 1845, Diary, **CFP-RIHS**.

42. Gettleman, *Dorr Rebellion*, 166, 171–73. CRW to Olney Ballou, Feb. 24, 1845, **SRC-BUL**. Frances H. Green to Lydia Dorr, Dec. 8, 1844, **SRC-BUL**.

43. CRW, "Recollections," 51; AM, May 16, 1842.

Part II. Party Dissolution and Formation

1. LL to Henry Spaulding, Apr. 3, 1852, Lucy Larcom Papers (SC 890), **ALPL**.

2. Pierson, *Free Hearts*, 10–13; Ryan, *Women,* 30–49.

Chapter 8. Sarah P. E. Hale as Enthused and Disaffected Whig

1. Remini, *Webster*, 570. *BDA*, Mar. 6, 1844. MF, Mar. 4, 1844, Diary, **LHS**. MP to JnP and LTP, May 5, 1844, **PFP-SL**.

2. MF, May 30, 1844, Diary. *CONST*, Sept. 11 and Oct. 2, 1844. LLN to Hester Newton, June 24, 1844, **NFP-AAS**. HHS, Nov. 1, 8, 1844, Diary, **CSL**. *CONST*, Sept. 11, 25, 1844. *BDA*, Sept. 18, 3, 30, Oct. 28, Sept. 20, 25, 11, 6, 24, 27, 30, Nov. 1,1844. *HDC*, Oct. 11, 1844. SEH to EEH, Nov. 1[?], 1844, **NYSL**.

3. E. Hale, *New England*, 198–99. SH to CBE, Sept. 30, 1844; SH to EEH, Sept. 20, 1844, and all letters by her unless otherwise indicated, **HFP-SSC**.

4. Holt, *Rise and Fall*, 194. SEH to EEH, Nov. 1[?], 1844, **NYSL**. SH to CBE, Sept. 30, 1844. SH to EEH, Sept. 20, 1844. SH to AHE, Nov. 3, 1844. *HDC*, Oct. 11, 1844. *BDA*, Sept. 24, 27, 20, Oct. 26, 1844.

5. SH to EdE, Dec. 13, 1844. Holt, *Rise and Fall*, 194–233, 954.

6. Pasley, *Tyranny*, 3, 7, 14, 5, 11.

7. Varg, *Edward Everett*, 15–16; P. Frothingham, *Edward Everett*, 4–7. E. Hale, *Memories*, 1:254, 114. Zboray, *Fictive People*, 84–85, 92–93. Kelley, *Learning*, 32. "Poetical Portraits," 460–61. E. Hale, *New England*, xxvi, 198–99. Somkin, "Alexander Hill Everett," 12–13. Fowle, "Boston," 109–10; *BDAv*, Apr. 6, 1814.

8. SH to AHE, Oct. 1, 1828. SH to EdE, Jan. 14, 1829, Mar. 24, 1828, Feb. 28, 1829, Feb. 8, 1828, Feb. 2, 1830, Dec. 5, 1828. AHE to SH, Jan. 17, 1829, July 4, 1828, June 1, 1829. **HFP-SSC**.

9. Zboray and Zboray, *Literary Dollars*, 5, 23, xxvii. On the vote, see *SG*, Feb. 24, 1835. SH to EdE, Feb. 21, 1835. Ellis, "Re-examination," 51–55. Schlesinger, *Age*, 174. P. Frothingham, *Edward Everett*, 149; Somkin, "Alexander Hill Everett," 117–18. SH to AHE, Feb. 14, 1836. Remini, *Adams*, 136. *NBM*, Nov. 16, 1838. SH to NHJ, Nov. 12, 1838.

10. *NBM*, Nov. 16, 1838. *HG*, Nov. 28, 1840. SH to EdE, May 30, 1841. *BG*, June 11, 1841. SH to AHE, Nov. 29, 1841. *BDA*, July 28, Nov. 9, 1841.

11. SH to EdE, Nov. 19, 1841. Darling, *Political Changes*, 240–42. Varg, *Edward Everett*, 93; P. Frothingham, *Edward Everett*, 155. SH to EdE, Oct. 15, Nov. 30, 1840. *NYH*, Nov. 19, 1840. EdE to SH, Jan 1, 1841, reel 26, *Edward Everett Papers, 1675–1910*, microfilm edition, 54 reels (Boston: Massachusetts Historical Society, 1972), **MHS**. P. Frothingham, *Edward Everett*, 173.

12. *BDA*, Sept. 17, 1841. Peterson, *Presidencies*, 89–90, 86. Chitwood, *John Tyler*, 226–51; Holt, *Rise and Fall*, 129–35; Watson, *Liberty*, 228. SH to EdE, Sept. 30, 1841.

13. SH to EdE, Dec. 14, 1841, Jan. 31, Apr. 22, 1842. *BDA*, Dec. 14, 2, 1841; *SG*, Nov. 19, 1841. Seager, *Tyler Too*, 169–70. Seager and others, *Papers*, 9:626. SH to EdE, May 15, 1842; Zboray and Zboray, *Literary Dollars*, 118–20.

14. Remini, *Webster*, 291, 533–35, 569–74. SH to EdE, Dec. 14, 1841, May 15, 1842, Sept. 30, 1842.

15. Seager, *Tyler Too*, 168. Remini, *Webster*, 570, 577, 586. SH to EEH, Mar. 8, Apr. 8, 1843, **NYSL**; SH to EEH, May 21, 1843. SH to EdE, Apr. 29, 1843, May 30, Sept. 21, 30, 1841. P. Frothingham, *Edward Everett*, 232, 227–30. *BDA*, Mar. 7, May 22, 23, 1843.

16. SH to NHS Dec. 12, 1843. SH to NHJ, Mar. 31, 1844. Remini, *Webster*, 586–87. *BDA*, July 17, 1849. *BS*, Jan. 5, 1844. *SP*, Apr. 30, 1844. *BDA*, Oct. 7, 1844. *Daily Picayune*, May 10, 1844.

17. SH to NHS, Feb. 13, Mar. 19, 1844. SH to EEH, Mar. 19, 1844. Holt, *Rise and Fall*, 168–70. Remini, *Henry Clay*, 631–69. Clay probably vetted the idea; Remini, *Henry Clay*, 636–39.

18. Seigenthaler, *James K. Polk*, 76, 82–84. SH to EdE, May 31, 1844. SH to CBE, Sept. 30, 1844. AHE to SH, Sept. 12, 1844.

19. SH to EEH, Oct. 11, 1844. See, for example, *BDA*, Oct. 5, 7, 1844. SH to AHE, Nov. 3, 1844.

20. Holt, *Rise and Fall*, 193–96; 212. HHS, Nov. 4, 1844, Diary. AP to MP, in LTP to LH, Nov. 24, 1844, **PFP-SL**. SH to EEH, Nov. 12, 1844. Remini, *Webster*, 597–99. *NYH*, Nov. 10, 1844.

21. SH to EEH, Nov. 12, 1844. SH to EdE, Dec. 13, 1844. *BDA*, Dec. 10, 1844.

22. [SH?] to EEH, Nov. 14, 1844, **NYSL**. Taslitz, *Reconstructing*, 246; *BDA*, Dec. 14, 1844. SH to EdE, Dec. 13, 1844.

23. SH to EEH, Jan. 7, 1845, Jan. 29, 1845, **NYSL**. SH to EEH, [Jan.?] 10, [1846?]. *BDA*, Jan. 9, 1845. *BP*, Jan. 31, 1845. Seigenthaler, *James K. Polk*, 99. Leonard, *James K. Polk*, 81, 75. Bauer, *Mexican War*, 18–24. *NHP*, Jan. 1, 1846.

24. SH to EEH, Feb. 23, 1846. Reilly, "American Reporters," 38–39, 43–45, 47, 48, 55, 63.

25. SH to EEH, July 29, 1846. SH to AHE and LE, Aug. 15, Oct. 1, Sept. 3, 1846. *NHSSJ*, June 26, 1846. *NHS*, June 3, 1846. *BS*, July 27, 1846. *BDA*, Aug. 14, 1846. Leonard, *James K. Polk*, 46–47, 170.

26. *BG*, Oct. 9, 1846. Darling, *Political Changes*, 334; Mayfield, *Rehearsal*, 57–59. Brauer, *Cotton*, chap. 9. *EM*, Sept. 30, 1846. SH to EEH, Sept. 24, Oct. [n.d.], 1846, and fragment, Oct. [n.d.], 1846. *ER*, Dec. 9, Nov. 11, Dec. 16, 1846. SH to AHE and LE, Oct. 1, 1846, Jan. 1, 1847. *ER*, Jan. 6, 1847. *BS*, Jan. 29, 1847.

27. SH to AHE and LE, Feb. 26, 1847. *Cleveland Herald*, Mar. 1, 1847. *DNI*, Feb. 26, 1847, Jan. 19, 1847. See, for example, *MN*, Feb. 11, 1847; *BDA*, Feb. 27, 1847.

28. LE to SH, Jan. 7, 1847, **HFP-SSC**. *BDA*, Apr. 1, 1847. *NHPSG*, Apr. 22, 1847. Lincoln, *History*, 385. Wilcox, *History*, 254. SH to AHE and LE, Apr. 29, 1847. SH to EEH, Apr. 2, 1847, **NYSL**.

29. LE to SH, June 30, 1847, **HFP-SSC**. SH to AHE, Sept. 30, 1847.

30. SH to EdE, Nov. 9, 1859. Bauer, *Zachary Taylor*, 225.

Chapter 9. Women, Mexico, and Taylor

1. HHS, 1848 retrospective (p. 95) and all HHS cites below, Diary, courtesy **CSL**. Zaeske, *Signatures*, 47, 109. HHS, Apr. 6, 1849

2. HHS, Sept. 15, Nov. 7, 1844; Aug. 10, 17, 1845; Sept. 20, 26, Dec. 14, 1846; Jan. 24, Dec. 26, 1847; Oct. 6, Dec. 9, 1848, Mar. 4, 1849.

3. Gonzalez, *Refusing*. On Mexican perspectives, see Vázquez, "Causes."

4. Greenberg, *Manifest Manhood*, 1–25, 198.

5. Johannsen, *Halls*.

6. ED to JD, Feb. 10, 1833, **JDP-AAS**.

7. PSA, June 2, 1844, Sept. 16, 1843, and all her cites below, Diary, courtesy **MeHS**.

8. PSA, Dec. 14, 1845; **CG**, 29/1/4–11 (1845).

9. PSA, May 24, 1846; *BS*, May 25, 1846; *MN*, May 26, 1846. Mexican casualties were "never determined" (52) according to Bauer, *Mexican War*, 49–52; *BS*, May 19, 1846; *NM*, May 23, 1846. Johannsen, *Halls*, 8, 10, 12, 78.

10. PSA, May 24, 31, 1846. *NHP*, June 4, 1846; *FC*, July 23, 1846. Hatch, *Maine*, 2:332–33; Hamlin, *Life*, 147–52.

11. HHS, Sept. 2, Oct. 25, Dec. 4–5, 11, 1846, Jan. 15, 17, 18, 22, 1847. *BDA*, Oct. 13, 1846. PSA, Dec. 20, 1846. **CG**, 29/2/3–11 (1846).

12. Bauer, *Mexican War*, 232, 245–52. EJ, Apr. 10, 1847, and all her cites below, Diary, **JFP-CHS**. *MN*, Apr. 12, 1847. The surrendering Mexican garrison was three thousand men; see Eisenhower, *So Far*, 263–65.

13. Bauer, *Mexican War*, 252. Heitman, *Historical Register*, 40. "Memoir of John R. Vinton," 601, 594. Mellen Chamberlain, July 24, 1847, Diary, **BPL**. AL, Jan. 1, Apr. 10, 1847, Diary, **LFP-MHS**.

14. Cutler, "President Polk's," 8–10, 25, 28–30. AL, June 29, 1847, Diary. *BG,* June 25, 1847; *SUN,* July 8, 1847. *NHPSG*, July 29, 1847. OW, July 2, 3, 1847, Diary, **SFP-SL**. PSA, July 4, 1847.

15. EJ, May 11, Sept. 15, 1847. Bauer, *Mexican War* (268), calculates 2,837; 300–301. *MN*, Sept. 23, 1847. Eisenhower, *So Far*, 327. Gue, *History of Iowa*, 386. Heitman, *Historical Register*, 31. **RH**.

16. HHS, Oct. 5, Dec. 9, 19, 1847, Jan. 14, 1848. **CG**, 30/1/96–100 (1848). Haynes, *James K. Polk*, 175–78.

17. Parsons, "Splendid Pageant," 465–72. *ER*, Mar. 15, Apr. 12, 1848. AgP to MAB, Apr. 17, 1848, **SFP-SL**. See also DFC and MDC, Apr. 21, 1848, Diary, **DFCP-MHS**.

18. W. White, "Our Soldier Dead." Bodenhamer, Barrows, and Vanderstel, *Encyclopedia*, 1001. **BD**. "Col. James S. McIntosh," **HM**. "Memoir of John R. Vinton," 599. AM, May 12, 1847, Journal, **OCHS**. SBE, May 11, 1848, Diary, **RIHS**. EJ, July 11, 1848; *BS*, July 7, 1848.

19. On Taylor's popularity in Maine, see Hatch, *Maine*, 341–42, and nationally, see Holt, *Rise and Fall*, 270–73. PSA, Aug. 1, 1847.

20. HFC to WSR, Aug. 10, [1847?], **RSP-SL**. Anonymous mother to her son, Mar. 23, 1848, Box 2, Folder 93, **HC-SL**. Cmiel, *Democratic Eloquence*. Charlotte Bostwick to Elizabeth Bostwick, Mar. 23, 1848, **HC-SL**. Remini, *Henry Clay*, 684–85, 700. Zboray and Zboray, *Literary Dollars*, chap. 3. Holt, *Rise and Fall*, 291, 298.

21. PSA, Aug. 20, 1847, May 28, 1848.

22. Silbey, *Martin Van Buren*, 190–93, 195–97; Lynch, *Epoch*, 2:510–17. Mayfield, *Rehearsal*, 105, 116–18. Holt, *Rise and Fall*, 341. Remini, *Webster*, 653–55. ED to JD, Sept. 3, 1848, **JDP-AAS**.

23. Huntoon, *History*, 531, 212–13. *BDA*, Jan. 4, 1849. CB, June 28, July 18, 19, 20, 1849, and all further cites to her, Diary, **SL**.

24. *BDA*, Sept. 8, 1848. CB, Sept. 4, 11, 22, 27, 1848.

25. CB, Oct. 24, 25, 1848. *BDA*, Oct. 25, 27, 28, 1848. *ER*, Nov. 1, 1848. Sterling, *Ahead*, 208–9; Morris, "Capital Aversion."

26. CB, Oct. 30, 1848. KL, Nov. 1, 1848, Diary, **LFP-MHS**. Advertisement, *BDA*, Oct. 21, 1848. SuH to Alexander Hale, Nov. 1, 1848, in Atkinson, *Letters*, 2. CB, Oct. 29, Nov. 2, 3, 1848. *BDA*, Nov. 2, 1848.

27. Mary Paul to Bela Paul, Nov. 5, 1848, Marion E. Blake and Tuttle Papers (MSC 12), **VHS**. OW, Nov. 6, 1848, Diary, **SFP-SL**.

28. CB, Nov. 4, 1848.

29. Donald, *Charles, Sumner*, 168; *Free Soil!*; Huntoon, *History*, 532, 536, 560–61. CB, Nov. 6, 1848. *BDA*, Aug. 25, Nov. 18, 1848.

30. Holt, *Rise and Fall*, 368. CB, Nov. 9, 10, 11, 12, 15, 18, 20, 1848. BD*A*, Jan. 4, 1849.

31. *BDA*, Nov. 30, 1848. CB, Nov. 23, 24, 1848.

32. HHS, Oct. 6, Nov. 10, 1848. PSA, Nov. 12, 1848. OW, Nov. 10, 1848, Diary, **SFP-SL.** Biographical note in Jocelyn Box, "Jocelyn, Eliz. Hannah; Jocelyn, Sarah," **JFP-CHS.** EJ, Nov. 16, 1848; FJ, Nov. 16, 1848, **JFP-CHS.** MP to JnP and LTP, Nov. 19, 1848, **PFP-SL.**

33. MP to JnP and LTP, Mar. 5, in Mar. 1, 1849, **PFP-SL.**

Chapter 10. Women Divert Their Attentions during the 1852 Campaign

1. Vaughan, "Preface," vii, x. EDC to ET, Nov. 7, 1852, and all their other letters below, **CFP-SL.** Holt, *Rise and Fall*, 698–700, 737–38, 762, 754 (quotes), 700–712, 726–27, 761–62.

2. The voter turnout was higher in Massachusetts; see Holt, *Rise and Fall*, 368.

3. OW, Mar. 5, 1849, Diary, **SFP-SL.** ED to NCP, Mar. 10, 1849, **JDP-AAS.** Bauer, *Zachary Taylor*, 256–57.

4. ED to NCP, Mar. 10, 1849, **JDP-AAS.** Bauer, *Zachary Taylor*, 256–58; McKinley and Bent, *Old Rough*, 225–26.

5. McKinley and Bent, *Old Rough*, 226–28. Bauer, *Zachary Taylor*, 257. Eisenhower, *Zachary Taylor,* 95–96. OW, Mar. 7, 1849, Diary. Holt, *Rise and Fall*, 388–90.

6. *WE,* Apr. 5, 1849. *NHP*, Apr. 26, 1849. Holt, *Rise and Fall*, 436–37. HHS, Apr. 6, 1849, **CSL.**

7. PSA, July 28, 1850, Diary, **MeHS.** Hamlin, *Life*, 234–49.

8. Richards, *California*, 20. Harlow, *California*, 279–86, 307, 317, 351. Holt, *Rise and Fall,* 437–39; Bauer, *Zachary Taylor*, 291–92.

9. AgP to MAB, Mar. 1, 1849, **SFP-SL.** HHS, July 6 (see also Aug. 10), Jan. 6, 15, Apr. 23, 1849, Diary, **CSL.** Martha Greene, Apr. 16, 1849, Diary, **NHHS.** Rolle, *Frémont,* 91. Harlow, *California*, 43–44. Sophronia Goodrich to Jared Goodrich, July 6, 1849, **CHS.**

10. HHS, 1848 retrospective (p. 95), Diary. Eisenhower, *Zachary Taylor*, 106. ACS, Jan. 29, 1850, Diary, **DFP-RIHS.** Remini, *Webster*, 665–80. ED to JD, [n.d.], 1850, **JDP-AAS.**

11. McKinley and Bent, *Old Rough*, 285. Smith, *Presidencies*, 156–57; Eisenhower, *Zachary Taylor*, 132–34. *Savannah Republican,* July 12, 1850; *CONST*, July 17, 1850; *SUN*, July 18, 1850; *BDA*, July 13, 1850; *NHG*, July 16, 1850. AL, July 9, 10, 1850, Diary, **LFP-MHS.**

12. ACS, July 9, 1850, Diary, **DFP-RIHS.** AMNL, July 10, 1850, Diary, **PEM.** ST, July 13, 1850, Journal (MSC 198), **VHS.** EO, July 13, 1850, Diary, **BHS.** Homans, *Sketches*, 219. *BDA*, July 10, 11, 18, Aug. 1, 14, 1850. HW, Mar. 22, July 10, 11, 18, Aug. 2, 13, 1850, Diary (Mss 595), **NEHGS.**

13. *ER*, Aug. 15, 22, 1850. Lincoln, *History*, 385. *BDA*, Aug. 17, 1850. HW, Aug. 15 and 19, 1850, Diary. SuH to Alexander Hale, Aug. 18, 1850, **SHC-URI.**

14. Holt, *Fate*, 82, 86–87.

15. *BS*, Dec. 20, 1850; Hatch, *Maine*, 350; PSA, Dec. 19, 1850, Diary.

16. Collison, *Shadrach*, 1–3, 139–42. Remini, *Webster*, 696. AnL to EGL, Feb. 23, 1851, Ellis Gray Loring Papers, **SL**. **CG**, 31/2/580, 596–600; 660–62; 675–76; app. 292, 294–95 (1851).

17. May, *Fugitive*, 16–17; he claims Sims departed the eleventh. Remini, *Webster*, 696. HW, Apr. 12, 13, 1851, Diary. *WE*, Apr. 17, 1851.

18. Remini, *Webster*, 697–98; *FC*, Apr. 24, 1851. Dall, Apr. 22, 1851, in *Daughter*, 144. *GPDRC* 1 (May 17, 1851): 37. *BDA*, Apr. 23, 1851.

19. KL, July 8, 1852, Journal, **LFP-MHS**. LGL to EGL, June 14, 1852, **LFP-SL**. Holt, *Rise and Fall*, 717, 720–23. Holt, *Fate*, 88. LGL to EGL and AnL, June 28, 1852, **LFP-SL**.

20. *BS*, July 10, 1852. The crowd included women that one engraver carefully depicted; *GPDRC* 3 (July 31, 1852), 73. J. Brown, *Beyond*, chap 1. LzB, July 9, 1852, Account Book, **FCLP-MHS**. Remini, *Webster*, 742–43. EAC, July 9, 1852, Journal, **DCD-MHS**. LGL to EGL and AnL, July 20, 1852, **LFP-SL**.

21. EJ, June 20, 1849, Diary, **JFP-CHS**; PSA, June 24, 1849, Diary. ACS, Apr. 1, 1850, Diary. MCM, June 30, 1852, Diary, **BPL**. ACS, July [n.d.], 1852, Diary; Mary G. Holbrook, July 2, 1852, Diary, Sterling Memorial Library, **YU**; LGL to EGL and AnL, July 20, 1852, **LFP-SL**. EO, Aug. 9, 1852, Diary, **BHS**; LGL to AnL, Aug. 25, 1852, **LFP-SL**.

22. EAC, Oct. 24, 1852, Journal. *BA*, Oct. 25, 1852. SLE, Oct. 24, 1852, Diary, **AAS**. Remini, *Webster*, 760; the time of death was 2:35 A.M. MCM, Oct. 24, 1852, Journal, **BPL**. On her father, Benjamin Crowninshield, see **PG**. CGCC, Oct. 24, 1852, **CFP-MHS**. On her husband, see *Vital Records of Massachusetts, 1841–1910*, vol. 62, p. 41, via **NEHGS**. Boutwell, *Reminiscences*, 71–72. ST, Oct. 25, 1852, Journal (MSC 198), **VHS**. KL, Oct. 29, 1852, Journal. Brauer, "Feud"; Remini, *Webster*, 603–4, 625, 635. OW, Oct. 30, 1852, Journal, **SFP-SL**. CC, Dec. 19, 1852, Journal, **CFP-RIHS**.

23. EDC to ET, Oct. 31, 1852. *BDA*, Oct. 27, 28, 1852. Voss, "Webster." Some of our diarists and correspondents saw the painting earlier: DFC and MDC, July 31, 1852, Diary, **DFCP-MHS**; Zboray and Zboray, "Reading." MCS, June 23, 1852, Diary, **MeHS**.

24. LzB, Oct. 28, 1852, Account Book. EAC, Oct. 29, 1852, Journal. EDC to ET, Oct. 31, 1852. *BDA*, Oct. 30, 1852. SLE, Oct. 29, 1852, Diary, **AAS**. KL, Nov. 7, 1852, Journal.

25. SLE, Nov. 30, 1852, Diary, **AAS**; MCM, Nov. 30, 1852, Diary; MCS, Nov. 30, 1852, Diary; EAC, Nov. 30, 1852, Journal. Mary Caroline Gardiner Davis, volume of poems, 1852–54, Gardner Family Papers, **SL**. Addison, *Lucy Larcom*, 96. Zboray and Zboray, *Literary Dollars*, 57–70. LL to Henry Spaulding, Apr. 3, 1852, **ALPL**.

26. Remini, *Webster*, 759. Daniel Webster to Mrs. James William Paige, Dec. 29, 1850, in *Writings*, 408. Harvey, *Reminiscences*, 310–312. [Eliza De Wolf Thayer], Oct. 16, 1854, Diary, Hill Family Papers, **SL** (the diary is catalogued as Catharine Rachel Childs Smith's).

27. ST, Nov. 2, 1852, Journal. ACS, Nov. [2?], 1852, Diary. PSA, Nov. 7, 1852, Diary. Holt, *Rise and Fall*, 754. "Ne'er Waved Beneath the Golden Sun," *Flag of Our Union*, [n.d.], [1852], identified as Mary Baker Glover, in Mary Baker Eddy, Scrapbook, **MBEL.**

Chapter 11. Women and Sectionalism

1. Davis, "Biographical Sketch," 321–22. SCH to HWC, Oct. 21, 1856, **CC-NEHGS**.

2. Davis, "Biographical Sketch," 321–23. HWC, June 2, 1854, Journal, **CC-NEHGS**. Holt, *Political Crisis*, 192, 196.

3. Gienapp, *Origins*, 38, 45–47. Mulkern, *Know Nothing*, 3.

4. **GWD**. ACS, Jan. 4, 1853, Diary, **DFP-RIHS**. Gienapp, *Origins*, 46. *SUN*, Nov. 11, 1852. Holt, *Rise and Fall*, 754.

5. Unidentified Salem Woman, Mar. 4, 6, 8, 7, 1853, Diary (ms.1946), **BPL**. *WH*, Mar. 12, 1853; Gienapp, *Origins*, 43. *SUN*, May 9, 1853, Apr. 6, 1854. MM, Mar. 30, 1854, Commonplace Book, **SL**. *BDA*, Apr. 1, 1854.

6. Holt, *Rise and Fall*, 805. *SUN*, Dec. 15, 1853. *BP*, Dec. 23, 30, 1853; *NHP*, Jan. 4, 1854. Mulkern, *Know Nothing*, 68. EAC, Jan. 19, 1854, Journal, **DCD-MHS**.

7. Gienapp, *Origins*, 47–50. Hatch, *Maine*, 326, 360–61. PSA, Jan. 30, 1853, Diary, **MeHS**. *BP*, Apr. 1, 1853. SBn to Mary Burnham Brown, Apr. 3, 1853, **BFP-MeHS**.

8. Holt, *Rise and Fall*, 785–86. Taft, *Vermont*, 3. ST, Jan. 3, 17, Sept. 6, Oct. 28, 1853, Journal (MSC 198), **VHS**. *NYT*, Oct. 13, 1854; *OS*, Sept. 12, 1853. *BS*, Oct. 29, 1853; *NHP*, Sept. 14, 1853.

9. LL to Ann Danforth Spaulding, Sept. 23, 1853, Lucy Larcom Collection, Clifton Waller Barrett Library of American Literature, **UVL**; John Greenleaf Whittier to the *National Era*, Aug. 25, 1853, in Whittier, *Letters*, 2:228–31. *NHP*, Aug. 24, 1853; *BS*, Aug. 27, 1853.

10. Gienapp, *Origins*, 80.

11. Stevenson, "Introduction," *Journals*, 3–33; Sumler-Lewis, "Forten-Purvis Women," 281–88. A. White, "Seedbed," 99–118. Yee, *Abolitionists*, 16. For Forten's biography, see Stevenson's introduction (3–55) and related items in Zboray and Zboray, *Literary Dollars*, 243–44n2.

12. Forten, May 25, 1856, in Stevenson, *Journals* (hereafter, *JCFG*), 60. Bacon, *Humblest*.

13. May 26, 27, 1854, *JCFG*, 60–62. Von Frank, *Trials*, 8–12, 54–69. *SUN*, June 1, 1854. Pease and Pease, *Fugitive*, 31–33.

14. May 27, 28, 30, 1854, *JCFG*, 62–63.

15. *JCFG*, 550n10. May 31, 1854, *JCFG*, 63–64.

16. *JCFG*, June 1, 1854, 64–65. MM, June 1, 1854, Commonplace Book. Pease and Pease, *Fugitive*, 11–12.

17. June 2, 1854, Jan. 1, 1863, *JCFG*, 65, 66, 428. LzB, May 30, June 2, 1854, Diary, **FCLP-MHS**. Von Frank, *Trials*, 189, 198–99. Pease and Pease, *Fugitive*, 48.

18. Holt, *Fate*, 92–109. Gienapp, *Origins*, 71, 77–78; Etcheson, *Bleeding Kansas*, 9–15.

19. LL to HHR, July 9, 1856, **RSP-SL**. ST, Feb. 13, 1854, Journal. ET to EDC, Sept. 7, June 29, July 19, 1854, in Twisleton, *Letters*, 233, 211, 218. *NYT*, Feb. 22, 1854.

20. Gienapp, *Origins*, 170–72. Etcheson, *Bleeding Kansas*, 69–75.

21. Etcheson, *Bleeding Kansas*, 91–92. Gienapp, *Origins*, 169–71. AP to MP, Feb 21, 1856, **PFP-SL**.

22. Etcheson, *Bleeding Kansas*, 67, 104–5. *BDAv*, June 18, 1856. EnC, June 17, 1856, Diary (Mss A 1924), **NEHGS**. *DG*, June 16, 1856. Oct. [n.d.] and 26, 1856, *JCFG*, 166. HHR, Oct. 29 and Sept. 3, 1856, Diary, **RSP-SL**; Petrulionis, *To Set*, 110–15.

23. Holt, *Fate*, 117. Charlotte Hyde to Sarah Amanda Ives Hyde, Sept. 23, 1856, Bradley-Hyde Papers, **SL**. EP to MP, Oct. 23, 1856, **PFP-SL**.

24. Gienapp, *Origins*, 133–36, 179.

25. Gienapp, *Origins*, 136–38. Mulkern, *Know Nothing*, 76. Holt, *Rise and Fall*, 892. MM, Nov. 14, 1854, Commonplace Book. EDC to ET, Nov. 13, 1854, **CFP-SL**.

26. EDC to ET, Feb. 27, 1855, May 14, 1854 [i.e., 1855], **CFP-SL**. Von Frank, *Trials*, 240–41. *BP*, Feb. 16 and 23, 1855; *BDA*, Feb. 18 and 21, Mar. 1, 2, and 7, 1855. *SUN*, Apr. 19, May 3, 1855. Mulkern, *Know Nothing*, 105, 102–3, and 117–18. Anbinder, *Nativism*, 155, 137.

27. Holt, *Rise and Fall*, 892, 923, 963. Gienapp, *Origins*, 240–46. MOB, July 2 and Dec. 30, 1855, Diary, **PEM**. Feb. 3, 1856, *JCFG*, 149.

28. Donald, *Charles Sumner*, 266–67. Sept. 14, 1854, Nov. 1, 1855, *JCFG*, 100, 143.

29. On the speech, see Pierson, "All." Donald, *Charles Sumner*, 290, 278–95, 312, 318–20. ACS, May 29, 1856, Diary. Lilian R. Clarke to Charles Sumner, [May 1856], quoted in Donald, *Charles Sumner*, 299. HHR, Sept. 3, 1856, Diary. Nov. 3, 1856, Dec 25, 26, 1854, Feb. 22, 1858, Feb. 27, 1858, *JCFG*, 166, 274, 287, 288–89.

30. Holt, *Political Crisis*, 171, 192, 196. Holt, *Rise and Fall*, 965–66. Gienapp, *Origins*, 317, 324.

31. FD, June 18, 1856, Diary, **MeHS**; Rolle, *Frémont*, 164. EnC, July 11, 1856, Diary. FD, Oct. 23, 1856, Diary. Gustafson, *Women*, 18–22. Cf. a Fillmore supporter from Maryland in Coryell, *Neither Heroine*, 13–29.

32. Pierson, *Free Hearts*, 140, and, for an inside glimpse into rally organizing, Pierson, "'Prairies.'" *BDA*, Sept. 12, Oct. 30, 1856.

33. Pierson, *Free Hearts*, 117, 119, 210n6. Denton, *Passion*, 236, 249. *FC*, Aug. 14, 1856; *BDA*, Aug. 8, 1856. HHR, Aug. 7, 1856, Diary. Martha Jane Averill, Sept. 10, 11, 1856, Diary, **PEM**. *BDA*, Sept. 12, 1856. EnC, Oct. 29, 1856, Diary;

BDA, Oct. 30, 1856. MOB, Sept. 1, 1856, Diary. LH to MP, Aug. 20, 1856, **PFP-SL.**

34. LH to MP, Aug. 20, 1856. PC, Nov. 3, 1856, Diary, **LyHS**. Mary Congdon, Oct. 23, 25, 29, 1856, Diary, **CFP-RIHS**. Mary Dawley, Sept. 24, Oct. 4, 23–30, Nov. 4, 1856, Diary, Misc. Manuscript Collection (MSS 9001-D), **RIHS**.

35. Feroline (Pierce) Fox to MP, Oct. 26, 1856, **PFP-SL**. HHR, Nov. 2, 1856, Diary.

36. Gienapp, *Origins*, 429, 414, 440–41. FJ, Nov. 6, 1856, Diary, **JFP-CHS**. PC, Nov. 13, 1856, Diary. HHR, Nov. 4, 1856, Diary. LL to HHR, Nov. 21, 1856, **RSP-SL.**

37. LL to HHR, Nov. 21, 1856.

Chapter 12. Women Face the Nightmare of Civil War

1. EDC to ET, Dec. 10, 1860, and all letters by her unless otherwise stated, **CFP-SL**. Donald, *Lincoln*, 257. Huston, *Panic*, 216. *Wisconsin Daily Patriot*, Dec. 1, 4, 1860; *NYH*, Dec. 10, 1860. *OS*, Dec. 1, 1860. *PI*, Nov. 29, 1860.

2. McPherson, *Battle*, 235. ET to EDC, Dec. 28, 1860, and subsequent letters from her unless otherwise indicated, **PTF-HL** (MS Am 2197, 118); specific item numbers are hereafter given in parentheses. Most of Ellen's letters from June 1855 to June 1860 are missing; see Twisleton, *Letters*, 292.

3. On their father's Whiggery, see *SUN*, Sept. 17, 1840; *NYH*, Sept. 14, 1848. Irving, *Sketch Book*, 1:83–85.

4. Rosina Houghton Moore, Mar. 4, 1857, Diary, 1857, **AAS**; EK, Mar. 4, 1857, Diary, **CHS**. FM, Mar. 7, 1857, Diary, **FMQP-SL**. Baker, *Buchanan*, 81–82.

5. EDC to ET, Sept. 26, 27, 1857, in Cabot, *Letters*, 2:187–89, 165. ET to Georgina Leigh, Mar. 25, 1858, in Twisleton, *Letters*, 292–93. Huston, *Panic*, 13–16. ACS, Sept. 22, 1857, Diary, **DFP-RIHS**. CGCC, Oct. 3, 1857, Diary, **CFP-MHS**. EK, Jan. 29, 1857, Diary. LL to HHR, Dec. 18, 1857, 56. Huston, *Panic*, 216.

6. NB to SB, Nov. 6, 1857, Dec. 7 [i.e. 6], 1856, and all her letters below unless otherwise indicated, **BroFP-SL**. FD, Feb. 23, 1857, Diary. Forten, Dec. 8, 25, 1856, Dec. 2, 25, 1857, Dec. 21, 1856, Jan. 13, 26, Oct. 17, Jan. 16, Apr. 29, May 1, Jan. 19, 1857, Nov. 19, 1858, in Stevenson, *Journals* (hereafter *JCFG*), 171, 175, 269, 273, 174, 182, 185, 262, 183, 215, 184, 345. HHR, Jan. 27, 1857, Diary, **RSP-SL**. SB to NB, Jan. 25, 1857, Sarah Ellen Browne Papers, **SL**. LGL to EGL, May 17, 1858, **LFP-SL**. EK, [c. 1857], Jan. 29, Feb. 14, May 26, Dec. 4, 1857, Diary; ACS, Dec. 2, 1858, Diary. MB to Emma Brown, Oct. 24, 1857, **BFP-MeHS**. Zboray and Zboray, *Literary Dollars*, 48. MP to LH, Nov. 6, 1860, and all subsequent letters by her below, **PFP-SL**.

7. EDC to ET, Dec. 13, 1858.

8. EDC to ET, Dec. 19, 1858, Jan. 4, 1859.

9. *Law Times*, Oct. 24, 1874, 439.

10. *BDAv*, Apr. 1, 1859. Baker, *Buchanan*, 60. EDC to ET, Apr. 3, 1859.

11. EDC to ET, Apr. 11, 1859; ET, Dec. 22, 1859, Commonplace Book (MS Am 2197, 77), **PTF-HL**. EDC to ET, Apr. 3, 1859, in Cabot, *Letters*, 2:219.

12. EDC to ET, June 23, Sept. 5, 1859. Donald, *Charles Sumner*, 345–47.

13. EDC to ET, Feb. 6, 1860. Venet, "Cry."

14. MOB, Nov. 24, Dec. 22, 1859, Feb. 19, 1860, Diary, **PEM**. MP to Feroline Fox, [n.d.], 1860, quoted in McGovern, *Yankee Family*, 91; see also MP to LH, Nov. 20, 1859. LL to HHR, Dec. 1, 1859, **RSP-SL**. Reynolds, *John Brown*, 415. EWG to MCW, Nov. 13, 1860, and all letters by her below, **GFP-SSC**.

15. EDC to ET, Apr. 9, 1859 [i.e., 1860], Apr. 16, May 13, 1860. Reynolds, *John Brown*, 428–31. ET, Sept. 30, 1859, Commonplace Book. EDC to ET, Apr. 16, 1860, in Cabot, *Letters*, 2:242. *NYH*, Apr. 5, Mar. 26, 1860. *BA*, Mar. 22, in *NYH*, Mar. 27, 1860.

16. Donald, *Lincoln*, 250–53. EDC to ET, June 18, May 21, 1860. Hamlin, *Life*, 8–9.

17. EDC to ET, May 21, 1860. EDC to ET, June 4, May 28, 1860, in Cabot, *Letters*, 2:247, 246. MP, Account Book, June 7, 1860, **PFP-SL**. *NYH*, June 8, 1860. NBD, Aug. 30, 1860, Diary, (Mss A 1931), **NEHGS**. SBn to CSB, Oct. 1, 1860, **BFP-MeHS**. EWG to William Wright, Dec. 4, in Nov. [n.d.], 1860.

18. SH to William Everett, Jan. 5, 1861, in Aaron, *Hales*, 16. Gillespie, *Politics*, 57. SH, Oct. 8, 12, Nov. 1, 1860, Diary, **HFP-SSC**. The family's paper supported Lincoln; *BDAv*, Nov. 5, 1860. CGCC, Sept. 12, 1860, Diary.

19. PSA, Jan. 1, 15, July 1, Aug. 26, Dec. 23, 1860, Diary, **DFP-MHS**.

20. PSA, Sept. 2, Aug, 26, Sept. 9, 30, 1860, Diary.

21. Donald, *Lincoln*, 255. McPherson, *Battle*, 229–30; Mansch, *Lincoln*, 70–73. EDC to ET, Nov. 6 [i.e., 5], 1860.

22. McPherson, *Battle*, 232; Holzer, *President*, 41. Mansch, *Lincoln*, 73–79. Johnson, *Patriarchal*, 17. EDC to ET, Nov. 11, 1860, in Cabot, *Letters*, 2:258. EDC to ET, Nov. 19, 1860. Baker, *Buchanan*, 122. Donald, *Lincoln*, 267.

23. EDC to ET, Nov. 19, 1860. MB to CSB, Nov. 19, 1860, **BFP-MeHS**. EWG to MCW, Nov. [n.d.], 1860. LL to HHR, Nov. 15, 1860, and all their correspondence below, **RSP-SL**.

24. Mansch, *Lincoln*, 77. PSA, Dec. 23, 1860, Diary. EDC to ET, Nov. 26, 1860. MP to LH, Dec. 30, 1860.

25. See, for example, EDC to ET, Nov. 11, 1860, in Cabot, *Letters*, 2:255–57. ET to EDC, Nov. 24, 1860 (113). EDC to ET, Dec. 10, 1860.

26. PSA, Jan. 6, 1861, Diary. For disinterestedness as a Whig value against Democratic self-interest on display at the Baltimore "Young Men's Whig Convention," see *CC*, May 16, 1840.

27. EDC to ET, Dec. 23, 1860. Donald, *Lincoln*, 267.

28. ET to EDC, Dec. 28, 1860 (118), Jan. 3, 1861 (119).

29. EDC to ET, Jan. 21, 1860 [i.e., 1861].

30. PSA, Jan. 6, 1861, Diary. EWG to Frank Wright, Jan. 5, 1861; EWG to MCW, Jan. 22, 1861. ADWM to Mrs. Henry de Wolf, in Middleton, *Life*, 113. Lettie H. Lewis to [Emma Brown?], Jan. 26, 1861, **BFP-MeHS**.

31. EDC to ET, Jan. 27, Feb. 3, 1861. Oakes, "Political Significance," 193–94. Donald, *Lincoln*, 268.

32. ET to EDC, Feb. 23 or 24, 1861 (123). EDC to ET Feb. 24, 1861.

33. MP to LH, Mar. 4, 1861; EWG to MCW, Mar. 6, 1861; Addison, *Lucy Larcom*, 86–87; LL to HHR, Mar. 8, 1861. See also: CGCC, Mar. 4, 1861, Diary; SH, Mar. 4, 1861, Diary; Cornelia Jocelyn Foster, Mar. 4 and 5, 1861, Diary, **JFP-CHS**. EDC to ET, Mar. 17, 1861.

34. Donald, *Lincoln*, 285–89. ET to EDC, Mar. 29, 1861 (127). Jones, *Union*, 1–9, chap. 1.

35. SH, Apr. 13, 14, 1861, Diary; SB, Apr. 14, 15, 1861, Diary, **BroFP-SL**; CCGC, Apr. 16, 1861, Diary; NBD, Apr. 16, 1861, Diary; Addison, *Lucy Larcom*, 87–88; PSA, Apr. 21, 1861, Diary.

36. EDC to ET, Apr. 15, 1861. Donald, *Lincoln*, 289, 296.

37. ET to "Family," May 11, 1861 (167).

38. EDC to ET, May 26, 1861; Zboray and Zboray, "Cannonballs," 254.

39. ET to EDC, May 4, June 14, Nov. 28 in Nov. 23, Apr. 26, 1861 (131, 133, 138, 130). Donald, *Lincoln*, 320–23. Edward Twisleton to EDC, Nov. 8, 1861 (74), **PTF-HL**. ET to "Sisters," Sept. 14, Dec. 21, 1861 (169, 170). EDC to ET, Dec. 30, 1861. Twisleton, *Letters*, 315.

40. FM to Catherine Prescott Merritt, Jan. 16, 1861, **FMQP-SL**; HLJC to Samuel Cabot, May 10 in May 9, 1862, **AFP-SL**; Laura Holmes Kingsbury to Isaac Franklin Kingsbury, Sept. 14, 1862, Mary K. Simkhovitch Papers, **SL**; SB to AGB, Oct. 13, 1863; BBA to SHB, July 21, 1861, in Ames, *Chronicles*, 77.

41. MP to Feroline Fox, Aug. 28, 1861, quoted in McGovern, *Yankee Family*, 91.

42. Attie, *Patriotic Toil*, 87–120. PSA, Nov. 17, 1861, Apr. 28, 1861, Sept. 7, 1862, Nov. 29, 1863, Diary.

43. EDC to ET, Aug. 26, 1861. *PI*, Aug. 22, 1861. *NHS*, Aug. 22, 1861. EDC to Edward Twisleton, Sept. 12, 1864.

44. CCGC, Aug. 31, 1, 8, and Oct. 10, 1864, Diary. ACS, Apr. 23, Oct. 24, Nov. 2 and 21, 1864, Diary. SB to AGB, Oct. 26, 1864.

45. EDC to [Mary Parkman], Sept. 1, 1862. Oct. 28, Nov. 10, 1862, *JCFG*, 389–90, 397. *Liberator*, Dec. 19, 1862. AGB to SB, Dec. 26, 1863, and AGB to family, Feb. 21, 1865, both in **BroFP-SL**; SB to AGB, Mar. 26, 1865. *PI*, Mar. 20, 1865.

46. SB to AGB, Apr. 20, 1865. SuH to Charles Hale, Apr. 21, 1865, Edward Everett Hale Papers (bMS 512, box 18, folder 11), **AHTL**. Elizabeth Ellery Dana, Apr. 15 and 19, 1865, Diary, **DFP-SL**. *BDAv*, Apr. 20, 1865. R. Brown, *Knowledge*, 253–65.

47. Gustafson, *Women*, 31–33.

Epilogue

1. About a thousand or more women did manage to serve illegally as combatants; Hall, *Women*, 11. Silber and Sievens, introduction, *Yankee Correspondence*, 8.

Alice Fahs, *Imagined*, chap. 4. Enloe, *Maneuvers*. McPherson, *For Cause*. Silber, *Daughters*, 52–68; Venet, *Ballots*, 48. Dubois, *Feminism*, 162–200.

2. Catt and Schuler, *Woman Suffrage*, esp. chap. 9; Blocker, "Separate Paths"; Deutsch, "Learning"; Kessler-Harris, *Gendering*, 21–39; Clinton, *Other Civil War*, 121–46.

3. Skocpol, *Protecting*; Bederman, *Manliness*; Hoganson, *Fighting*.

4. Harriet Bailey Blaine to Walker Blaine, Sept. 8, 1871, in Blaine, *Letters*, 29–30; BBA to AA, Sept. 25, 1871, in Ames, *Chronicles*, 316; Caroline Clapp Briggs to unidentified recipient, Oct. 19, 1884, in Briggs, *Reminiscences*, 285–86; Charlotte Howard Conant to Chester C. Conant, Oct. 30, 1884, in Conant, *Girl*, 178–79; Elizabeth Parsons Channing, Oct. 31, 1896, Diary, in Channing, *Autobiography*, 187; Louise Imogen Guiney to Herbert E. Clarke, Nov. 8, 1896, in Guiney, *Letters*, 151; Helen Adams Keller to George Frisbie Hoar, Nov. 25, 1901, in Keller, *Story*, 280.

5. Edwards, *Angels*, 52–58.

6. Gustafson, *Women*, 34–89; Edwards, *Angels*, 39–90.

7. Conforti, *Imagining*, 203–62.

8. Cooke, "Miss Dorcas's Opinion." Linkon, "Saints." Fetterley and Pryse, *Writing*, 184–86.

9. Frances Elizabeth Willard, Nov. 1860, Diary, in Willard, *Glimpses*, 156. Leeman, *Do Everything*.

10. Butler, *Autobiography*, 82; BBA to SHB, June 6, 1861, in Ames, *Chronicles*, 73–74. Pierson, *Mutiny*, 156–60. BBA to AA, Nov. 3, 1873, in Ames, *Chronicles*, 626. Clark, *My Dear*, 13.

11. *NYT*, Apr. 3, 1944. Brooks, *Flowering*, 485. SH to AHE, July 6, 1843, **HFP-SSC**. *Lowell Daily Citizen and News*, Dec. 16, 1874. Penney and Livingston, *Very Dangerous*; Avery, *Proceedings*, 60; *NYT*, Aug. 4, 1912.

12. Olick and Robbins, "Social Memory."

13. Cabot, *Letters*, 1:146–48, iii. ED to ET, Nov. 13, 1854, **CFP-SL**.

14. Stanton and Anthony, *History*. Williams, "In the Garden." Hannaford, *Daughters*; Willard and Livermore, *Woman*. On the Quincy event and its speakers, see Zboray and Zboray, "Gender Slurs," 429.

15. Norton, *Great Revolution*, 357–58. Ginzberg, "Hearts." Zboray and Zboray, "Gender Slurs," 442.

16. PSA, Feb. 11, 1841, Diary, **MeHS**.

17. Alcott, *Young Woman's Guide*, 320–22. A diary provides "a faithful picture of our former lives"; quoted in HW, Jan. 18, 1850, Diary, (Mss 595), **NEHGS**.

18. Glenn and Goldthwaite, *St. Martin's Guide*, 153.

19. RS to SS, Feb. 25, 1840, **SFP-AAS**.

Bibliography

Aaron, Daniel, ed. *The Hales and the "Great Rebellion"-Letters: 1861–1865*. Northampton, Mass.: Smith College, 1966.

Addison, Daniel Dulany. *Lucy Larcom: Life, Letters, and Diary*. Boston: Houghton, Mifflin, 1894.

Alcott, William A. *The Young Woman's Guide to Excellence*. Boston, G. W. Light, 1841.

Allgor, Catherine. *Parlor Politics: In Which the Ladies of Washington Help Build a City and a Government*. Charlottesville: University Press of Virginia, 2000.

Almond, Gabriel A., and Sidney Verba. *The Civic Culture: Political Attitudes and Democracy in Five Nations*. Princeton, N.J.: Princeton University Press, 1963.

Altschuler, Glenn C., and Stuart M. Blumin. *Rude Republic: Americans and Their Politics in the Nineteenth Century*. Princeton, N.J.: Princeton University Press, 2000.

Ames, Blanche Butler. *Chronicles from the Nineteenth Century: Family Letters of Blanche Butler and Adelbert Ames Married July 21st, 1870*. Vol. 1. Clinton, Mass.: privately published, 1957.

Anbinder, Tyler. *Nativism and Slavery: The Northern Know Nothings and the Politics of the 1850's*. New York: Oxford University Press, 1992.

Ashworth, John. *"Agrarians" and "Aristocrats": Party Political Ideology in the United States, 1837–1846*. New York: Cambridge University Press, 1987.

Atkinson, Caroline P., ed. *Letters of Susan Hale*. Boston: Marshall, Jones, 1919.

Attie, Jeanie. *Patriotic Toil: Northern Women and the American Civil War*. Ithaca, N.Y.: Cornell University Press, 1998.

Augur, Helen. *Tall Ships to Cathay*. Garden City, N.Y.: Doubleday, 1951.

Austin, J. L. *How to Do Things with Words*. Cambridge, Mass.: Harvard University Press, 1962.

Avery, Rachel Foster, ed. *Proceedings of the Thirtieth Annual Convention of the National American Woman Suffrage Association*. Philadelphia: Ferris, 1898.

Bacon, Jacqueline. *The Humblest May Stand Forth: Rhetoric, Empowerment, and Abolition*. Columbia: University of South Carolina Press, 2002.

Baker, Jean H. *Affairs of Party: The Political Culture of Northern Democrats in the Mid-Nineteenth Century*. Ithaca, N.Y.: Cornell University Press, 1983.

———. *James Buchanan*. New York: Henry Holt, 2004.

Baker, Paula. "The Midlife Crisis of the New Political History." *Journal of American History* 86.1 (June 1999): 158–66.

Baldwin, Christopher Columbus. *Diary of Christopher Columbus Baldwin, Librarian of the American Antiquarian Society, 1829–1835*. 1901; New York: Johnson Reprint, 1971.

Banner, Lois W. *American Beauty*. Chicago: University of Chicago Press, 1983.

Bartlett, Irving H. "Daniel Webster as a Symbolic Hero." *New England Quarterly* 45.4 (Dec. 1972): 484–507.

Basch, Norma. "Marriage, Morals, and Politics in the Election of 1828." *Journal of American History* 80.3 (1993): 890–918.

Bauer, K. Jack. *The Mexican War, 1846–1848*. New York: Macmillan, 1974.

———. *Zachary Taylor: Soldier, Planter, Statesman of the Old Southwest*. Newtown, Conn.: American Political Biography Press, 1994.

Bederman, Gail. *Manliness and Civilization: A Cultural History of Gender and Race in the United States, 1880–1917*. Chicago: University of Chicago Press, 1995.

Beecher, Catharine. *Educational Reminiscences and Suggestions*. New York: J. B. Ford, 1874.

Belohlavek, John M. *Broken Glass: Caleb Cushing and the Shattering of the Union*. Kent, Ohio: Kent State University Press, 2005.

Blaine, Harriet Bailey. *Letters of Mrs. James G. Blaine*. Vol. 1. Edited by Harriet S. Blaine Beale. New York: Duffield, 1908.

Blanchard, Michael D. "The Politics of Abolition in Northampton." *Historical Journal of Massachusetts* 19.2 (1991): 175–96.

Blocker, Jack S., Jr. "Separate Paths: Suffragists and the Women's Temperance Crusade." *Signs* 10.3 (Spring 1985): 460–76.

Bodenhamer, David J., Robert Graham Barrows, and David Gordon Vanderstel. *Encyclopedia of Indianapolis*. Bloomington: Indiana University Press, 1994.

Boutwell, George S. *Reminiscences of Sixty Years in Public Affairs*. Vol. 1. New York: McClure, Phillips, 1902.

Boylan, Anne M. "Women and Politics in the Era before Seneca Falls." *Journal of the Early Republic* 10.3 (Fall 1990): 363–82.

Branson, Susan. *These Fiery Frenchified Dames: Women and Political Culture in Early National Philadelphia*. Philadelphia: University of Pennsylvania Press, 2001.

Brauer, Kinley J. *Cotton versus Conscience: Massachusetts Whig Politics and Southwestern Expansion, 1843–1848*. Lexington: University Press of Kentucky, 1967.

———. "The Webster-Lawrence Feud: A Study in Politics and Ambitions." *Historian* 29.1 (1966): 34–59.

Briggs, Caroline Clapp. *Reminiscences and Letters of Caroline C. Briggs*. Edited by George S. Merriam. Boston: Houghton, Mifflin, 1897.

Brooke, John L. *The Heart of the Commonwealth: Society and Political Culture in Worcester County, Massachusetts, 1713–1861*. Amherst: University of Massachusetts Press, 1992.

Brooks, Van Wyck. *The Flowering of New England, 1815–1865*. New York: E. P. Dutton, 1936.

Brown, Joshua. *Beyond the Lines: Pictorial Reporting, Everyday Life, and the Crisis of Gilded Age America*. Berkeley and Los Angeles: University of California Press, 2002.

Brown, Richard D. *Knowledge Is Power: The Diffusion of Information in Early America, 1700–1865*. New York: Oxford University Press, 1989.

Browne, Stephen H. *Angelina Grimké: Rhetoric, Identity, and the Radical Imagination*. East Lansing: Michigan State University Press, 1999.

Brummett, Barry. "Towards a Theory of Silence as a Political Strategy." *Quarterly Journal of Speech* 66 (1980): 289–303.

Bulkley, Robert D., Jr. "Robert Rantoul, Jr., 1805–1852: Politics and Reform in Antebellum Massachusetts." PhD diss., Princeton University, 1971.

Burke, Edmond. *Rhode Island-Interference of the Executive in the Affairs of June 7, 1844*. Washington, D.C.: Blair and Rives, 1844.

Butler, Benjamin F. *Autobiography and Personal Reminiscences of Major-General Benj. F. Butler: Butler's Book*. Boston: A. M. Thayer, 1892.

[Cabot, Richard Clarke, ed.] *The Letters of Elizabeth Cabot*. 2 vols. Boston: privately printed, 1905.

Campbell, Karlyn Kohrs. *Man Cannot Speak for Her*, vol. 1, *A Critical Study of Early Feminist Rhetoric*. Westport, Conn.: Praeger, 1989.

Carlson, A. Cheree. "Limitations on the Comic Frame: Some Witty American Women of the Nineteenth Century." *Quarterly Journal of Speech* 74.3 (1988): 310–22.

Carter, Jane G. Avery, and Susie P. Holmes. *Genealogical Record of the Dedham Branch of the Avery Family in America*. Plymouth, Mass.: Winslow W. Avery, 1893.

Carwardine, Richard. "Evangelicals, Whigs and the Election of William Henry Harrison." *Journal of American Studies* 17.1 (Apr. 1983): 47–75.

Catt, Carrie Chapman, and Nettie Rogers Schuler. *Woman Suffrage and Politics: The Inner Story of the Suffrage Movement*. New York: Charles Scribner's Sons, 1926.

Catterall, Ralph C. H. *The Second Bank of the United States*. Chicago: University of Chicago Press, 1902.

Chambers, William Nisbet. "Election of 1840." In *History of American Presidential Elections, 1789–1968*, 1:643–90. Edited by Arthur M. Schlesinger, Jr., and Fred L. Israel. New York: Chelsea House, 1971.

Channing, Elizabeth Parsons. *Autobiography and Diary of Elizabeth Parsons Channing: Gleanings of a Thoughtful Life*. Boston: American Unitarian Association, 1907.

Chase, Charles A. "Worcester." In *History of Worcester County, Massachusetts*, 2:548–667. Edited by Abijah Perkins Marvin. Boston: C. F. Jewett, 1879.

Chitwood, Oliver Perry. *John Tyler: Champion of the Old South*. New York: D. Appleton-Century, 1939.

Clapp, Elizabeth J. "'A Virago-Errant in Enchanted Armor?': Anne Royall's 1829 Trial as a Common Scold." *Journal of the Early Republic* 23.2 (Summer 2003): 207–32.

Clark, Anne Biller. *My Dear Mrs. Ames: A Study of Suffragist Cartoonist Blanche Ames Ames*. New York: Peter Lang, 2001.

Clinton, Catherine. *The Other Civil War: American Women in the Nineteenth Century*. 2nd ed. New York: Hill and Wang, 1999.

Cmiel, Kenneth. *Democratic Eloquence: The Fight over Popular Speech in Nineteenth-Century America*. New York: W. Morrow, 1990.

Coates, Austin. *A Macao Narrative*. 1978; Oxford: Oxford University Press, 1999.

Cockrell, Dale. *Demons of Disorder: Early Blackface Minstrels and Their World*. New York: Cambridge University Press, 1997.

Cohen, Daniel A. "Introduction." In *The Female Marine and Related Works: Narratives of Cross-Dressing and Urban Vice in America's Early Republic*, 1–45. Edited by Daniel A. Cohen. Amherst: University of Massachusetts Press, 1997.

Collison, Gary. *Shadrach Minkins: From Fugitive Slave to Citizen*. Cambridge, Mass.: Harvard University Press, 1998.

Conant, Charlotte Howard. *A Girl of the Eighties at College and at Home from the Family Letters of Charlotte Howard Conant and from Other Records*. Edited by Martha Pike Conant. Boston: Houghton, Mifflin, 1931.

Conforti, Joseph A. *Imagining New England: Explorations of Regional Identity from the Pilgrims to the Mid-Twentieth Century*. Chapel Hill: University of North Carolina Press, 2001.

"Constitution of the State of Maine, Adopted by the People. January 5, 1820." In *Documentary History of the State of Maine: The Farnham Papers, 1698–1871*, 8:153–96. Compiled by Mary Frances Farnham. Portland, Maine: Lefavor-Tower, 1902.

Cooke, Rose Terry. "Miss Dorcas's Opinion." *Congregationalist*, Apr. 17, 1884, 125.

Coryell, Janet L. *Neither Heroine nor Fool: Anna Ella Carroll of Maryland*. Kent, Ohio: Kent State University Press, 1990.

———. "Superseding Gender: The Role of the Woman Politico in Antebellum Partisan Politics." In *Women and the Unstable State in Nineteenth-Century America*, 84–112. Edited by Alison M. Parker and Stephanie Cole. College Station: Texas A&M University Press, 2000.

Cott, Nancy F. *The Bonds of Womanhood: "Woman's Sphere" in New England, 1780–1835*. 1977; New Haven, Conn.: Yale University Press, 1997.

Crapol, Edward P. *John Tyler: The Accidental President*. Chapel Hill: University of North Carolina Press, 2006.

Crocker, Matthew H. *The Magic of the Many: Josiah Quincy and the Rise of Mass Politics in Boston, 1800–1830*. Amherst: University of Massachusetts Press, 1999.

Cutler, Wayne. "President Polk's New England Tour: North for Union." In *Essays on the Mexican War*, 8–33. Edited by Douglas W. Richmond. College Station: Texas A&M University Press, 1986.

Dall, Caroline Healey. *Daughter of Boston: The Extraordinary Diary of a Nineteenth-Century Woman*. Edited by Helen R. Deese. Boston: Beacon, 2005.

Darling, Arthur B. *Political Changes in Massachusetts, 1824–1848: A Study of Liberal Movements in Politics*. New Haven: Yale University Press, 1925.

Davis, George T. "Biographical Sketch of Hon. Henry W. Cushman." *New England Historical and Genealogical Register* 18.24 (1864): 321–25.

DeFiore, Jayne Crumpler. "'Come, and Bring the Ladies': Tennessee Women and the Politics of Opportunity during the Campaigns of 1840 and 1844." *Tennessee Historical Quarterly* 51 (Winter 1992): 197–212.

Dennett, Tyler. *Americans in Eastern Asia: A Critical Study of the Policy of the United States with Reference to China, Japan, and Korea in the 19th Century*. New York: Macmillan, 1922.

Dennison, George M. *The Dorr War: Republicanism on Trial, 1831–1861*. Lexington: University Press of Kentucky, 1976.

Denton, Sally. *Passion and Principle: John and Jessie Frémont, the Couple Whose Power, Politics, and Love Shaped Nineteenth-Century America*. New York: Bloomsbury, 2007.

de Pina-Cabral, João. *Between China and Europe: Anthropological Essays on Macao*. London: Athlone, 2001.

Deutsch, Sarah. "Learning to Talk More Like a Man: Boston Women's Class-Bridging Organizations, 1870–1940." *American Historical Review* 97.2 (Apr. 1992): 379–404.

Dickinson, Emily. *The Letters of Emily Dickinson*. Edited by Mabel Loomis Todd. Boston: Roberts Brothers, 1894.

Dinkin, Robert J. *Before Equal Suffrage: Women in Partisan Politics from Colonial Times to 1920*. Westport, Conn.: Greenwood, 1995.

Donald, David Herbert. *Charles Sumner*. Part 1. New York: Da Capo, 1996.

———. *Lincoln*. New York: Simon and Schuster, 1995.

Dublin, Thomas. *Women at Work: The Transformation of Work and Community in Lowell, Massachusetts, 1826–1860*. New York: Columbia University Press, 1993.

———. "Women, Work, and Protest in the Early Lowell Mills: 'The Oppressing Hand of Avarice Would Enslave Us.'" *Labor History* 16.1 (1975): 99–116.

Dubois, Ellen Carol. *Feminism and Suffrage: The Emergence of an Independent Women's Movement in America, 1848–1869*. 1978; Ithaca, N.Y.: Cornell University Press, 1999.

Earle, Edward Mead. "American Interest in the Greek Cause, 1821–1827." *American Historical Review* 33.1 (Oct. 1927): 44–63.

Earle, Jonathan Halperin. *Jacksonian Antislavery and the Politics of Free Soil, 1824–1854*. Chapel Hill: University of North Carolina Press, 2004.

Eaton, Clement. *Henry Clay and the Art of American Politics*. Boston: Little, Brown, 1957.

Edwards, Rebecca. *Angels in the Machinery: Gender in American Party Politics from the Civil War to the Progressive Era*. New York: Oxford University Press, 1997.

Eisenhower, John S. D. *So Far from God: The U.S. War with Mexico, 1846–1848*. New York: Random House, 1989.

———. *Zachary Taylor*. New York: Henry Holt, 2008.

Elkins, Stanley, and Eric McKitrick. *The Age of Federalism.* New York: Oxford University Press, 1993.

Ellis, Mary B. "The Re-examination of a Reputation: A Biography of Alexander Hill Everett." MA thesis, George Washington University, 1955.

Enloe, Cynthia. *Maneuvers: The International Politics of Militarizing Women's Lives.* Berkeley: University of California Press, 2000.

Epstein, Barbara Leslie. *The Politics of Domesticity: Women, Evangelism, and Temperance in Nineteenth-Century America.* Middletown, Conn.: Wesleyan University Press, 1981.

Etcheson, Nicole. *Bleeding Kansas: Contested Liberty in the Civil War Era.* Lawrence: University Press of Kansas, 2004.

Fahs, Alice. *The Imagined Civil War: Popular Literature of the North and South, 1861–1865.* Chapel Hill: University of North Carolina Press, 2001.

Feller, Daniel. "Politics and Society: Toward a Jacksonian Synthesis." *Journal of the Early Republic* 10 (Summer 1990): 135–61.

Fetterley, Judith, and Marjorie Pryse. *Writing Out of Place: Regionalism, Women, and American Literary Culture.* Urbana: University of Illinois Press, 2003.

Field, Edward, ed. *State of Rhode Island and Providence Plantations at the End of the Century: A History.* Vol. 1. Boston and Syracuse: Mason Publishing, 1902.

Fischer, Roger A. *Tippecanoe and Trinkets Too: The Material Culture of American Presidential Campaigns, 1828–1984.* Urbana: University of Illinois Press, 1988.

Flammang, Janet A. *Women's Political Voice: How Women Are Transforming the Practice and Study of Politics.* Philadelphia: Temple University Press, 1997.

Formisano, Ronald P. *For the People: American Populist Movements from the Revolution to the 1850s.* Chapel Hill: University of North Carolina Press, 2008.

———. "The Invention of the Ethnocultural Interpretation." *American Historical Review* 99.2 (Apr. 1994): 453–77.

———. "The New Political History and the Election of 1840." *Journal of Interdisciplinary History* 23.4 (Spring 1993): 661–82.

———. "The Role of Women in the Dorr Rebellion." *Rhode Island History* 51.3 (1993): 89–104.

———. *The Transformation of Political Culture: Massachusetts Parties, 1790s-1840s.* New York: Oxford University Press, 1983.

Fowle, Priscilla Hawthorne. "Boston Daily Newspapers, 1830–1850." PhD diss., Radcliffe College, 1920.

Free Soil! Grand Rally! Broadside. Boston: Dickinson Printing, 1848.

Frothingham, Paul Revere. *Edward Everett: Orator and Statesman.* Boston: Houghton Mifflin, 1925.

Frothingham, Richard. *History of the Siege of Boston, and of the Battles of Lexington, Concord, and Bunker Hill.* 1849; New York: De Capo Press, 1970.

Gabriel, Ralph Henry. *Elias Boudinot, Cherokee, and His America.* Norman: University of Oklahoma Press, 1941.

Gaillet, Lynée Lewis, and Elizabeth Tasker. "Recovering, Revisioning, and Regendering the History of 18th- and 19th-Century Rhetorical Theory and Practice." In *The Sage Handbook of Rhetorical Studies*, 67–84. Edited by Andrea Lunsford, Kirt H. Wilson, and Rosa A. Eberly. Los Angeles: Sage, 2009.

Gelles, Edith B. *Abigail Adams: A Writing Life*. New York: Routledge, 2002.

———. *Abigail and John: Portrait of a Marriage*. New York: William Morrow, 2009.

Gettleman, Marvin E. *The Dorr Rebellion: A Study in American Radicalism, 1833–1849*. New York: Random House, 1973.

Gienapp, William E. "Abolitionism and the Nature of Antebellum Reform." In *Courage and Conscience: Black and White Abolitionists in Boston*, 21–46. Edited by Donald M. Jacobs. Bloomington: Indiana University Press, 1993.

———. *The Origins of the Republican Party, 1852–1856*. New York: Oxford University Press, 1987.

———. "'Politics Seem to Enter into Everything': Political Culture in the North, 1840–1860." In *Essays on American Antebellum Politics, 1840–1860*, 15–69. Edited by Stephen E. Maizlish and John J. Kushma. College Station: Texas A&M University Press, 1982.

Gilbert, Abby L. "Of Banks and Politics: The Bank Issue and the Election of 1840." *West Virginia History* 34.1 (1972): 18–45.

Gillespie, J. David. *Politics at the Periphery: Third Parties in Two-Party America*. Columbia: University of South Carolina Press, 1993.

Gilmore, William J. "Elementary Literacy on the Eve of the Industrial Revolution: Trends in Rural New England." *Proceedings of the American Antiquarian Society* 92, pt. 1 (1982): 87–178.

Ginzberg, Lori D. "'The Hearts of Your Readers will Shudder': Fanny Wright, Infidelity, and American Freethought." *American Quarterly* 46.2 (1994): 195–226.

———. *Women and the Work of Benevolence: Morality, Politics, and Class in the Nineteenth-Century United States*. New Haven, Conn.: Yale University Press, 1990.

Glenn, Cheryl, and Melissa A. Goldthwaite. *The St. Martin's Guide to Teaching Writing*. New York: St. Martin's, 2008.

Goebel, Dorothy Burne. *William Henry Harrison: A Political Biography*. Philadelphia, Porcupine Press, 1974.

González, Deena J. *Refusing the Favor: The Spanish-Mexican Women of Santa Fe, 1820–1880*. New York: Oxford University Press, 1999.

Gordon, Beverly. *Bazaars and Fair Ladies: The History of the American Fundraising Fair*. Knoxville: University of Tennessee Press, 1998.

Graham, Susan H. "'Call Me a Female Politician, I Glory in the Name!' Women Dorrites and Rhode Island's 1842 Suffrage Crisis." PhD diss., University of Minnesota, 2006.

Green, Frances H. *Might and Right*. Providence: A. H. Stillwell, 1844.

Greenberg, Amy S. *Manifest Manhood and the Antebellum American Empire*. New York: Cambridge University Press, 2005.

Grimsted, David. *American Mobbing, 1828–1861.* New York: Oxford University Press, 1998.

Gring-Pemble, Lisa M. "Writing Themselves into Consciousness: Creating a Rhetorical Bridge between the Public and Private Spheres." *Quarterly Journal of Speech* 84.1 (1998): 41–61.

Gue, B. F. *History of Iowa from the Earliest Times. . . .* Vol. 4. New York: Century History, 1903.

Guest, Ivor. *Fanny Elssler.* Middletown, Conn.: Wesleyan University Press, 1970.

Guiney, Louise Imogen. *Letters of Louise Imogen Guiney.* Vol. 1. Edited by Grace Guiney. New York: Harper and Row, 1926.

Gunderson, Robert Gray. *The Log-Cabin Campaign.* Lexington: University of Kentucky Press, 1957.

Gustafson, Melanie Susan. *Women and the Republican Party, 1854–1924.* Urbana: University of Illinois Press, 2001.

Hale, Edward Everett. *Memories of a Hundred Years.* Vol. 1. New York: Macmillan, 1903.

———. *A New England Boyhood.* New York: Cassell, 1893.

[Hale, Sarah Josepha]. "The Worth of Money." *Ladies' Magazine and Literary Gazette* 3.2 (Feb. 1830): 49.

Hall, Richard. *Women on the Civil War Battlefront.* Lawrence: University Press of Kansas, 2006.

Hamlin, Charles Eugene. *The Life and Times of Hannibal Hamlin.* Cambridge, Mass.: Riverside Press, 1899.

Hammond, Bray. "Jackson, Biddle, and the Bank of the United States." *Journal of Economic History* 7.1 (May 1847): 1–23.

Hampel, Robert L. *Temperance and Prohibition in Massachusetts, 1813–1852.* Ann Arbor: UMI Research Press, 1982.

Hanaford, Phebe A. *Daughters of America; or, Women of the Century.* Augusta, Maine: True, 1883.

Handlin, Lilian. *George Bancroft: The Intellectual as Democrat.* New York: Harper and Row, 1984.

Hansen, Debra Gold. "The Boston Female Anti-Slavery Society and the Limits of Gender Politics." In *The Abolitionist Sisterhood: Women's Political Culture in Antebellum America*, 45–66. Edited by Jean Fagan Yellin and John C. Van Horne. Ithaca, N.Y.: Cornell University Press, 1994.

Hansen, Karen V. *A Very Social Time: Crafting Community in Antebellum New England.* Berkeley: University of California Press, 1994.

Harlow, Neal. *California Conquered: The Annexation of a Mexican Province, 1846–1850.* Berkeley: University of California Press, 1982.

Hart, Roderick P. *Campaign Talk: Why Elections Are Good for Us.* Princeton, N.J.: Princeton University Press, 2000.

Harvey, Peter. *Reminiscences and Anecdotes of Daniel Webster.* Boston: Little, Brown, 1877.

Hatch, Louis Clinton. *Maine: A History*. Vol. 2. New York: American Historical Society, 1919.

Haynes, Sam W. *James K. Polk and the Expansionist Impulse*. New York: Longman, 1997.

Heitman, Francis B. *Historical Register and Dictionary of the United States Army, 1789–1903*. Vol. 2. Washington, D.C.: U.S. Government Printing Office, 1903.

Hershberger, Mary. "Mobilizing Women, Anticipating Abolition: The Struggle against Indian Removal in the 1830s." *Journal of American History* 86.1 (June 1999): 15–40.

Hewitt, Nancy A. *Women's Activism and Social Change: Rochester, New York, 1822–1872*. Ithaca, N.Y.: Cornell University Press, 1984.

Hill, Hamilton Andrews, ed. *Memoir of Abbott Lawrence*. 1883. 2nd ed., Boston: Little Brown, 1884.

Hillard, Katharine, ed. *My Mother's Journal: A Young Lady's Diary of Five Years Spent in Manilla, Macao, and the Cape of Good Hope from 1829–1834*. Boston: George H. Ellis, 1900.

Hodges, Nan P., and Arthur W. Hummel, eds. *Lights and Shadows of a Macao Life: The Journal of Harriett Low, Travelling Spinster*. 2 vols. Woodinville, Wash.: History Bank, 2002.

Hoganson, Kristin. *Fighting for American Manhood: How Gender Politics Provoked the Spanish-American and Philippine-American Wars*. New Haven, Conn.: Yale University Press, 1998.

Holloway, Jean. *Edward Everett Hale: A Biography*. Austin: University of Texas Press, 1956.

Holt, Michael F. "The Election of 1840, Voter Mobilization, and the Emergence of the Second American Party System: A Reappraisal of Jacksonian Voting Behavior." In *A Master's Due: Essays in Honor of David Herbert Donald*, 16–85. Edited by William J. Cooper, Michael F. Holt, and John McCardell. Baton Rouge: Louisiana State University Press, 1985.

———. *The Fate of Their Country: Politicians, Slavery Extension, and the Coming of the Civil War*. New York: Hill and Wang, 2004.

———. *The Political Crisis of the 1850s*. New York: John Wiley and Sons, 1978.

———. *The Rise and Fall of the American Whig Party: Jacksonian Politics and the Onset of the Civil War*. New York: Oxford University Press, 1999.

Holzer, Harold. *Lincoln President-Elect: Abraham Lincoln and the Great Secession Winter, 1860–1861*. New York: Simon and Schuster, 2008.

Homans, Isaac Smith. *Sketches of Boston, Past and Present. . . .* Boston: Phillips Sampson, 1851.

hooks, bell. "'When I Was a Young Soldier for the Revolution': Coming to Voice." In her *Talking Back: Thinking Feminist, Thinking Black*, 10–18. Boston: South End, 1989.

Horward, Donald D. "The American Press and the Death of Napoleon." *Journalism Quarterly* 43.4 (1966): 715–21.

Howe, Daniel Walker. "The Evangelical Movement and Political Culture in the North during the Second Party System." *Journal of American History* 77 (Mar. 1991): 1216–39.

———. *The Political Culture of the American Whigs*. Chicago: University of Chicago Press, 1979.

Hudson, Frederic. *Journalism in the United States, from 1690 to 1872*. New York: Harper and Brothers, 1873.

Huntoon, Daniel T. V. *History of the Town of Canton*. Cambridge, Mass.: John Wilson, 1893.

Huspek, Michael, and Kathleen E. Kendall. "On Withholding Political Voice: An Analysis of the Political Vocabulary of a 'Nonpolitical' Speech Community." *Quarterly Journal of Speech* 77.1 (Feb. 1991): 1–18.

Huston, James L. *The Panic of 1857 and the Coming of the Civil War*. Baton Rouge: Louisiana State University Press, 1987.

Irving, Washington. *The Sketch Book of Geoffrey Crayon, Gent.* 2 vols. New York: C. S. Van Winkle, 1819.

Isenberg, Nancy. *Sex and Citizenship in Antebellum America*. Chapel Hill: University of North Carolina Press, 1998.

Jabour, Anya. *Marriage in the Early Republic: Elizabeth and William Wirt and the Companionate Ideal*. Baltimore: Johns Hopkins University Press, 1998.

Jeffrey, Julie Roy. *The Great Silent Army of Abolitionism: Ordinary Women in the Antislavery Movement*. Chapel Hill: University of North Carolina Press, 1998.

Jesus, C. A. Montalto de. *Historic Macao*. 1926; New York: Oxford University Press, 1984.

Johannsen, Robert Walter. *To the Halls of the Montezumas: The Mexican War in the American Imagination*. New York: Oxford University Press, 1985.

"John Chandler Bancroft Davis." *Proceedings of the American Antiquarian Society* 19 (1909): 13–17.

Johnson, Michael P. *Toward a Patriarchal Republic: The Secession of Georgia*. Baton Rouge: Louisiana State University Press, 1977.

Johnson, Nan. *Gender and Rhetorical Space in American Life, 1866–1910*. Carbondale: Southern Illinois University Press, 2002.

Jones, Howard. "Anglophobia and the Aroostook War." *New England Quarterly* 48.4 (1975): 519–539.

———. *Mutiny on the Amistad: The Saga of a Slave Revolt and Its Impact on American Abolition, Law, and Diplomacy*. New York: Oxford University Press, 1987.

———. *Union in Peril: The Crisis over British Intervention in the Civil War*. Chapel Hill: University of North Carolina Press, 1992.

Kann, Mark E. *The Gendering of American Politics: Founding Mothers, Founding Fathers, and Political Patriarchy*. Westport, Conn.: Praeger, 1999.

Keller, Helen Adams. *The Story of My Life: With Her Letters (1887–1901)*. New York: Doubleday, 1903.

Kelley, Mary. *Learning to Stand and Speak: Women, Education, and Public Life in America's Republic*. Chapel Hill: University of North Carolina Press, 2006.

Kennett, Lee. "Le Culte de Napoléon aux États-Unis Jusqu'á la Guerre de Sécession." *Revue de l'Institut Napoléon* 125 (1972): 145–56.

Kerber, Linda K. *No Constitutional Right to Be Ladies: Women and the Obligations of Citizenship*. New York: Hill and Wang, 1998.

———. "Separate Spheres, Female Worlds, Woman's Place: The Rhetoric of Women's History." *Journal of American History* 75.1 (1998): 9–39.

———. *Women of the Republic: Intellect and Ideology in Revolutionary America*. Chapel Hill: University of North Carolina Press, 1980.

Kessler-Harris, Alice. *Gendering Labor History*. Urbana: University of Illinois Press, 2007.

Kincheloe, Joe L., Jr. "Transcending Role Restrictions: Women at Camp Meetings and Political Rallies." *Tennessee Historical Quarterly* 40 (Summer 1981): 158–69.

Klein, Philip Shriver. *President James Buchanan, a Biography*. University Park: Pennsylvania State University Press, 1962.

Kohl, Lawrence Frederick. *The Politics of Individualism: Parties and the American Character in the Jacksonian Era*. New York: Oxford University Press, 1989.

Kraditor, Aileen. "The Introduction." In her *Up from the Pedestal: Selected Writings in the History of American Feminism*, 3–24. Chicago: Quadrangle Books, 1968.

Kruman, Marc W. "The Second American Party System and the Transformation of Revolutionary Republicanism." *Journal of the Early Republic* 12 (Winter 1992): 509–37.

Lamas, Rosmarie W. N. *Everything in Style: Harriet Low's Macau*. Hong Kong: Hong Kong University Press, 2006.

Laurie, Bruce. *Beyond Garrison: Antislavery and Social Reform*. New York: Cambridge University Press, 2005.

Lawes, Carolyn J. *Women and Reform in a New England Community, 1815–1860*. Lexington: University Press of Kentucky, 2000.

Lawson, John D. *American State Trials*. Vol. 2. St. Louis: F. H. Thomas, 1914.

Le Duc, Thomas. "The Maine Frontier and the Northeastern Boundary Controversy." *American Historical Review* 53.1 (1947): 30–41.

Leeman, Richard W. *"Do Everything" Reform: The Oratory of Frances E. Willard*. Westport, Conn.: Greenwood, 1992.

Leonard, Thomas M. *James K. Polk: A Clear and Unquestionable Destiny*. Wilmington, Del.: Scholarly Resources, 2001.

Lincoln, William. *History of Worcester, Massachusetts, from Its Earliest Settlement to September, 1836. . . .* Worcester, Mass.: M. D. Phillips, 1837.

Linkon, Sherry Lee. "Saints, Sufferers, and 'Strong-Minded Sisters': Anti-Suffrage Rhetoric in Rose Terry Cooke's Fiction." *Legacy* 10.1 (1993): 31–46.

Loines, Elma, ed. *The China Trade Post-Bag of the Seth Low Family of Salem and New York, 1829–1873*. Manchester, Maine: Falmouth, 1953.

———, ed. "Hard Cash; or a Salem Housewife in the Eighteen Twenties." *Essex Institute Historical Collections* 91 (1955): 246–65.

Lynch, Denis Tilden. *An Epoch and a Man: Martin Van Buren and His Times*. 2 vols. 1929; Port Washington, N.Y.: Kennikat Press, 1971.

Lystra, Karen. *Searching the Heart: Women, Men, and Romantic Love in Nineteenth-Century America*. New York: Oxford University Press, 1989.

Mahon, John K. *The History of the Militia and the National Guard*. New York: Macmillan, 1983.

Maine Council. *Aroostook War: Historical Sketch and Roster of Commissioned Officers and Enlisted Men. . . .* Augusta, Maine: Kennebec Journal Print, 1904.

Mansch, Larry D. *Abraham Lincoln, President-Elect: The Four Critical Months from Election to Inauguration*. Jefferson, N.C.: McFarland, 2005.

Marszalek, John F. *The Petticoat Affair: Manners, Mutiny, and Sex in Andrew Jackson's White House*. New York: Free Press, 1997.

Martin, Lawrence. "Women Fought at Bunker Hill." *New England Quarterly* 8.4 (Dec. 1935): 467–79.

Mattelart, Armand, and Michèle Mattelart. *Theories of Communication: A Short Introduction*. Translated by Susan Gruenheck Taponier and James A. Cohen. London: Sage, 1998.

Mattingly, Carol A. *Appropriate[ing] Dress: Women's Rhetorical Style in Nineteenth-Century America*. Carbondale: Southern Illinois University Press, 2002.

May, Samuel. *The Fugitive Slave Law and Its Victims*. New York: American Anti-slavery Society, 1861.

Mayfield, John. *Rehearsal for Republicanism: Free Soil and the Politics of Antislavery*. Port Washington, N.Y.: Kennikat Press, 1980.

McGerr, Michael. "Political Style and Women's Power, 1830–1930." *Journal of American History* 77.3 (Dec. 1990): 864–85.

McGovern, James R. *Yankee Family*. New Orleans: Polyanthos, 1975.

McKinley, Silas Bent, and Silas Bent. *Old Rough and Ready: The Life and Times of Zachary Taylor*. New York: Vanguard, 1946.

McKivigan, John R. "Series Introduction." In *History of the American Abolitionist Movement: A Bibliography of Scholarly Articles*, vii-xiv. Edited by John R. McKivigan. New York: Garland, 1999.

McPherson, James M. *Battle Cry of Freedom: The Civil War Era*. New York: Oxford University Press, 1988.

———. *For Cause and Comrades: Why Men Fought in the Civil War*. New York: Oxford University Press, 1997.

Melder, Keith E. *Hail to the Candidate: Presidential Campaigns from Banners to Broadcasts*. Washington, D.C.: Smithsonian Institution Press, 1992.

"Memoir of John R. Vinton." *American Review* 5 (June 1847): 594–602.

Middleton, Allecia Hopton, ed. *Life in Carolina and New England during the Nineteenth Century, as Illustrated by Reminiscences and Letters of the Middleton Family of Charleston, South Carolina, and of the DeWolf Family of Bristol, Rhode Island*. Bristol, R.I.: private printing, 1929.

Miller, Hildy, and Lillian Bridwell-Bowles, eds. *Rhetorical Women: Roles and Representations*. Tuscaloosa: University of Alabama Press, 2005.

Mitchell, Thomas G. *Antislavery Politics in Antebellum and Civil War America.* Westport, Conn.: Praeger, 2007.

Monroe, Dan. *The Republican Vision of John Tyler.* College Station: Texas A&M University Press: 2003.

Moore, Lillian. "Ballet Slippers and Bunker Hill." *Dance* 10 (Sept. 1937): 11, 42.

Morris, Charles E., III. "'Our Capital Aversion': Abigail Folsom, Madness, and Radical Antislavery Praxis." *Women's Studies in Communication* 24.1 (Spring 2001): 62–89.

Motz, Marilyn Ferris. "Folk Expression of Time and Place: 19th-Century Midwestern Rural Diaries." *Journal of American Folklore* 100 (1987): 131–47.

Moulton, Janice. "A Paradigm of Philosophy: The Adversary Method." In *Women, Knowledge, and Reality: Explorations in Feminist Philosophy*, 5–20. Edited by Ann Garry and Marilyn Pearsall. London: Routledge, 1992.

Mowry, Arthur May. *The Dorr War: The Constitutional Struggle in Rhode Island.* Providence: Preston and Rounds, 1901.

Mulkern, John R. *The Know Nothing Party in Massachusetts: The Rise and Fall of a People's Movement.* Boston: Northeastern University Press, 1990.

Nash, Gary B. *The Urban Crucible: The Northern Seaports and the Origins of the American Revolution.* Cambridge, Mass.: Harvard University Press, 1979.

Neely, Mark E., Jr. *The Boundaries of American Political Culture in the Civil War Era.* Chapel Hill: University of North Carolina Press, 2005.

Niven, John. *John C. Calhoun and the Price of Union.* Baton Rouge: Louisiana State University Press, 1988.

Norton, Anthony Banning. *The Great Revolution of 1840: Reminiscences of the Log Cabin and Hard Cider Campaign.* Mount Vernon, Ohio: private printing, 1888.

Nystrand, Martin, and John Duffy, eds. *Towards a Rhetoric of Everyday Life: New Directions in Research on Writing, Text, and Discourse.* Madison: University of Wisconsin Press, 2003.

Oakes, James. "The Political Significance of Slave Resistance." In *African-American Activism before the Civil War: The Freedom Struggle in the Antebellum North*, 188–205. Edited by Patrick Rael. New York: Routledge, 2008.

Olick, Jeffrey K., and Joyce Robbins. "Social Memory Studies: From 'Collective Memory' to the Historical Sociology of Mnemonic Practices." *Annual Review of Sociology* 24 (1998): 105–40.

Olsen, Christopher J. "Respecting 'The Wise Allotment of Our Sphere': White Women and Politics in Mississippi, 1840–1860." *Journal of Women's History* 11.3 (Autumn 1999): 104–25.

Packard, Alpheus S. *History of the Bunker Hill Monument.* Portland, Maine: B. Thurston, 1853.

Parsons, Lynn Hudson. "The 'Splendid Pageant': Observations on the Death of John Quincy Adams." *New England Quarterly* 53.4 (Dec. 1980): 464–82.

Pasley, Jeffrey L. "Minnows, Spies, and Aristocrats: The Social Crisis of Congress in the Age of Martin Van Buren." *Journal of the Early Republic* 27.4 (Winter 2007): 599–653.

———. *"The Tyranny of Printers": Newspaper Politics in the Early American Republic*. Charlottesville: University Press of Virginia, 2001.

Pease, Jane H., and William H. Pease. *The Fugitive Slave Law and Anthony Burns: A Problem in Law Enforcement*. Philadelphia: Lippincott, 1975.

Penney, Sherry H., and James D. Livingston. *A Very Dangerous Woman: Martha Wright and Women's Rights*. Amherst: University of Massachusetts Press, 2004.

Peterson, Norma Lois. *The Presidencies of William Henry Harrison and John Tyler*. Lawrence: University Press of Kansas, 1989.

Petrulionis, Sandra Harbert. *To Set This World Right: The Antislavery Movement in Thoreau's Concord*. Ithaca, N.Y.: Cornell University Press, 2006.

Pierson, Michael D. "'All Southern Society Is Assailed by the Foulest Charges': Charles Sumner's 'The Crime against Kansas' and the Escalation of Republican Anti-Slavery Rhetoric." *New England Quarterly* 68 (1995): 531–57.

———. *Free Hearts and Free Homes: Gender and American Antislavery Politics*. Chapel Hill: University of North Carolina Press, 2003.

———. *Mutiny at Fort Jackson: The Untold Story of the Fall of New Orleans*. Chapel Hill: University of North Carolina Press, 2008.

———. "'Prairies on Fire': The Organization of the 1856 Mass Republican Rally in Beloit, Wisconsin." *Civil War History* 48.2 (2002): 101–22.

Plumstead, A. W. *The Wall and the Garden: Selected Massachusetts Election Sermons, 1670–1775*. Minneapolis: University of Minnesota Press, 1968.

"Poetical Portraits with Pen and Pencil, No. XXX: Alexander H. Everett." *Democratic Review* 10.47 (May 1842): 460–79.

Popkin, Samuel L. *The Reasoning Voter: Communication and Persuasion in Presidential Campaigns*. 2nd ed. Chicago: University of Chicago Press, 1994.

Portnoy, Alisse. *Their Right to Speak: Women's Activism in the Indian and Slave Debates*. Cambridge, Mass.: Harvard University Press, 2005.

Powell, Kimberly A. "The Association of Southern Women for the Prevention of Lynching: Strategies of a Movement in the Comic Frame." *Communication Quarterly* 43.1 (Winter 1995): 86–99.

Prescott, William. *The Prescott Memorial; or, A Genealogical Memoir of the Prescott Families in America, in Two Parts*. Boston: W. Dutton, 1870.

Pugh, David G. *Sons of Liberty: The Masculine Mind in Nineteenth-Century America*. Westport, Conn.: Greenwood Press, 1983.

Purcell, Sarah J. *Sealed with Blood: War, Sacrifice, and Memory in Revolutionary America*. Philadelphia: University of Pennsylvania Press, 2002.

Putala, Claire White. *Reading and Writing Ourselves into Being: The Literacy of Certain Nineteenth-Century Young Women*. Greenwich, Conn.: Information Age, 2004.

Putnam, James Jackson. *A Memoir of Dr. James Jackson, with Sketches of His Father. . . .* Boston and New York: Houghton Mifflin, 1905.

Raikes, Thomas. *The City of the Czar: or, A Visit to St. Petersburg, in the Winter of 1829–30*. Philadelphia: Lea and Blanchard, 1838.

Ray, Angela G. *The Lyceum and Public Culture in the Nineteenth-Century United States*. East Lansing: Michigan State University Press, 2005.

———. "What Hath She Wrought? Woman's Rights and the Nineteenth-Century Lyceum." *Rhetoric and Public Affairs* 9.2 (Summer 2006): 183–213.

Reed, John J. "Battleground: Pennsylvania Antimasons and the Emergence of the National Nominating Convention, 1835–1839." *Pennsylvania Magazine of History and Biography* 122.1/2 (Jan./Apr. 1998): 77–115.

Reilly, Thomas. "American Reporters and the Mexican War." PhD diss., University of Minnesota, 1975.

Remini, Robert V. *Andrew Jackson and His Indian Wars*. New York: Viking, 2001.

———. *Andrew Jackson and the Course of American Democracy, 1833–1845*. New York: Harper and Row, 1984.

———. *Andrew Jackson and the Course of American Freedom, 1822–1832*. New York: Harper and Row, 1981.

———. *Daniel Webster: The Man and His Time*. New York: W. W. Norton, 1997.

———. *Henry Clay: Statesman for the Union*. New York: W. W. Norton, 1991.

———. *John Quincy Adams*. New York: Times Books, 2002.

Repousis, Angelo. "'The Cause of the Greeks': Philadelphia and the Greek War for Independence, 1821–1828." *Pennsylvania Magazine of History and Biography* 123.4 (Oct. 1999): 333–63.

Reynolds, David S. *John Brown, Abolitionist: The Man Who Killed Slavery, Sparked the Civil War, and Seeded Civil Rights*. New York: Knopf, 2005.

Richards, Leonard L. *The California Gold Rush and the Coming of the Civil War*. New York: Knopf, 2007.

Robotti, Frances Diane. *Chronicles of Old Salem: A History in Miniature*. Salem, Mass.: Newcomb and Gauss, 1948.

Rohrs, Richard C. "'Public Attention for . . . Essentially Private Matters': Women Seeking Assistance from President James K. Polk." *Journal of the Early Republic* 24 (Spring 2004): 107–23.

Rolle, Andrew F. *John Charles Frémont: Character as Destiny*. Norman: University of Oklahoma Press, 1991.

Ryan, Mary P. *Cradle of the Middle Class: The Family in Oneida County, New York, 1790–1865*. New York: Cambridge University Press, 1981.

———. *Women in Public: Between Banners and Ballots, 1825–1880*. Baltimore: Johns Hopkins University Press, 1990.

Sacher, John M. "'The Ladies Are Moving Everywhere': Louisiana Women and Antebellum Politics." *Louisiana History* 42.4 (Autumn 2001): 439–57.

Saxton, Alexander. *The Rise and Fall of the White Republic: Class Politics and Mass Culture in Nineteenth-Century America*. 1990; London: Verso, 2003.

Schantz, Mark S. *Piety in Providence: Class Dimensions of Religious Experience in Antebellum Rhode Island*. Ithaca, N.Y.: Cornell University Press, 2000.

Schlesinger, Arthur M., Jr. *The Age of Jackson*. Boston: Little, Brown, 1945.

Scott, Anne Firor, and Andrew MacKay Scott. *One Half the People: The Fight for Woman Suffrage*. Philadelphia: Lippincott, 1975.

Seager, Robert, II. *And Tyler Too: A Biography of John & Julia Gardiner Tyler.* New York: McGraw-Hill, 1963.

Seager, Robert, II, Robert Seager, James F. Hopkins, Melba Porter Hay, and Mary W. M. Hargreaves, eds. *The Papers of Henry Clay*, vol. 9, *The Whig Leader, January 1, 1837–December 31, 1843*. Lexington: University Press of Kentucky, 1988.

Seigenthaler, John. *James K. Polk*. New York: Times Books, 2003.

Sheidley, Harlow W. "The Webster-Hayne Debate: Recasting New England's Sectionalism." *New England Quarterly* 67.1 (Mar. 1994): 5–29.

Shover, Kenneth B. "Another Look at the Late Whig Party: The Perspective of the Loyal Whig." *Historian* 48 (Aug. 1986): 539–58.

Silber, Nina. *Daughters of the Union: Northern Women Fight the Civil War*. Cambridge, Mass.: Harvard University Press, 2005.

Silber, Nina, and Mary Beth Sievens, eds. *Yankee Correspondence: Civil War Letters between New England Soldiers and the Home Front*. Charlottesville: University Press of Virginia, 1996.

Silbey, Joel H. *Martin Van Buren and the Emergence of American Popular Politics*. Lanham, Md.: Rowman and Littlefield, 2002.

———. *The Partisan Imperative: The Dynamics of American Politics before the Civil War*. New York: Oxford University Press, 1985.

Silverman, Kenneth. *Lightning Man: The Accursed Life of Samuel F. B. Morse*. New York: Alfred A. Knopf, 2003.

Simon, Paul. *Freedom's Champion: Elijah Lovejoy*. Carbondale: Southern Illinois University Press, 1994.

Skocpol, Theda. *Protecting Soldiers and Mothers: The Political Origins of Social Policy in the United States*. Cambridge, Mass.: Belknap Press of Harvard University Press, 1992.

Smith, Elbert B. *The Presidencies of Zachary Taylor and Millard Fillmore*. Lawrence: University Press of Kansas, 1988.

Smith-Rosenberg, Carroll. "The Female World of Love and Ritual: Relations between Women in Nineteenth-Century America." *Signs* 1.1 (Autumn 1975): 1–29.

Somkin, Fred. "Alexander Hill Everett." MA thesis, American University, 1961.

Sprague, John Francis. *The North Eastern Boundary Controversy and the Aroostook War*. Dover, Maine: Observer Press, 1910.

Stanton, Elizabeth Cady, and Susan B. Anthony. *History of Woman Suffrage*. 6 vols. Rochester, N.Y.: Anthony, 1881–1922.

Stavely, Keith, and Kathleen Fitzgerald. *America's Founding Food: The Story of New England Cooking*. Chapel Hill: University of North Carolina Press, 2004.

Steffens, Lincoln. *The Struggle for Self-Government: Being an Attempt to Trace American Political Corruption to Its Sources in Six States of the United States*. New York: McClure, Phillips, 1906.

Sterne, Evelyn Savidge. *Ballots and Bibles: Ethnic Politics and the Catholic Church in Providence*. Ithaca, N.Y.: Cornell University Press, 2004.

Sterling, Dorothy. *Ahead of Her Time: Abby Kelley and the Politics of Anti-slavery*. New York: W. W. Norton, 1991.

Stevenson, Brenda, ed. *The Journals of Charlotte Forten Grimké*. New York: Oxford University Press, 1988.

Sumler-Lewis, Janice. "The Forten-Purvis Women of Philadelphia and the American Anti-slavery Crusade." *Journal of Negro History* 66.4 (Winter 1981–1982): 281–88.

Taft, Russell Wales. *The Vermont Prohibitory Law*. Burlington, Vt.: Free Press Association, 1902.

Taketani, Etsuko. *U.S. Women Writers and the Discourses of Colonialism, 1825–1861*. Knoxville: University of Tennessee Press, 2003.

Taslitz, Andrew E. *Reconstructing the Fourth Amendment: A History of Search and Seizure, 1789–1868*. New York: New York University Press, 2006.

Taylor, Alan. "'The Art of Hook and Snivey': Political Culture in Upstate New York during the 1790s." *Journal of American History* 79 (Mar. 1993): 1371–96.

Taylor, William R. *Cavalier and Yankee: The Old South and American National Character*. New York: G. Braziller, 1961.

Temin, Peter. "The Economic Consequences of the Bank War." *Journal of Political Economy* 76.2 (Mar.-Apr. 1968): 257–74.

———. *The Jacksonian Economy*. New York: W. W. Norton, 1969.

Templin, Mary. "Panic Fiction: Women's Responses to Antebellum Economic Crisis." *Legacy* 21.1 (2004): 1–16.

Thornton, Tamara Plakins. *Cultivating Gentlemen: The Meaning of Country Life among the Boston Elite, 1785–1860*. New Haven, Conn.: Yale University Press, 1989.

———. *Handwriting in America: A Cultural History*. New Haven, Conn.: Yale University Press, 1996.

Tilly, Louise A., and Patricia Gurin, eds. *Women, Politics, and Change*. New York: Russell Sage Foundation, 1990.

"To the Women of New England." *Ladies' Magazine and Literary Gazette* 3.4 (Apr. 1830): 171–73.

Travers, Len. *Celebrating the Fourth: Independence Day and the Rites of Nationalism in the Early Republic*. Amherst: University of Massachusetts Press, 1997.

Troy, Gil. *See How They Ran: The Changing Role of the Presidential Candidate*. New York: Free Press, 1991.

Twisleton, Ellen Dwight. *Letters of the Hon. Mrs. Edward Twisleton, Written to Her Family, 1852–1862*. Edited by Ellen Twisleton Vaughan. London: John Murray, 1928.

Upham, Timothy, Horatio Hill, and Cyrus Barton. *Report of the Case of Timothy Upham Against Hill and Barton, Publishers of the New-Hampshire Patriot*. Dover, N.H.: G. W. Ela, 1830.

Uviller, H. Richard, and William G. Merkel. *The Militia and the Right to Arms, or, How the Second Amendment Fell Silent*. Durham, N.C.: Duke University Press, 2002.

Van Broekhoven, Deborah Bingham. *The Devotion of These Women: Rhode Island in the Antislavery Network*. Amherst: University of Massachusetts Press, 2002.

Van Deusen, Glyndon. "The Whig Party." In *History of U.S. Political Parties*, 1:331–63. Edited by Arthur M. Schlesinger, Jr. New York: Chelsea House, 1973.

VanVugt, William E. *Britain to America: Mid-Nineteenth-Century Immigrants to the United States*. Urbana: University of Illinois Press, 1999.

Varg, Paul A. *Edward Everett: The Intellectual in the Turmoil of Politics*. Selinsgrove, Pa.: Susquehanna University Press, 1992.

Varon, Elizabeth R. "'The Ladies Are Whigs': Lucy Barbour, Henry Clay, and Nineteenth-Century Virginia Politics." *Virginia Cavalcade* 42.2 (Autumn 1992): 72–83.

——. "Tippecanoe and the Ladies, Too: White Women and Party Politics in Antebellum Virginia." *Journal of American History* 82.2 (Sept. 1995): 494–521.

——. *We Mean to Be Counted: White Women and Politics in Antebellum Virginia*. Chapel Hill: University of North Carolina Press, 1998.

Vaughan, Ellen Twisleton. "Preface." In Twisleton, *Letters*, v-xii.

Vázquez, Josefina Zoraida. "Causes of the War with the United States." In *Dueling Eagles: Reinterpreting the U.S.-Mexican War, 1846–1848*, 41–66. Edited by Richard V. Francaviglia and Douglas W. Richmond. Fort Worth: Texas Christian University Press, 2000.

Venet, Wendy Hamand. "'Cry Aloud and Spare Not': Northern Antislavery Women and John Brown's Raid." In *His Soul Goes Marching On: Responses to John Brown and the Harpers Ferry Raid*, 98–118. Edited by Paul Finkelman. Charlottesville: University Press of Virginia, 1995.

——. *Neither Ballots nor Bullets: Women Abolitionists and the Civil War*. Charlottesville: University Press of Virginia, 1991.

Verba, Sidney. "Women in American Politics." In Tilly and Gurin, *Women*, 555–72.

Von Frank, Albert J. *The Trials of Anthony Burns: Freedom and Slavery in Emerson's Boston*. Cambridge, Mass.: Harvard University Press, 1998.

Voss, Frederick. "Webster Replying to Hayne: George Healy and the Economics of History Painting." *American Art* 15.3 (Autumn 2001): 34–53.

Watson, Harry L. "Humbug? Bah! Altschuler and Blumin and the Riddle of the Antebellum Electorate." *Journal of American History* 84.3 (Dec. 1997): 886–93.

——. *Liberty and Power: The Politics of Jacksonian America*. New York: Hill and Wang, 1990.

Webster, Daniel. "The Character of Washington." *National Intelligencer*, Mar. 6, 1832.

——. *The Writings and Speeches of Daniel Webster*, vol. 18, *Private Correspondence*. Edited by Edward Everett. Boston: Little, Brown, 1903.

Welter, Barbara. "The Cult of True Womanhood, 1820–1860." *American Quarterly* 18.2 (Summer 1966) 151–74.

White, Arthur O. "Salem's Antebellum Black Community: Seedbed of the School Integration Movement." *Essex Institute Historical Collections* 108 (Apr. 1972): 99–118.

White, William R. "Our Soldier Dead." *Quartermaster Review* (May-June 1930): 10–15.

Whittier, John Greenleaf. *The Letters of John Greenleaf Whittier*. 3 vols. Edited by John B. Pickard. Cambridge, Mass.: Belknap Press of Harvard University Press, 1975.

Wilcox, Cadmus M. *History of the Mexican War*. Washington, D.C.: Church News, 1892.

Wilentz, Sean. *The Rise of Democracy: Jefferson to Lincoln*. New York: Norton, 2005.

Willard, Frances Elizabeth. *Glimpses of Fifty Years: The Autobiography of an American Woman*. Chicago: Woman's Temperance Publication Association, 1889.

Willard, Frances Elizabeth, and Mary Ashton Rice Livermore. *A Woman of the Century: Fourteen Hundred-Seventy Biographical Sketches*. Buffalo: Moulton, 1893.

Williams, Susan Reynolds. "In the Garden of New England: Alice Morse Earle and the History of Domestic Life." PhD diss., University of Delaware, 1992.

Willingham, William F. "Deference Democracy and Town Government in Windham, Connecticut, 1755 to 1786." *William and Mary Quarterly* 3d ser. 30.3 (July 1973): 401–22.

Wilson, Clyde N., ed. *The Papers of John C. Calhoun*. Vol. 13. Columbia: University of South Carolina Press, 1980.

Wilson, Major L. *The Presidency of Martin Van Buren*. Lawrence: University Press of Kansas, 1984.

Wilson, Richard W. "The Many Voices of Political Culture: Assessing Different Approaches." *World Politics* 52.2 (Jan. 2000): 246–73.

Yee, Shirley J. *Black Women Abolitionists: A Study in Activism, 1828–1860*. Knoxville: University of Tennessee Press, 1992.

Zaeske, Susan. "The 'Promiscuous Audience' Controversy and the Emergence of the Early Woman's Rights Movement." *Quarterly Journal of Speech* 81.2 (1995): 191–207.

——. *Signatures of Citizenship: Petitioning, Antislavery, and Women's Political Identity*. Chapel Hill: University of North Carolina Press, 2003.

——. "Unveiling Esther as a Pragmatic Radical Rhetoric." *Philosophy and Rhetoric* 33.3 (2000): 193–220.

Zagarri, Rosemarie. *Revolutionary Backlash: Women and Politics in the Early American Republic*. Philadelphia: University of Pennsylvania Press, 2007.

Zboray, Ronald J. *A Fictive People: Antebellum Economic Development and the American Reading Public*. New York: Oxford University Press, 1993.

Zboray, Ronald J., and Mary Saracino Zboray. "Cannonballs and Books: Reading and the Disruption of Social Ties on the New England Home Front." In *The*

War Was You and Me: Civilians in the American Civil War, 237–61. Edited by Joan E. Cashin. Princeton, N.J.: Princeton University Press, 2002.

———. *Everyday Ideas: Socioliterary Experience among Antebellum New Englanders*. Knoxville: University of Tennessee Press, 2006.

———. "Gender Slurs in Boston's Partisan Press during the 1840s." *Journal of American Studies* 34.3 (2000): 413–46.

———. "Is It a Diary, Commonplace Book, Scrapbook, or Whatchamacallit?: Six Years of Exploration in New England's Manuscript Archives." *Libraries and the Cultural Record* 44.1 (Feb. 2009): 101–23.

———. *Literary Dollars and Social Sense: A People's History of the Mass Market Book*. New York: Routledge, 2005.

———. "Political News and Female Readership in Antebellum Boston and Its Region." *Journalism History* 22.1 (Spring 1996): 2–14.

———. "Reading and Everyday Life in Antebellum Boston: The Diary of Daniel F. and Mary D. Child." *Libraries and Culture* 32.3 (Summer 1997): 285–323.

———. "Transcendentalism in Print: Production, Dissemination, and Common Reception." In *Transient and Permanent: The Transcendentalist Movement and Its Contexts*, 310–81. Edited by Charles Capper and Conrad Edick Wright. Boston: Massachusetts Historical Society, 1999.

———. "Whig Women, Politics, and Culture in the Campaign of 1840: Three Perspectives from Massachusetts." *Journal of the Early Republic* 17.2 (Summer 1997): 277–315.

Zelizer, Julian E. "Beyond the Presidential Synthesis: Reordering Political Time." In *A Companion to Post-1945 America*, 345–70. Edited by Jean-Christophe Agnew and Roy Rosenzweig. Malden, Mass.: Blackwell, 2006.

Zuckerman, Michael, and others. "Deference or Defiance in Eighteenth-Century America? A Round Table." *Journal of American History* 85.1 (1998): 13–97.

Index

abolitionists, 148, 184; as anti-Dorr, 119; and Burns case, 178–79; and District of Columbia slave trade ban, 69; and elections, 68–69, 72, 106, 145, 148; Faneuil Hall denied to, 172; meetings of, 185, 200–201; mob attacks on, 73; as percentage of population, 72; and petitions, 62, 72; and school boards, 215; at Sims extradition, 171; and Texas annexation, 145–46; vote-scattering by, 138; and Whig Party, 139, 148; and women, 14, 44, 65, 72, 145, 171. *See also* antislavery; slavery issue
Acorn (ship), 171
Adams, Abigail, 71, 90
Adams, Charles Francis, 71, 148
Adams, John Quincy, 25, 38, 43, 48, 53, 55, 58–59, 62, 140, 156
Adams, Thomas, 89
"Address Delivered at Faneuil Hall, July 4, 1828" (Prince), 25
"Address Delivered before the American Institute" (Cushing), 60
Advertiser (Boston), 144, 145, 155
Aesop, 56
African Americans, 119, 134, 136, 146, 171, 184–86, 188, 216, 235n9
Aikin, Lucy, 24–25
Alabama, 34
Alabama (ship), 214
Altschuler, Glenn, 4
American Anti-Slavery Society, 72
American Party, 2, 133, 146, 180, 189–90, 192, 205, 224
American Review (New York), 154
American Revolution, 6, 10, 71, 199, 222, 225, 237n37
American system (Henry Clay), 37, 53, 55
Ames, Adelbert, 222
Ames, Blanche Ames, 223
Ames, Blanche Butler, 222
Amistad case, 73
Ammidon, Philip Jr., 24, 25
Anderson, Robert, 211–12
Andersonville Prison, 216
Andrews, Charles, 106; as clerk of courts, 110; courtship of, 99, 101; death of, 110; as Democrat, 98–99, 158; and Democratic filibuster, 100–101; 1843 run for U.S. representative of, 105–6; on 1844 Democratic victories, 109; estate purchased by, 108; letters and story papers exchanged by, 103; marriage of, 102–103, 105, 107; new county argued by, 107; and partisan meetings, 108, 170–71; on Polk's visit to Maine, 155; and religion, 105; as speaker of the Maine house, 104; as state representative, 103; as U.S. representative, 110–111, 171
Andrews, Charlotte, 106, 108, 110
Andrews, Persis Sibley, 98–111; and Andrews, 100, 102–4; on banking policy, 104; bible quoted by, 208; and bipartisanship, 98, 111, 171; and campaigns, 106–7; as chronicler of partisan events, 205; and Civil War, 209, 212, 214–15; courtship of, 99, 101; and Democratic Party, 205, 208, 214; on 1861 National Fast Day, 210; on elections, 107–9, 153, 162, 166–67, 177, 182, 206; and Harrison, 98, 102; and housework, 101; as husband's legal secretary, 110; legislative interests deemed unladylike by, 101; letters and story papers received by, 103; lionized in husband's absence, 158; on love of

Andrews, Persis Sibley *(continued)* politics, 110; at Maine legislature, 100–1; on marriage, 101–3, 104–5, 110, 205; and mass meetings, 109–10, 170–71; on mudslinging against Clay, 108; newspapers read by, 100–1; on New Year's Day, 107–8; on office seeking, 100, 104; partisan debates in family circle of, 101; partisan ethos of, compared with Tyler, 99; partisanship in 1860 diary of, 206; as Peace Democrat, 214; and political conversations, 103; political discussion, attended by, 206; as political wife, 99, 107, 111; on Polk's visit to Maine, 155; portrait of, 108; as schoolteacher, 102, 104; on secession, 207–8; sermons read aloud by, 105; Shakespeare quoted by, 157; on Taylor, 157; Texas annexation opposed by, 108; on Tyler's bank veto, 103; as unionist willing to compromise, 199; as Whig, 98–99, 106, 108; Whig disaffiliation of, 110
Anglo-American diplomacy, 73–74, 77, 96, 143, 152, 202, 211, 213
Anthony, Burrington, 117, 120
anti-Catholicism, 36, 115, 146, 181, 190
anti-Jacksonianism, 36–38, 41
Anti-Masonic Party, 37, 56, 242n13
antislavery, 10, 15, 65; and Burns case, 179, 183–86, 203; and editors, 73; and elections, 69, 73, 148, 153, 158, 164, 166, 182–83; and fairs, 72, 192, 200; and Kansas issue, 186–89; newspapers devoted to, 73, 151; and partisan women, 73, 133, 180; petitions concerning, 44, 62; Seward speech on, 201; societies, 63, 72, 171, 243n30; speeches about read by women, 154; and U.S.-Mexico War, 152; and Whigs, 148; and women, 10, 15, 72–73, 164, 205; and women's rights addressed by speakers, 201. *See also* abolitionists; Free-Soil Party; slavery issue
antiwar sentiment: in Aroostook War, 77–78; in Civil War, 199, 212, 214; in U.S.-Mexico War, 78, 134, 145, 147–49, 151–52, 155, 160
Appleton, Jane Sophia Hill, 74–75
Appleton, John, 75
Appleton, Moses Larke, 74–75
Appleton, William, 175
Aroostook War, 63–65, 73–76, 152
Atlantic (ship), 29
Atlas (Boston), 67, 122, 123, 161, 169
Attucks, Crispus, 200
audiences (promiscuous) and women speakers, 7, 8, 185, 225. *See also* speeches
Austin, John T., 57
Austin, William, 48

Ballou, Olney, 128
Bancroft, Aaron, 41, 53, 63
Bancroft, George: bank investments of, 66; and *Bay State Democrat,* 80; as Boston port collector, 50, 69; and Davis, 59–60, 81, 84–85; as Democratic convert, 59–60; and election fraud, 70; and elections, 64, 66, 81, 127; and family fracas over Whig acquaintance, 83; Independence Day speech of, 89; as National Republican, 59; and political fight with sister, 63; as rhetor, 81–82; on U.S. bank, 81; U.S. representative run of, 60
Bancroft, Lucretia, 60, 63–64, 70, 83–84, 89
Bancroft, Lucretia Chandler, 50, 53, 61, 66
Bancroft, Sarah, 63
banking, 3, 34, 42, 49, 69, 104, 141
Bank of the United States, 34, 37, 41–42, 47, 81, 141, 246n8
Bankruptcy Bill (1841), 142
Banks, Nathaniel P., 190–91
Banquo's ghost (Shakespeare's *Macbeth*), 102
Barnburners, 158. *See also* Democratic Party
Barnes, Cordelia P., 120
Barney, Mary, 41–42
Barney, William B., 41
Barre (Mass.), 86–87, 89
Barrett, Martha Osborne, 190, 193, 203
Barrett, Samantha, 47–48
Barrett, Zeloda, 47–48
Bartlett, Frederick K., 74–77
"Battle Hymn of the Republic" (Howe), 216

Baynes, William, 29
Bay State Democrat (Boston), 80, 88, 122–23
Beecher, Catharine, 38
Bell, John, 63
benevolent work, 3, 11, 44, 214
Benger, Elizabeth Ogilvy, 25
Benton, Thomas Hart, 61, 193
Berbineau, Lorenza, 173, 175, 186
Berrien, John McPherson, 29, 137
Bible: quoted, 32, 33, 39–40, 48–49, 56, 187, 208; reading of, 173; referenced, 185
Bigelow, John, 192
Bigelow, John P., 169
Billings, Calista, 152, 158–62
Billings, Jarvis, 158–59
Black, Alvah, 205–6
Black, Persis Sibley Andrews. *See* Andrews, Persis Sibley
Blaine, James G., 220
Bleeding Kansas, 187–88
Blumin, Stuart, 4
Bonds of Womanhood (Cott), 9
Boston: Burns trial in, 184, 186; Compromise of 1850 disliked in, 183; elections in, 46, 67, 142, 181–82; Polk's visit to, 155; protest meeting on post-office hard-money policy, 66; public events in, 97, 136, 159, 173, 193; public mourning in, 102, 169, 175–76, 216–17; women at 1844 Whig mass meeting in, 136–37, 145
Boston Massacre Commemorative Festival, 200
Boston Post, 84
Boston School Committee, 223
Boston Times, 143
Bostwick, Charlotte, 157
Boudinot, Elias, 41
Bouquet (Bangor literary society), 70
Boutwell, George S., 174
Bowen, Harriet, 118
Boylan, Annie, 200
Bradbury, James Ware, 153
Bradford, Dr. James, 29
Branch, John, 29
Breckinridge, John C., 204
Briggs, George N., 162
Briggs, Jeremiah, 124
Brooklyn Equal Rights Association (N.Y.), 223
Brooks, Preston, 191
Brown, Catherine, 39
Browne, Sarah Smith (Cox), 72, 212, 214, 216
Browning, Elizabeth Barrett, 185
Brown, John, 199, 203, 205, 216
Brown University, 118, 120
Buchanan, James: congressional speech of, 53; and Davis, 61, 83–84; and Dorrite-Democratic events, 123, 127; as 1856 Democratic presidential candidate, 2, 192, 179, 195; and Jackson's censure, 61; as lame duck, 207; Lincoln compared with, 211; National Fast Day proclaimed by, 209–210; pamphlets of, 85; Panic of 1857 blamed on, 200; post-office flag depiction of, 195; Quincy picnic attack on, 90; as secretary of legation to England, 202; torchlight procession for, 192; and U.S. Constitution's terminus, 197; and women, 199–200
Buena Vista, Battle of, 149, 157, 170
Bunker Hill, Battle of, 83
Bunker Hill Monument Association, 45
Bunker Hill Monument (Charlestown, Mass.), 37, 45, 94, 222
Bunker Hill Monument Ladies' Fair (1840), 46, 94
Bunker Hill Whig Convention (1840), 46, 90, 92–93
Burns, Anthony, 179–80, 184–85
Burnside, Samuel M., 62
Burns, Robert, 107
Burr, Aaron, 60
Butler, Andrew, 191
Butler, Benjamin Franklin, 222
Butler, Blanche. *See* Ames, Blanche Butler
Butler, Sarah Hildreth, 222–23
Buxton, Althea, 100
Buxton, William, 100
Byron, George Gordon Lord, 104–5

Cabot, Elizabeth Dwight, 197–99, 200–4, 206–13, 215–16, 224; on American Party, 190; and antislavery, 190, 197, 203; on Boston mourning for Webster, 175–76; on Brown's Harpers

Cabot, Elizabeth Dwight *(continued)*
Ferry raid, 203; Civil War position of, and sister, 198–99, 202, 209–10, 212–13; Crittenden Compromise rejected by, 210; on elections, 163, 189, 204, 206–7, 215, 224; escapist reading of, 201; Everett's speechmaking criticized by, 202; on Fort Sumter, 212; on Hamlin family names, 204; on independent judiciary, 190; on Lincoln, 204, 207, 210–11; marriage of, 200; and news, 197, 201–2, 224; and Panic of 1857, 200; politicization of, muted in published letters, 224; politics and military affairs conflated by, 215; on removal of Burns's judge, 190; on Sickles murder case, 202; sister's illness and abbreviated correspondence of, 204; sister's Republican affiliation denied by, 210; on secession, 207–9; Sumner speech sent by, 187; war work of, 216; from Whiggery to Republicanism, 198–99
Cabot, Hannah Lowell Jackson, 66, 216
Cabot, James Elliot, 200, 204, 208
Cabot, Joseph S., 68
Cabot, Richard, 224
Calderón de la Barca, Fanny, 95
Calhoun, John C., 29, 54, 62, 140, 156, 174
California, 147, 155, 164, 167–68
Call, Charles, 159
Callé, Richard K., 62
campaign talk, 3, 12–13, 220
Canton Free-Soil Club, 160
Canton Taylor Club, 159
Carlyle, Thomas, 201
Carpenter, Thomas F., 124, 127
Carrie Harrison Clubs, 220
Cass, Lewis, 158, 161
Cerro Gordo, Battle of, 155
Chadbourne, John R., 100
Chalmers, George, 25
Chandler, Anson G., 182
Chandler, Louisa, 170
Chapman, John, 142
Charles H. Mills and Company, 200
Charter government (R.I.), 111, 114, 116–20, 122, 128
Charter of 1663 (R.I.), 114
Cheever, Elizabeth, 73
Cherokee Nation, 39, 41, 67
Cherokee Nation v. Georgia (1831), 41
Cherokee Phoenix (New Echota, Ga.), 39, 41
Child, Lydia Maria, 45
Childs, Henry H., 127
Choate, Rufus, 102
Christian Reflector (Boston), 170
Cilley, Jonathan, 67
"Circular Addressed to Benevolent Ladies of the U. States" (Beecher), 38–39
citizenship and women, 3, 24, 235n4
Citizen's Union, 181
City of the Czar (Raikes), 63
civic culture, 6. *See also* political culture
civic holidays. *See* holidays (civic)
Civil War, 198–99, 211–19; and marital relations, 214; military service evasions during, 215; onset of, 211–12; and private counterparts, 198; Republican women's reactions to coming of, 196; as terminus of study, 5; Union arrests of spies and traitors in, 215; women as illegal combatants in, 262n1; women's martial spirit in, 213; women's partisanship and patriotism in, 134, 214, 218; women's reaction to onset of, 199, 212, 222; and women's workforce participation, 218
clambakes (partisan), 8, 89, 122–24, 127, 129
Clapp, Elizabeth Atherton, 173–75, 181–82
Clarke, James Freeman, 203
Clark, Harriet, 39–40
Clay, Cassius M., 148
Clay, Henry, 41; and African Americans, 136; and American System, 37, 53; antiannexationism of, 108, 144; bank bill of, vetoed, 103, 141; campaign clubs of, 144; and Compromise of 1850, 168; and Compromise Tariff of 1833, 56–57; death of, 174; and death of son, 157; Dorrite women's opposition to, 128; on Eliza Davis, 241n1; in Harrison administration, 102, 141; Jackson censure resolution of, 61; Massachusetts Whigs' support for, 135; Minkins resolution of, 171; on playing to ladies' gallery, 171; as presidential candidate, 43, 46, 56, 108, 110,

138, 143–46; as presidential hopeful, 157; senate committee chair taken from, 61; speeches of, 36, 55; before U.S. Supreme Court, 91; and Whig Party's origins, 1, 36; youngsters' support for, 135, 194
Clay, Henry Jr., 170
Clement, Ann, 95
Clement, Elizabeth, 95
Cleveland, Chauncey Fitch, 123
Cleveland, Frances, 220
Cleveland, Grover, 219–20
Clifford, John Henry, 181
coalitions (political), 2, 133–34, 180–81, 183, 190
Cobb, Eunice Hale (Waite), 188, 192–93
Collins, Amos M., 157
Colver, Nathaniel, 171–72
Combe, George, 71
Compromise of 1850, 164, 168, 199
Compromise Tariff of 1833, 32–33, 56–57
Confederate States of America, 209, 211, 213, 216
Congdon, Cynthia Sprague, 175, 195
Congdon, John R., 128
Congdon, Mary Remington, 195
Congregational Church, 53
Congressional Globe (Washington, D.C.), 34
Connecticut Horse Guards, 47
Conscience Whigs, 138, 148, 156, 158
Constitutional Union Party, 205, 215
contagion effects, 7, 226
Cooke, Rose Terry, 221–22
Cooley, Frances, 124
Cott, Nancy, 9, 15
Coulter, John, 54
Courier and Enquirer (New York), 125
Courier (Bangor), 69
Cowper, William, 185
Crawford, William H., 140
Creek Nation, 34
"Crime Against Kansas" (Sumner), 191
Crittenden, John J., 144, 210
Crockett, Davy, 43
Crosby, William George, 182
currency reform, 34, 85, 95
Curtis, Caroline Gardiner, 205, 212
Curtis, Charles Pelham, 212
Curtis, George T., 171, 175
Curtis, George W., 201
Curtis, Harriot F., 157
Cushing, Caleb, 60, 90, 94, 148
Cushman, Henry Wyles, 179–80
Cutter, Ammi Greely, 103
Czar of Russia, 224

Daily Advertiser (Boston), 96, 136, 139
Dallas, George M., 109, 126–27, 146
Dana, Elizabeth Ellery, 217
Dana, Mary Rosamond, 217
Dana, Richard Henry Jr., 186, 188
Dana, Sarah Watson, 46, 216–17
Daoguang, Emperor of China, 28
Davis, Eliza Bancroft, 50–63, 81–88; on Adams, 55; on American System, 53, 55; and antislavery, 63, 73; as "Aunt John," 63; and brother, 60, 81–85; Butler compared with, 222; and Calhoun newspaper subscription, 62; as campaigner, 63, 80–81; on Cherokee antiremoval advocates speaking, 41; on chessplaying and political strategizing, 82; and Clay, 55–56, 241n15; correspondence of, with husband, 51, 53; on Democrats replacing committee chairs, 61; and 1840 Whig State Convention, 81, 83, 85–87, 93; on elections, 46, 70, 85, 246n9; ennui over politics, 62–63; on Independence Day partisan events, 56, 89; and Independent Treasury, 62, 82, 84–85; and Jackson, 42, 46, 54, 56–57, 59, 61, 152; and letters of, publicized through publication, 96; metaphorical use of Jacksonian argot by, 55; and new home, 62; on nullification, 56–57; on paratactical political conversation, 81; as partisan without apology, 57; and political faith in the people, 88; political savvy of, 52; as politician's wife, 49, 51, 53–55, 57–58, 242n19; politicization of, 63; on popularity of husband, 57; as preacher against doughfaces, 56; public role of, 86–87; reading of, 60; as rhetor, 88; and sister, 60, 63, 83–85; and slavery debates in congress, 62; and speeches, 54–55, 63, 82, 85; and tariff-debate overload, 56; and Taylor, 164–66; and 25th U.S. Congress Second Session, 62; and

Davis, Eliza Bancroft *(continued)*
Van Buren, 49, 50, 53, 56, 59, 61–62, 87, 158; and Webster's pro-Fugitive Slave Law stance, 168; as Whig, 47, 51, 53; as Worcester Committee Chair at Bunker Hill Monument Ladies' Fair, 94
Davis, John: and Bancroft, 59–61; and Buchanan, 61, 83–84; as candidate for office, 52, 57–58, 63, 80–81, 91, 124, 140–41, 242n18; Compromise Tariff of 1833, 57; correspondence of, with wife, 51, 53; Dorrite extraditions by, 123; and Eaton scandal, 54; and Fugitive Slave Law, 171; health problems of, 57, 59; as "Honest John," 63; and House Committee on Commerce appointment, 54; Independent Treasury speech of, 62, 82, 84–85; as Massachusetts governor, 58; on nullification, 57; portrait of, 90; speeches of, 55, 57, 63; on Taylor inauguration committee, 165; and Taylorism over Van Burenism, 158; and 24th U.S. Congress special session, 61; as U.S. Representative, 51, 53; as U.S. Senator, 49, 50–52, 58; and Van Buren, 54; and veterans appropriation, 63; and Webster, 88, 168; and Webster-Hayne debate, 54; at Whig victory celebration, 97; wife as political advisor of, 46, 53–54, 57–58, 86–87; on wife's assumed disinterest in speeches, 54
Davis, Mary Gardiner, 176
Davis, Matthew Livingston ("Spy in Washington"), 59–60
Davis, Sarah, 160
Dawley, Mary Matilda, 195
Dean, William, 123
Dearborn, Henry A. S., 45, 71
Declaration of Independence, 24, 187, 223
deference democracy, 6, 23
DeFiore, Jayne Crumpler, 11
Democratic Party: Bancroft as organizer for, 59; and Compromise of 1850, 163; control of congress by, 60; declension from nation's founding principles of, 96; and Dorrites, 113, 116, 122–23, 125; and Douglas, 187, 201, 204–6; and 1840 elections, 79, 81–82, 90, 92, 246n9; and 1841 elections, 103; 1841 filibustering of, 100–1; and 1844 elections, 109, 126–27, 145–46; 1848 National Convention of, 157–68; 1849 victories of, in Free-Soil coalitions, 166; and 1853 elections, 181, 183; 1854 coalition with American Party, 2, 190, 224; 1856 presidential nomination and platform of, 192; and 1860 elections, 204–6; 1864 prospects for, 215; 1884 presidential candidate of, 219; electoral corruption of, 69, 204; and 15 Gallon Law in Massachusetts elections, 68, 70; gender style of, 20; hunkers versus barnburners in, 158; inadequacy of, in addressing Depression of 1837 and 1840 losses, 96; Jacksonian economic policies of, and Whigs in 1841, 98–99; and Kansas-Nebraska Act, 187; and Maine elections, 106, 153, 166–67, 182; monetary policy of, 65; Panic of 1857 blamed on, 200; and Polk, 108, 145; press of, 41, 43, 46, 84, 94, 108, 125, 225; principles of, 64, 200; and Rantoul women, 68; Republican Party as chief rival of, 195–96; secession crisis blamed on, 210; and sectional divisions, 133; and temperance issue, 181; and Texas annexation, 152; and third-party challenges, 133; and Third Party System, 133; and union meetings, 170–71; and U.S.-Mexico War, 149, 157; vernacular speaking in, 157; and Walker Tariff, 147; Whig Party compared with, 47; and women, 8, 19, 37, 123, 128. *See also* Democratic women; Dorrite women
Democratic-Republicans, 19, 23
Democratic Review (New York), 145
Democratic women: addressed by speakers, 127; campaign event procession led by, 126; and Davis's Independent Treasury speech, 85; diffidence of, 20, 164; in Dorr Rebellion, 19, 121–28; and 1838 election, 68; in 1844 elections, 19, 127–28, 135; evidence of, 20; fictional depictions of, 221–22; in Frances Cleveland Influence Clubs, 220; and Jacksonian gender mystique,

20; partisanship of versus that of Whig women, 20; and party affiliation, 80; voice of, 42, 128. *See also* Democratic Party
diaries: as evidence of reading, 3; as faithful pictures, 263n17; in letters, 235n1; moral mimesis in, 226; as not private, 12; and women's partisanship, 98, 225. *See also* women's partisanship
Dickens, Catherine, 142
Dickens, Charles, 142
Dickinson, Anna Elizabeth, 218
Dickinson, Emily, 8
Dixon, George Washington, 67
"Don Juan" (Byron), 104–5
Dorrite women, 121–28; as activists and speakers, 123–24; assessment of, 129; and Charterist parade of Chepachet prisoners, 120; class diversity of, 123; Clay campaigned against by, 128; as Democrats, 113; Dorr as correspondent of, 123; and Dorr Liberation Society, 127–28; 1843 arrests of, 125; and elections, 112, 122, 124, 128; and partisan essays, 113; at partisan events 1844, 124, 127; and "petticoat revolution," 122; on political corruption, 125; political voice of, 129; and postmaster appointment, 128; Republican women compared to, 193; on Texas annexation, 125; Whig women compared to, 112–13, 129. *See also* Dorr Rebellion; Dorr, Thomas Wilson
Dorr Liberation Society, 127–28
Dorr Rebellion, 8, 112–27; beginning of, 117; and Bleeding Kansas, 187; and Chepachet, 118, 120; as class conflict, 119; Democratic women's role in, 19, 121–28; as 1844 campaign issue for Whigs, 135; and treason trials, 124; women as speakers during, 8; and women's partisanship, 112–13. *See also* Charter government (R.I.); Dorr, Thomas Wilson; Dorrite women; people's government (R.I.)
Dorr, Sullivan, 128
Dorr, Thomas Wilson, 124; arsenal attack led by, 117; Chepachet abandoned by, 120; and Democratic Party, 113, 116, 124–27; and Dorrite women, 113, 121, 123–25, 127; 1843 return of, 125; freedom of, sought via petition to Polk, 128; inauguration as governor, 116; Morton alliance urged upon, 124; motives of, 119; pardon of, 128; as People's Convention delegate, 115; people's government in Chepachet reconvened by, 118; people's militia called up by, 117; Providence return of, 112, 117; and Rhode Island Constitutional Party, 114; Rhode Island fled by, 117; as Suffrage Party gubernatorial candidate, 116; sword of, 120; treason trial of, 125–26; and Tyler, 116, 123. *See also* Dorr Rebellion; Dorrite women; people's government (R.I.)
Dorr War. *See* Dorr Rebellion
Douglass, Frances A. C. (Small), 192
Douglas, Stephen A., 187, 201, 204, 205
Dover Gazette and Strafford Advertiser (Dover, N.H.), 128
Dunbar, James, 159
Durfee, Calvin, 91
Dwight, Edmund, 199
Dwight, Elizabeth. *See* Cabot, Elizabeth Dwight
Dwight, Ellen. *See* Twisleton, Ellen

East India Company, 28–30
Eaton, Horace, 187
Eaton, John, 29
Eaton, Margaret O'Neale Timberlake ("Peggy"), 29, 54
economy. *See* banking; currency reform; Panic of 1837; Panic of 1857
Eddy, Mary Baker Glover, 177
Edes, Henry Augustus, 176
Edes, Sarah Louisa (Lincoln), 174, 176
Edwards, Bel, 205
Election Day, 38, 47–48
elections, 6, 16, 46, 65, 73; of 1828, 25, 46; of 1832, 30–31, 43, 46; of 1834, 1, 36, 46; of 1835, 47, 140; of 1836, 47, 49, 64, 163; of 1837, 65–67; of 1838, 67–69; of 1839, 70; of 1840, 1, 8, 11–10, 19, 36, 78–81, 85, 91, 96, 114, 141; of 1841, 103; of 1842, 116, 122; of 1843, 106, 113, 124; of 1844, 11, 108–10, 113, 125, 127, 135, 145–46, 152; of 1845, 128; of 1846, 148, 153; of 1848, 149,

elections *(continued)*
152, 161; of 1849, 151, 166; of 1850, 166; of 1852, 163–64, 177; of 1853, 180–83; of 1854, 2, 181, 189–90; of 1856, 179, 188, 193, 195–96; of 1859, 150; of 1860, 196, 199, 204–7; of 1864, 215; of 1871, 219; of 1873, 223; of 1884, 219–20; of 1896, 220
election sermons, 47–48
Eliot, Samuel A., 67
Elizabeth I (of England), 25
Ellis, Charles Mayo, 186
Ellis, Nathan, 76
Emancipator (New York and Boston), 73
Embargo Act of 1807, 23
Emerson, Ralph Waldo, 203
"Epistle to James Smith" (Burns), 107
Esther (O.T.), 39–40
Eulogy on Lafayette (Cushing), 60
Europe During the Middle Ages (Hallam), 67
Evans, George, 153, 155, 160
Evarts, Jeremiah, 40
Everett, Alexander Hill, 38, 138–41, 145, 147–49
Everett, Charlotte Gray Brooks, 44, 145
Everett, Edward, 44–45, 56, 70, 137–38, 140–43, 145, 149, 156, 202, 205
Everett, Lucretia Orne Peabody, 38, 45, 46, 149
Everett, Oliver, 139
Exploring Expedition to the Rocky Mountains (Frémont), 167

Fairfield, John, 69, 74, 77, 109
"Fair Play for Women" (Curtis), 201
Fanny Wrightists, 225
Farrar, Caroline, 77
Faust (Goethe), 201
Federalists, 19, 23, 125
Fénelon, François de Salinac de la Mothe-, 26
Fenner, James, 127
fiction (genre), 24, 66, 101, 221–22
Field, George, 103
15 Gallon Law, 67–68, 70, 140. *See also* temperance issue
Fillmore, Millard, 165, 171, 192, 195
First Congregational Church (Worcester, Mass.), 53
First Ladies, 71, 91, 146–47, 193, 220
Fiske, Mary, 89, 135
Fitch, Samuel Sheldon, 156
Flagg and Fales' Band, 162
Flag of Our Union (Boston), 177
Fletcher, Richard, 67
Folsom, Abby, 159
Forten, Charlotte: abolitionist rhetoric of, 185; and American Revolutionary legacy, 186; at antislavery fair, 192; on Banks's election as speaker, 191; and Burns case, 184–86; diary of, 184; on freedom as natural right, 184; introduced, 184; *Liberator* article by, 216; at New England Anti-Slavery Society annual convention, 185; parodic song by, 200; and Port Royal Experiment, 216; speeches heard by, 185, 188, 191; on Sumner, 191–92
Forten-Purvis family, 184
Forten, Robert, 185
Fortification Bill, 140
Fort Sumter (S.C.), 211–12
Fort Texas siege of, 153
Foster, Abby Kelley, 185
Foster, Ezekiel, 76
Foster, George, 181
Fourth of July. *See* Independence Day
"Fox and the Hedgehog" (Aesop), 56
Frances Cleveland Influence Clubs, 220
franchise, 2, 6, 12, 19, 23, 112, 114–15, 119, 121, 127, 219
Free-Soil Party: and barnburners, 158; and Conscience Whigs, 138, 158; and Democratic Party, 133; 1849 victories of, 166; and 1853 Massachusetts Constitutional Convention, 181; and elections, 151–52, 158–61, 166–67, 181, 183; Kansas-Nebraska Act opposed by, 187; and Liberty Party, 158; New Hampshire Democrats wooed by, 183; principles of, 158; as pro-temperance, 181; and Rantoul's death, 174; supporters of, vote American Party, 190; and women, 160, 164
Frelinghuysen, Theodore, 40
Frémont, Jessie Benton, 178, 180, 193
Frémont, John C.: biography of, 192; and Bleeding Kansas, 188; campaign poem for, 189; and 1856 election, 2, 179, 192,

195; as former Democrat, 192; as future Republican candidate, 168; meetings for, 193, 195; as pathfinder, 192; and women, 167–68, 178, 180, 192–94; writings of, 167
French Revolution of 1830, 27
Fugitive Slave Law, 168, 170–72, 183, 186, 189
Fuller, William, 160

Gardner, Henry Joseph, 189, 192
Garita de San Antonio (Mexico City), 155
Garrison, Eleanor, 223
Garrison, Ellen Wright, 203, 207, 210–11, 223
Garrison, William Lloyd, 191
Gaston, William, 55
Geographical Memoir Upon Upper California (Frémont), 167
Gleason's Pictorial Drawing Room Companion (Boston), 173
Globe. See *Congressional Globe*
Glover, Mary Baker. *See* Eddy, Mary Baker Glover
Goodrich, Mary Boott, 90
Goodrich, Samuel G., 90
Gorham, Margaret Champlin Jones (Coles), 146
Gothic Seminary (Northampton, Mass.), 44
Grandy, George W., 183, 187
"Grave of Washington" (anon.), 170
Graves, William Jordan, 67
Greek War for Independence, 27, 37, 44
Greene, Nathaniel, 142, 144
Green, Frances Whipple, 125, 128
Grimké, Charlotte Forten. *See* Forten, Charlotte
Grote, George, 187
Grundy, Felix, 43
Gunderson, Robert Gray, 10

"Hail Columbia!" (Hopkinson), 87
Hale, Edward Everett, 150
Hale, John P., 171, 183
Hale, Lucretia Peabody, 223
Hale, Nathan, 43, 136, 139, 140, 144, 146, 150
Hale, Nathan Jr., 144, 146
Hale, Sarah Josepha, 45–46, 94
Hale, Sarah Preston Everett, 38, 44; ambassadorial characterization of, 142; as anti-Jacksonian, 140; as anti-war, 149, 152; and brothers' political careers, 137, 140–41, 145, 147, 205; and Bunker Hill Monument Association, 45; and Clay, 138, 145; daughter of, on Lincoln assassination, 216; early life of, 139; on early Whig Party, 140; on 1841 Bankrupt Bill, 142; on elections, 67, 96, 145–46; on expulsion of Hoar, 146; on 15 Gallon Law, 140; on Fort Sumter, 211–12; and Greek meeting, 44; and Harrison, 97, 102, 141; on Haywood's resignation, 147; letters of, as political communication, 139; and news accuracy, 140; as newspaperman's wife, 136, 139; on Oregon boundary, 152; and political disengagement, 138; political voice of, 138; on political wifedom, 95; on politics versus family, 141; on Polk's Texas annexation policy, 147; on Polk's wife as First Lady, 146; Republican and Union 1860 campaign events noted by, 205; on slavery issue, 138, 146; and son as editor, 144, 152–53; speeches read by, 140; and Story, 223; and stump speaking, 137, 150; on torchlight processions, 145; as translator, 145; and Tyler, 141–42; and U.S.-Mexico War, 138–39, 142, 147–49; and Webster, 142–43, 145, 223; and Webster-Hayne debate, 43; Websters received by, 144; and Whiggery, 97, 138–40, 145; Whig glorification of military exploits rejected by, 149; women's rights and politics disclaimed by, 150; as writer, 140
Hale, Susan, 159
Hallam, Henry, 67
Hall, Basil, 26
Hall, Edward Brooks, 116, 118–19
Hallett, Benjamin F., 64, 82, 85
Hall, Louisa Park, 113, 116–20, 127
Hall, Mary, 42, 47–48
Hamilton-Gordon, George (4th Earl of Aberdeen), 224
Hamlet (Shakespeare), 157
Hamlin Family, 204
Hamlin, Hannibal, 153, 166–67, 182, 204–5

Hammond, James Henry, 201
Hancock School (Boston), 169
Harding, William Burton, 144
hard money, 34–35, 66
Harpers Ferry (Va.), raid on, 199, 203, 216
Harrington, Clarissa, 95–96
Harris, Lydia A., 128
Harrison, Benjamin, 220
Harrison, Carrie, 220
Harrison, William Henry, 35, 63, 136; African American support for, 136; cabinet of, 141; death of, 99, 102, 113; inauguration of, 8, 98, 101; in material culture of 1840 campaign, 79, 94; obsequies for, 102, 113; and partisan melodies, 90, 95; as president, 37, 141; as "Tippecanoe," 78; victory celebrations for, 81, 97; as Whig presidential candidate, 60, 80–81, 88, 91
Harris, Westcott, 128
Harvard College, 43
Harvey, John, 76–77
Hayne, Robert Y., 43, 54, 175
Haynes, Caroline Jemima Williamson, 74, 77
Haywood, William Henry Jr., 147
Healy, George P. A., 175
Hedge, Frederic Henry, 77
Hedge, Lucy Pierce, 70, 77
Henry, Patrick, 127
Henshaw, David, 123
Higginson Grammar School (Salem, Mass.), 184
Hill, Alonzo, 85, 168
Hillard, John, 35
Hill, Benjamin Munro, 48
Hillside Frémont Club (East Greenwich, R.I.), 195
Hiss, Joseph, 190
History of Worcester (Lincoln), 61
Hoar, Samuel, 146
Hoffman, Ogden, 91
holidays (civic), 47–49
Holmes, John, 41
Hopkinson, Francis, 87
Horticultural Rooms (Massachusetts Horticultural Society), 93
Howe, John, 88–90
Howe, Julia Ward, 216
Howe, Samuel Gridley, 44
Hubbard, Henry, 42, 126–27
Hubbard, John, 170, 182
Hubbard, Sarah, 42
humor, 54, 68, 88–89
Hunkers, 158. *See also* Democratic Party
Hunter, Robert M. T., 210
Huntington, Asahel, 181
Huntress (ship), 155
Hurlburt, Sarah, 179–80
Hyde, Charlotte E. Burnap, 189

immigrants, 115–16, 127, 181, 221
Independence Day: celebrations of, 6, 24–25, 48, 56, 88–89, 115, 162, 168, 223; as civic holiday, 38, 48
Independent Treasury, 61–62, 81–85, 90
Indian Removal, 37–41, 43–44, 49
Ingham, Samuel D., 29
Innis, John A., 191
internal improvements, 37, 95, 138, 166
Irving, Washington, 199

Jackson, Andrew: and bank war, 34; cabinet resignations under, 29; and controversy over 1818 Florida invasion, 54; and Dorrite-Democratic mass meeting, 127; and Eaton scandal, 29; economic downturn blamed on, 42; election of 1832, 30, 46; and Eliza Davis, 50, 56, 59; and executive removal, 41; first inauguration of, 38; and Fortification Bill, 140; and Independence Day, 48; and Indian Removal, 37–38, 40–41; as "King," 6, 25; and Napoleon, 25, 140; northeastern tour of, 34, 42; "Message of the President" (1829), 39; opposition to, 19, 23, 53; presidency of, 1, 5, 21, 37, 49, 51; proclamation on nullification of, 32–33; public opinion of, 19, 42; and recess appointments, 41; reelection of, 31; senate censure of, 61; as sick head of state, 49; and spoils system, 41; territorial exile wished for, 152; vacillation of, likened to women's, 42; as Van Buren's puppet, 42–43; versus Calhoun, 54; and veto, 41, 55; and workingclass women, 42
Jackson, Hannah Lowell. *See* Cabot, Hannah Lowell Jackson

Jackson, Patrick Tracy, 66
Jefferson College (La.), 141
Jefferson, Thomas, 23, 60
Jocelyn, Elizabeth, 76, 77, 154–55, 157, 162
Jocelyn, Frances, 162
Jocelyn, Sarah, 77, 95–96, 97, 102
"John Brown's Body" (anon. song), 216
Johnson, Andrew, 215
Johnson, Richard M., 61
Jones, Moses, 88
Josselyn, Lewis, 122–23
Journal of Commerce (New York), 35

Kansas, 180, 187–89, 192
Kansas-Nebraska Act, 179, 186–87, 189, 190–92
Keller, Helen, 220
Kendall, Amos, 59
Kent, Edward, 69
Kerber, Linda, 9
Key, Philip Barton, 202
King, Charles William, 27
King, Samuel Ward, 116, 117, 119, 123
King, William R., 61
Kinsley, Adelaide, 160
Kinsley, Louisa Billings, 158–59
Kinsley, Lyman, 158–61
Knapp, John Francis, 43
Knowlton, Ebenezer, 153
Know-Nothings. *See* American Party

Ladies' Benevolent Suffrage Association (Providence), 120, 123, 127–29
Ladies Free Suffrage Association of Pawtucket, 123
ladies' galleries, 7, 94, 100, 156, 165, 170–71, 175
Ladies' Magazine and Literary Gazette, 45
Lafayette, Marie Joseph Paul Yves Roch Gilbert Du Motier, marquis de, 27, 60, 115, 222
Landholders' Convention (Providence), 115
"Landmark of Freedom" (Sumner), 187
Larcom, Lucy: as disunionist, 207; on 1856 election outcomes, 195; on Fort Sumter and divine hand, 212; as Free-Soiler, 133, 183; on John Brown's execution, 203; Kansas-Nebraska Act poem by, 187; on Lincoln's manliness, 211; on Monica McCarty, 176; Republican president predicted by, 196; on union's prospects upon Lincoln's inauguration, 211; Webster estate visited by, 176
Law and Order Party (R.I.), 115
Lawrence, Abbott, 45, 67, 71, 81, 92, 95–96, 174
Lawrence, Amos, 95
Lawrence, Annie Bigelow, 67–68, 71–72, 91–97; and Abigail Adams, 71–72, 91; Boston return of, in 1838, 68; at Bunker Hill Monument Ladies' Fair, 94; and Clay, 91; and Cumberland Road speech, 91; on Democrats, 96; and 1840 election events, 80, 92–94, 97; and father's career, 71–72, 81, 95–96; illness of, 91–92; as lecture-goer, 71; marriage of, and partisan occlusion, 96; mother's politicization efforts toward, 67; and political sociabilities, 71, 91; on Polk's Boston visit, 155; on Taylor's death, 168–69; on U.S.-Mexico War, 154–55; on Vinton, 154; as Whig, 91, 95
Lawrence Company, 48
Lawrence (Kansas), 189
Lawrence, Katharine Bigelow Jr., 159, 173–76
Lawrence, Katherine Bigelow, 45, 67–68, 91, 94–95, 142, 147
Law, Tellulah, 205
Leavett, Arvilla, 105, 107
lectures, 7, 41, 44, 65, 71–72, 80, 91, 95, 102, 182, 188. *See also* lyceums
Leighton, Charles, 142
letters, 235; in diary form, 235n1; as evidence of reading, 3; and moral mimesis, 226; as news vehicles, 7; as not private, 12; and women's partisanship, 225. *See also* women's partisanship
Liberator (Boston), 73, 216
Liberty Almanac (1847), 154
Liberty Party, 106, 145, 158
Life of Anne Boleyn (Benger), 25
Life of Mary Queen of Scots (Chalmers), 25
Life of Napoleon Buonaparte (Scott), 25
Lincoln, Abraham, 2, 14, 196–97, 204–5, 207, 211–13, 215–18
Lincoln, Caroline, 160–61
Lincoln, Frederick Walter, 160–61

Lincoln, George, 149, 169–70
Lincoln, Levi Jr., 46, 58, 59, 95, 149
Lincoln, William, 58, 60
literacy, 4, 7, 24, 39, 161, 204, 236, 236n23
Little, Jacob S., 100
Livingston, Edward, 32
locofocos. *See* Democratic Party
locos. *See* Democratic Party
Logan, John A., 220
Log Cabin Campaign. *See under* elections
Loines, Mary Hillard, 223
Longfellow, Henry Wadsworth, 192
Lord, Abby, 123–24, 127
Lord Aberdeen. *See* Hamilton-Gordon, George (4th Earl of Aberdeen)
Lord, Henry, 124
Lord, Nathan, 47
Loring, Anna, 171
Loring, Edward, 184, 186, 190
Loring, Ellis Gray, 171
Loring, Louisa Gilman, 173–74
Louis XV (France), 30
Lovejoy, Elijah, 73, 78
Lovejoy, Joseph C., 77–78
Low, Abigail, 24, 26, 28, 34
Lowell Institute, 71
Low family, 35
Low, Harriett, 21–35: on American prosperity, 30; anti-Jacksonianism of, 21, 23–24, 36, 38, 46; Canton factory visited by, 28; and courtships, 30; education of, 24; as epitome of republicanism, 22; on European politics, 32; Hall's *Travels* criticized by, 26; and Independence Day, 24–25, 30, 33, 48; on Jackson, 24, 27, 29–35; on Macao's aristocracy compared to Calcutta's, 27; marriage of, 35; on Napoleon, 25; on nullification crisis, 33, 56; political talk of, 31; and political voice, 21; political women among descendants of, 223; reading of, 23–27, 29, 33; and Republican motherhood, 24; Twisleton compared with, 201; unsociability of, due to politics, 32; voyage home of, 34; as Whig, 33, 35; and woman's sphere, 23
Low, Mary Ann, 23
Low, Seth, 23, 35
Low, William Henry, 24, 26–27, 30, 34
Lucifer, 56
Lummis, Abigail, 72
Luther, Martin, 201
Luther, Seth, 114
lyceums, 71, 182–83, 187. *See also* lectures

Macbeth (Shakespeare), 102
Madison, James, 108
Maine: Aroostook War in, 73–74; boundary settlement of with Canada, 96; and 1850 Democratic Party split, 166; 1851 law prohibiting liquor sales in, 181; elections in, 69, 88, 90–91, 100, 103, 105, 107, 109–10, 153, 205; feminine influence used to sway voters in, 90–91; gerrymandering in, 105; gubernatorial elections in, 47, 182, 205, 219; Militia Act (1792) of, 74; selection of speaker of the house in, 10
Maine Law, 182
Manifest Destiny, 152
Martineau, Harriet, 35
Mason Committee, 203
Mason, James M., 203
Massachusetts, 139; attorneyship general of, 57; claims against U.S. from War of 1812, 55; Cushman as lieutenant governor of, 179; 1820 constitutional convention in, 139; 1840 Whig victories in, 91; 1842 Democratic state convention in, 123; 1845 antiannexationist meeting in, 147; 1846 Whig convention in, 148; 1848 election in, 158; 1853 Whig control of legislature in, 181; 1854 electorate in, and American Party, 190; Free-Soil climate in, 168; governorship of, 57; gubernatorial elections in, 46, 58, 70, 81, 124, 181; legislature of, and Hiss removal, 190; and political effect of Conscience Whigs, 148
Massachusetts Anti-Slavery Society, 72
Massachusetts Birth Control League, 223
Massachusetts Constitutional Convention of 1853, 181
Massachusetts Woman Suffrage Association, 223
Massapoag Hotel (Canton, Mass.), 159, 161–62
mass meetings (partisan), 7, 109–10, 127, 136, 145, 204, 206, 215, 225

mass politics, 6, 10, 80
Matamoros, Battle of, 153
material culture (partisan), 7–8, 79, 160, 205
McCarty, Monica, 176–77
McClellan, George B., 215
McIntire, Rufus, 74
McKinley, William, 220
McNeil, John, 123
Memoir of Catharine Brown (Brown), 39
Memoir of the Life and Public Services of John Charles Frémont (Bigelow), 192
Memoirs of Aaron Burr (M. Davis), 60
Memoirs of the Court of Queen Elizabeth (Aikin), 24–25
Mephistopheles (Goethe's *Faust*), 201
"Message of the President" (Jackson), 39
methods, 3–5
Mexican Cession, 158, 166
Mexico, 147, 152. *See also* U.S.-Mexico War
Mexico City, 149, 155
Middleton, Annie De Wolfe, 210
Might and Right (Green), 125
military and women, 3, 214, 218–19
Mills, Charles H., 200
Mills, Frederick D., 155
Minkins, Shadrach, 171
"Miss Dorcas's Opinion" (Cooke), 221
Missouri Compromise of 1820, 179–80, 187, 210
Moffitt, Aurilla, 89, 115–18, 120, 156
Moffitt, Orson, 112, 117, 120
Monterrey, Battle of, 154
Monument (Boston), 94
Moral and Political Philosophy (Paley), 26
moral reform, 3, 15, 44, 237n35
Mordecai (O.T.), 39–40
Morehead, James T., 144
Morrill Tariff, 213
Morris, Emily, 154
Morse, Freeman H., 107, 110
Morton, Marcus, 42, 70, 81, 85, 123–24, 127
Morton, Perez, 57
Moseley, Emily, 151
Mrs. Ward's school (Salem, Mass.), 24
Mudge, Mary, 186, 189
music in campaigns, 90, 95, 97, 159

Napoleon, 25, 140
National Boston Lancers, 186
National Convention of the Whig Young Men (Baltimore, 1840), 92
National Era (Washington, D.C.), 183, 187
National Fast Day (1861), 209–210
National Guards (France), 27
National Intelligencer (Washington, D.C.), 156
National Republican Convention (Baltimore, 1831), 46
National Republican Party, 23, 37–38, 53, 55–56, 57, 242n13
National Women's Republican Association, 220–21
Native Americans, 39
nativism, 115, 134, 146, 157, 180–82
New Age and Constitutional Advocate (Providence), 114
New England, 6, 188, 221, 226, 236n23
New England Anti-Slavery Society, 185
New Englanders, 3–4, 101, 157, 170, 183, 188, 195, 210
New England women: and abolitionism, 65; and American Party, 189; and Bleeding Kansas, 186–87; and Buchanan, 199–200; and Bunker Hill Monument, 45–46; and Civil War as Cause, 217; and 1856 election, 193; ideology of, 221–22; and Independence Day, 48; life writings of, 1, 9; as news readers, 11; and Panic of 1857, 200; and pre-1840 elections, 46; as proto-Whigs, 37; and regional political culture, 6–7, 9; representational problems of partisanship, 224; and Republican Party, 180; and Second Party System, 133–34; and sectional crisis, 200; and side-taking, 65, 73; and Sumner's caning, 191; and voice in politics, 14–16; and Webster myth, 177; and women's civic future, 14. *See also* Dorrite women; Democratic women; Republican women; Whig women; women; women's partisanship
New Hampshire, 46–48, 123–24, 128, 183, 194
New Hampshire Patriot (Concord N.H.), 46
New Jersey (ship), 27
New Mexico, 147, 155, 168
Newport Artillery (R.I.), 119

new social history, 9
newspapers, 7; and Barney letter, 41; Crimean War in, 224; and Davis's Independent Treasury speech, 82; editors of, 70, 103, 122, 136, 139, 144, 147, 155, 172, 188, 211; and Fort Sumter, 212; and Lovejoy murder, 73; militarization of content in, 138; political clips from, mailed, 201; as private postal communication, 101; representation of political women in, 225; and secession, 208–9; and Sickles murder case, 202; and Taylorism, 162; and telegraphy, 158; and U.S.-Mexico War, 147, 151, 153–54; Webster's death in, 175; and women, 11, 76, 225; women's reading of, 4, 73, 100–101, 197, 220, 224
New York Evangelist, 73, 151
New York Herald, 204
New York State, 66, 158
New York Times, 223
New York Tribune, 151
North American Review (Boston), 40, 44–45
North American Woman Suffrage Association, 223
Northern Light (ship), 175
Notes of Travel in California (Frémont), 167
Noyes, Samuel Bradley, 159–61
nullification, 31–34, 56, 62

Oglesby, Minnie, 205, 210
Ohio Life Insurance and Trust Company, 200
Oliphant, Carolina, 193
Opium Wars, 34
Oregon, 152
organization of presentation, 5, 14
Otis, Harrison Gray, 46
Ottoman Empire, 44

Paine, Nancy C., 165
Paley, William, 26
Palfrey, John Gorham, 148
Palmerston, Lord. *See* Temple, Henry John
Palo Alto, Battle of, 153
Panic of 1837, 1, 35, 61, 66, 216
Panic of 1857, 200
Papers of James Madison, 108
parades (partisan), 86–87, 114, 127, 215; and women, 7, 112, 159, 170, 193–94. *See also* torchlight processions
Parker, Theodore, 185
Park, John, 116, 119, 127
Parliament (England), 39, 202, 213
Parlin, Ann, 123–24
"Parody on 'Red, White, and Blue'" (Forten), 200
Parris, Virgil Delphini, 106
partisan songs, 8, 79, 95, 97, 159–60, 162, 206
"Pass of the Sierra" (Whittier), 189
Patton Resolution (gag law), 62
Paul, Mary Stiles, 160
Peabody, George, 181
Peabody, Sophia, 42, 44, 46
Peckham, Eliza, 118–19
Peckham, Samuel, 118
Pennsylvania, 81, 144
People's Constitution, 115
People's Convention (Providence), 115
people's government (R.I.), 111, 116, 118
persuasion (by women), 3, 13, 19, 23, 65, 81, 90–91
Peter Parley (i.e., Samuel G. Goodrich), 90
petitions (political) 38–39, 44, 62, 72, 190, 221–22
Phillips, Stephen C., 95
Phillips, Wendell, 185, 201, 203
Pierce, Abigail, 146, 188
Pierce, Elizabeth, 38–40, 46, 48, 189
Pierce, Franklin, 163–64, 176–77, 187–88, 199
Pierce, Julia, 195
Pierce, Mary. *See* Poor, Mary Pierce
Pierpont, John, 182
Pingree, Andrew, 103–4
political culture, 3, 6–7, 9, 11, 14, 219, 235n4
political wives, 49, 51, 53, 55, 62–63, 72, 98–100, 107, 158, 222–23
Polk, James K.: death of, 174; and Dorr petitions, 128; in 1844 campaign, 108–9, 126, 127–28, 145–46; election of, 99, 110, 128, 146; messages to congress by, 147, 153–56; New England tour of, 155; and Texas annexation, 138, 147; U.S.-Mexico War, 78, 147,

151, 155; as young hickory, 127; and wife as political team, 147
Polk, Sarah Childress, 146–47
Polonious (*Hamlet*), 157
Poor, Agnes Blake, 135, 194
Poor, Alfred, 69
Poor, Henry Varnum, 69, 75, 81, 88–90, 97
Poor, Mary Pierce, 74–79, 88–91; and antiremoval activism, 40; on antislavery lecturer, 72; and Aroostook War, 74, 75–77; on Civil War versus Revolutionary era women, 214; and childrens' politicization, 135, 201; on Democratic banking policy, 88–89; and elections, 69–70, 80, 91, 146, 204; and John Brown, 203; on Lincoln's 1861 inaugural, 210; partisan awakening of, 44, 69–70; and rational argument, 81, 91; and secession, 207; on Taylor, 162; and U.S.-Mexico War, 78; and Webster's school visit, 44; at Whig events, 79, 88–90, 93, 97, 162
popular sovereignty, 158, 192, 200
Porter, David R., 81
Port Royal Experiment (S.C.), 216
Prescott, Harriet, 41, 46–48
Prescott, Joseph, 76
Prince, Joseph Hardy, 25
Progressive Party, 223
promiscuous audiences. *See* audiences (promiscuous)
protectionism, 37, 55, 57
Psalter, Der (Luther), 201
public opinion, 7–8, 63, 210, 213
public speaking, 12, 13, 53, 82. *See also* speeches
Punch (London), 224

Quincy, Edmund, 173–74
Quincy, Josiah Jr., 90
Quincy, Josiah III, 6, 43, 46, 114
Quincy (Mass.), 1840 Whig "ladies" picnic in, 79, 89, 225
Quincy Patriot (Quincy Mass.), 89, 225

Raikes, Thomas, 63
Rantoul, Charlotte, 68–69, 72
Rantoul, Jane Woodbury, 42, 68
Rantoul, Robert, 68
Rantoul, Robert Jr., 68–69, 95, 174
Reading: advice about, 63; about California, 164, 167–68; of diaries or letters, 12, 88; about electoral outcomes, 107, 110; for escapism, 210; of foreign newspapers, 224; and government appointments, 27, 41–42, 143; in groups, 80, 210; and Indian removal 38–40; among New Englanders, 2–4, 7, 11; of newspapers, 3–4, 11, 41, 88, 118, 151, 197, 236n12; as oral performance, 73, 100–1, 103; and persuasion, 65, 67; of poetry, 39, 170, 185; and politicization, 24–26, 33, 37, 49, 51, 67; in public, 123; of public documents, 32–33, 39, 104, 154–55, 223; and republicanism, 23, 29; and secession, 210; and sectionalism, 200; of sermons, 105; of speeches, 1, 41, 54–55, 57, 61, 82, 140, 156, 202, 207, 210–11; and war, 77, 148, 151. *See also* literacy; newspapers; speeches
reading rooms (partisan), 90, 135, 247n33
Reeder, Andrew, 188
reform. *See* moral reform
Reformer (Washington, D.C.), 62
Remond, Charles Lenox, 184, 188
Republican Herald (Providence), 124
republicanism, 6, 94, 179
Republican Journal (Belfast, Me.), 108
Republican motherhood, 9–11, 24
Republican Party, 192; American Party eclipsed by, 195; Dana as midwife of, 188; and Democratic Party, 195–96, 204; disunionism of, 212; election campaigns of, 188, 192, 204–6, 220; and Kansas aid societies, 188; and party factioning, 134; press of, 200; speeches of, 210; and Sumner, 191; territorial extension of slavery opposed by, 180; and Third Party System, 133; and war spirit, 213; and women, 178, 180, 214
Republican women, 178, 180, 193, 196, 199, 203–4, 207, 220–21
Resaca de la Palma, Battle of, 153
Revere House (Boston), 172–73
Rhetoric: of abolitionists, 185; of agency in women's partisan affiliation, 8; of anti-Jacksonianism, 23, 29; of benevolence, 3; biblical references in (*see*

Rhetoric *(continued)*
Bible); comic frame in, 13; of democracy, 82, 157; of denying political interest in order to express it, 13; of diffidence, 12–13, 166, 179, 215, 225–26; of feigned ignorance, 13; feminine influence in, 81, 91; feminine style of, 12; and Jacksonian argot, 55; of moral reform, 3; parataxis in, 81; of parties in newspapers, 139; of partisan women, 3, 5, 8, 12–13, 68, 80–81, 91, 149, 225–26; and personal disclosure, 13; pragmatic, 12; of republicanism, 6, 73, 94, 179; strategic silence in, 13; versus naturalized feminine diffidence, 13; of violence by women, 203; of Whig womanhood, 11; of woman's sphere, 3, 15; of woman suffrage, 223; of women compared with that of men, 225; of women on Independence Day, 48
Rhode Island: and Charter of 1663, 114; constitutional reform in, 115, 124; Dorr Rebellion in (*see* Charter government; Dorrite women; Dorr Rebellion; Dorr, Thomas Wilson; people's government); elections in, 124, 127; franchise in, 6, 19, 112, 127, 144; and repatriation of war dead, 156
Rhode Island Constitutional Convention (1834), 114
Rhode Island Constitutional Party, 114
Rhode Island Suffrage Association, 113–114
Rhode Island Supreme Court, 115
Richardson, Thomas Page, 181
Ridge, Major, 41
"The Right of the People of Rhode Island to Form a Constitution," 115
"Rip Van Winkle" (Irving), 199
Rives, William Cabell, 61
Robinson, Harriet Hanson, 188, 191, 193
Robinson, John Staniford, 183
Rogers, Richard S., 181
Rotch, Annie Bigelow Lawrence. *See* Lawrence, Annie Bigelow
Royall, Anne, 43
"Runaway Slave at Pilgrim's Point" (Browning), 185
Russell and Company, 24, 28, 34
Russell, Nancy, 101
Russo-Turkish War, 27
sabbatarianism, 46, 48
Salisbury family, 57, 87
Salisbury, Rebekah Scott Dean, 82–84
Salisbury, Stephen II, 83–84, 92
Saltonstall, Leverett, 68–69
Sanborn, Franklin B., 203
San Juan de Ulúa, Battle of, 154
Santa Ana, Antonio López de, 148–49, 155
Saturday Review of Politics, Literature, Science, and Art, 208
Sayles, Welcome Ballou, 123, 128
schools, 95, 205, 214–15, 220, 223. *See also* women, and education
Scott, Walter, 25
Scott, Winfield, 71, 77, 149, 154–55, 163, 177
secession, 2, 168, 197, 199–210, 206–8, 209–10
Second Congregational Church (Worcester, Mass.), 53
Second Party System, 6, 14; birth of, 19, 36–37, 49; and death of statesmen, 174; demise of, 164, 180; instability of, in late 1840s, 133; peaceful transfer of power in, 165; side-taking in, 64; slavery issue suppressed under, 15; and women, 65, 167. *See also* Democratic Party; Whig Party
Sedgwick, Elizabeth Buckminster Dwight, 203
Sedgwick school for girls (Lenox, Mass.), 210–11
separate spheres ideology. *See* woman's sphere
Sequoyah, 39
Sergeant, John, 46
sermons, 6–7, 47–48, 56, 105–6, 174
"Seventh of March Speech" (Webster), 168
Seward, William Henry, 201
Shakespeare, William, 13, 102, 157
Shepard, Mary, 185
Sibley, Charlotte Buxton, 101
Sibley, Persis. *See* Andrews, Persis Sibley
Sibley, William, 101, 108
Sibley, William George, 101
Sickles, Daniel E., 202
Silsbee, Nathaniel, 58
Sims, Thomas, 171–72, 175

Six Lectures on the Uses of the Lungs (Fitch), 155–56
Slave Power (Palfrey), 148
slavery issue, 134, 138, 143, 146, 168, 180, 192. *See also* abolitionists; antislavery
Slidell, John, 147
Smart, Ephraim K., 205
Smith College, 223
Smith, Gerrit, 201
Smith, Hannah Hicock, 72, 146, 151, 153, 154–56, 162, 166–68
Smith, Jerome V. C., 181–82, 185–86
Smith, Sarah Cassey, 185
Socrates, 91
South Carolina, 31–32, 34, 55–56, 146, 197, 207–8
Southey, Robert, 149
Spain, 27, 38, 95
speeches: Democratic women addressed in, 127; and Dorrite women, 212, 123; by girls for candidates, 195; at inaugurations, 70, 101, 210–11; at Independence Day celebrations, 6, 56; newsclips of, mailed, 201; slang used in, 157; and women, 150, 200; by women, 5, 7, 8, 159, 185, 193, 221–22; women as auditors of, 7–8, 59, 71, 82, 95, 101, 136, 159, 160–61, 183, 191; women as critics of, 55, 82; women as editors or writers of, 8; women as readers of, 1, 40, 55, 140, 166, 187, 191, 202, 210; and women depicted as auditors, 173; women's putative disinterest in, 54; women's rights and antislavery combined in, 201; by women to congress, 218. *See also* public speaking; reading; stump-speaking
Speeches on the Passage of the Bill for the Removal of the Indians (Evarts), 40
speechifying. *See* public speaking; speeches; stump-speaking
Sprague, Peleg, 40
Standish Guards (Plymouth, Mass.), 212
Stanley, Albert Fiske, 105
Stetson, Hannah, 160, 162
Stevenson, Andrew, 54
St. Helena Island (S.C.), 216
Stiles, Mary, 86
Stimson, Abigail M. (Clarke), 168, 177, 181, 191, 200, 215
Storrs, Henry Randolph, 40
Story, Joseph, 140, 223
story papers, 101, 103
strategic silence, 13
study group, 235n8–9, 236n12
stump-speaking, 6, 82, 137, 150, 159, 160–61. *See also* public speaking; speeches
Subtreasury. *See* Independent Treasury
Suffrage Association. *See* Rhode Island Suffrage Association
Suffrage Party (R.I.), 115
Sumatra (ship), 23–24
Sumner, Charles, 92, 148, 152, 160–61, 187, 191–92, 202
Swan, Margaret Bradley, 61
Swan, William H., 61
Swasey, Benjamin B., 27

Talbot, Charles Nicoll, 27
Talleyrand-Périgord, Charles Maurice de, 50
Taney, Roger B., 165
Tappan, Anne, 39
Tappan, Benjamin, 39–40
Tariff Bill of 1832, 31
Tariff (protective), 55, 95, 135, 220. *See also* protectionism
"The Task" (Cowper), 185
Taylor, Zachary: death of, 164, 168–69, 170, 174; 1848 Whig presidential campaign of, 138, 149, 157–68; Fillmore as successor to, 192; final words of, 169; as general, 147, 153, 157; inauguration of, 162, 164–66; speeches on behalf of, 159–60; victory celebrations for, 152, 162
teacher-training schools, 1, 95
Teackle, Abby, 203
Telegraph (Washington, D.C.), 29
telegraphy, 158, 174, 211, 216
Télémaque (Fenélon), 26
temperance issue, 10, 15, 63, 134, 142, 181–82, 189
Temperance Union, 181
"Tempest" (country dance), 162
Temple, Henry John (3rd Viscount Palmerston), 77
Texas annexation, 62, 125, 135, 143–44, 146–47, 152, 155

Thayer, Eliza De Wolfe, 176–77
third-partyism, 56
Third Party System, 14, 133, 180, 195–96, 220–21
Ticknor, George, 164, 175
Timberlake, John, 2
Times (London), 213, 224
Topeka Constitution, 187
torchlight processions, 136, 145, 159, 192–93, 220. *See also* parades (partisan)
trade unions and women, 219
Trail of Tears, 41
Transcript (Boston), 66–67
Travels in North America (Hall), 26
treason, 115, 124
Treaty of Cusseta, 34
Treaty of Guadalupe Hidalgo, 151, 156
Treaty of Paris (1783), 73
Trent affair, 213
Tribune (New York), 204
Tuck, Amos, 183
Tucker, Susan, 174, 182–83
Tudor, William, 45
Twisleton, Edward Turner Boyd, 199, 201–2, 204, 213, 215
Twisleton, Ellen, 204; and American Party coalition victory, 189; as anti-aristocratically republican, 202; and anti-Republican news stories, 204; Civil War position of, and sister, 198–99, 212–13; death of, 213; depression of, 208; and 1860 Republican victory as unthreatening, 206; and English opinion, 201, 213; Everett speech praised by, 202; illnesses of, 203–4, 213; introduced, 163; on Kansas-Nebraska speeches, 187; on Lincoln, 211, 213; Low compared with, 201; marriage of, 199; on newspapers' indifference to secession, 209; and nonpolitical correspondence with sister, 204; as political Rip Van Winkle, 199; Republican nonaffiliation of, 210; and secession, 207, 209–10; and Sickles case, 202; on Sumner's English visit, 202; as unionist, 197, 199, 203; and U.S.-Confederate affairs, 211; U.S. visit planned by, 208; war spirit of, and tranquil autonomy, 213; Webster obsequies account read by, 175; and Whiggery, 198–99, 202
Twisleton-Wykeham-Fiennes, Frederick Benjamin, 10th Baron Saye and Sele, 201
two-step information flow, 236n25
Tyler, John, 78; as anti-bank, 99, 103, 141; cabinet resignations during administration of, 141; and Dorr, 112, 116, 123; and 1844 presidential election, 108; exchequer plan of, 104; and Massachusetts Whigs, 143; messages to congress of, 104, 142; partisan ethos of, 99; presidential succession of, 99; and Texas annexation, 143, 147; as vice-presidential candidate, 81, 91; Whig Party excommunication of, 99, 141

United States Armory and Arsenal (Harpers Ferry, Va.). *See* Harpers Ferry
Universal History (Willard), 67
Upham, Timothy, 46
Ursuline Convent (Charlestown, Mass.), 45
U.S. Congress, 61; anti-Jacksonians in, 36, 41; antislavery in, and threat of internecine warfare, 73; Aroostook War appropriation by, 74, 77; and Compromise of 1850, 168; Davis as most useful man in, 57; debates in, read by women, 140; and Dorr Rebellion, 122, 128; 1840 party conventions occasion recess of, 92; first woman speaker before, 218; Fugitive Slave Law passed by, 170; insider view of, by political wife, 51; members of, described, 43; and Mexican cession, 166; and overtime pay, 54; peace overtures of, questioned, 148; presidential messages to, 99, 101, 142, 143, 147, 153, 154; session length of, 51; and slavery issue, 62; Southerners in, advocate overturning the Missouri Compromise, 186–87; speeches of, read by women, 40, 54, 151, 154; territorial exile wished for, 56–57, 152; and Texas annexation, 147, 152; 24th special session of, 61, 66; 27th special session of, 102–3; and U.S.-Mexico War, 147; and Whig agenda, 95–96;

veto threats' effect upon, 33; and Wilmot Proviso, 158; and women's antiremoval petitions, 38
U.S. Constitution: Buchanan and end of, 197; and Dorr Rebellion, 128; and executive removal, 33; Fourteenth Amendment of, 219; and Fugitive Slave Law, 170; loose construction of, 41–42, 46; Nineteenth Amendment of, 219; nullification as subversive of, 32, 56; Sumner's defense of, 191; and veto power, 33; as Webster's mantra, 143
U.S. federal judiciary, 219
U.S. House of Representatives: Adams's hemorrhage on floor of, 156; Committee on Commerce of, 54; Davis's fear of speaking in, 53; 1841 Whig majority in, 98; and 1856 speakership, 190–91; Fugitive Slave Bill passed in, 170; gag laws in, 62; ladies' gallery in, 94; members of, criticized by women, 55; removal bill passed in, 38; speakership of, 81; Ways and Means Committee of, 67
U.S.-Mexico War: American casualties in, 149; battles of, 153–55; declaration of, 147; and Democratic Party, 157; and 1844 election, 152; end of, 151; news of, 148; and print culture, 152; repatriation and burial of dead from, 156; as unjustified, 151; Whig candidate Scott as hero of, 163; women read of casualties in, 154; women's opposition to, contrasted with women's pro-Civil War stance, 199; and women's partisanship, 134, 138, 150
U.S. Sanitary Commission, 214, 216
U.S. Senate: caning of Sumner in, 191; debates on floor of, 54–55, 84, 171; 1846 Civil and Diplomatic Bill in, 148; executive appointments during recess of, 41; Harpers Ferry investigation of, 203; Independent Treasury Bill in, 81, 84; and Jackson's censure, 34–35, 61; Jackson's dismissal of cabinet members approved by, 29; Mexico commissioner funded by, 148; removal bill passed in, 38; Treaty of Guadalupe Hidalgo ratified in, 156; vice-president-elect's inauguration in, 165; "Whig" origination in 1834 speech in, 36; women hearing speeches in, 44, 171
U.S. Supreme Court, 41, 91
Utah, 168

Van Buren, Martin, 29, 51; and Aroostook War, 73–74; and 1837 Democratic state assembly loss, 66; and 1844 Dorrite-Democratic mass meeting, 127; and elections, 46, 60, 64–65, 81, 108, 145, 152, 158; and Eliza Davis, 47, 49, 50, 52, 56, 59, 64, 87; Free-Soil candidacy of, questioned, 160–61; and Indian Removal, 41; and Jackson, 42, 59; public reception of, 50, 56, 59, 71, 83; slavery mentioned in inaugural speech by, 62; territorial exile wished for, 152; and 24th U.S. Congress special session, 66; and women's partisanship, 49
Varon, Elizabeth, 11
veracity (news), 7, 144
Vera Cruz, Battle of, 154
Vermont, 84, 95, 179, 182–83, 218
Vermont Prohibitory Law, 182
viceroy of Kwangtung and Kwansi provinces (China), 28
Vigilance Committee (Boston), 185
Vinton, John Rogers, 149, 154, 156, 170
Virginia, 11
"Virginia Reel" (country dance), 162
voice (political) of women, 2, 3, 16; and changing party systems, 14, 133; collective versus individual, 5; defined as partisan, 5; in Dorr Rebellion, 129; in 1850s, 164; inarticulate women represented by, 226; and literary quotation, 149; as resistance to disfranchisement, 235n4; stifling of, in postbellum era, 225; and U.S.-Mexico War, 138; and women's self construction, 226. *See also* women; women's partisanship; women's writing
voting, 91, 96; and apathy, 163; corruption in, 69; scattering in, 16, 106, 138; turnout in, 7, 65, 163

Walker, Robert J., 84, 147
Walker Tariff, 147
Ward, Samuel, 70

Warner, Helen M., 169–72
War of 1812, 55, 124
War of the Spanish Succession, 149
Warren, Abby B. Hedge, 61
Warren, Charles Henry, 61, 83
Washburn, Israel, 205
Washington, George, 55, 122, 170, 188, 197
Washington, Martha, 89–90
Washington Monument (Washington, D.C.), 168
Water Celebration (Boston), 159
Waterhouse, Louisa Lee, 70–71
Waterloo (ship), 34
Watie, Buck. *See* Boudinot, Elias
Watson, Sarah. *See* Dana, Sarah Watson
Wayland, Francis, 118
Wayland, Hepsy, 118
Webb, James Watson, 125
Webster-Ashburton Treaty, 77, 143
Webster, Caroline Le Roy, 144
Webster, Daniel, 222; and Annie Lawrence, 71; as "Black Dan," 173; and Bunker Hill Monument Association, 45; Clay's antiannexationism revealed by, 144–45; death and funeral of, 164, 174–76, 199, 217; distrust of, 139, 145; and elections, 43, 47, 60, 64, 143, 164, 173; and Eliza Davis, 55, 59, 88; and emoluments for speaking, 158; and Everett, 143; family of, and Sarah Hale, 142, 144; Faneuil Hall denied for speech of, 172; festival for, 67; Free-Soil turn contemplated by, 168; and Fugitive Slave Law, 168, 171, 176; Gothic Seminary visited by, 44; and Knapp trial, 43; and Minkins' rescue, 171; moral features of, criticized, 172; return of, and mass meeting for, 173; Secretary of State office of, goes to Everett, 149; senate committee chair lost by, 61; speeches of, 55, 62, 89, 137, 139, 146, 158, 168, 172–73, 222–23; and Tyler administration, 141–43; and Webster-Ashburton Treaty, 77, 143; and Webster-Hayne debates, 43, 54, 175; as Whig bellwether, 49; on Wilmot Proviso, 168; and women, 20, 37, 43–44, 49, 146, 172–77, 222
Webster Replying to Hayne (Healy), 175
Wells, Jonathan, 154
Weybosset (ship), 128
"Wh'all be King But Charlie?" (Oliphant), 193
Whig (Boston), 148
Whig Jubilee (New York), 67
Whig Party, 37, 140; as Algerines, 122, 125; as antiannexationist, 152; and anti-Jacksonianism, 23, 36, 38; antipartyism of, 106; as aristocratic, 64; banking policy of, 61, 82, 95; Brookline (Mass.) reading room of, 90; Bunker Hill convention of, 93; congressional agenda of, 99; and constitutional reform in Rhode Island, 114; and Constitutional Union Party, 205; demise of, 133, 180, 199, 205; Democratic Party compared with, 47; Democratic vernacular speaking opposed by, 157; and 1840 elections, 79, 81, 90, 97; 1841 election losses after ascendancy of, 98, 103; 1843 victories of, 107, 124; and 1844 elections, 108, 110, 135, 145; and 1846 convention in Massachusetts, 148; and 1848 elections, 149, 157, 159, 161; and 1852 elections, 163–64, 168, 173, 177, 182; in 1853–54 elections, 181, 189–90; and 15 Gallon Law, 70, 140; formation of, 1, 34, 36; gender style of, 20; Kansas-Nebraska Act opposed by northerners in, 187; and Low family, 33, 35; and Maine elections, 69, 167, 183; Manifest Destiny opposed by, 152; and Massachusetts Conscience Whigs, 148; and Morton's clambake letter, 123; name of, 36; National Republican roots of, 51; press of, attacks Dorrite women, 123; pro-Fugitive Slave Law members of, and multi-partisan union meetings, 170–71; and Quincy picnic, 79, 89, 225; and temperance, 67, 181; Tyler excommunicated by, 99, 141; unity of, challenged by abolitionists, 139; and U.S.-Mexico War, 138, 149; and Vermont prohibition, 182–83; and women, 8, 19–20, 37, 113. *See also* Whig women
Whig State Convention (Worcester, Mass., 1840), 49, 52, 81, 83, 86

Whig women, 20, 135; and American Revolution, 225; Democratic and Dorrite women compared to, 20, 112–13, 127–28, 135; Democrats married to, 97; at 1844 Whig meetings, 136; and elections, 10–11, 78, 80–97, 135–39, 145, 160–62, 164; evidence of, preserved in Whig-oriented institutions, 20; and mass politics, 19, 79–80, 86–90, 92–95; at opposition party events, 161; and party affiliation, 80; and party demise, 134, 164, 178; on Polk as inciting U.S.-Mexico War, 78; and Quincy picnic, 79, 89; and Revolutionary republicanism in 1840, 94; and tendency toward written political expression, 20; Whig men's glorification of militarism rejected by, 152; and Whig Party gender style, 20; and Whig womanhood, 11. *See also* Whig Party; women's partisanship

White, Aaron Jr., 113, 115, 117–18, 120

White, Hugh Lawson, 60

White, Mary Avery, 113, 115, 117, 120

Whitmarsh, Seth, 123

Whittier, John Greenleaf, 183, 189

Willard, Calvin (Sheriff of Worcester County, Mass.), 53

Willard, Emma, 67

Willard, Frances, 222

Willard, Mary Thomas, 50, 59

Williams, Catherine R., 113, 121, 123–25

Williams, Reuel, 69, 100

Wilmot Proviso, 158, 166, 168

Winthrop, Robert C., 81, 141, 147

Woman's Christian Temperance Union, 219, 222, 236n32

Woman's sphere, 2–3, 9–12, 14–15, 23, 80, 137. *See also* women's history (as field)

woman suffrage, 3, 10, 12, 219–24

women: and anti-Jacksonianism, 38, 41; as anti-Manifest Destiny, 152; and antislavery, 10, 44, 72–73; as antiwar, 134, 152; and association leadership, 37; and benevolent work, 2–3, 10, 44, 214, 216; and citizenship, 3, 24, 235n4; civic identity of, 3, 220, 225; and Civil War, 213–14, 217, 262n1; and Compromise of 1850, 164; and debate, 2, 43, 51, 56, 59, 62, 95, 140, 171, 187, 204–5; and education, 7, 70, 139 (*see also* schools); and elections (*see* Democratic women; Dorrite women; elections; Republican women; Whig women); and handwriting, 68; and honorifics, 183; literacy of, 7, 236n23; and militarization, 214, 218–19; and moral reform, 2–3, 44; news-accuracy of, 7; and nonpartisan activism, 7, 10, 15, 40–45, 65, 134, 189, 218–19; number of, in study group, 235n8; and parades (*see* parades; torchlight processions); as participants in political culture, 6; and petitions (*see* petitions); political consciousness of, 5, 11, 13–14, 36–38, 49 (*see also* women's partisanship); and political discourse networks, 8, 19, 77; as political history chroniclers, 7; politicization of, as exigent, 225; politics redefined with inclusion of, 235n4; pro-Civil War versus anti-U.S.-Mexico War among, 214; at public events, 102, 156, 159; as readers of antislavery newspapers, 73; as readers of political news, 11, 76, 151, 207, 210, 224 (*see also* newspapers; reading); and Republican motherhood, 9; role of, in Civil War versus Revolution, 214; and sectionalism, 134, 180, 202; and speeches, 5, 7–8, 59, 220 (*see also* reading, speeches; stump-speaking); and statesmen's careers, 37; stigmatized for political extremism, 225; and "two-step" information flow, 236n25; and U.S.-Mexico War, 151–54; and U.S. Sanitary Commission, 214; and Yankee "old maid" caricature, 221–22. *See also* New England women; women's partisanship

women's history (as field), 9–10, 14, 16, 224

women's life writings. *See* diaries; letters; women's partisanship; women's writing

women's partisanship: antecedents of, 6, 9–10, 214; collective biographers' neglect of, 224–25; in collective memory, 224; as contagion effect, women's partisanship *(continued)* 226; and decorum, 79–80; and Democratic Party (*see* Democratic Party; Democratic women; Dorrite women); and diaries, 4, 5, 9, 11–12, 14–15, 98, 108; diversification of, 133; in 1830s, 1, 21–78; in 1840s, 1–2, 79–162; in 1850s, 2, 163–202; 1850s political confusion reflected in, 164; from 1857 to 1861, 199; in 1860s, 2, 203–18; and elections (*see* Democratic women; Dorrite women; elections; Republican women; Whig women); evidence of, in diaries and letters, 134, 225–26; and families, 8, 222–23; and genres of romantic self-disclosure, 226; and humor, 88–89; impact of, upon the polity, 16; and letter writing, 4, 9, 11–12, 14–15; and low-information voters, 7; via Lysistrata strategy, 91; and mass party politics, 10–11, 14, 19, 49, 80, 85, 93, 114, 122 ; via material culture of campaigns, 7–8, 205, 160; and newspaper reading (*see* newspapers; reading); opposition to, 89; and parlor politics, 10; via party affiliations, 8, 19, 42, 65, 80, 99, 113, 164, 180, 189; and party realignment during the 1850s, 14, 133–34,167, 180; party stability unnecessary for, 133; and persuasion, 8, 13; and political disclaimers, 150; and political wifedom (*see* political wives); in postbellum years, 219, 222; as pragmatic, 220; and public speaking, 7–8, 10, 218, 222 (*see also* public speaking; speeches; stump-speaking); representational problems of, 225; and Republican Party (*see* Republican women); rhetoric of (*see* rhetoric); and Second Party System, 6, 14–15, 19, 35, 37, 46, 49, 64–65, 133–34, 164, 167, 174, 180; and temperance issue, 10, 15, 70, 181–83, 189, 219; and third-party politics, 166, 183; and Third Party System, 14, 133, 180; twentieth-century occlusion of, 14; voice of (*see* voice); and Whig Party (*see* elections; Whig Party; Whig women); Whig versus Democrat in (*see* Democratic women; Whig women); and woman's sphere role restrictions (*see* woman's sphere); women's historians and problem of, 10, 236n32 (*see also* women's history); in workingclass, 15, 42, 47, 127, 133, 219; among youngsters, 159, 193–94

women's rights, 10, 185, 201, 223

women's writing, 42, 193; as argument for civic participation, 225; and decorum in political productions, 12; on Dorr, 124–25; of letters as political, 139; and moral mimesis, 226; policy change advocated in, 41; as political expression transgressing gender norms, 11; on politics similar to men's, 80. *See also* diaries, letters, women's partisanship

Woodbury, Levi, 42, 68

Worcester Central Bank, 62

Worcester, Olive Gay, 155, 160, 162, 165–66, 175

"Worth of Money" (Hale), 45

Wright, Ellen. *See* Garrison, Ellen Wright

Wright, Martha Coffin, 223

Wright, Silas, 61

Young Men's League, 181

Young Women's Suffrage Fair, 121